WEIMAR AND NAZI GERMANY

We work with leading authors to develop the
strongest educational materials in History,
bringing cutting edge thinking and best learning
practice to a global market.

Under a range of well-known imprints,
including Longman, we craft high quality
print and electronic publications which help
readers to understand and apply their content,
whether studying or at work.

To find out about the complete range of our
publishing please visit us on the World Wide Web at:

www.pearsoneduc.com

WEIMAR AND NAZI GERMANY

Continuities and Discontinuities

Edited by
PANIKOS PANAYI

An imprint of **Pearson Education**

Harlow, England · London · New York · Reading, Massachusetts · San Francisco
Toronto · Don Mills, Ontario · Sydney · Tokyo · Singapore · Hong Kong · Seoul
Taipei · Cape Town · Madrid · Mexico City · Amsterdam · Munich · Paris · Milan

Pearson Education Limited
Edinburgh Gate
Harlow
Essex CM20 2JE
England

and Associated Companies throughout the World.

Visit us on the World Wide Web at:
www.pearsoneduc.com

First published 2001

ISBN 0 582 32780 6 LIMP
     0 582 32778 4 CASED

British Library Cataloguing-in-Publication Data
A catalogue record for this book can be obtained from the British
Library

Library of Congress Cataloging-in-Publication Data
A catalog record for this book can be obtained from the Library of Congress

10 9 8 7 6 5 4 3 2 1
05 04 03 02 01 00

Typeset by 35 in 11/13pt Baskerville
Produced by Pearson Education Asia Pte Ltd.
Printed in Singapore

CONTENTS

PART THREE: ECONOMICS, SOCIETY, POLITICS
AND DIPLOMACY, 1919–1945: KEY THEMES

LIST OF MAPS

LIST OF TABLES

ACKNOWLEDGEMENTS

The publishers wish to thank the following for permission to reproduce the following material:

Maps 1 and 2 from *A History of Germany 1815–1990, 4th edition,* (William Carr, 1991), reproduced by permission of Arnold Publishers.

Extract from speech by Otto Wels (translated by Stefan Berger) from Stenograpische Berichte über die Verhandlungen des Deutschen Reichstages, Vol. 457 (1933) pp. 322–4 with permission of Bundesarchiv, Berlin.

PREFACE

This may represent yet another book on Germany under the Weimar Republic and the Third Reich, but it does take an interesting approach, which has several novel features. First, authors were asked to examine not only the continuities and discontinuities between inter-war Germany and the years before and after, but also between Weimar and Nazi Germany. Second, the structure of the book divides into two sections after my introductory essay. The articles in the second part consist of outlines of the economic, social, political and diplomatic history of Germany between 1919 and 1945. The third section contains a variety of essays on specific aspects of the economic, social, political and diplomatic history of the Federal Republic, many of them based on original archival research. The authors consist of a mixture of some of the most important historians of Germany in the last four decades, a selection of some of those who are currently establishing themselves as leading authorities on Germany, and a few who have just started out on their academic careers.

My introductory essay sets the agenda for the articles that follow, pointing to the historical background, the links and breaks between Weimar and Nazi Germany and the legacy of the years between 1919 and 1945 on the Federal Republic and the German Democratic Republic. I consider economic, social, political and diplomatic developments.

Part Two begins with an outline essay on the inter-war economy by Richard Overy, one of the leading experts on the subject. As well as describing the pattern of development, Overy also examines specific issues in the form of the role of the state, industry and labour and Nazi economic policy towards other countries. Hartmut Berghoff's essay reopens the debate about the effects of Nazi policy on social structure and living standards and, by examining individual classes, comes to the conclusion that the Third Reich had a limited impact in these areas. Edgar Feuchtwanger's piece is an examination of the political history of Germany between 1919 and 1945, focusing specifically upon the elements of continuity and discontinuity between Weimar and Nazi Germany through the examination of both policy and bureaucracy. The final essay in Part Two, by Imanuel Geiss, consists of a detailed examination of the diplomacy of Germany under the Weimar

Republic and the Third Reich by contextualizing it within the foreign policy of the *Kaiserreich*.

The third section on specific themes within the history of Germany between 1919 and 1945 opens with an essay by Adam Tooze, 'Big Business and the Continuities of German History', which is both a historical and a historiographical piece examining several aspects of German business history between 1900 and 1945. There then follow two essays on the social history of Weimar and Nazi Germany. Lisa Pine's article on 'Women and the Family' utilizes the latest lines in research on this subject to examine the racist ways in which the Nazis tackled issues such as eugenics, marriage and family welfare. Similarly, my own essay on 'Continuities and Discontinuities in Race' examines the differing methods by which both Weimar and Nazism excluded Jews, gypsies and Slavs. There are then two articles on aspects of the political history of Germany between 1919 and 1945. Lee McGowan examines both the ideology and the reality of Nazism, while Stefan Berger tackles the SPD both before 1933 and under the Nazis, contextualizing the events of these years in developments in the party's history both before 1919 and after 1945. Finally, G.T. Waddington's article is an original primary source-based examination of Anglo-German relations between 1919 and 1939, one of the few essays written on this subject.

It is hoped that the book will appeal to the student, the general reader and the specialist on German history. The editor would like to thank all of the contributors for their promptness in delivering their essays and the effort they put into their individual pieces. He would also thank the Longman editors who took on the project in the form of Andrew MacLennan, who commissioned it, and Emma Mitchell, who saw it to fruition.

Panikos Panayi
Oadby, Leicestershire
October 1999

NOTES ON THE CONTRIBUTORS

Stefan Berger was born in Langenfeld/Rhineland in 1964. He studied history, political science and literature at the universities of Cologne and Oxford. In 1991 he obtained his DPhil from the University of Oxford. He is currently Professor of History at the University of Glamorgan. His major research interests are in the areas of comparative labour history and historiography. More recently he has published *Social Democracy and the Working Class in Nineteenth and Twentieth Century Germany* (London, 2000); ed. with Angel Smith, *Labour, Nationalism and Ethnicity, 1870–1939* (Manchester, 1999); ed. with Mark Donovan and Kevin Passmore, *Writing National Histories: Western Europe Since 1800* (London, 1999); and *The Search for Normality: National Identity and Historical Consciousness in Germany Since 1800* (Oxford, 1997). His current projects include a book entitled *From Radical Nationalism to Postnationalism? The Invention of German National Identities in the Nineteenth and Twentieth Centuries.*

Hartmut Berghoff was born in Herford in Germany in 1960 and studied in Bielefeld, Berlin and London. He is a *Privatdozent* at the University of Tübingen where he teaches modern history and economic history. His 1989 Bielefeld PhD thesis on the social history of British businessmen before the First World War appeared as *Englische Unternehmer, 1870–1914: Eine Kollektivbiographie führender Wirtschaftsbürger in Birmingham, Bristol und Manchester* (Göttingen, 1991). His other major books include: *Zwischen Kleinstadt und Weltmarkt: Hohner und die Harmonika, 1857 bis 1961: Unternehmensgeschichte als Gesellschaftsgeschichte* (Paderborn, 1997); and, ed., *Konsumpolitik: Die Regulierung des privaten Verbrauchs im 20. Jahrhundert* (Göttingen, 1999). Together with Cornelia Rauh-Kühne he recently finished a biography of a German businessman who was a functionary within the Nazi economic administration: *Fritz K. Ein deutsches Leben im zwanzigsten Jahrhundert* (Stuttgart, 2000).

Edgar Feuchtwanger was born in Munich in 1924. He was educated at a German *Gymnasium* and at Winchester and Magdalene College, Cambridge. He was Deputy Director of Adult Education from 1964 and Reader in History from 1973 at the University of Southampton. His areas of research and teaching are British political history in the Victorian period and modern German history. His publications on British history include *Disraeli, Democracy and the Tory Party* (Oxford, 1968); *Democracy and Empire: Britain, 1865–1914* (London, 1985); and biographies of Gladstone (London, 1975, 1989) and Disraeli (London, 2000). On German history he has published. *Prussia: Myth and Reality* (London, 1970), *From Weimar to Hitler: Germany, 1918–33* (London, 1993, 1995) and *Germany, 1916–1941* (Sempringham, 1997). He is at present working on Imperial Germany and Bismarck.

Imanuel Geiss was born in Frankfurt am Main in 1931. He read History and English at the universities of Munich and Hamburg and received his doctorate in 1959. He was lecturer and assistant professor in Hamburg from 1968 to 1973 and became Professor at the University of Bremen in 1973, a position he occupied until his retirement in 1996. He has also held visiting positions at the universities of Gdansk, Tel Aviv, Brisbane and Hong Kong. His major works include: *Der polnische Grenzstreifen, 1914–1918* (Hamburg, 1960); *Juli 1914* (Munich, 1965); *The Pan-African Movement* (London and Boston, 1974); *Geschichte griffbereit*, 6 vols, 2nd edn (Dortmund, 1993); *German Foreign Policy* (London, 1976); *Geschichte im Überblick* (Reinbek, 1986); *Die Lange Weg in die Katastrophe: Vorgeschichte des Ersten Weltkrieges, 1815–1914* (Munich, 1990); *The Question of German Unification* (London, 1997); and *Geschichte im Oratorium* (Berlin, 1999). Current projects include a third enlarged edition of *Geschichte griffbereit* and a critique of the Goldhagen thesis.

Lee McGowan was born in Londonderry in 1964. After studying West European Studies as an undergraduate at the University of Ulster he obtained a masters degree at the University of Reading in 1987. In 1991 he completed his PhD at the same university on the theme of right-wing political violence in Germany during the 1980s. He has held research and lecturing positions at the universities of Exeter and Ulster and is currently a lecturer at the Institute of European Studies at the Queen's University of Belfast. His research has focused on German right-wing extremism, as well as European integration with special emphasis on competition policy. He is currently working on an ESRC-sponsored project on Northern Ireland and the EU. He has published widely in journals such as the *Journal of Common Market Studies, the European Journal of Political Research* and *Governance.* He co-authored (with M. Cini) *Competition Policy in the EU* (London, 1998).

Richard Overy was born in London in 1947. He studied at Gonville and Caius College, Cambridge, where he began research on aircraft production in the German war economy. He has been Professor in Modern History at King's College, London, since 1992, where he moved to a lectureship in 1980 after teaching at Churchill and Queens' colleges in Cambridge. He has written extensively on the German economy before and after 1945. His interests have also extended to air power and the origins and course of the Second World War. He has written or edited sixteen books, including *The Nazi Economic Recovery, 1932–1938*, 2nd edn (London, 1996); *War and Economy in the Third Reich* (Oxford, 1994); *Why the Allies Won* (London, 1995); *The Origins of the Second World War*, 2nd edn (London, 1998); and *Russia's War* (London, 1998). He is currently preparing an edition of the pre-Nuremberg Trial interrogations and the *Oxford History of the Second World War*.

Panikos Panayi was born in London in 1962. After graduating with a degree in history from the Polytechnic of North London in 1985, he completed his PhD in 1988 at the University of Sheffield, which was published in 1991 as *The Enemy in Our Midst: Germans in Britain during the First World War* (Oxford, 1991). After a one-year post as a temporary lecturer in Modern History at the University of Keele (1989–90), he took up a post at De Montfort University, where he is now Professor of European History. He also holds a Visiting Fellowship at the University of Osnabrück, where he has carried out research on several occasions with the assistance of funding from the Alexander von Humboldt Foundation. His most recent publications include *Outsiders: A History of European Minorities* (London, 1999) and *An Ethnic History of Europe Since 1945* (London, 2000). He recently completed a history of ethnic minorities in Germany during the nineteenth and twentieth centuries and is currently carrying out research on the town of Osnabrück between 1933 and 1949.

Lisa Pine was born in London in 1966. She was educated at the London School of Economics where she obtained a BSc in Government and History, and an MSc and PhD from the Department of International History. She is Senior Lecturer in Modern European History at South Bank University. Her major publication is *Nazi Family Policy, 1933–1945* (Oxford, 1997). In addition, she has published several articles for *History Today*, as well as others in *German History* and *History of Education*. She is currently carrying out research for a book on Nazi education policy, as well as writing a number of articles on various aspects of Nazi social policy and the Holocaust.

J. Adam Tooze was born in London in 1967 and grew up in Heidelberg. He took a double first in economics from King's College, Cambridge, in 1989 and continued his studies at the Free University of Berlin. He received his PhD from the London School of Economics in 1996 with a dissertation on 'Official Statistics and Economic Governance in Inter-war Germany'. He has published articles on the history of economic statistics in English, German and French, including 'Statistical Economics in Weimar Germany:

Ernst Wagemann and the Institute for Business-Cycle Research, 1924–1933', *Economic History Review* 52 (1999). He is currently completing a monograph on 'The Making of Modern Economic Knowledge: Statistics and the German State, 1900–1945'. Adam Tooze lectures in modern European economic history at the University of Cambridge and directs studies in history at Jesus College.

G.T. Waddington was born in Manchester in 1958. He is a graduate of the University of Leeds, where he gained his PhD in 1987 on the pre-war career of Joachim von Ribbentrop. From 1987 to 1989 he was a Teaching Fellow in the School of History at the University of Leeds, where since 1989 he has been a Lecturer in International History specializing in the inter-war period and German foreign policy during the Nazi era. He translated the memoirs of Reinhard Spitzy, *So Haben Wir das Reich Verspielt*, which appeared in 1997 under the title *How We Squandered the Reich*. He is the author of several articles and contributions to collected volumes on Ribbentrop, Anglo-German and German–Soviet relations. He is currently completing a monograph for Cambridge University Press on *Ribbentrop and the Evolution of German Foreign Policy, 1933–45* and is engaged in the writing of two further books, one on Germany, its allies and satellites before and during the Second World War and the other (with Dr Frank Magee) on Anglo-German relations between the wars.

PART ONE

Introduction

CHAPTER ONE

Continuities and discontinuities in German history, 1919–1945

PANIKOS PANAYI

Introduction

An examination of Germany between 1919 and 1945 clearly reveals both continuities and discontinuities. On the one hand we can see the Weimar Republic and the Nazi dictatorship as firmly rooted in the evolution of the German nation state which came into existence in 1871. The years between 1919 and 1945 brought to the surface latent characteristics of the *Kaiserreich*. At the same time one could make comparisons with the other dictatorships that existed in inter-war Europe, including Stalinism and Italian Fascism. Weimar specifically may be said to have similarities with contemporary European liberal democracies of the years 1919–45. Finally, developments in Germany after the Second World War indicate that Nazism had such a profound impact upon the country that it could never fully escape from its Nazi past.

An alternative view would stress the uniqueness of Nazism. While it may have roots in German and European history, it has various characteristics which make it stand out from any other state. This line of argument would not only see the Nazi dictatorship as detached from other modern European regimes, but would also clearly delineate the Nazi years from the Weimar Republic.[1] The uniqueness of Nazism according to this line of argument would lie in a number of central aspects of the regime. These would include the ideology, which has both backward- and forward-looking elements. The centrality of race in Nazi Germany, both ideologically and in terms of practical implementation, would also appear to make it unique.[2] A third element which would appear to distinguish Nazism from other modern European regimes would consist of the level of control, intolerance, and, during the Second World War, brutality. After 1939 the Nazi regime entered a period in which killing became its central function. While such an assertion may apply to all states that become involved in war, the treatment of the Jewish and Slavic populations of eastern Europe, which involved an organized bureaucratic system of mass murder, would certainly appear to make Nazism unique.

In reality, both of the above points of view have validity. No period of history, even one as apparently unique as Nazism, can be regarded as rootless. Clearly, it did bring to the surface many latent developments characteristic of German evolution before 1918. Racism and anti-Semitism had played a central role in German history from the creation of the first modern state in 1871. On the other hand, the practical *implementation* of racism appears to make Nazism unique. Similar statements can be made about any number of Nazi policies. But other characteristics of the years 1933–45 place them firmly in the context of German history. A good example would be economic development. If anything, the Weimar period, with the economic disasters which characterize it, would represent the unique period in modern German history. The economic success of peacetime Nazism links it closely with the *Kaiserreich* and the Federal Republic.

There are several possible ways of examining the continuities and discontinuities in German history, with particular reference to the years 1919–45. Apart from contextualizing this period within German history before 1919 and after 1945, we can also draw comparisons with other regimes that existed simultaneously within Europe, particularly Stalinism and Italian Fascism. In addition, an examination of contemporary European liberal democracies reveals that similarities existed with such systems of government. The discussion will revolve around the four divisions of the present book, namely economics, society, politics and foreign policy. It will also examine specific issues within these areas, as well as some of the core questions which would point to the uniqueness of Nazism, including those of race and intolerance.

The historical background

The central political development in nineteenth-century central Europe was the foundation of the first German nation state in 1871. Unlike Britain and France, which had existed as monarchies since the medieval period and which evolved, by a process sparked off by revolution, into liberal nation states, no unitary German state, with executive control over all German areas of Europe, had ever existed. In this sense Germany represents the norm, becoming, as it did, a nation state during the nineteenth century, when nationalism in Europe began to emerge as the dominant political ideology.[3] Hand in hand with the political transformation that took place in Germany during the nineteenth century went economic, social and intellectual revolutions, which acted as the roots for the German states that would emerge after the First World War.

Underlying all the other changes in nineteenth-century Germany was the process of industrialization, which, by 1914, had made the country the dominant economy on the continent. While Britain may have industrialized first, Germany made up for lost time. During the period 1882–96 annual industrial growth rates averaged 4.5 per cent per annum, remaining at 3.1 per cent from 1896 to 1913. By the outbreak of the First World War Germany produced more iron ore and coal than Britain. The industries that would play a dominant role in the economic history of Germany during the twentieth century had come into existence, especially in the areas of engineering, electrical engineering and chemicals. In the last of these Germany reigned supreme in terms of the quantity and quality of its products, based on the strength of chemistry as an academic subject in German universities.[4]

The spread of industrialization inevitably meant a transformation of German society. German demography underwent dramatic changes characteristic of an industrializing state. In the first place, largely as a result of declining death rates, the population increased from its pre-industrial base of 23,520,000 in 1816 to 37,956,000 in 1865 and 67,883,000 in 1915.[5] In addition, population was highly mobile. This meant emigration to America, internal movement to German industrial areas, and a general internal east–west movement under the *Kaiserreich*. By the beginning of the twentieth century, as economic growth outstripped the increase in domestic labour supplies, emigration to the USA ceased, while the *Kaiserreich* began a process which all of its German successors would copy: importing foreign labour.[6] As a result of industrialization, employment structure clearly changed so that the overwhelming majority of Germans moved from working in rural to urban occupations. Thus a town such as Dortmund saw an increase in its population from 57,752 in 1875 to 214,226 in 1910, or a growth of 271 per cent. The overall proportion of Germans living in settlements of less than 2,000 decreased from almost two-thirds in 1871 to two-fifths by 1910.[7] Such changes meant an increase in the size of the working classes and the various shades of the German *Mittelstand* (middle class) at the expense of the peasantry. By 1907 over half of German employees belonged to the working classes, meaning an increase from 12.4 million workers in 1882 to 19.6 by 1907.[8] The middle-class occupations of businessmen, professionals and bureaucrats also saw significant expansion in the same period.[9] By the outbreak of the First World War, German society had the characteristics that would survive into the Weimar and Nazi periods and that would play a role in the rise of Hitler.[10] This meant that while the urban working classes may have represented the largest social group, the relatively large size of the bourgeoisie and the peasantry, as well as the continued survival of a Prussian aristocracy, determined the political development of Germany both before and after 1918.

The creation of the German nation state of 1871 clearly took place against the background of the economic and social transformations that affected central Europe during the course of the nineteenth century. The growth of liberal nationalism before 1848 would fit into classic interpretations of rising national movements dependent upon an emerging bourgeoisie. Had the revolutionaries of 1848 succeeded, the course of German history would have been quite different.[11] However, they did not, meaning that the first German nation state came into existence due to intervention from above, in the form of the Prussian autocracy, personified initially by Bismarck and then by Kaiser Wilhelm II. State creation from above, rather than, as in the British and French cases, the emergence of a new nation state due to revolution from below, meant that the *Kaiserreich* had strong autocratic tendencies. Although the Constitution of 1871 established a Reichstag elected by universal manhood suffrage, the executive, in the form of Kaiser and Chancellor, held real power between 1871 and 1918.[12]

Nevertheless, whether or not the *Kaiserreich* represented a sham democracy, the fact that all males could vote led to the emergence of mass parties. Much to the chagrin of the Kaiser, by the outbreak of the First World War the largest of these was the Social Democratic Party (SPD). Its share of the vote increased from 19.7 per cent in the Reichstag elections of 1890 to 34.8 per cent in 1912. By this time it had widened its support beyond its traditional urban centres of strength to make some impact (though often minimal) in rural Germany.[13] In 1912 it had 1,085,000 members and had become a truly mass party in terms of its organizational structure and its social and cultural activities, as well as its membership.[14] In addition, there also existed various shades of liberals and conservatives, as well as the Catholic Centre Party, which survived the anti-Catholic, Bismarckian *Kulturkampf*. The three groups had much in common. In the first place, they played a role in government between 1870 and 1914, with the Catholic Centre Party gradually coming back into favour. However, all three witnessed a decline in their share of the vote as the working classes and support for the SPD grew. Furthermore, the three parties were influenced, to a greater or lesser extent, by the growth of grass-roots politics.[15]

Finally, the *Kaiserreich* also witnessed a mushrooming of anti-Semitic parties, which fed off the endemic Judeophobia of Germany. While official anti-Semitism, depriving Jews of their civil rights, had always existed in Germany, the nineteenth-century emancipation of the Jews went hand in hand with a rise in popular hatred of them, surfacing in the Napoleonic and *Vormärz* periods in the works of Fichte, Jahn and Arndt and reaching new peaks after Jews became fully emancipated in the 1871 Constitution. A direct line certainly exists from Fichte, through the anti-Semitic parties of the *Kaiserreich*, to Hitler.[16] Nevertheless, this does not mean that Nazism was inevitable in 1830 or 1890. If anything, Germany was less anti-Semitic in the three decades before 1914 than either Russia, which witnessed a series of bloody pogroms,[17] or France, in which support or opposition for the Jewish soldier Alfred Dreyfus became the central political issue during the 1890s.[18]

Nevertheless, we must still accept the link between the anti-Semitic parties of the *Kaiserreich* and those of the Weimar Republic. In addition, the former period left a further political legacy to the latter in the polarization of political discourse from the anti-Semites to the extreme left. The latter became increasingly divided on ideological grounds during the First World War and its aftermath, as the SPD split, resulting in the emergence of the Communist Party (KPD).[19] Thus, in 1919 every political ideology had its supporters in Germany.

Apart from industrialization, the emergence of modern class society and the existence of an autocratic state, which, nevertheless, gave rise to numerous political parties, the other major characteristic of the *Kaiserreich* was its aggressive foreign policy, which played the determining role in the outbreak of the First World War. This aggressiveness has several explanations, including the fact that the first German state emerged from a series of wars of conquest, which, it may be argued, would inevitably mean that the newly created state would be too dynamic to rest on its laurels. In fact, it did remain peaceful for a short period while Bismarck served as Chancellor, but, when he lost his position following the crowning of Kaiser Wilhelm II, the new course in German foreign policy, in fact a return to the aggression of the period 1863–71, meant that Germany demanded her 'place in the sun',[20] which scared the other leading European state, Britain, as this implied that Germany would become the strongest power on the continent, as well as an imperial power, therefore threatening British world dominance.[21] The aggressive foreign policy of the years leading up to the First World War also finds explanation in the nature of the Constitution. Unable to satisfy the demands of the working classes and their representatives, the SPD, external expansion represented a way of 'buying off' the workers, by refocusing their attention away from their own unenviable position towards pride in German greatness.[22] The outbreak of the First World War in many ways resulted from the internal contradictions of the *Kaiserreich*, and therefore resembles the 1939–45 conflict, the underlying cause of which was a crisis in Nazi economy and society.[23]

Nevertheless, in describing continuities and discontinuities, vast differences exist between the two world wars. While the Imperial armies of 1914–18 may have committed some atrocities in both western and eastern Europe, they did not carry out the brutal acts that characterized Hitler's armies in eastern Europe. The First World War was a traditional expansionist conflict, with the central aim, evolving as the conflict progressed, of seizing territory in *Mitteleuropa*.[24] In contrast, the Second World War represented a struggle for racial purity for the Nazis, which meant that they devoted enormous attention to killing as many Jews as possible, as well as exploiting the labour power of eastern Europeans. While some use of eastern and western European workers took place in the First World War, it was on a much smaller scale.[25] Furthermore, the years 1914–18 did not result in extreme brutality against the native populations of eastern Europe, which would become fair game for the Nazis. The First World War also did not mean the same level of control as the Second. While mobilization for a Total War certainly took place almost immediately after the outbreak of hostilities, war weariness had emerged by 1917 and the defeat of 1918 came about against a background of dissension from below.[26] The level of control exercised by the Nazis meant that the home front remained basically loyal until the bitter end.

The Weimar Republic

While interpretations of Nazism often stress the years 1933–45 as unique, some aspects of the history of the Weimar Republic suggest that the period it covers can also be regarded as having distinctive characteristics when compared with other periods in modern German history. On the other hand, while Weimar has direct links with the regimes that preceded and followed it, as a liberal democracy it also has connections with the Federal Republic and roots in the *Vormärz* period and the 1848 revolutions.

Economically, the Weimar Republic can be regarded as a unique period in German history. The economic development of modern Germany essentially consists of the irresistible rise of German industry. Several setbacks have occurred, including the Great Depression of the 1870s and 1880s, which affected the whole of Europe, the years immediately after the Second World War, and various short periods during the Federal Republic's history, including 1974–5, after the hike in international oil prices, and the 1990s, due to reunification and the attempt to meet the Maastricht convergence criteria. Nevertheless, success rather than failure is the dominant characteristic of the economic history of both the *Kaiserreich* and the Federal Republic. While the economic system established in the German Democratic Republic (GDR) may have ultimately proved disastrous when opened up to western markets, even this system had a large measure of economic success, especially when compared with other Eastern Bloc regimes. Only the Weimar Republic is characterized by economic failure rather than success.[27]

Apart from the recovery period of 1924–9, when the world economy emerged from the postwar slump (helped by the Dawes Plan, which allowed Germany to pay reparations according to her ability to do so), the rest of the Weimar period is characterized by economic stagnation, collapse and disaster, the memory held by Nazi voters about the whole period 1919–33. Even during the recovery of 1924–9, growth remained patchy and basic structural problems had not been solved.[28] In the early postwar years Germany faced problems of starvation and fiscal collapse. The neglect of agriculture during the war, as mass mobilization took place, and the consequences of the Allied blockade, meant widespread food shortages in 1919. The financial burden of reparations led to the currency collapse and inflation of the early Weimar years. In addition, Germany also faced the same demobilization problems as the other states that had participated in the First World War. Nevertheless, the Germany of 1919 looked much healthier than the Germany of 1945, because it had not been destroyed by Allied bombers.[29]

The patchy recovery of 1924–9 collapsed with the Wall Street Crash, leading to more financial disaster as German banks, dependent on US support, dropped like flies. Unemployment represented the most concrete manifestation of the 1929–33 crisis, reaching an official total of six million by the time the Nazis came to power, although the real figure may have been much higher.[30] The callous policies of the various short-lived governments of the period 1929–33, uncharacteristic in the history of German economic and social policy, did not help the unemployed. For instance, 'The Brüning Government moved to deal with the situation by reducing benefits, increasing contributions and providing financial support from the Reich all at the same time, in the emergency decree of 26 July 1930'. In the winter of 1932–3 there may have been 'over a million people capable of work who were without either a job or any form of support'.[31]

In social terms, perhaps the most unusual characteristic of the Weimar Republic consisted in the fact that the middle classes suffered particularly badly as a result of the inflation of the early 1920s, one of the reasons for their over-representation in support for the Nazis. Nevertheless, it could not be said that they endured the worst deprivation, as the peasantry and the working classes also became victims of the international agricultural crisis of the 1920s and the rise in unemployment respectively.[32]

The Weimar Republic broke new ground in various aspects of social policy which, while reversed by the Nazis, would essentially be reinstated by both the Federal Republic and the German Democratic Republic. The SPD-founded Republic, while certainly not revolutionary, put much effort into guaranteeing workers' rights. In the words of Detlev J. Peukert, it created a 'welfare state', resulting, in 1927, in the introduction of unemployment insurance, although measures introduced in the early 1920s had attempted to help the unemployed. Other reforms were aimed at the rehabilitation of young offenders.[33] In addition, while the Weimar Republic may have remained, in feminist discourse, a traditional patriarchal society, women made more progress in the Germany of the 1920s than in virtually any other contemporaneous state, a process begun by the First World War, 'the father of women's emancipation'. Consequently, 112 women were elected to the Reichstag between 1919 and 1932, and by 1929 there were 2,500 women physicians, 300 lawyers and several dozen judges and professors.[34]

In political terms Weimar has elements of both continuity and discontinuity. Born in revolution, its creation resembles events in 1848, not only because of the uprising from below, but because the old order regained the initiative, both in the short run, in 1919, and in the long run, in 1933. The events in Germany in 1918 remained quite different from those in the Russian Empire in the previous year. The German revolution did not result in a root and branch reconstruction of society, but meant, instead, essentially a change in the nature of government, from a sham democracy to a 'real' democracy, in which the legislature had power but where the President replaced the Kaiser at the top of the executive, with the ability to act independently in times of emergency. In the context of both German and European history the Weimar Republic represents a progressive liberal democracy.

In fact, it may have been too progressive, perpetuating the plethora of parties covering all sections of the political spectrum. The system of proportional representation meant that any party could, in theory, rise from nothing to seize power, which true liberals must have viewed positively. As we know, this did actually happen, but the group that managed to succeed in this way completely despised and destroyed the free and open democracy that had allowed it to come to power. As a result of this experience, the Federal Republic was a less democratic state than the Weimar Republic, although one might argue that it just has more checks and balances.[35]

The birth of the Weimar Republic in defeat may also be viewed as unique (but then we would have to remember that the Federal Republic emerged out of a background of complete devastation). The Nazis made much of this fact with their stab-in-the-back theory, so that they got rid of a regime unloved by virtually all sections of society. In contrast, the Federal

Republic and the GDR survived. How loved these regimes actually were, especially the latter, is open to question, but they survived as separate entities until 1989. The reason for this lies in the second bitter experience of defeat, but also in the Cold War conflict, in which Germany was simply a tool.

This last point would also point to the fact that while the Weimar Republic may have represented a new departure in the history of German foreign policy, an emasculated Germany existed for much of the postwar period. Nevertheless, when German nationalists looked back to the glory days of the *Kaiserreich* after 1918, the humiliation proved unbearable. The Wilhelminian Empire had represented the strongest power on the continent, and one that threatened Britain's world dominance. In contrast, the vindictive Treaty of Versailles, which rubbed Germany's face in the humiliation of defeat, turned the country into a leper excluded from the international community and placed limits on the size of its armed forces. While all Weimar politicians may have wanted to escape from the Versailles straitjacket, they were not prepared, and not in a position, to ignore its provisions, preferring to work through diplomatic methods. Hitler, in contrast, simply acted as he pleased once he developed enough confidence.[36]

Nazism

More than 50 years after its demise Nazism appears one of the most murderous and totalitarian regimes in history, which, by implication, also makes it unique. While these aspects of Nazism certainly do separate it from its immediate German predecessor and successors, mass murder and control have characterized other regimes throughout the twentieth century, not the least of these being contemporaneous Stalinism. This regime, especially between 1929 and 1945, eliminated millions of its ethnic, social and political enemies through a combination of deportation, collectivization, industrialization and purging.[37] The centrality of race would also appear to make the Nazi period unique, but race has played a major role throughout twentieth-century Germany, as well as in locations all over the world. What is unquestionably unique is the effort Nazism put into the implementation of murderous racial goals, culminating in the establishment of the death camps. On the other hand, Nazism did not spring from nowhere: it had ideological, economic, social and diplomatic roots in the nineteenth century and even before. It also left a legacy which, in many cases, manifested itself in the desire never to return to the years 1933–45; in others, it left more negative traces.

Economically, Nazism is often regarded as a new path. The direct inter-vention of the state to solve economic problems in a Keynesian manner may appear new, but the state had always played a central role in the German economy, going back at least to the eighteenth-century Prussian monarchy and its investment in armaments, as well as linen and iron ore, especially in the newly acquired territory of Silesia.[38] During the nineteenth century government had played a large role in, for instance, the construction of railways,[39] and the building of municipal facilities.[40] The maintenance of the German armed forces and the attempt to build a navy during the *Kaiserreich* also meant considerable central government investment, which intensified during the First World War.[41] While the governments of the last years of Weimar may have remained relatively aloof, those of the 1920s introduced measures such as job creation, control of foreign exchange, and inter-vention in banking and agricultural production.[42]

Nazi economics therefore needs to be seen against the above historical background. Even so, the Nazi state does appear to have taken new economic paths, partly explained by its contrast with the laissez-faire policies of the last years of the Weimar period. The Nazis determined to solve unemploy-ment by deficit financing of public works in the short run and rearmament over a longer period of time. The number of people without jobs declined rapidly and by 1938 the unemployment problem had disappeared as the Nazi state began to enter a period of labour shortages and an overheating economy. By the outbreak of the Second World War, the German economy also became yet more tightly controlled with the introduction of a four-year plan. Furthermore, the attempt to achieve autarky, characteristic of late nineteenth-century imperial economic policy through the use of tariffs, now reached its logical conclusion, as the attempt to become self-sufficient formed a central tenet in Nazi ideology and meant the takeover of much of Europe, reducing the First World War problems of a lack of agricultural produce and raw materials.[43]

As the Nazis invaded central and eastern Europe they had an opportun-ity to implement their autarchic policies, which meant the plunder of natural resources, agriculture and manpower in the controlled areas. As Omer Bartov has written, 'The German Army marched into the Soviet Union with explicit orders to "live off the land", regardless of the effects this would have on the civilian populations. This method of supplying the army led to terrible impoverishment, famine and destruction, and caused millions of deaths in the occupied territories.'[44] On the home front, the economy became increasingly geared towards the production of armaments as the war pro-gressed, so that, in 1945, the economy focused upon nothing else.[45]

The Nazis invested much effort in transforming society, a central core of their ideology. They opposed the social divisions that had characterized the past and wanted, instead, to create a *Volksgemeinschaft*, in which social differences would disappear. In reality, the Nazis did little to break down class barriers among Aryans. During their twelve years of power, background continued to determine levels of economic success and German society remained divided.[46] Class-consciousness lessened because of the elimination of left-wing political parties and trade unions. In their place came a series of organizations to make people feel good about themselves and forget about their loss of liberty. At the top of this pyramid was the German Labour Front, which essentially represented an official trade union. The Beauty of Labour movement improved working conditions in factories, while the Strength Through Joy movement put much effort into providing subsidized activities, especially holidays.[47]

While Nazi rhetoric remained rhetoric with regard to breaking down class, the Nazis achieved extraordinary success in the most central core of their ideology, the creation of a racial state. As we have seen, racism had always played a central role in German history. But under an overtly racial party, proud of its ideology, German racism moved into a new phase, worse than anything seen even in the history of medieval persecuting anti-Semitism. By the outbreak of the Second World War the Nazis had managed to isolate all racial inferiors living within their borders, including Jews, gypsies and Slavs, so that, in the racial sense, they certainly had reconstructed German society.[48]

The Second World War allowed the Nazis to implement a system of murderous control never seen before even in the bloody history of Europe. In the invaded areas of eastern Europe, the Nazis played the role of God, deciding who would live and die, a decision determined by racial origin. Jews stood very little chance, as the Nazis saw them as the lowest form of human life and made every effort to eliminate them, either by shooting them, concentrating them, or placing them in death camps. Slavs fared somewhat better, as Nazi ideology dictated their exploitation rather than their murder, but the policy of the armies that invaded the Soviet Union was to take as few prisoners as possible. The eastern European gypsies, also regarded as racial inferiors by the Nazis, had a similar experience to the Jews, although they did not face quite the same population losses.[49] If the Nazi period is to be regarded as unique, then the fate of the populations of eastern Europe between 1939 and 1945 must play a large role in the reasons for this. Systematic factory killing, meaning the use of business methods for the implementation of Nazi racial goals,[50] as well as the shooting of men, women and children, point to the most bloody, ruthless and callous phase in European history. In fact, such actions on such a scale could only have happened in Europe from 1939 to 1945, and, as we have seen, the only regime that compares with the Nazis was the USSR under Stalin, which eliminated its enemies in an equally ruthless way. Both undemocratic and ideologically driven regimes saw the creation of a new society as their aim, which meant little concern for those regarded as outsiders.[51]

The implementation of a racial state did not simply mean the persecution of ethnic minorities in core and expanded Germany, but also had an impact on Aryans regarded as problematic, especially those with 'hereditary' diseases, who could face euthanasia or sterilization.[52] Members of the medical profession forgot about their Hippocratic oath as they worked in the service of the Nazi state, concerned with racial purity, euthanasia and genetics rather than the welfare of their patients. This meant the establishment of research institutes to look at all aspects of 'racial hygiene' and, during the Second World War, involved members of the medical profession carrying out experiments on humans.[53]

Also in accordance with their ideological goals, the Nazis devoted much attention to the position of women. The ideal German woman would not work but would, instead, produce as many children as possible, necessary for the expansion of the German *Reich* into eastern Europe. Women obtained medals for having large numbers of children and the Nazis tightened up abortion legislation. The liberation that women had enjoyed during the 1920s was reversed so that they disappeared from politics, except in Nazi women's organizations, and from many of the professions. Nevertheless, ideology and reality differed, as the Nazis had little success in either increasing the birth rate, which actually fell, or in taking women out of employment, although, unlike the situation in Britain, the Second World War did not mean mass mobilization of women.[54] Despite the rhetoric, the position of women can hardly be regarded as unique in Nazi Germany when compared either with other German states, or with the situation in other parts of inter-war Europe, whether fascist, liberal democratic or communist, in which patriarchy remained in control.[55]

The political changes implemented by the Nazis point to new directions in German history, as well as indicating continuities. For instance, the suspension of democracy would appear to be, in many ways, a return to the past as much as a new departure, especially in the context of nineteenth-century German history, during which time progressive forces vied with reactionary ones, with the latter holding the upper hand until 1919. Even in the Weimar Republic the old order, particularly in the form of the Prussian aristocracy, continued to play a role. In fact, this struggle between progressive and reactionary forces, epitomised in events such as the suppression of the revolutionaries of the early 1920s and the light treatment of Hitler after the Munich Beer Hall Putsch, played a large role in the failure of the Weimar Republic because the regime satisfied the wishes of nobody.[56]

The seizure of power by the Nazis meant the elimination of the forces of the left – once and for all, or so it would have appeared after the purges of

1933. On the other hand, the suppression of the KPD and the SPD would appear to resemble the Anti-Socialist Laws of 1878. Nevertheless, the 1878 actions were not as draconian and violent as those of 1933[57] and did not act as the prelude to the elimination, by various methods (not always violent), of all parliamentary parties except one, which Hitler had achieved by the middle of 1933. The exception, of course, was the Nazis. At no other time in German history, except during the GDR, did one party have sole control of the state.[58]

Did the personality cult of Hitler represent a unique development in German history? It proves difficult to find any political figure who attracted quite the same amount of adulation as the Führer. In the 'Hitler Myth', he remained distinct from everyday politics and stood out as a pinnacle of virtue compared with his infighting subordinates.[59] If ever a substitute human God existed in European history, Hitler represented such a person. To the forces of the extreme right he was a Messiah, rescuing Germany from the chaos into which it had fallen after the end of the First World War. Yet Hitler hardly represents a unique cult figure in the context of the twentieth century. The inter-war Soviet Union created two earthly Gods in the form of Lenin and Stalin.[60] While Hitler may have experienced more adulation than anybody else in German history, he has both predecessors and successors. If we went back to the period before the First World War, we could point to Bismarck, Kaiser Wilhelm I and Kaiser Wilhelm II. Bismarck worship is still indicated by the presence of Bismarck statues and towers in cities throughout Germany.[61] In the postwar period figures such as Adenauer, Ulbricht and Honnecker also attracted cult followings, if not quite on the scale of Hitler.[62]

One of the explanations for the scale of the Hitler cult may lie in Nazi propaganda. But it would be naive to suggest that the Nazis had a more sophisticated publicity machine than either the Federal Republic or the GDR.[63] However, the Nazis had an extraordinarily tight control over information and also made use, for the first time, of new methods of mass media, especially radio and film, to indoctrinate the population.[64] While straightforward political brainwashing took place through propaganda films, it also involved more subtle methods such as film drama. In a situation in which the Nazis had ultimate control over all cultural production in Germany, they could, for instance, encourage stories which pointed to the benefits of euthanasia,[65] as well as releasing such crude documentary racist potboilers as *The Eternal Jew* (1940).[66]

The propaganda films may have played a large role in the obedience of Germans under the Third Reich, for, unlike the areas occupied by the Nazis throughout Europe, no organized mass resistance movement with the aim of overthrowing the regime developed among Germans.[67] The real explanation for this state of affairs may essentially lie in the power of twentieth-century nationalism, because, however evil a regime may be, if it works in the name of those with the right ethnic credentials within its own borders, any attempt to challenge it represents treason. The French resistance, like other resistance movements all over Europe, ultimately fought in the name of nationalism.[68] A German opposition group would have fought against the legitimate government, and would therefore have attracted limited support.

Other reasons present themselves for the obedience of the Germans under the Nazis. One of these would point to the level of repression. After all, immediately after seizing power the Nazis eliminated all of their opponents, especially the left-wing ones, who went either into camps or exile. This meant that the working classes, a major source of potential opposition, remained leaderless.[69] Furthermore, even after the elimination of opposition in 1933, the Nazis practised surveillance and used brutal methods to eliminate anyone who demonstrated any dissent, however mild, especially during the Second World War. Apart from utilizing the already existing instruments of control, the Nazis had their own security forces in the form of the SA, the SS, which gradually took over the state as the war progressed, and the Gestapo.[70] In addition, the Nazis established a system of camps, which varied in size and numbers held before the Second World War but took off both within German borders and throughout Nazi-occupied Europe from 1939.[71] How was resistance possible in such a tightly controlled system? In fact, as Robert Gellately has demonstrated, the Nazi system worked through a system of informers and consequently needed to employ few 'policemen' of various sorts. In March 1937 the Düsseldorf Gestapo employed 291 persons, 242 of them bureaucrats, to control a population of approximately 500,000.[72] But from the point of view of absence of resistance, Nazi Germany represents normality. Even in the 'normal' circumstances of a liberal democracy, German people tend to undertake relatively few heroic political acts. It therefore seems unlikely that they would do so during the most intolerant regime in German history. In the same way, people in the second most tightly controlled regime in German history, the GDR, displayed little resistance for most of the period of its existence, perhaps because it had an even more advanced surveillance system in the form of the Stasi, which employed 260,000 people as informers between January 1985 and October 1989. Proportionate to the population, there may have been seven times as many informers in the GDR as there were under the Nazis.[73] However, unlike the Third Reich, the GDR did eventually collapse through people power. The explanation for this may simply be that the citizens of the former were more scared and disorganized, fighting a war, than those of the latter.

While surveillance in the Third Reich may have rooted out some fairly innocent activities that could result in severe punishment,[74] the Nazis could not possibly standardize everybody, no matter how brutal and tightly controlled their years of power. Therefore, we would have to regard groups such as Swing Youth and Eidelweiss Pirates as examples of youth subculture typical of twentieth-century liberal democracies.[75] Furthermore, while constant changing of jobs under conditions of full employment during the late 1930s may have irritated the Nazis, it hardly threatened the regime. Such actions simply represent normal life in the twentieth century.[76]

A final political aspect of the Third Reich that has received attention since the 1960s concerns the question of the efficiency of the Nazi bureaucracy. Led by Martin Broszat[77] and Ian Kershaw,[78] a series of historians have developed the idea of a pluralistic regime led by a lazy Hitler, rather than one in which an efficient Führer had complete control. This would point to Nazism as a fairly normal system of government, with a large bureaucratic structure in which civil servants played a leading role in determining policy. Nevertheless, Hitler's Germany was as efficient as any other modern German state, indicated by the efficiency of its killing and persecuting machines.

Foreign policy under the Nazis would, like all else, point to elements of continuity and discontinuity.[79] In the context of the expansionist policy of Bismarck and Wilhelm II, Hitler's aggression seems completely normal. It was the Weimar Republic that pursued an unusual path by acting cautiously, rather than the Third Reich. This argument seems to have much going for it. The difference may simply lie in the level of Hitler's expansionist goals, his willingness to carry them out, and the central role of racist ideology.

In terms of the ambition of Hitler, this may differ from the Weimar Republic, but it seems to have close similarities with the *Kaiserreich*. After all, Wilhelm II dreamt of an international German empire, and did not care whom he irritated in his attempts to obtain world dominance from the 1890s onward, a policy which played a large role in causing the outbreak of the First World War. When the conflict began, elaborate plans developed for the creation of a German-controlled *Mitteleuropa* and the takeover of much of Africa. The Treaty of Brest Litovsk, signed with the Bolsheviks in 1918, provided the clearest indication of Imperial ambitions, as it meant that Germany annexed much of western Russia.[80] Therefore, even in terms of ambition and the carrying out of these ambitions, there seems relatively little difference in the aims of Germany during the two world wars. In the Second, the Nazis, because of the initial superiority of their military machine, seized far more territory, throughout Europe and North Africa, than they did during the First.[81]

The centrality of racial ideology would have to point to a real difference in the way in which war was fought in 1914–18 compared with 1939–45. The Germans certainly did carry out some atrocities during the First World War, as was stressed by the Allied propaganda machine, such as the sinking of the *Lusitania*, the mistreatment of civilians in Belgium and the use of chemical weapons.[82] But the armies of the Emperor did not invade eastern Europe for the purpose of enslaving the native slavic populations and murdering the local Jews. While the *Kaiserreich* made some use of Polish and Russian labour, it ignored the Jews. Although ideologically motivated, racist, eastward-looking anti-Semites certainly existed in Germany during the First World War, they did not control power.[83] The Second World War grew out of the First in many ways, not the least of which was the change in the level of brutalization. The Second built upon the precedents of the First.

The legacy of Weimar and the Third Reich

In view of the seismic impact of the Third Reich and, to a lesser extent, the changes implemented by the Weimar Republic, it is unlikely that any state which followed these two systems of government could remain completely free of their influence. It may be fair to say that Nazism has cast a shadow upon all subsequent German states from which they could never really escape. As well as leaving negative traces of intolerance, the legacy of Nazism has also acted positively, because the states that have followed the Nazis have been determined not to make the same calamitous errors.

Economically, the connections between the inter-war regimes and their successors may not appear that obvious, but they do exist. In fact, in the case of the Federal Republic, it had traces of both Weimar and Nazism, as well as taking new departures. State intervention continued, as it had done, in fact, since the *Kaiserreich*. But the postwar Federal Republic had the central concern of avoiding a return to the last disastrous years of the Weimar Republic, when the callousness of welfare policy helped the Nazis to gather votes. This meant, among other things, an advanced welfare programme, although this would have connections with the *Kaiserreich*, the Weimar Republic and the Third Reich.[84] The Federal Republic also had a sophisticated system of industrial relations, with workers sitting on company boards. This was a reaction against the lack of worker representation under the Nazis, although it also displays links with Weimar. In terms of the success of the German economy and the basis of this success, patterns established during the nineteenth century continued into the postwar period.

As in the years before 1945, the economic dynamism of the Federal Republic depended heavily upon chemicals, engineering and electrical engineering. Unlike other Western states, the Federal Republic remains a leading manufacturing state, despite competition from globalization due, largely, to the quality of its products and the marketing that has persuaded international customers of this fact. The motor car has represented a leading sector in this process.[85] Even the GDR, despite the relatively poor quality of its products, could sell in the West, as the example of Zeiss photographic goods indicates.[86]

As time progressed, the fear of the Nazi past lessened and German economic power showed some decline. Changes did take place, especially under the impact of unification, which, in the east, meant the reappearance of unemployment on a significant scale for the first time since the Weimar Republic. The newly reunified state was also not as caring, in welfare policy terms, as its immediate predecessors, although there was no return to late Weimar callousness.

Assessing the legacy of Weimar and the Third Reich upon society in the postwar German states proves difficult. As we have seen, eliminating class differences and implementing an Aryan *Volksgemeinschaft* represented a central aim of Nazi social policy. The former did not happen and the Federal Republic certainly had gradations within it, so that, as in all capitalist societies, those born into wealthy bourgeois families enjoyed the greatest level of success. Nevertheless, the Federal Republic did not have the type of archaic class-consciousness characteristic of Britain. The Allied bombers of the Second World War had played a large part in eliminating such ideas, while the ceding of East Elbia to Poland killed off the Prussian aristocracy.[87] Similarly, the GDR had no time for social gradations.[88]

On the other hand, we may ask if the legacy of the *Volksgemeinschaft* concept survived into both the postwar German states. Twelve years of racial brainwashing could not disappear overnight. At the same time, both the Federal Republic and the GDR imported foreign labour, the former on a massive scale. In both cases the immigrants and their offspring remained outsiders. While the level of exploitation differed in the Federal Republic from the Nazi period, the importation process remained similar. Furthermore, once within the Federal Republic the newcomers and their offspring have been denied German citizenship, emphasizing their marginal position. Throughout the history of the Federal Republic, a clear cleavage has existed between Germans and foreigners.[89]

After reunification a new division emerged between *Ossis* and *Wessis*. This manifested itself, above all, in economic differences. The events of 1989-90 meant that one of the most advanced capitalist states in the world unified with one of the most successful communist ones. However, this could never be an equal match, with the west essentially taking over the east. Apart from the higher living standards of *Wessis* and the superiority of their accommodation and consumer goods, they did not face the collapse of industry that occurred in the GDR and that resulted in truly mass unemployment.[90]

German society at the start of the twenty-first century therefore has three clear groups in the form of *Wessis*, *Ossis* and *Ausländer*. Even within these groups, divisions exist, not least in relation to the position of women, who have, however, made massive advances in their position compared with either the Nazi period or the Weimar Republic. Nevertheless, as in most states, they face disadvantage.[91]

The inter-war years had a massive impact upon the political history of the postwar German states in numerous ways. Most obviously, the defeat of Nazism led to the creation of two new states. These new states lived very much in the shadow of the Nazi past, and their history displayed an obsessive desire to avoid a return to the horrors of Nazism, as well as evading the pitfalls of the Weimar Republic. The Constitution of the Federal Republic contains numerous clauses aimed at preventing a return to the arbitrary, totalitarian state of Nazism. For instance, it contains a charter of fundamental rights and freedoms. Article 1 declares that 'The dignity of man shall be inviolable', while article 2 states that 'Everyone shall have the right to life and to inviolability of his person. The liberty of the individual shall be inviolable.'[92] In addition, the establishment of the Federal Constitutional Court was partly aimed at preventing the re-emergence of a new Nazi party because it can ban undemocratic groupings. Furthermore, political parties cannot gain representation in the Bundestag unless they obtain 5 per cent of the vote.[93] Such actions have played a large role in preventing a return to Nazism, but then so has the economic success of the Federal Republic and the positive attitude of the Western Allies towards it, especially when compared with inter-war views towards Germany.

Nevertheless, negative legacies have remained from the Nazi period. In the case of the GDR, the Stasi seems to have had close connections with the Gestapo, although even in the Federal Republic various types of surveillance have existed.[94] Furthermore, the Federal Republic has always counted numerous extreme right-wing groups, ranging from nationalists to Neo-Nazis, even though, for the reasons outlined above, none of them has ever gained representation in the Bundestag. Nevertheless, this offers little consolation for the victims of racial attacks, which peaked in both east and west Germany immediately after reunification, indicating that the legacy of Nazism had remained repressed within the GDR and exploded in the early 1990s.[95]

By this time, some change had taken place in attitudes towards the Nazi past, epitomised in the *Historikerstreit* of the 1980s, which essentially involved left- and right-wing historians offering their differing views of German history and the centrality of Nazism within it.[96] Following German reunification, a new type of German self-confidence emerged, in which the memory of Nazism began to drift away, epitomized by the switching of the capital from the 'village' of Bonn to 'imperial' Berlin.

Germany's international position changed forever as a result of the experience of the Third Reich, never to return to the aggression and bullying that had characterized Imperial and Nazi Germany. In order to prevent a return to such tactics the foreign policy of the Federal Republic has involved cooperation with former enemies, especially France, in the formation and subsequent development of the European Economic Community.[97] Of course, both the Federal Republic and the GDR had little room for manoeuvre in the Cold War international division of power after 1945, in which they formed core parts of the Great Power blocs of the period 1945–89.[98] Nevertheless, during this period attitudes towards eastern Europe changed, not just in the GDR, which had no choice in the matter as a member of the Warsaw Pact, but also in the west, so that both Adenauer and Willy Brandt put much effort into the development of an *Ostpolitik*, epitomized by the latter's kneeling before the memorial to the Warsaw ghetto uprising. While *Ostpolitik* may have had the ultimate aim of reunification, it also aimed at mending fences with the eastern victims of Nazism.[99]

The foreign policy of the new Federal Republic after 1990 is little different to that of the old one of 1949–89. Certainly, there have been no serious indications that the ghosts of the Nazi past are about to return to steer a different course for German diplomacy, although German foreign policy has become more self-confident, and has shaken off some of the guilt feeling of before 1989. This would help to explain the use of German troops in UN and NATO action during the 1990s. The new reunified Germany remains absolutely central to the development of Europe, with the largest economy and one of the largest populations. It is completely committed to the European Union, to the UN and to NATO.[100]

At the start of the twenty-first century Germany has reached the status of a secure liberal democracy, a process which has involved the shedding of millions of gallons of German and non-German blood. Born out of the ashes of Nazism and defeat, it would appear, over five decades later, that the demons of the German past have been exorcised forever. Nevertheless, while Germany may never return to Nazism, its Nazi past, together with the legacy of the Weimar Republic and the *Kaiserreich*, continue to play a role in German history.

Notes

1. See the various interpretations of Nazism outlined by Ian Kershaw, *The Nazi Dictatorship: Problems and Perspectives of Interpretation*, 3rd edn (London, 1993), pp. 17–39.

2. This is the argument of Michael Burleigh and Wolfgang Wippermann, *The Racial State: Germany, 1933–1945* (Cambridge, 1991).

3. See Eric Hobsbawm, *Nations and Nationalism Since 1780: Programme, Myth, Reality*, 2nd edn (Cambridge, 1992), pp. 101–30.

4. See Clive Trebilcock, *The Industrialization of the Continental Powers, 1870–1914* (London, 1981), pp. 46–7.

5. Peter Marschalck, *Bevölkerungsgeschichte Deutschlands im 19. und 20. Jahrhundert* (Frankfurt, 1984), pp. 145–6.

6. Klaus J. Bade, 'Labour, Migration, and the State: Germany from the Late 19th Century to the Onset of the Great Depression', in Bade, ed., *Population, Labour and Migration in 19th- and 20th-Century Germany* (Oxford, 1987), pp. 59–76.

7. Thomas Nipperday, *Deutsche Geschichte, 1866–1918*, I, *Arbeitswelt und Bürgergeist* (Munich, 1990), pp. 34–7.

8. Ibid., p. 291.

9. Ibid., p. 374.

10. A good analysis of support for the Nazis is Michael H. Kater, *The Nazi Party: A Social Profile of Members and Leaders* (Oxford, 1983).

11. See James J. Sheehan, *German Liberalism in the Nineteenth Century* (London, 1982); Jonathan Sperber, *Rhineland Radicals: The Democratic Movement and the Revolution of 1848–1849* (Princeton, NJ, 1991).

12. See Hans-Ulrich Wehler, *The German Empire, 1871–1918* (Oxford, 1985), pp. 52–65.

13. W.L. Guttsman, *The German Social Democratic Party, 1875–1933: From Ghetto to Government* (London, 1981), pp. 78–81.

14. Ibid., pp. 130–66.

15. For a general account of these three parties see Thomas Nipperday, *Deutsche Geschichte, 1866–1918*, II, *Machstaat vor der Demokratie* (Munich, 1992), pp. 451–757. A good account of the National Liberals is David S. White, *The Splintered Party: National Liberalism in Hessen and the Reich, 1867–1918* (Cambridge, MA, 1976). For the conservatives see James N. Retallack, *Notables of the Right: The Conservative Party and Political Mobilization in Germany, 1876–1918*

(London, 1988). One of the best accounts of the Catholic Centre Party is David Blackbourn, *Class, Religion and Local Politics in Wilhelmine Germany: The Centre Party in Württemberg before 1914* (Wiesbaden, 1980).

16. This is the view of Lucy Dawidowicz, *The War Against the Jews, 1933–45* (Harmondsworth, 1987), esp. pp. 27–77.

17. See John Doyle Klier, *Imperial Russia's Jewish Question* (Cambridge, 1995).

18. For a thorough account see Jean-Denis Bredin, *The Affair: The Case of Alfred Dreyfus* (New York, 1986).

19. See Abraham Joseph Berlau, *The German Social Democratic Party, 1914–1921* (New York, 1970).

20. See, for instance, Imanuel Geiss, *German Foreign Policy, 1871–1914* (London, 1976).

21. Paul M. Kennedy, *The Rise of the Anglo-German Antagonism, 1860–1914* (London, 1980).

22. See contributions to Gregor Schöllgen, ed., *Escape into War? The Foreign Policy of Imperial Germany* (Oxford, 1990).

23. The problems of Nazi economy and society in peacetime are brilliantly summed up by Tim Mason in his essay 'Internal Crisis and War of Aggression, 1938–1939', reprinted in his posthumously published *Nazism, Fascism and the Working Class* (Cambridge, 1995), pp. 104–30.

24. See Fritz Fischer, *Germany's Aims in the First World War* (London, 1967).

25. Ulrich Herbert, *A History of Foreign Labour in Germany, 1880–1980: Seasonal Workers/Forced Labourers/Guest Workers* (Ann Arbor, MI, 1990), pp. 87–119.

26. Roger Chickering, *Imperial Germany and the Great War, 1914–1918* (Cambridge, 1998).

27. A good introduction to various aspects of the German economy during the nineteenth and twentieth centuries is Knut Borchardt, *Perspectives on Modern German Economic History and Policy* (Cambridge, 1991).

28. See, for instance, Theo Balderston, *The Origins and Course of the German Economic Crisis, 1923–32* (Berlin, 1993).

29. For the condition of German society and economy during the early Weimar years see Richard Bessel, *Germany After the First World War* (Oxford, 1993).

30. Richard J. Evans, 'Introduction: The Experience of Unemployment in the Weimar Republic', in Richard J. Evans and Dick Geary, eds, *The German Unemployed: Experiences and Consequences of Mass Unemployment from the Weimar Republic to the Third Reich* (London, 1987), pp. 1–22.

31. Ibid., pp. 7–8.

32. The experience of the middle classes is looked at by Gerald D. Feldman, *The Great Disorder: Politics, Economics and Society in the German Inflation, 1914–1924* (Oxford, 1993), pp. 527–55. For the peasantry see Harold James, *The German Slump: Politics and Economics* (Oxford, 1986), pp. 246–82. For unemployment in the Weimar Republic see contributions to Evans and Geary, *German Unemployed.*

33. See Detlev J. Peukert, *The Weimar Republic: The Crisis of Classical Modernity* (New York, 1991), pp. 130–4; Evans, 'Introduction', pp. 1–7; Elizabeth Harvey, *Youth and Welfare State in Weimar Germany* (Oxford, 1993).

34. See Claudia Koonz, *Mothers in the Fatherland: Women, the Family and Nazi Politics* (London, 1987), pp. 19–49; Ute Frevert, *Women in German History: From Bourgeois Emancipation to Sexual Liberation* (Oxford, 1989), pp. 168–204.

35. For the Weimar constitution see Helmut Heiber, *The Weimar Republic* (Oxford, 1993), pp. 24–42; Peukert, *Weimar Republic,* pp. 35–42.

36. See John Hiden, *Germany and Europe, 1919–1939,* 2nd edn (London, 1993).

37. For an introduction see Hélène Carrère D'Encausse, *Stalin: Order Through Terror* (London, 1981).

38. Trebilcock, *Industrialization,* pp. 24–9.

39. An extremely thorough account is Dieter Ziegler, *Eisenbahnen und Staat im Zeitalter der Industrialisierung: Die Eisenbahnpolitik der Deutschen Staaten im Vergleich* (Stuttgart, 1996).

40. See Brian Ladd, *Urban Planning and Civic Order in Germany, 1860–1914* (Cambridge, MA, 1990).

41. For naval investment see Gary E. Weir, *Building the Kaiser's Navy: The Imperial Naval Office and German Industry in the von Tirpitz Era, 1890–1919* (Annapolis, MD, 1992). For wartime investment and financing see Feldman, *Great Disorder,* pp. 25–96.

42. For the early Weimar economy see Peukert, *Weimar Republic,* pp. 107–28. Peukert actually speaks of 'corporatism', suggesting even closer connections with the Third Reich and the postwar German states. For economic policy in the final years of Weimar see Carl-Ludwig Holtfrerich, 'Economic Policy Options and the End of the Weimar Republic', in Ian Kershaw, ed., *Weimar: Why Did German Democracy Fail?* (London, 1990), pp. 58–91.

43. See Richard Overy, *War and Economy in the Third Reich* (Oxford, 1994). For Germany's problems in the First World War see Avner Offer, *The First World War: An Agrarian Interpretation* (Oxford, 1989).

44. Omer Bartov, *The Eastern Front, 1941–1945: German Troops and the Barbarization of Warfare* (London, 1985), pp. 129–30.

45. Overy, *War and Economy,* pp. 133–375.

46. See the contribution of Hartmut Berghoff to the present volume.

47. See David Schoenbaum, *Hitler's Social Revolution: Class and Status in Nazi Germany, 1933–39* (London, 1967), which remains a major study of all aspects of Nazi society.

48. See my essay below on 'Continuities and Discontinuities in race: Jews, gypsies and Slavs under the Weimar Republic and the Third Reich', pp. 218–45.

49. Ibid., pp. 218–45.

50. Two of the most important works on this issue are: Zygmunt Bauman, *Modernity and the Holocaust* (Cambridge, 1989); and Omer Bartov, *Murder in Our Midst: The Holocaust, Industrial Killing, and Representation* (Oxford, 1996).

51. See the range of essays on this subject in Ian Kershaw and Moshe Lewin, eds, *Stalinism and Nazism: Dictatorships in Comparison* (Cambridge, 1997).

52. Michael Burleigh, *Death and Deliverance: 'Euthanasia' in Germany, 1900–1945* (Cambridge, 1994). As the dates in the subtitle indicate, and as Burleigh makes clear, the killing of disabled people did not start with the Nazis.

53. Paul Weindling, *Health, Race and German Politics Between National Unification and Nazism, 1870–1945* (Cambridge, 1989), pp. 489–564.

54. See Koonz, *Mothers in the Fatherland*; Frevert, *Women in German History*, pp. 205–52; and the contribution by Lisa Pine to the present volume.

55. See contributions to Part One of Françoise Thébaud, ed., *A History of Women in the West*, V, *Toward a Cultural Identity in the Twentieth Century* (London, 1994).

56. A good political history of Weimar is Edgar Feuchtwanger, *From Weimar to Hitler: Germany, 1918–33* (London, 1993).

57. The SPD quickly recovered after the 1878 laws, despite the ban which meant that some of its members faced imprisonment or exile. At the 1884 Reichstag elections the party gained 9.71 per cent of the votes cast, even though the SPD remained officially illegal until 1890, after which the Anti-Socialist Laws no longer operated. See Vernon Lidtke, *The Outlawed Party: Social Democracy in Germany, 1878–1890* (Princeton, NJ, 1966).

58. For the elimination of opposition by the Nazis see, for instance, Karl Dietrich Bracher, *The German Dictatorship: The Origins, Structure and Consequences of National Socialism* (Harmondsworth, 1973), pp. 243–87. For government in the GDR see Mary Fulbrook, *Anatomy of a Dictatorship: Inside the GDR, 1949–1989* (Oxford, 1995).

59. The Hitler cult is brilliantly analysed by Ian Kershaw in his *The 'Hitler Myth': Image and Reality in the Third Reich* (Oxford, 1987).

60. For Lenin see Nina Tumarkin, *Lenin Lives! The Lenin Cult in Soviet Russia* (London, 1983). For Stalin see Robert C. Tucker, 'The Rise of Stalin's Personality Cult', *American Historical Review* 84 (1979), pp. 347–66. I would

like to thank my De Montfort colleague Mark Sandle for pointing me to these sources.

61. Kershaw, *Hitler Myth*, pp. 13–16.

62. For a hagiography of Adenauer see Wilhelm von Sternburg, *Adenauer: eine deutsche Legende* (Frankfurt, 1987). An excellent account of the Ulbricht cult can be found in Carola Stern, *Ulbricht: Eine politische Biographie* (Cologne and Berlin, 1964), pp. 237–53. One of the manifestations of the cult, typical of postwar Eastern bloc dictators, was the production of poetry and songs in Ulbricht's honour. Many of these linked Ulbricht with the heroes of the Communist past, including Karl Liebknecht, Rosa Luxemburg, Ernst Thälmann and Lenin. See ibid., pp. 249–51.

63. See the wide range of contributions to Gerald Diesener and Rainer Gries, eds, *Propaganda in Deutschland: Zur Geschichte der politischen Massenbeeinflussung im 20. Jahrhundert* (Darmstadt, 1996). This contains sections on the Third Reich, the GDR and the Federal Republic.

64. See David Welch, *The Third Reich: Politics and Propaganda* (London, 1993).

65. Burleigh and Wippermann, *Racial State*, pp. 153–62.

66. See Eric Rentschler, *The Ministry of Illusion: Nazi Cinema and Its Afterlife* (London, 1996), pp. 149–69, who makes comparisons between *The Eternal Jew* and the other infamous Nazi anti-Semitic film, the fictional *Jude Süss* (1940).

67. However, there were various types of resistance, including numerous attempts to kill Hitler, one of which, in the summer of 1944, came very close to succeeding. German opposition to the Nazis has received much attention: see, for instance, Francis R. Nicosia and Lawrence D. Stokes, eds, *Germans Against Nazism: Opposition and Resistance in the Third Reich* (Oxford, 1988); David Clay Large, ed., *Contending With Hitler: Varieties of German Resistance to the Third Reich* (Cambridge, 1991); and Michael Balfour, *Withstanding Hitler in Germany, 1933–45* (London, 1988).

68. For an account of resistance in countries throughout Europe see Jørgen Hæstrup, *Europe Ablaze: An Analysis of the History of the European Resistance Movements, 1939–45* (Odense, 1978).

69. However, some underground left-wing organizations did survive within Germany, even into the war, but did not regenerate a mass working-class movement. For details of such groups see F.L. Carsten, *The German Workers and the Nazis* (Aldershot, 1995).

70. For the SA see, for instance, Richard Bessel, *Political Violence and the Rise of Nazism* (London, 1984), esp. pp. 97–118, which deals with the role of the SA in eliminating opposition immediately after the Nazis seized power. For the SS see Heinz Höhne, *The Order of the Death's Head* (London, 1980). Different perspectives on the Gestapo can be found in Gerhard Paul and Klaus-Michael Mallmann, eds, *Die Gestapo: Mythos und Realität* (Darmstadt, 1995).

71. As early as 31 July 1933 the Nazis held 26,879 people in 'protective custody'. While this figure subsequently declined, it rose to 60,000 immediately after *Kristallnacht*, but fell back to 21,400 at the outbreak of war. See Wolfgang Sofsky, *The Order of Terror: The Concentration Camp* (Princeton, NJ, 1997), pp. 28, 34. For the camp system during the Second World War, which claimed millions of victims, see Panayi, 'Continuities and Discontinuities in Race', below, pp. 230–7.

72. Robert Gellately, *The Gestapo and German Society: Enforcing Racial Policy, 1933–1945* (Oxford, 1990), p. 45.

73. David Childs and Richard Popplewell, *The Stasi: The East German Intelligence and Security Service* (London, 1967), pp. 82–6.

74. Gellately, *Gestapo*, pp. 129–58.

75. See the discussion of youth groups in Detlev J.K. Peukert, *Inside Nazi Germany: Conformity, Opposition and Racism in Everyday Life* (Harmondsworth, 1993), pp. 145–74.

76. Tim Mason points out in *Social Policy in the Third Reich: The Working Class and the 'National Community'* (Oxford, 1993), p. 230, that the Nazis required workers to gain permission before finding new employment. However, in a condition of full employment by the late 1930s, workers changed jobs once every twelve months on average. Mason views this as a way of defying the regime and industry in 'The Workers' Opposition in Nazi Germany', *History Workshop* 11 (1981), pp. 120–37.

77. Martin Broszat, *The Hitler State: The Foundation and Development of the Internal Structure of the Third Reich* (London, 1981).

78. See Ian Kershaw, *Hitler* (London, 1991).

79. This is the view of Imanuel Geiss in his contribution to the present volume.

80. One of the best accounts of late nineteenth-century Imperial expansion, Germany's First World War aims, and the Treaty of Brest-Litovsk is Fischer, *Germany's Aims*.

81. See Gerhard L. Weinberg, *A World at Arms: A Global History of World War II* (Cambridge, 1994).

82. For the myth and reality of German warfare between 1914 and 1918 see, for instance, Thomas A. Bailey and Paul B. Ryan, *The Lusitania Disaster: An Episode in Modern Warfare and Diplomacy* (New York, 1975); Alan Kramer, '"Greueltaten": Zum Problem der deutschen Kriegsverbrechen in Belgien und Frankreich 1914', in Gerhard Hirschfeld, Gerhard Krumeich and Irina Renz, eds, *Keiner fühlt sich hier mehr als Mensch: Erlebnis und Wirkung des Ersten Weltkrieges* (Essen, 1993), pp. 85–114; and L.F. Haber, *The Poisonous Cloud: Chemical Warfare in the First World War* (Oxford, 1986).

83. In fact, organized anti-Semitism had declined by 1914, compared with its strength in the peacetime *Kaiserreich*, as pointed out by Richard S. Levy, *The Downfall of Anti-Semitic Parties in Imperial Germany* (New Haven, CT, 1975).

84. See contributions to Jochen Clasen and Richard Freeman, eds, *Social Policy in Germany* (London, 1994).

85. See Richard Overy, 'The Economy of the Federal Republic: A Survey', in Klaus Larres and Panikos Panayi, eds, *The Federal Republic of Germany Since 1949: Politics, Society and Economy Before and After Unification* (London, 1996), pp. 3–34.

86. Nevertheless, from a capitalist viewpoint the economy of the GDR had serious economic problems. While some products were of high quality even by Western standards, most could not compete, as can be evidenced by comparing the Trabant with the Mercedes. Furthermore, the GDR economy had serious structural problems. Although it had impressive growth rates for national income, low rates of productivity meant that consumer demand could not be satisfied. However, the GDR did not face the perpetual economic crisis characteristic of Weimar. For an account of economics in the GDR see Günter Kusch, Rolf Montag, Günter Specht and Konrad Wetzker, *Schlusbilanz-DDR: Fazit einer verfehlten Wirtschafts- und Sozialpolitik* (Berlin, 1991).

87. Two starting points for society and class in the Federal Republic are J. Fijalkowski, 'The Structure of German Society After the Second World War', in J.P. Payne, ed., *Germany Today: Introductory Studies* (London, 1971), pp. 84–110, and David Childs and Jeffrey Johnson, *West Germany: Politics and Society* (London, 1981), esp. pp. 86–109.

88. The GDR had an advanced welfare system, for which see, for instance, Jonathan Steele, *Inside East Germany: The State that Came in From the Cold* (New York, 1977), pp. 167–98. However, as in other Eastern bloc states there certainly were social gradations according to occupation, for which see Dietrich Staritz, *Geschichte der DDR, 1949–1985* (Frankfurt am Main, 1985), pp. 165–75.

89. For an introduction to the situation in the Federal Republic see Panikos Panayi, 'Race in the Federal Republic of Germany: Immigration, Ethnicity and Racism Since the Second World War', in Larres and Panayi, *Federal Republic*, pp. 191–208. For the GDR see Maria and Lothar Elsner, *Zwischen Nationalismus und Internationalismus: Über Ausländer und Ausländerpolitik in der DDR, 1949–1990* (Rostock, 1994).

90. For a statistical outline see Alun Jones, *The New Germany: A Human Geography* (Chichester, 1994). A good oral history of East German changes is Jürgen A.K. Thomaneck, 'From Euphoria to Reality: Social Problems of Post-Unification', in Derek Lewis and John R.P. Mackenzie, eds, *The New Germany: Social, Political and Cultural Changes of Unification* (Exeter, 1995), pp. 7–30.

91. A good introduction is Eva Kolinsky, *Women in Contemporary Germany: Life, Work and Politics*, 2nd edn (Oxford, 1993).

92. Quoted and translated in Carl-Christoph Schweitzer, Detlev Karsten, Robert Spencer, R. Taylor Cole, Donald Kommers and Anthony Nicholls, eds, *Politics and Government in Germany, 1944–1994: Basic Documents* (Oxford, 1995), p. 302.

93. For an outline of the history of the extreme right in the Federal Republic see David Childs, 'The Nationalist and Neo-Nazi Scene Since 1945', in Larres and Panayi, *Federal Republic*, pp. 209–29.

94. Most importantly the Amt für Verfassungsschutz, which, in its annual report, the *Verfassungsschutzbericht*, publishes a list of extreme right- and left-wing groups in existence, as well as keeping tags on the existence of foreign extremist groups active within Germany. The annual report has detailed information on all such organizations. Furthermore, the individual German Länder also keep track of extremist groupings, with their own 'Office for the Protection of the Constitution'. These may have employed 4,000 officials in 1980 according to H. Busch, A. Funk, U. Kauß, W.D. Narr and F. Werkenten, *Die Polizei in der Bundesrepublik* (Frankfurt, 1988), p. 107, whose book represents a critical examination of all aspects of policing in the Federal Republic.

95. Panikos Panayi, 'Racial Violence in the New Germany 1990–93', *Contemporary European History* 3 (1994), pp. 265–87.

96. See Richard J. Evans, *In Hitler's Shadow: West German Historians and the Attempt to Escape from the Nazi Past* (London, 1989).

97. In fact, we may see the entire history of European integration as the evolution of the Franco-German axis, which has dominated postwar continental western Europe. Every development that has taken place, from the formation of the European Coal and Steel Community in 1952 to the launch of the Euro in 1999, has been driven by the two states acting together. Studies on Germany, the European Union and France include Clemens Wurms, ed., *Western Europe and Germany: The Beginnings of European Integration, 1949–1960* (Oxford, 1995), and Patrick McCarthy, ed., *France–Germany, 1983–1993* (London, 1993).

98. See, for instance, A. James McAdams, *Germany Divided: From the Wall to Reunification* (Princeton, NJ, 1993).

99. See, for instance, William E. Griffith, *The Ospolitik of the Federal Republic of Germany* (Cambridge, MA, 1978).

100. See, for instance, Lothar Gutjahr, *German Foreign and Defence Policy After Unification* (London, 1994); Arnulf Baring, ed., *Germany's New Position in Europe: Problems and Perspectives* (Oxford, 1994); and Paul B. Stares, ed., *The New Germany and the New Europe* (Washington, DC, 1992).

PART TWO

Weimar and Nazi Germany: A Survey

CHAPTER TWO

The German Economy, 1919–1945

RICHARD OVERY

Shortly after the end of the war in Europe in May 1945 the writer James Stern was posted to Frankfurt-am-Main, a city he had known before the war, a centre of German finance, and home to the chemicals giant IG Farben. Stern found the city reduced to 'acres of corpse-like buildings with their black, hollow eyes . . . fallen roofs and collapsed ceilings'. The destruction was comprehensive: 'Nothing I saw in Frankfurt', Stern continued, 'remained in so unharmed a state as to convince me I'd really been there before'.[1] In Frankfurt 52 per cent of the built-up area was destroyed in eleven attacks. Other cities were devastated even more completely: Würzburg 89 per cent destroyed, Bochum 83 per cent, Hamburg and Wuppertal each 75 per cent.[2]

The destruction of half the urban area of Germany's major cities was the most visible evidence of the extent to which Germany's economic development had been hostage to the fortunes of war for over 30 years. The Weimar economy was severely dislocated by the effects of defeat in the First World War; economic revival in the 1930s was distorted by the decision to build Germany into a military superpower; defeat in a second world war faced Germany in 1945 with the bleak prospect of territorial division, unpredictable levels of economic reparation, and occupying powers determined to reduce Germany's productive might. For the German economy the era of the two world wars created exceptional domestic and external circumstances. Development was conditioned by political objectives or military ambitions that undermined conventional patterns of productive growth and wealth creation. Expressed in crude statistical terms, the net national product of Germany was the same in 1947 as it had been in 1896: 33 billion marks at constant prices. By comparison, Britain's domestic national product in 1947 was almost 100 per cent higher than it had been in 1896.[3]

The pattern of development

The overall development of the German economy from the First World War to the end of the Second was characterized by an underlying stagnation, punctuated by two short periods of more sustained growth. In 1913 net national product was 52 billion marks. In 19 of the next 30 years net national product, expressed in constant prices, fell below this level. Only in 1927–9, and from 1935 to 1944, was the 1913 figure exceeded. In the first case it was overtaken only narrowly, though both area and population were smaller than pre-war, as a result of the terms of the Versailles settlement. In the second case the figures are substantially distorted by the acquisition of additional territory and population, from the Austrian *Anschluss* in 1938 to the final creation of Greater Germany in 1940 following the re-occupation of Alsace-Lorraine. Taking account of population changes, output per head in Germany grew between 1913 and 1950 at an average of only 0.4 per cent a year, compared with an average of 1.8 per cent achieved between 1870 and 1913 and 5.3 per cent during the 'economic miracle' of 1950–70.[4]

Before the First World War the German economy underwent a rapid process of economic modernization. The proportion of the population working on the land in 1870 was approximately two-thirds; by 1914 the figure had fallen to one-third. According to the census of 1907, industry and services employed 62.8 per cent of the workforce, agriculture 37.0 per cent. This distribution reflected the rapid growth in Germany from the 1890s of manufacturing industry, commercial services and foreign trade. Germany's capital stock more than doubled between 1890 and 1913, with most of the growth occurring in the last ten years; exports grew at 8.5 per cent a year from 1900 to 1913. The German economy was internationalized during the period; large flows of capital moved into and out of Germany, and the manufacturing economy became heavily export-dependent. As a result of the world boom German living standards rose steadily. Real earnings for German workers doubled between the founding of the Reich and the outbreak of war.

The upward trajectory of economic development was sharply interrupted by the First World War and its aftermath. The failure to anticipate a war of any length was compounded with the sheer lack of government experience in mobilizing and directing national economic resources. Industrial output fell 43 per cent, private consumption fell by almost one-third, Germany's capital stock declined, and German exports fell by three-quarters. Government expenditure for the war effort could only be met by creating high levels of debt, 151 billion RM by 1918. Real earnings declined for all groups, but the effect on living standards was uneven given the distortion of the labour

Table 2.1 Basic statistics for the German economy, 1913–1950

Year	Net National Profit (NNP)	Govt expend (bn marks, 1913 prices)	Govt debt (bn marks)	Index of industrial production (1928 = 100)	Unemployment rate (%)
1913	52.4	5.13	5.2	98	2.9
1919	[28.3]	[14.70]	199.7	37	3.7
1920	[31.9]	[9.30]	263.5	54	3.8
1921	[35.7]	[6.70]	352.2	65	2.8
1922	[39.1]	[4.00]	667.5	70	1.5
1923	[29.7]	[11.40]	–	46	9.6
1924	[39.3]	[5.50]	2.7	69	13.5
1925	46.9	5.80	7.1	81	6.7
1926	46.6	6.13	7.3	78	18.0
1927	53.1	6.38	7.1	98	8.8
1928	54.0	6.69	8.2	100	8.4
1929	51.7	6.57	9.6	100	13.1
1930	49.3	6.50	11.3	87	15.3
1931	43.9	6.32	11.4	70	23.3
1932	41.8	6.28	11.6	58	30.1
1933	47.4	7.72	11.7	66	26.3
1934	52.1	9.77	12.6	83	14.9
1935	58.7	13.37	14.4	96	11.6
1936	64.5	15.69	16.1	107	8.3
1937	71.9	16.25	19.1	117	4.6
1938	79.8	22.46	30.7	125	2.1
1939	[83.6]	[31.59]	47.9	135	0.4
1940	[77.2]	[41.53]	85.9	140	0.2
1941	[76.2]	[48.96]	137.6	155	–
1942	[75.3]	[60.91]	195.6	160	–
1943	[73.3]	[69.80]	273.4	175	–
1944	[68.5]	[74.96]	379.8	180	–
1945	[41.7]	[43.06]	387.3	–	–
1950	[44.9]	7.81	7.3	102	10.2

Figures in brackets are estimates. NNP from 1939 does not include the new areas incorporated into Greater Germany. Unemployment rate is for union members 1913–29, registered unemployed 1930–40.

Adapted from: A. Sommariva and G. Tullio, *German Macroeconomic History, 1880–1979* (London, 1987), pp. 226–7, 237–8; D. Petzina, 'Was There a Crisis Before the Crisis?', in J. von Kruedener, ed., *Economic Crisis and Political Collapse: The Weimar Republic, 1924–1933* (Oxford, 1990), p. 6; R. Berthold, ed., *Produktivkräfte in Deutschland, 1917/18 bis 1945* (Berlin, 1988), p. 15; B. Mitchell, *European Historical Statistics, 1750–1970* (London, 1978), pp. 65, 68.

market produced by the concentration of productive effort on a narrow range of war-related products. The internationalization of the German economy was reversed by the blockade and the freezing of German overseas assets.

This was the unhappy situation inherited by the new democratic regime in 1919. The process of postwar demobilization and industrial restructuring carried the risk of large-scale unemployment, but the decision to increase public debt in order to buy off potential social unrest succeeded in reducing unemployment rapidly. The government opted to penalize savers by encouraging the productive economy through sustained inflationary spending. This decision, in sharp contrast to the deflationary policies pursued in other major economies, has to be understood against the background of German defeat, revolution and a punitive peace settlement. The widespread political and industrial unrest of the winter of 1918–19 was fuelled by severe shortages of foodstuffs, high black-market prices and rising unemployment. The Allied blockade remained in force, pending the peace settlement, and Germany was denied access to assets abroad including much of the German merchant marine. Under the terms of the peace settlement Germany was subject to severe penalties: she lost 13 per cent of her territory, three-quarters of her iron ore deposits, 26 per cent of her coal and 38 per cent of steel capacity. Germany was also required to pay reparations for war damage. A final schedule of 132 billion gold marks established in 1921 (denominated thus to prevent the German government paying in depreciating paper marks) was added to very substantial reparations in kind seized between 1919 and 1921. The transfers in kind have been estimated at approximately 20 billion between 1919 and 1922, representing around one-tenth of German national income.[5]

Under these circumstances the Weimar governments gambled that creditors were a less dangerous political force than a hungry and unemployed workforce. In 1919 the state spent 55 billion marks, only 11 billion of which was covered by revenue. By 1923 all but 1 per cent of government expenditure was met by deficit spending. The reform of the tax system in 1920, pushed through by the Centre Party politician Matthias Erzberger, did far too little to stem the tide. The *Reichsbank* was permitted to provide generous credits for German industry at low rates of interest to encourage the investment necessary to re-establish the civilian economy and expand employment. Following a brief pause in 1920/1 the currency depreciated rapidly. At the beginning of 1919 the dollar was worth 8.9 RM; by the beginning of 1923 it stood at 17,972 RM; when the currency collapsed in November the figure was 4.2 billion marks to the dollar.[6]

Government financial policy was not the only cause of inflation, however. There remained a severe shortage of goods as industrial and agricultural production failed to return to anything like pre-war levels. Price controls on key foodstuffs were retained, encouraging a widespread black market and escalating prices. The postwar expansion of the trade union movement strengthened labour demands for wage increases. A large inflow of funds from abroad, speculating on German stabilization and revival, encouraged the atmosphere of easy money. The shift to hyperinflation was bound up with external factors. When confidence abroad in German revival finally cracked in the summer of 1922, the value of the mark plummeted on world currency markets. German firms began to denominate in dollars and frightened German investors tried to unload their own marks as quickly as possible. The accelerated velocity of circulation created the final downward spiral. When French and Belgian troops occupied the Ruhr in January 1923 to enforce reparation deliveries, the currency was doomed. During 1923 German leaders accepted that destruction of the currency would at least eliminate the primary cause of inflation – high government debt. In November 1923 the 154 billion RM of government debt was worth precisely 15.4 pfennig.[7]

It is possible, as some historians have argued, to see the inflation in positive terms, rather than in conventional terms as a catastrophic aftershock of war. The gamble on inflation did have the effect of reviving employment, investment and output, while the low cost of German exports produced a trade revival that saw exports quadruple between 1919 and 1922 from the low postwar base.[8] Moreover the redistributive effects of the inflation favoured manual workers at the expense of white-collar and state employees, and imposed a crippling 'inflation' tax on the rich, while freeing the republican regime from the burden of war debts.

There remain nonetheless serious objections to such a view. Hjalmar Schacht, the banker appointed as Reich currency commissar in November 1923 to oversee the stabilization of the mark, described the inflation period as 'a moral poisoning of the whole of business life'.[9] The political and psychological impact of the inflation lived on in Germany for decades. The economic effects were immediate. While businesses scrambled to invest at negative rates of interest, levels of real net investment remained well below those achieved pre-war or after 1924. At the Krupp works in Essen investment in the years 1919–23 was on average only 36 per cent of the 1909–14 level.[10] Living standards developed very unevenly, but millions of Germans experienced declining real income and poor levels of consumption compared with 1913. In 1923 per capita consumption of meat was only 54 per cent of pre-war, of potatoes only 62 per cent.[11] The impact of the loss of savings and investments went well beyond the rich in Germany. Estimates based on tax returns suggest a loss of 90 per cent of personal wealth during the inflation.[12] The German financial system after 1924 was permanently scarred

Table 2.2 Statistics on the 'golden years', 1925–1929

	1913	1925	1926	1927	1928	1929
Index of real national income per head	100	90	92	99	102	101
Unemployment (000s)	348	682	2025	1312	1391	1899
Gross fixed investment (bn RM)	–	10.31	10.67	12.97	13.68	12.79
Share prices (1926–8 = 100)	113	86	101	98	101	77
Real weekly net earnings (1925 = 100)	–	100	99	107	110	111
Agricultural output (1928 = 100)	113	86	85	95	100	101
Industrial output (1928 = 100)	98	83	76	96	100	100

Adapted from: T. Balderston, *The Origins and Course of the German Economic Crisis: November 1923 to May 1932* (Berlin, 1993), pp. 16, 334; R. Berthold, ed., *Produktivkräfte in Deutschland, 1917/18 bis 1945* (Berlin, 1988), p. 15; V. Berghahn, *Modern Germany: Society, Economy and Politics in the Twentieth Century* (Cambridge, 1982), p. 269.

by the collapse. In 1913 savings in Germany had totalled 19 billion RM; in 1925 they amounted to a mere 608 million.

Above all, the period of stabilization that began in early 1924 with the refounding of the currency led to higher levels of investment, output and trade, and to a sharp rise in real earnings compared with the inflation period. The years from 1924 to 1929 are usually regarded as the 'golden years' of the German inter-war economy, but the achievement should not be exaggerated. By 1928 the process of 'catching up' with the economic performance of the pre-1914 economy was finally completed, but at the peak of the stabilization boom the national product was only 4 per cent larger than in 1913, with higher levels of unemployment and a lower investment ratio than pre-war. The 'golden years' masked a fragile economic revival. This was partly a reflection of weaknesses in the wider world economy. The failure fully to re-establish the pre-war currency and trading system based on gold, and the decline in primary product prices, penalized the German economy with its high export dependence and revalued currency. Germany's share of world exports fell by 31 per cent between 1913 and 1927–9, and trade with primary producers by more than a third. Germany also found herself heavily dependent on foreign investment to compensate for the collapse of private domestic savings and the continued capital flight abroad by German investors wary of renewed inflation. Between 1924 and 1930 net foreign investment of over 17 billion RM was attracted by high interest rates. In 1929 some 38 per cent of German bank deposits were foreign-owned. Slow trade growth and high interest rates in turn reduced the domestic incentive to invest. Capital invested as a share of national income fell from an estimated 12.5 per cent in 1913 to 2 per cent in 1925, rising only to 4.2 per cent by 1929.[13]

What investment was undertaken helped to create a modern industrial core using more modern equipment and work processes, but the effect was to create higher levels of technological unemployment, while profit levels remained historically low. It has been argued that the profit squeeze owed a great deal to the growth of unionized labour which pressured employers into granting excessive wage deals which made German goods uncompetitive. However, the evidence based on the relationship between productivity growth and wage increases is ambiguous. Moreover, the number of unionized workers fell from 7.8 million in 1922 to 4.6 million in 1928, along with a decline in strike activity, while some wage increases were the result of local labour shortages caused by rigidities in the labour market.[14] Other factors also explain poor profitability. Taxation levels on industry were considerably higher than in other developed economies, and employers bore a substantial share of the cost of welfare provision. Though entrepreneurs blamed workers for pushing up costs, the problems they faced stemmed as much from deficient demand as they did from high wage costs. Foreign markets were restricted by tariffs and falling income, while home markets were depressed by the loss of middle-class savings and the existence of sizeable economic sectors – agriculture, craft industries – characterized by declining net income and rising debt. These are the elements of what Knut Borchardt has called 'the crisis before the crisis'.[15]

The evidence that Germany had never fully recovered from the distorting effects of war and postwar inflation was cruelly exposed in the slump. Though the downturn in Germany is conventionally associated with the Wall Street Crash of October 1929, the signs of impending recession in Germany were evident from 1928. Indeed poor expectations of continued German revival helped to undermine the confidence of American speculators, a cause rather than a consequence of the Great Crash. Investment activity slowed down and share prices fell steadily from the spring of 1928; by the spring of 1929 there were 2.9 million unemployed.[16] Increased state and municipal investment helped to soften the blow, but well before the Crash the German economy was in crisis. Nevertheless, the Crash when it came made the German situation much worse. Once again the economy was plunged into a prolonged period of economic uncertainty from which it slowly recovered only seven or eight years later. As late as the spring of 1936 there were still 2.5 million unemployed. Living standards barely revived even by the end of the 1930s. Though Hitler's dictatorship in 1933 provided an evident political break with the Weimar period, the economic crisis, and the attempts to overcome it, form much more of a unity from the late 1920s to the mid-1930s. The issue that faced all governments, Hitler's included, was simply how to create an economy that would function effectively after almost twenty years of economic dislocation.

The German slump was in this sense the end point of a period of economic turmoil rather than an interruption to a trajectory of steady economic progress, which helps to explain the climate of utter despair that it engendered. The slump was not the cause of many of Germany's problems but simply intensified them – the fragile capital and banking sector, weak underfunded agriculture, industrial overcapacity, slow trade growth were all inherited from the 1920s. The collapse of world trade and the withdrawal of foreign short-term lending in 1930–2 exposed these structural weaknesses and led to historically exceptional falls in employment, output and investment. The trough of the recession was reached in the autumn and winter of 1932–3 against the background of German political crisis, but revival proved uncertain and patchy for another two years.

The historical debate surrounding the German slump has focused chiefly on the question why recovery could not have been achieved sooner. It is often assumed that the failure of the government or the German business community to work for a radical solution to the crisis paved the way for Hitler and the NSDAP's crude promise of economic justice – 'Bread and Work' for all. The issue at the time, however, was much less clear-cut. When Heinrich Brüning was appointed chancellor in March 1930 he saw it as his responsibility to solve Germany's economic crisis in the terms in which he understood it. His aim was to put downward pressure on prices, wages and welfare payments in order to boost exports, balance the budget and restore German creditworthiness. He also hoped that the deflationary platform would encourage German flight capital to return, and persuade German creditors abroad to renegotiate German debt repayment and, above all, reparations.[17]

Brüning's strategy succeeded in slowing export decline and balancing the budget, but only at the cost of further job losses. Deflation was politically unpopular and forced Brüning to rule by presidential decree, which compromised efforts to make Germany look a stable haven for overseas investors. The hope that international agreement could be reached over questions of trade and indebtedness foundered on the rapid introduction of protectionist policies abroad and the panic withdrawal of foreign funds from central Europe. The financial crisis precipitated by these withdrawals in June and July 1931 destroyed any chance that Germany could be helped

Table 2.3 Statistics on the German slump, 1929–1933

	1929	1930	1931	1932	1933
Gross National Product (bn RM)	79.3	73.1	60.2	48.4	49.9
Gross National Product (1900 prices)	44.4	43.2	39.2	35.5	37.8
Registered unemployed (000s)	1899	3076	4520	5603	4804
Industrial output index (1928 = 100)	100	87	70	58	66
Total state spending (bn RM, 1900 prices)	13.5	14.4	13.9	12.9	13.9
Exports (current value, bn RM)	13.5	12.0	9.6	5.7	4.9
Exports (1913 prices, bn RM)	10.6	9.5	7.8	6.9	6.9

Unemployment figures are annual averages. Figures for GNP (at current and constant prices) are estimates. Other calculations show a considerably higher figure, though the proportions are similar. See B.H. Klein, *Germany's Economic Preparations for War* (Cambridge, MA, 1959), pp. 242–53.

Adapted from: S. Andic and J. Veverka, 'The Growth of Government Expenditure in Germany', *Finanzarchiv* 25 (1964), pp. 242, 243–5; R. Berthold, ed., *Produktivkräfte in Deutschland, 1917/18 bis 1945* (Berlin, 1988), p. 15; A. Sommariva and G. Tullio, *German Macroeconomic History, 1880–1979* (London, 1987), p. 227.

by substantial new foreign loans and paved the way for state regulation of the German credit structure.

The panic was triggered by the collapse of the Austrian Creditanstalt bank in May, and the announcement in June of German and Austrian plans for a customs union in defiance of the terms of Versailles. Heavy losses of foreign exchange – 700 million RM in one week – forced the *Reichsbank* to adopt exchange controls. An international moratorium was declared on debt movements, and the *Reichsbank* negotiated 'standstill' agreements with Germany's major creditors to prevent any further outflow of funds. At the same time the big German banks came under increasing pressure as major commercial customers faced bankruptcy. In July the Darmstädter und Nationalbank collapsed, followed shortly by the Dresdner Bank. The government was compelled to bail out the banking system. In February 1932 the major credit banks were re-organized under government supervision and with government money. Some 1.3 billion RM was used to subsidize the banking sector.[18]

Much of this crisis was imported from the wider world recession and was beyond the German government's control. Brüning's strategy for bringing Germany out of the slump was hostage to these conditions and foundered on them. From 1931 to 1932 the recession in Germany deepened to the point late in 1932 where almost nine million fewer Germans were employed than in 1929. This figure represented two-fifths of the workforce.[19] A further quarter of all those still employed were working on short time. Could this disaster have been averted by adopting policies of deficit spending for work creation, or through devaluation of the mark to make exports more competitive, as many critics of the Brüning era have argued?

The short answer is that the government covertly did both of these things, but the effect was not to solve the recession, only to prevent things getting worse still. Government spending in real terms was a higher proportion of the national product in 1931 and 1932 than in any year of the 1920s. Secret permission was given to the *Reichsbank* to relax the rules agreed in the stabilization *Reichsbank* law of 1924 on the balance between its gold holdings and its note issue, in order to create veiled credit expansion.[20] Subsidies for export industries had the same effect as devaluation with none of the dangerous consequences which might have flowed from any measure interpreted as inflationary. Foreign investors with frozen assets in Berlin were encouraged to take German exports in place of money as a further boost to Germany's embattled export sectors. But the real problem facing German traders was not price – for many German heavy industrial or infrastructure products were not particularly price-sensitive – but the feeble level of foreign demand and the widespread use of discriminatory tariffs and controls abroad.

The failure to reduce the impact of the slump was as much a product of politics as it was of economics. Foreign governments had little interest by 1932 in continuing to fund a state in the process of debt default while trying to cope with their own domestic crises, while the will to collaborate to solve the wider problems of the world economy could not be conjured out of the growing mood of economic nationalism. At home the economic crisis fuelled the collapse of the parliamentary system. Both the German Communist Party (KPD) and the National Socialists (NSDAP) were the beneficiaries of a growing radical temper among the German population, while Brüning, despite his liberal economic inclinations, found himself the butt of criticism from big business and the banks for intervening in entrepreneurial affairs. In May 1932 Brüning was pressured to resign over aristocratic resentment at his plans for peasant resettlement. Shortly after his dismissal the former wartime Allies agreed at the Lausanne Conference in June to suspend reparations; by the autumn there appeared the first signs that the business cycle was about to turn up again.[21]

Over the next four years the economy slowly returned to the level it had reached when the slump hit in 1928. The direct beneficiary of that revival was Hitler, who was appointed chancellor in January 1933 with unemployment at its peak. Why Hitler, the leader of a mass populist movement with an unsophisticated grasp of economic policy, should have succeeded where Brüning failed is a complex question. There is no doubt that the political revolution ushered in with Hitler's appointment created a sense of political stabilization absent since the late 1920s, while the authoritarian character of the regime brought the forcible suppression of the labour opposition and trade unions and satisfied a great many conservatives in the business community and the ministerial apparatus that the main political barriers to revival had been set aside. The psychological impact of a government with a single-minded commitment to re-employment at all costs, as the price of its own political survival, should not be overlooked. Nor did Hitler allow either his ambitions for extensive German rearmament, expressed at his opening cabinet meeting, or his desire for treaty revision to destabilize the pursuit of recovery in the early stages of the regime.

There were, however, important continuities. The finance minister in Hitler's cabinet, Count Schwerin von Krosigk, had been a career civil servant in the ministry since 1920 and served in the post in the cabinets of Brüning's short-lived successors, Franz von Papen and Kurt Schleicher. The man Hitler chose as President of the *Reichsbank*, Hjalmar Schacht, had served in that office from 1924 to 1929 and was, like von Krosigk a man of conservative instincts. The Economics Ministry was headed first by the German National People's Party (DNVP) leader, Alfred Hugenberg, then from 1933 to 1934 by Kurt Schmitt, head of Alliance Insurance, and finally from the summer of 1934 by Schacht himself, none of whom were Nazi Party members. Indeed Schacht, though clearly sympathetic to the national revolution ushered in in 1933, was called to office as he had been in November 1923, to rescue the German economy from a crisis that was beyond the politicians.

The instruments for achieving recovery were also inherited from the pre-Hitler period. The growing *dirigisme* evident in state economic policy during the recession was extended and refined but did not differ in principle. In 1933 and 1934 Germany's relationship to the wider world economy was institutionalized along the lines established since 1931 with the network of exchange controls, bilateral exchange and trade agreements, and licensing of imports and exports to prevent serious balance-of-payments problems.[22] Formal controls on all capital movements, which had so weakened the German economy during the vulnerable inflation and depression years, were finally instituted in the so-called 'New Plan' introduced by Schacht in September 1934. Above all Schacht, with the government's blessing, confirmed the implicit debt default engineered during the banking crisis by refusing any longer to service the foreign debt, except on terms negotiated to Germany's advantage. The result was to insulate the German economy from world financial markets and to end dependence on foreign loans, but it also created an environment in which it was difficult to generate higher levels of trade. German exports throughout the 1930s failed to reach the value achieved in 1931. Revival from 1932 was not export-led.

The recovery depended instead much more on Germany's own resources than had been the case at any time since 1919. The government's approach was to tackle directly the structural problems inhibiting growth. No doubt the natural working of the business cycle would have produced some revival in 1933, but left to itself the market did not guarantee either full employment or a higher investment ratio. This could only be done by initiating a range of policies that amounted in aggregate to an early experiment in macro-economic steering. In essence the strategy was to raise domestic demand while maintaining a stable currency and increasing investment in high employment sectors such as agriculture and construction. This was achieved first by a strict ceiling on wage rates, which were pegged at depression levels, controls over dividends, and high levels of taxation in order to prevent a short-term consumer boom from sucking in imports or reducing funds needed for investment. Controls were maintained over the capital market and the banks to ensure that funds were targeted at projects that would provide high employment and stimulate the heavy industries that had suffered most during the recession.

The increase in investment activity was vital to the success of the strategy. The share of net investment in national income increased from 9.3 per cent in 1928 to 11.5 per cent by 1936 and 15.7 per cent in 1938. Over the period 1933–8 45 per cent of all investment was supplied by the state. In the early years of recovery these funds were targeted at infrastructure investment (railways, roads, electricity grid) and construction projects (including the building of a military infrastructure which had been proscribed under the Versailles settlement). Some 4.8 billion RM was spent on work creation programmes which had begun in the summer of 1932, but were enlarged with additional resources in September 1933.[23] Agriculture was given special assistance with tax cuts, debt reduction and price support in order to encourage rural modernization.[24] The net effect of the government investment programme was to shift the balance in the economy sharply towards heavy industry. The capital goods sector grew 197 per cent between 1932 and 1938, while consumer goods grew only 38 per cent. Even allowing for the fact that demand for consumer goods was more inelastic than for

Table 2.4   Statistics on the German recovery, 1933–1938

	1933	1934	1935	1936	1937	1938
Gross National Product (bn RM)	49.9	56.3	63.3	70.6	78.9	87.6
Gross National Product (1900 prices)	37.8	41.3	45.6	49.7	55.0	61.1
Registered unemployed (000s)	4804	2718	2151	1593	912	429
Gross investment (bn RM)	5.7	9.3	13.6	17.3	18.9	22.5
Industrial output index (1928 = 100)	66	83	96	107	117	125
Consumer goods index (1928 = 100)	83	93	91	98	103	108
Producer goods index (1928 = 100)	54	77	99	113	126	136
Total state spending (bn RM)	9.4	12.8	13.9	15.8	19.3	29.3

Adapted from: S. Andic and J. Veverka, 'The Growth of Government Expenditure in Germany', *Finanzarchiv* 25 (1964), pp. 242, 243–5; R. Berthold, ed., *Produktivkräfte in Deutschland, 1917/18 bis 1945* (Berlin, 1988), p. 15; R. Erbé, *Die nationalsozialistische Wirtschaftspolitik 1933–9 im Lichte der modernen Theorie* (Zurich, 1958), p. 67; S. Lurie, *Private Investment in a Controlled Economy: Germany, 1933–1939* (London, 1947), pp. 23, 38.

capital goods, the disparity is marked. It can largely be explained by the introduction of higher military spending, consistent with Hitler's ambition to embark on very high levels of remilitarization once the economic recovery was secure.

The chief result of the investment campaign was to increase employment rapidly during 1933–5 (see Table 2.4) with relatively modest increases in government debt. Rising tax revenues helped to avoid higher deficits, as Schacht intended, while the government also found ways of stimulating the private sector to contribute to the revival either through generous tax concessions (for example on motor-vehicle purchases) or through matching private investment activity with state loans. Kurt Schmitt shared the widespread hope in the business community in 1933 that the state would provide the 'first spark' (*Initialzündung*) to make possible 'a genuine private economic revival'.[25] The results were mixed. After years of low investment and poor share yields the private sector responded slowly to the evidence of recovery. Private share issues totalled 2.5 billion RM in 1928, but only 100 million RM in 1933 and 1934, and 400 million in 1935, while private investment only reached the 1928 level in 1937, after which it began to exceed public investment by a growing margin.[26]

From 1936 until the outbreak of the Second World War the German economy entered on a period of sustained high growth. By 1938 the net national product was 48 per cent greater in real terms than it had been a decade before. This outcome suggests that once freed of the structural constraints restricting development there had always been substantial growth potential in the economy. But in reality the achievement was a largely artificial one, produced not by expanded exports and consumer demand as it was later in the 1950s, but by the decision taken in 1936 to subvert the 'private economic revival' altogether by directing the economy towards large-scale military preparation under the increased direction of the state authorities. There was considerable resistance to this decision not only from conservatives such as Schacht, who saw economic revival as a means to secure social peace and a renewed entry into world markets, but from businessmen who also looked to expanded trade and feared the consequences of a second armaments boom after the disruptions occasioned by the first before 1914.[27]

It is impossible not to see 1936 as the starting point of almost a decade of economic exceptionalism. The conventional determinants of economic development were subverted by the ideological and military ambitions of the regime, and in particular of Hitler himself. In October 1936 the Second Four Year Plan was launched (following the 1933 First Four Year Plan for re-employment) under the direction of the party leader, Hermann Göring. Its secret purpose was to prepare both the armed forces and the economy for war. Hitler based economic militarization on the concept, long supported by the German armed forces, of *Wehrwirtschaft*, or the defence-based economy. The military–economic strategy took the form of expanding domestic output of all resources deemed essential to free Germany from the threat of wartime blockade, particularly food and raw materials, and building up the industrial capacity and trained manpower to sustain high levels of military output.[28] It was a strategy suited to the declining internationalization of the economy already evident from the slump.

Goering was able to use the Plan organization as a platform to subvert the position of Schacht and the conservative opponents of rearmament and autarky, and by 1938 had become a virtual economic dictator. Under his authority between 1936 and 1939 some 6.4 billion RM were invested by state authorities and private companies in gigantic industrial ventures.[29] An estimated two-thirds of all industrial investment went into war-related projects with the result that civilian consumption failed to match the great increase in the size of the economy. Per capita civilian consumption increased only 4 per cent between 1928 and 1938 and trade remained stagnant. Almost all the additional growth of the national product was diverted to state purposes, the bulk of it to feed Hitler's ambition to turn Germany into a military superpower.

The renewed distortion of the economy by war had a number of effects. The technical threshold of the economy was raised with the build-up of the aviation, motor-vehicle, electronics and chemical industries, though some

Table 2.5 Statistics on the German war economy, 1939–1944

	1939	1940	1941	1942	1943	1944
Govt expenditure						
(bn RM, 'war' years)*	57.5	81.3	102.3	126.8	149.3	97.5
Military expenditure						
(bn RM, 'war' years)	38.0	55.9	72.3	86.1	99.4	62.1
Consumer expenditure p.c.						
(1938 = 100)	95.0	88.4	81.9	75.3	75.3	70.0
Consumer expenditure						
(bn RM, 1938 prices)	71.0	66.0	62.0	57.0	57.0	53.0
Industrial output						
(1928 = 100)	132	128	131	132	149	146
Industrial labour force on						
war orders (%)**	21.9	50.2	54.5	56.7	61.0	–
Armaments output as %						
of industrial output	12.0	14.0	19.0	26.0	37.0	48.0

* 'war' years were calculated by the *Reich* Finance Ministry from Sept to August
** figure for May of each year
Adapted from: R.J. Overy, *War and Economy in the Third Reich* (Oxford, 1994), pp. 278, 294;
W. Boelcke, *Die Kosten von Hitlers Krieg* (Paderborn, 1985), p. 269; F.-W. Henning,
Das industrialisierte Deutschland, 1914 bis 1992 (9th edn, Munich, 1997), p. 177.

at least of this change would have occurred regardless of the military imperative. The Four Year Plan also participated in nationwide efforts to raise the skill threshold of German labour through retraining schemes, while the coming of full employment brought into the workforce large additional numbers of women, many of whom acquired industrial skills for the first time.[30] Growth on such a scale and at such speed began to expose new problems. High levels of government debt were needed to fund the additional military expansion. Industrial productivity grew slowly since many firms, locked into the uncompetitive world of cartelized industry and secure state contracts, had few incentives to rationalize factory practices. Labour productivity remained low in the 1930s by comparison with the revival of the 1950s.[31] The result was a veiled inflation that was suppressed only by tight price controls and the informal rationing of consumer output. One consequence was a sharply rising savings ratio which allowed the government to fund state expenditure by compelling the savings banks to buy government bonds. The economic regime became increasingly coercive as macro-economic steering evolved into a more rigid structure of micro-economic controls.

This regime was by 1939 almost indistinguishable from a war economy. During the war the proportion of the economic product devoted to military purposes expanded rapidly, while the forms of finance, material rationing and price and wage control already utilized before 1939 were extended in order to prevent inflation and to siphon resources towards the war effort. Many of the inefficiences evident before 1939 persisted, while new ones emerged in the wake of German territorial expansion. The efforts to rationalize the war economy begun in 1941 produced a substantial improvement in the productivity performance across the industrial economy, but by that point the use of forced and slave labour, the vast programme of ethnic cleansing, the onset of heavy bombing and the increasing use of terror created a temporary form of emergency economy quite distinct from anything that had preceded it.[32] Defeat in 1945 left Germany with most of the raw resources necessary for the revival of economic life but with little say over the conditions that now governed it.

The 'primacy of politics':
state, ideology and economics

In 1937 an article appeared in *Foreign Affairs* on the 'Destruction of Capitalism in Germany'. Its thesis was simply that Germany had ceased since 1933 to be a capitalist country: 'The German industrialist has no more control over the means and ends of production than the German worker has over the conditions of his job.' This was not, the author argued, a result of Nazism, but was the consequence of the First World War in which the relation of state and economy had been permanently altered. It was the democratic Weimar Republic 'that was already in control of the banks, the railroads, the power sources, the urban transit systems, the municipal gas and water, vast housing developments and large parts of heavy industry'.[33]

The growing role of the state is a key element running through the entire history of Germany's economy from 1919 to 1945. This was not simply a German phenomenon, for state claims on the economy expanded in every industrialized country after 1919. Total state spending as a proportion of GNP (calculated at constant prices) rose from a pre-war peak of 17 per cent in 1913 to an average of 27.9 per cent between 1925 and 1929, and an average of 36.2 per cent between 1930 and 1938 (see Table 2.1). The higher threshold in the 1920s reflects the growth of the Weimar welfare state; in the 1930s the increases had diverse causes. Before 1935 government spending was statistically more significant simply because of the decline of private sector activity; from 1936 the increase was a result of absolute increases in state spending on rearmament and prestige projects, including the autobahns and the remodelling of German cities. Actual expenditure per head at constant prices increased far more dramatically, from 42 RM in 1913 to 109 RM in 1929 and 298 RM in 1938. The 1938 figure included 161 RM (54 per cent) per head spent on defence.[34]

The expansion of state spending generated higher levels of state employment, which in the 1930s helped to absorb a proportion of the German unemployed. In 1925 central state administration and services employed 648,000; by 1939 the figure was 1,039,000. Local government employment expanded from 544,000 in 1934 to 741,000 in 1938. The NSDAP developed its own administrative apparatus during the 1930s, which included by 1934 373,000 full-time employees. During the Second World War administrative employment continued to expand to meet the needs of the military apparatus and to cope with the mobilization and provisioning of the civilian population, rising from a total of 3,359,000 in 1939 to 3,522,000 in 1944, when it constituted 12.2 per cent of the total workforce.[35]

The growth of state employment can be explained by the expansion of German social services during the inter-war years. In 1913 social expenditure absorbed only 1.8 per cent of GNP and 10.3 per cent of all government expenditure, but during the inter-war years (1925–38) it averaged 6.7 per cent of GNP, and 20.2 per cent of government expenditure.[36] Growth also resulted from the increase in direct state intervention in the productive economy. This took a number of forms. Many utilities were directly owned by central and local state authorities; employment in 1925 stood at 1.18 million. The German rail network was nationalized in 1920 and developed into the largest transport undertaking in the world by 1939, when it employed 600,000 people.[37] During the slump and particularly under the Nazi regime the state began to penetrate into industrial production in areas previously dominated by large private firms. The capital assets of state firms doubled between 1933 and 1943, when they stood at 4.1 billion RM, with total debts of 16 billion RM. By 1943 some 531 firms were state-owned, including the giant Junkers Flugzeug- und Motorenwerke, nationalized in 1935, and the state holding company Reichswerke 'Hermann Göring', which by 1940 employed 600,000 people and had gross assets in excess of 5 billion RM, mostly acquired in the captured areas of Europe.[38] There was a clear link between the increase in direct state ownership and the growth of the military–industrial complex in Germany from the 1930s. Many private firms relied on funds supplied by the state during the rearmament and war period, blurring the distinction between the public and private sectors altogether.

Yet not all state ownership was directly related to war. During the slump industrial and banking businesses were taken over temporarily by the state until they could be returned to private hands. Banks were reprivatized in 1936–7, but only on terms governed by the new Law on Credit issued in December 1934 which gave a government agency, the Aufsichtsamt für Kreditwesen (Supervisory Office for Credit Affairs), regulatory powers over the banking sector.[39] In other non-war sectors state ownership also increased. The decision in 1938 to establish the publicly owned Volkswagen works as Europe's largest vehicle producer had little direct bearing on war preparation, but stemmed from Hitler's frustration with the attitude of the private car-makers to his ideas on mass motorization. Volkswagen was finally privatized in 1960.[40] Plans to nationalize the coal industry, German insurance companies and German energy supply were mooted during the Third Reich but came to nothing.

The growth of the state's share in the economy in the inter-war years masked profoundly different conceptions of the relationship between state and economy. In the early 1920s there was a widespread belief that the traditional liberal conception of the free market was no longer viable. This was a view shared by socialists, who wanted a larger welfare system and greater social control over industry, and by politicians from the new democratic right. The influential industrialist Walther Rathenau, who became German foreign minister in 1921, argued that the war experience showed the importance of developing a state-regulated capitalism: 'Our policy is a transition from the principle of private economy into that of the state.'[41] To Rathenau the state, through the application of rational planning, would create a collectivist economic system sensitive to wider social needs, while maintaining the framework for 'free competition', a view not very distant from the 'social market economy' of the 1950s.

There also emerged in the 1920s a very different conception of the German economic system which drew its strength from the rise of popular radical nationalism, but was not confined to it. The centrepiece of this conception was the idea that economies should not be governed by the principles of economic individualism or autonomous market forces but by the needs of the community or race. Werner Sombart was among the most influential economists to argue in the 1920s that the 'national economy' (*Volkswirtschaft*), collectively organized under the principle of the primacy of politics, should supersede the outdated liberal conception which satisfied neither the practical issues confronting nations in the 1920s, nor the spiritual needs of the *Volk*.[42] This instrumental view of the economy in the service of the people had a long and respectable intellectual pedigree and was widely shared by important sections of Germany's academic establishment; it was central to the view of the economy adopted by popular anti-capitalist and anti-Marxist circles, including the NSDAP. Hitler, who was familiar with Sombart's work, showed his debt to the economic discourses of the 1920s in the so-called Four Year Plan memorandum, which he wrote in August 1936 to explain his decision to redirect economic policy:

> Just as the political movement among our people only knows one aim, to make possible the assertion of the life of the *Volk* and the Reich, that is to say, to secure the spiritual and other prerequisites for the self-assertion of our people, so the economy too has only this one objective.[43]

The idea of 'national economy' serving the needs of the people or race incorporated other important elements of the anti-liberal and radical nationalist outlook. These included: the building of an 'organic' economy based on corporatist traditions in German social and political thought; the neo-mercantilist view that economic development depended on the physical expansion of territory and resources (or 'living-space'); the complementary argument that the national 'space' (*Raum*) should be economically self-sustaining (autarky); and the pernicious argument that modern international capitalism was a product of a Jewish-dominated modernization process designed to dissolve national economies and to enslave their populations.[44]

Almost none of this economic conception was original to the NSDAP, but it proved entirely compatible with the ideas on economic justice, social organization and race that many in the party shared. All of its elements were adopted by the regime at some point after 1933. The corporatist restructuring of economic life was pushed through in 1933–4 with the establishment of compulsory industrial associations and chambers, and the creation of the German Labour Front (DAF) and the Reich Food Estate (Reichsnährstand) to represent productive workers and peasants respectively.[45] The pursuit of an autarkic economic bloc dominated by German national interests was begun even before the Four Year Plan gave it a formal frameworks and was extended from 1938 onwards with the incorporation of Austria, Czechoslovakia and western Poland and the war in the east. The racial interpretation of the economy led first to the exclusion of Jews from business life, then to the expropriation of Jewish wealth and finally to the deportation and extermination of millions of Jews who could not be tolerated by the regime in the fantastic project to reconstruct the ethnic and economic geography of Europe around the German national economy begun in 1939.[46]

Historians and political scientists have argued since the 1930s about how to characterize the German economy under Hitler. There is little to be gained from trying to fit the National Socialist economic conception somewhere on a recognizable scale between free-market capitalism and communism. In the first place that conception was intellectually unstable, a loose alliance of ideas borrowed from the anti-capitalist and anti-liberal academic establishment in the 1920s. Second, it is easier to understand economic developments after 1933 not in terms of the imposition of a 'system' but as a *process*. The early years of the regime represented a necessary compromise with other social and intellectual forces; in economic policy, as in other areas of state, there was a progressive radicalization as the regime became institutionalized and its wider racial and military agenda became more prominent. It is perhaps no accident that Jewish expropriation or 'aryanization' was begun systematically at that point in the mid-1930s when Hitler shifted the economy to a formal strategy of *Wehrwirtschaft*, autarky and expansion.

By the late 1930s Nazi economists were at pains to distinguish their economy from both liberal capitalism and the Marxist planned economy. Otto Ohlendorf, who rose to prominence in the economic offices of the SS, defined the system as one dominated by national priorities rather than economic egoism, in which 'the state *leads* the economy' (italics in original) through policies of 'fully planned economic management (*planvolle Lenkung*)'.[47] The term 'managed national economy' (*die gelenkte Volkswirtschaft*) became the prevailing description of the new economic form. It embraced the reality of extensive state control and macro-economic direction in the late 1930s, through which the market was effectively set aside in favour of a system of economic coercion. In 1946 Ludwig Erhard, the future economics minister and chancellor of the Federal Republic, reflecting on the differences between the National Socialist economy and the 'social market economy' with which his name was closely associated, argued that the chief contrast was not between planning and the free market, which were in principle far from incompatible, but between 'market economy with the free formation of prices and state command economy . . . This economic principle leads to the subversion of the market and of free consumer choice.'[48] In truth the concept of a command economy committed to racial economics and military expansion was *sui generis*, a product of the tradition in German political economy that disliked economic egoism and the supposed anarchy of the market, and linked economic well-being with territorial expansion and necessary violence. It can be defined more easily in terms of its ends than its means.

Industry and labour

The development of German industry was overshadowed, with the economy as a whole, by the effects of war and war preparation. The decline of industrial output during the 1914–18 war to a little over half the level of 1913 took a further ten years to make good. Output then fell sharply again during the slump, to be revived by the rearmament boom after 1936 and the demands of the war economy, which raised the aggregate output of the non-consumer sectors by 80 per cent between 1936 and 1943 (see Table 2.1).

The failure to sustain the pre-war pattern of industrial growth was a direct result of the dislocation caused by war, inflation and the later slump, but it masked important changes in the structure and geographical distribution of industry. Smaller manufacturing and craft firms were squeezed out during the war, and in the 1920s the processes of consolidation and rationalization continued. Between 1925 and 1939 employment in the major consumer sectors (food, textiles, light industry) fell from 47 to 41 per cent of total industrial employment, while employment in heavy industry (chemicals, energy supply, electrotechnical industries, machinery and metalwares) increased from 30 to 35 per cent.[49]

Germany's industrial structure, despite persistent low levels of aggregate output, followed other industrial economies in the 1920s in developing new technologies and factory processes, which were extended in the 1930s under the impact of rearmament and autarky. In the post-slump years Germany developed the synthetic production of oil from coal, synthetic rubber production, synthetic textiles, and established Europe's leading aeronautical and aluminium industries. The motor industry, which had lagged far behind other industrial states in the 1920s, expanded faster than any other major sector after 1932.[50] The new industries were less reliant on coal and steel and had higher demands for traditional craft labour. This change was reflected in a geographical redistribution of industry, away from the Ruhr and the older industrial regions to Berlin and the southern and south-western provinces with their strong artisan traditions. In the mid-1920s some 2.4 million artisans worked in large industrial and commercial enterprises.[51] This shift was already under way before the Hitler government actively encouraged relocation to avoid the possible threat from enemy bombing.

The long-term stagnation of industrial output and the low level of foreign trade growth had the effect of encouraging German industry to intensify the defensive organizational structures already developed before 1914. German industry became heavily concentrated and cartelized in the interwar years. By 1922 there were approximately three times as many cartel agreements as there had been pre-war, spreading out from the traditional area of 'organized capitalism' in heavy Ruhr-based industry to embrace a wide range of other manufacturing sectors. There existed a widespread assumption in business circles that the optimum way to cope with the harsh postwar circumstances and the unpredictable growth of the world market

Table 2.6 Output of cars and commercial vehicles, 1925–1939

Year	Cars	Commercial vehicles	Total
1925	39 080	10 304	49 384
1926	31 958	5 211	37 169
1927	84 668	11 972	96 640
1928	101 701	20 960	122 661
1929	96 161	31 577	127 738
1930	71 960	9 985	81 945
1931	58 744	8 734	67 478
1932	43 430	8 234	51 664
1933	92 160	13 261	105 421
1934	147 350	27 325	174 675
1935	205 092	41 528	246 620
1936	244 289	57 312	301 601
1937	269 005	62 404	331 409
1938	276 592	64 127	340 719
1939*	143 602	32 994	176 596

* Jan–Jun only
Adapted from: Statistisches Jahrbuch für das Deutsche Reich (Berlin, 1926–40).

was to protect prices and profits by organizing trade associations that agreed fixed prices and allocated production quotas or market areas. The German government estimated that there were at least 3,000 such associations by 1925, covering a wide range of products in both the older and newer industrial sectors.[52] The effect was to keep many prices artificially high, but at the same time to spread the risk equally for all firms and to protect profit levels. They were encouraged by government early in the 1920s as a means to secure higher employment and output, and as a means to regulate the development of key industrial sectors by avoiding what was seen as high levels of socially irresponsible competition. The coal industry cartel (Rheinisch-Westfälischen Kohlensyndikat) was strongly influenced by the state as a major mine-owner, and here, as in other industrial sectors, the state insisted on maintaining the cartel form.

The industrial system inherited in 1933 was already highly organized. The Hitler regime only followed Weimar governments in favouring cartelization as a means of coping with crisis conditions. In 1933 a Compulsory Cartel Law protected existing associations and created the basis for a further 1,600 cartel agreements. By 1936 an estimated 66 per cent of all German industry was cartelized. At the same time the state sustained the pre-1933 commitment to price regulation first begun under Brüning in 1931 in order to prevent industry from exploiting the associations to maintain artificially high prices. In October 1936 a Commissioner for Price Formation, Joseph Wagner, was appointed with responsibility for monitoring and regulating all price changes, with the result that official price movements, even during the period of full employment from 1937, remained modest.[53]

A second defensive response came through the process of industrial concentration. This process was accelerated by the First World War as marginal producers were squeezed out or compulsorily closed down, and continued in the 1920s as smaller firms found increasing difficulty in getting access to capital or sustaining pre-war market shares. Amalgamation was most marked in iron and steel, chemicals and the electrical industry. The consolidation of the country's three largest chemical firms in IG Farbenindustrie AG in 1925, the formation of Vereinigte Stahlwerke AG (United Steel) in 1926, and the pre-war development of the electrical giant Siemens & Halske, produced three of the four largest concerns in the world.[54]

The gradual development of large integrated concerns was not entirely compatible with the domestic cartel system, since their leaders preferred to absorb small or unsuccessful firms rather than subsidize their survival, but they were important in the establishment of international cartels and market agreements where all sides had a vested interest, particularly during and after the slump, in regulating competition abroad.[55] The establishment of larger concerns also permitted the adoption of rational organizational and managerial practices, many borrowed from the United States. Vereinigte Stahl in the early 1930s decentralized the concern by creating a number of discrete operating divisions with a central head office to direct overall strategy. IG Farben adopted a mixed system of divisional and territorial decentralization. When the German state established the Reichswerke concern in 1937 to safeguard the development of domestic iron ore exploitation it rapidly evolved into a vast integrated concern producing iron, steel, coal and armaments. Here, too, organizational reform in 1941 adopted the practice of decentralized product divisions with a central strategy group based in Berlin.[56] These reforms avoided the danger of adopting large scale simply for its own sake, and prepared the ground for the transition after 1945 to a more aggressive and Americanized industrial structure in the Federal Republic.[57]

The generally defensive outlook of Germany's industrial leadership reflected not only the relative weakness of the German economy between the wars and the peculiar nature of the world market, but fears among the business community about the long-term stability of the domestic political situation and the prospects for the survival of capitalism. Businessmen were by no means neutral politically, for the leaders of heavy industry and the major export industries represented important lobby-groups in their own right. They collaborated with the new republic in 1919–20 in buying social peace by rapid expansion of employment well beyond the levels that could be used productively. This was partly to offset the prospect of socialization, which had been part of the social-democratic platform in 1919. An uneasy peace was maintained between state and business during the mid-1920s, but the growth of industrial conflict in 1928, symbolized by the prolonged lock-out in the steel industry, and the onset of domestic recession in 1929 sharpened business fears for the survival of industrial capitalism and undermined business confidence in the republic.[58]

It has often been argued that this crisis drove German business into the arms of the NSDAP. While it is certainly the case that a number of prominent businessmen, including Fritz Thyssen, one of the leaders of Vereinigte Stahlwerke, came to see salvation in the movement's economic nationalism and corporativism, there is little evidence that leading business circles either directly supported the NSDAP with funds or favoured a National Socialist government. The strong under-current of anti-capitalism in the movement and its large working-class membership alienated many business leaders. Support was much more widespread among the struggling craft firms and smaller manufacturing businesses which saw themselves as equally the victims of the international capitalist system as the radical working-class membership.[59]

The relationship between industry and the state after 1933 was diverse and fragmented, as it had been under Weimar. Many businessmen, it must be assumed, welcomed the closure of trade unions and the wage controls instituted in 1934. But business leaders remained wary of the growth of state controls and the persistent fear of 'backdoor' socialization, while price controls, the Dividend Limitations Law of 1934 (which prevented the payment of share dividends above 6 per cent as a means to compel firms to plough money back into their businesses), and the system of *Reichstellen* (Reich offices) for state supervision of raw materials imports, introduced the same year, all combined to undermine what remained of business autonomy. Some businessmen reacted with an opportunistic enthusiasm, adapting themselves to the new conditions and collaborating directly with the autarkic and rearmament goals of the regime. This was especially true of companies such as IG Farben which worked on war-related product fields and whose prospects for growth abroad were limited. IG Farben was closely integrated with Goering's Four Year Plan after 1936, and was its main private beneficiary. There was little open business resistance, but much evidence that leading business circles would by 1939 have preferred a more conventional conservative system with greater entrepreneurial autonomy preserved. This did not necessarily imply complicity, but was a recognition by businessmen of the limited sphere of action they enjoyed and of the prevailing conviction that the economy in some sense served the state. Gustav Krupp no doubt spoke for a great many of his business colleagues when he claimed that 'primacy always belongs to politics'; business priority in the 1930s was to avoid anything that might unhinge what they hoped would be a period of economic equilibrium following twenty years of instability.[60]

Yet the ambitions of the regime compelled complicity or made complicity desirable. Businessmen were not immune from the terror imposed under the dictatorship. A disillusioned Fritz Thyssen fled from Germany in 1939 with his vast industrial holdings forfeit to the state.[61] Hjalmar Schacht ended up in Dachau. The pressures to conform were no less for businessmen than for other Germans, and the opportunities available for those who did so were tangible and real. This was most evidently so in the history of so-called 'aryanization', the expropriation of Jewish businessmen and wealth-owners. There is little to suggest that the driving force in the exclusion of Jews from German economic life came from the business elite itself, in which Jews played a prominent role before 1933. The process of exclusion and expropriation was slow and uneven, if remorseless, but it was driven principally by the anti-Semitic radicals in the NSDAP drawing on the crude association of anti-Semitism and anti-capitalism.[62]

The assault on Jewish business and wealth took a number of forms. All firms were encouraged to exclude Jews from boards of directors, but this process occurred haphazardly until January 1938, when a new law was brought in defining any company with a Jewish director as 'Jewish', and subject to aryanization. Second, Jews were encouraged to emigrate and to sell their businesses and assets at reduced real values. Thousands did so, and Jewish-owned assets declined by an estimated half by 1938. Larger Jewish firms, including banks and insurance companies, lasted longer, but in 1937–8 the process of aryanization was given greater legal sanction. Jewish owners began to seek 'aryan' purchasers who were able to buy up assets at a substantial discount, while the state, abusing the capital flight tax introduced by Brüning in 1931, compelled Jewish owners who fled from the Reich to give up an estimated 939 million RM in tax between 1933 and 1939. Finally, the state moved to open expropriation and sale of Jewish businesses following the *Anschluss*. By 1939 110,000 Jewish firms had been closed down, and only 15.6 per cent of German Jews remaining were gainfully employed.[63] After the outbreak of war the process was completed. In November 1941 a new legal instrument gave the Reich the right to take all the assets of Jews 'whose usual place of residence was abroad'. The instrument was applied in practice to all those Jews already deported, and to those who were to be deported on the day they were entrained for the camps.[64] The expropriation did not end there. Gold taken from Jewish victims was melted down and deposited with the *Reichsbank*, whence much of it was sent to Switzerland to fund German purchases of essential wartime resources.[65]

German business also collaborated in the exploitation of foreign and camp labour during the war. Some foreign labour was voluntary – from Italy, for example – but the conditions for volunteers became little different from conditions for those compelled to work in Germany. By September 1944 there were 5.9 million foreign workers in Greater Germany, 1.9 million of them women. They were drawn from all over Europe, but the bulk were Poles (1.7 million) and Soviet peoples (2.2 million). Their mobilization was organized by the NSDAP leader Fritz Sauckel. Further labour was recruited from the network of camps and sub-camps set up under the direction of SS leader Heinrich Himmler. The camps had 200,000 inmates in May 1943, but 714,000 in January 1945, the number of prisoners swollen with an influx of Jews retained for work and Russian and Polish labourers accused of misdemeanours. The camp workers were placed under a harsh regime which few were expected to survive. Armaments firms were allotted batches of prisoners under SS supervision. Other camps, most notoriously Auschwitz-Birkenau, had their own industrial undertakings, some run by the SS, some by private German firms, whose compliance with the programme of enforced and slave labour showed the powerful corrupting influence of the regime on a business elite compelled ultimately to endorse atrocity.[66]

The longer history of labour during the 1918–45 period was also one of defence, first against declining postwar living standards, then against a business establishment that sought to undo the gains made by organized labour on issues of wage arbitration and labour participation in the workplace, finally against the rising tide of political radicalism which in 1933 engulfed the entire labour movement. The labour force itself underwent a slow process of change which matched the sectoral changes in the industrial and service economy. By 1939 the number working in agriculture had fallen from the 1925 figure of 30 per cent of the workforce to 26 per cent; industrial labour took up 42 per cent in both years; there was an increase in service and administrative employment from 25 to 32 per cent. Industrial employment expanded fastest in the engineering, chemical and electrical industries, and fell in a whole range of more traditional sectors such as textiles, woodworking and leather.[67] There was an overall increase in female employment, which, despite the Third Reich's unwarranted reputation as a regime committed to eradicating female work, grew from 11.4 million in 1925 to 12.7 million by 1939, when women supplied 37 per cent of all those employed. Much of the growth came in female industrial employment which expanded by one-fifth in six years, thanks largely to the rearmament boom.[68]

The skill ratio of the workforce also changed with the decline of the craft- and skill-based industries and the rise of modern factory-based production of consumer and engineering goods. Between the late 1920s and the late 1930s the proportion of the workforce composed of skilled workers (mostly men) fell in most industrial branches. To some extent this reflected simply the reality of full employment, since labourers were more likely to have been out of work than skilled machinists. But it also reflected a change in working patterns, with the coming of rationalized production and the assembly belt. Rationalization in this sense was slower to develop in Germany than elsewhere because of the capital shortages and weak demand of the 1920s, but by the 1930s with the growth of the motor, aviation and electrical industries more use could be made of less skilled labour, using general purpose tools and closely supervised by skilled foremen. The sharp decline of the skill ratio during the 1939–45 war was due entirely to wartime circumstances with the growing proportion of female, youth, foreign and POW labour drafted in to take the place of conscripted men. This process was exacerbated by the requirements of modern armed forces for large numbers of skilled workers of their own.[69]

The structure of German wages over the period did not entirely reflect either the productivity performance of German industry or the prevailing conditions in the labour market. The data on wage rates and real earnings are set out in Table 2.7. Wage rates were as much a function of politics as of economics. In the inflation period workers were re-employed in numbers that could not be justified except in political terms. The establishment of the eight-hour day, the development of wage-bargaining agreements across entire industries, and the creation of arbitration tribunals helped to keep up the chase of wages after prices, though real wages remained well below 1913 levels. In the stabilization period wage rates were created at levels higher than 1913, and earnings expanded up to 1929, partly due to the inherited structure of wage agreements, partly due to local demand for labour. In the slump they fell again sharply, nominal weekly earnings falling by one-third compared with 1929. Wage rates were subsequently pegged at recession levels, the trade unions were abolished in May 1933, and the DAF took over responsibility for setting wages through a system of Labour Trustees. As hours worked increased steadily, weekly earnings rose in line, but high taxation and compulsory levies taken at source kept real net income below the 1929 level until the late 1930s. The war then created artificial conditions for wage formation with the influx of millions of low-paid foreign workers and compulsory rationing and price control. Nevertheless a

Table 2.7 German wage and price statistics, 1928–1944

	Cost of living index	Real wage rate index (1913/14 = 100)	Real weekly earnings index (1932 = 100)**
1928	151.7	110	–
1929	154.0	115	118
1930	148.1	122	–
1931	136.1	125	–
1932	120.6	120	100
1933	118.0	119	104
1934	121.1	116	109
1935	123.0	114	110
1936	124.5	112	112
1937	125.1	112	110
1938	125.6	112	114
1939	126.2	112	118
1940	130.1	109	116
1941	133.2	107	121
1942	136.6	105	119
1943	138.5	104	118
1944*	139.6	102	114

* figure for Feb 1944
** after deductions for compulsory levies and cost-of-living underestimates
Adapted from: IWM Reel 168, BA-RD 51/21–3, Deutsche Reichsbank, volkswirtschaftliche Abteilung, graphisch-statistische Tabellen, Jan 1944, p. 20; G. Bry, *Wages in Germany, 1871–1945* (Princeton, NJ, 1960), pp. 264, 362.

substantial reform of the entire wage system was begun in the war by the DAF to try to end the traditional distinction between skilled, semi-skilled and unskilled worker in favour of a system based on achievement (*Leistung*). Eight separate wage categories were devised to allow greater reward for particular skills and to encourage the acquisition of new skills. The system was introduced into the metal-producing industry in 1943, but was extensively adopted in the Federal Republic in the 1950s.[70]

There has been much argument over the development of living standards, particularly during the Third Reich. The workforce was far from homogeneous; some groups fared better at some times than others. In general the differentials between skilled, semi-skilled and unskilled narrowed, though women continued to earn substantially lower wages than men. Earnings in the heavy industrial sectors and the new industries expanded faster than in the consumer sector, a situation that became marked during the period of large-scale rearmament after 1936. What is not in doubt is that German workers at all levels spent long periods after 1914 worse off in terms of living standards than they had been in 1913. The impact of war, inflation and slump created large areas of poverty which the revival after 1933 did not entirely alleviate. This situation was reflected in the comparatively low level of consumer durable sales during the period. Car sales lagged far behind levels in France or Britain, and even in the improved climate of the 1930s most car sales were for business use rather than for personal motoring. By 1938 real wages in Germany had grown 9 per cent since 1913, but they had grown 53 per cent in the USA and 33 per cent in Britain. In 1939 average per capita incomes in Germany were two-thirds of British levels and less than half American levels. Moreover throughout the 1930s there had been a decline in the variety and quality of consumer goods, due partly to the diversion of trade to military purposes, partly to official government efforts to sponsor *ersatz* or substitute products.[71]

Little could be done to reverse this trend. From 1936 the government in effect rationed the expansion of the civilian consumer economy, while labour lacked any formal means for renegotiating its share of the cake. It was possible for workers to put pressure on employers through go-slows or veiled strikes; some workers actively participated in the operation of the DAF; as members of the NSDAP they could bring direct political pressure to bear on bosses. In practice many firms offered generous bonuses and gifts in kind, or increased social expenditure, in order to reduce labour mobility and to circumvent the wage laws. Yet the overall result was a higher savings ratio, not more consumption. The consumer boom was postponed to the 1950s.[72]

Germany and the world economy

In November 1937, in the meeting famously recorded by Colonel Hossbach, Hitler analysed for his listeners the economic options faced by Germany. German participation in the world economy, he argued, was 'severely impeded' because it was dominated by established economic empires and subject to the damaging effects of 'market fluctuations'. Reliance on German self-sufficiency was one solution, but the autarkic economy was 'untenable' because it could not permanently satisfy German needs. 'The only remedy', Hitler continued, 'lay in the acquisition of more living space . . .'. Rather than 'the liberal–capitalist view' which favoured overseas colonies, Hitler told his audience that space could 'only be sought in Europe' and could 'only be solved by means of force'.[73]

Hitler was summarizing an argument about the future of Germany's role in the world economy that stretched back to the pre-1914 period. Although Germany had enjoyed unprecedented trade growth since the 1870s, and the economy had become progressively internationalized with the inter-locking of patterns of trade and foreign investment and a high export ratio, there were already critics of Germany's dependence on the wider world market. The leader of the Pan-German League, Heinrich Class, wrote in 1912 about Germany's 'unbearable dependence' on overseas supply and the necessity of acquiring colonial areas in Europe 'to the east of the Empire'.[74] The collapse of German trade during the wartime blockade, and its slow revival in the 1920s, encouraged simultaneously both economic nationalism and ideas of economic imperialism. The view that there was a necessary relationship between economic well-being and territorial expansion, encapsulated in the popular idea of *Lebensraum*, came to compete successfully with the idea that trade growth and international economic collaboration would solve Germany's problems.[75]

The internationalization of the German economy did not end in 1919, but sustained trade growth was inhibited both by external market conditions and domestic political choices. In real terms (1913 prices) exports failed to reach the pre-war level at any time between 1919 and 1945, and only exceeded 1913 for the first time in 1956. At the same time German foreign direct investment, which rose steeply before 1914, declined to negligible amounts in the 1920s and 1930s. Most German capital abroad was flight capital, and much of it was repatriated either voluntarily or, in the 1930s, under compulsion.[76] Major German companies preferred to protect trade through international cartel agreements rather than invest abroad and run once again the danger of expropriation.

The international links that survived in the 1920s were deeply resented by many Germans. Dependence on foreign speculative capital after 1924 was widely interpreted, and not only by the economic spokesmen of the NSDAP, as a form of economic enslavement. Reparations were viewed by Germans across the political spectrum as unjust tribute, and every effort was made to circumvent fulfilment of the reparations terms. The total sum paid in cash and kind has been calculated at 22.8 billion RM, or 2.7 per cent of national income 1919–31, though the value of deliveries in kind has been much disputed. This was not a negligible sum, but it was more than compensated by the inflow of an estimated 44 billion RM from foreign investors over the same period. Reparations were resented so much not only because of the economic burden but also because they constituted a

Table 2.8 German trade statistics, 1913, 1920–1943

Year	Exports (bn RM)	Imports (bn RM)	Balance of trade
1913	10.10	10.75	−0.65
1920	3.70	3.93	−0.23
1921	2.98*	5.75	n.a.
1922	6.20	6.31	−0.11
1923	5.35	4.82	+0.53
1924	6.67	9.13	−2.46
1925	9.28	12.43	−3.15
1926	10.42	9.98	+0.44
1927	10.80	14.11	−3.31
1928	12.05	13.93	−1.88
1929	13.50	13.36	+0.14
1930	12.04	10.35	+1.69
1931	9.59	6.71	+2.88
1932	5.74	4.65	+1.09
1933	4.87	4.20	+0.67
1934	4.18	4.45	−0.27
1935	4.27	4.16	+0.11
1936	4.78	4.23	+0.55
1937	5.92	5.49	+0.43
1938	5.26	5.45	−0.19
1939	5.65	5.20	+0.45
1940	4.87	5.01	−0.14
1941	6.84	6.93	−0.09
1942	7.56	8.69	−1.13
1943	8.59	8.26	+0.33

* estimated figure only

Adapted from: B. Mitchell, *European Historical Statistics, 1750–1970* (London, 1978), p. 304; C.-L. Holtfrerich, 'Die Konjunkturanregenden Wirkungen der deutschen Inflation auf die US-Wirtschaft in der Weltwirtschaftskrise 1920/21', in G. Feldman *et al.*, *Die Deutsche Inflation* (Berlin, 1982), p. 213.

formal acknowledgement of German war guilt, which few Germans would accept.[77]

The one-sided character of the international economic ties of the 1920s were exposed in the slump when German trade was hit by foreign tariffs and devaluations, while large amounts of short-term lending to Germany were withdrawn, bringing the national economy close to bankruptcy in 1931. Economic nationalism in Germany was a direct response to what was regarded as the economic selfishness of other powers, but it was nourished by popular ideas of autarky and economic imperialism which pre-dated the slump. The alternative to the open liberal economic order was found in the concept of the closed economic bloc (*Grossraumwirtschaft*), a large, self-contained economic region which could as far as possible supply its own requirements of industrial goods, food and raw materials, and would engage in trade with other blocs on a regulated basis. The pre-Nazi concept was based on the assumption that Germany's less developed neighbours in central and eastern Europe would recognize economic reality and join a German-centred bloc of their own accord. Trade agreements negotiated in central Europe in the 1920s, and later in the 1930s, were political as well as economic instruments, designed to revive Germany's pre-war great power status.[78]

Under Brüning the growth of German–Soviet trade, the attempt to establish a customs union with Austria and the search for closer economic ties with the Danube states all pointed in the direction of *Grossraumwirtschaft*. The decline of external trade and Germany's low level of gold and foreign currency reserves (from 2.8 billion in 1930 to 0.16 billion by 1934) added economic compulsion to the attractions of an autarkic economy. From 1931 exchange controls and regulated trade replaced what remained of the free market, and every effort was made to raise domestic output of food and raw materials. Imports as a proportion of the net national product (1913 prices) were 16.5 per cent in 1932 but only 11.6 per cent in 1935 and 10.5 per cent by 1937. Raw materials produced domestically increased by 49 per cent between 1932 and 1935, while imported raw materials increased only 12 per cent. By 1937 the figures were 108 per cent and 14 per cent respectively.[79] While the rate of autarkic development expanded under the Second Four Year Plan, the roots of self-sufficiency lay in the economic experience of the slump and the rejection of the liberal trading model by a great many German economists and politicians.

The difference between the initial conception of the autarkic *Grossraumwirtschaft* and the *Lebensraum* programme outlined by Hitler in 1937 lay in its militarization. Hitler did not want to rely on economic coercion to bring other states into a German bloc but wanted to acquire them by force. Economic motives were central to the foreign policy project that Hitler outlined. The seizure of Austria, the occupation of Czechoslovakia and the war with Poland in 1939 conformed with the vision of a militarized economic area, self-reliant to a substantial degree in food and materials, in which Germany produced high-value industrial goods and armaments while the other areas supplied food, labour and materials.[80] Some states – Hungary,

Romania and Yugoslavia – retained their independence but built up a heavy reliance on German trade and funds. The trade agreements with the Soviet Union made at the same time as the German–Soviet Pact of August 1939 was also consistent with this pattern. Hitler then launched the assault on his Soviet trade partner which was to secure control of the vast resources of the western and southern USSR to lay the foundation for the complete economic restructuring of the whole area under the direction of a German apparatus for economic planning and regulation.[81]

The colonial economic system imposed in the East after 1939 had much in common with Class's pre-1914 ideas on economic imperialism and with the economic nationalists of the 1920s, with the important qualification that the German New Order economy extended right across Europe and was not confined to the closed bloc in central and eastern Europe. Moreover Hitler's new economic model was driven by a crude racial vision in which Jews were to be violently expelled and exterminated and other peoples subjected to a crude process of demodernization and economic expropriation. Whatever efforts are made to see the German economic experiment as a proto-Common Market, they founder on the grim reality of German *dirigisme*, racism and spoliation. The New Order was exclusive and predatory, its links with the wider world economy merely residual by comparison with the internationalized economy of the 1920s.[82]

The *Grossraumwirtschaft* as a function of Germany's relationship with the global economy ultimately rose or fell on the issue of war. German defeat highlighted the contradiction between the attempt to find a modern form of economic organization that would restore economic health and stability and the belief that only a militarized, expanding state, like the Prussia of the nineteenth century, could supply it. The consequence was an economy in which the process of modernization, expressed in terms of technological, scientific and managerial innovation, was largely maintained for the sake of the military economy, to be appropriated after 1945 as the foundation for future German prosperity. But the cost of steering Germany towards the new economic order resulted in the loss for Germany's population of years of economic well-being, the destruction of German cities, the deaths of six million Germans, the expulsion of millions more from the East and the division of the state for almost half a century. It may well be that welfare capitalism and the free market could not have been sustained under any circumstances after the slump – and the British economist J.M. Keynes believed that some kind of New Order on German lines was inevitable, even desirable[83] – but the violent and racist economic strategy finally adopted from the mid-1930s was unquestionably the least functionally sufficient of the many anti-liberal and neo-mercantilist strategies that populated German political economy in the crisis years after 1919.

Notes

1. J. Stern, *The Hidden Damage* (London, 1990), p. 83.

2. J. Diefendorf, *In the Wake of War: The Reconstruction of German Cities after World War II* (New York, 1993), pp. 11–14.

3. A. Sommariva and G. Tullio, *German Macroeconomic History, 1880–1979* (London, 1987), pp. 226–7; C. Feinstein, *Statistical Tables of National Income, Expenditure and Output of the U.K., 1855–1965* (Cambridge, 1972), Tables T-18, T-19.

4. Sommariva and Tullio, *Macroeconomic History*, p. 227; A. Maddison, *Phases of Capitalist Development* (New York, 1982), p. 44.

5. C.-L. Holtfrerich, *The German Inflation, 1914–1923* (Berlin/New York, 1986) pp. 146–9.

6. H. Kellenbenz, *Deutsche Wirtschaftsgeschichte: Band II* (Munich, 1981), p. 360.

7. See in particular G. Merkin, 'Towards a Theory of the German Inflation: Some Preliminary Observations', in G. Feldman, C.-L. Holtfrerich and P.-C. Witt, eds, *Die Deutsche Inflation* (Berlin, 1982), pp. 25–48.

8. H.-J. Schröder, 'Zur politische Bedeutung der deutschen Handelspolitik nach den Ersten Weltkrieg', in Feldman *et al.*, *Deutsche Inflation*, p. 21.

9. H. Schacht, *76 Jahre meines Lebens* (Bad Wörishofen, 1953), p. 208.

10. D. Lindenlaub, 'Maschinenbauunternehmen in der Inflation 1919 bis 1923: unternehmenshistorische Überlegungen zu einigen Inflationstheorien', in Feldman *et al.*, *Deutsche Inflation*, p. 95.

11. Holtfrerich, *German Inflation*, pp. 249–52.

12. K. Borchardt, *Perspectives on Modern German Economic History and Policy* (Cambridge, 1991), p. 141.

13. S. Schuker, *American 'Reparations' to Germany, 1919–33: Implications for the Third-World Debt Crisis* (Princeton, NJ, 1988), pp. 30, 114–15.

14. T. Balderston, *The Origins and Course of the German Economic Crisis: November 1923 to May 1932* (Berlin, 1993), pp. 39–41, 80–1, 401–2.

15. See Borchardt's essay 'Economic Causes of the Collapse of the Weimar Republic', in *idem*, *Modern German Economic History*, pp. 161–83; see too the general discussion of the 'Borchardt thesis' in J. von Kruedener, ed., *Economic Crisis and Political Collapse: The Weimar Republic, 1924–1933* (Oxford, 1990), in particular the articles by Holtfrerich and von Kruedener.

16. P. Temin, 'The Beginning of the Depression in Germany', *Economic History Review*, 2nd ser., 24 (1971), pp. 246–8.

17. Schuker, *American 'Reparations'*, pp. 53–4; W.L. Patch, *Heinrich Brüning and the Dissolution of the Weimar Republic* (Cambridge, 1998), pp. 150–1, 205–6. In general see W. Jochmann, 'Brünings Deflationspolitik und der Untergang der Weimarer Republik', in D. Stegmann, B.-J. Wendt and P.-C. Witt, eds, *Industrielle Gesellschaft und politisches System* (Bonn, 1978), pp. 97–112.

18. G. Hardach, 'Banking and Industry in Germany in the Interwar Period, 1919–1939', *Journal of European Economic History* 13 (1984), pp. 219–24. See too B. Eichengreen, *Golden Fetters: The Gold Standard and the Great Depression, 1919–1939* (New York, 1992), pp. 270–6.

19. The figure for registered unemployment peaked in February 1932 at 6.12 million. This figure greatly understated actual unemployment, since many had left the register by 1932. Employment in July 1929 was 20.75 million; in January 1933 it was 11.4 million, a difference of 9.35 million (seasonally unadjusted) (*Statistisches Jahrbuch für das Deutsche Reich 1940* [Berlin, 1940], p. 389).

20. H. James, *The Reichsbank and Public Finance in Germany, 1924–1933* (Frankfurt/Main, 1985), pp. 326–31.

21. On the onset of revival see F.-W. Henning, 'Die zeitliche Einordnung der Überwindung der Weltwirtschaftskrise in Deutschland', in H. Winkel, ed., *Finanz- und wirtschaftspolitische Fragen der Zwischenkriegszeit* (Berlin, 1973), pp. 135–73. On Brüning see Patch, *Brüning*, pp. 215–19; H. James, *The German Slump: Politics and Economics, 1924–1936* (Oxford, 1986), pp. 34–5, 273–4.

22. In general see G. Radiis, *Die deutsche Aussenhandelspolitik unter dem Einfluss der Devisenbewirtschaftung von 1931 bis 1938* (Vienna, 1939); F. Child, *The Theory and Practice of Exchange Control in Germany* (London, 1958).

23. On work creation see M. Schneider, 'The Development of State Work Creation Policy in Germany, 1930–1933', in P. Stachura, ed., *Unemployment and the Great Depression in Weimar Germany* (London, 1986), pp. 173–80; on the regional impact see D. Silverman, *Hitler's Economy: Nazi Work Creation Programs, 1933–1936* (Cambridge, MA, 1998), esp. chs 4, 6.

24. On help for agriculture see J. Farquharson, *The Plough and the Swastika: The NSDAP and Agriculture in Germany, 1928–1945* (London, 1976), pp. 59–67; James, *German Slump*, pp. 335–7. See in general G. Corni, *Hitler and the Peasants* (Oxford, 1990).

25. K.H. Minuth, ed., *Akten der Reichskanzlei: Regierung Hitler 1933–1938: Band II 1933* (Boppard am Rhein, 1983), p. 754, speech to the first session of the General Economic Council, 2 Sept 1933.

26. Details in W. Reichardt, 'Kapitalbildung und Kapitalmarkt in Deutschland', in Deutsches Institut für Bankwissenschaft und Bankwesen, *Probleme des Deutschen Wirtschaftslebens* (Berlin, 1937), pp. 587–97; R. Erbé, *Die nationalsozialistische Wirtschaftspolitik 1933–9 im Lichte der modernen Theorie* (Zurich, 1958), p. 67;

S. Lurie, *Private Investment in a Controlled Economy: Germany, 1933–1939* (London, 1947), pp. 23, 38.

27. See for example R.J. Overy, 'Heavy Industry in the Third Reich: the Reichswerke Crisis', *European History Quarterly* 15 (1985), pp. 313–14, 317–23.

28. See W. Stern, 'Wehrwirtschaft: a German Contribution to Economics', *Economic History Review*, 2nd ser., 13 (1960–1), pp. 270–81; H.-E. Volkmann, 'Aspekte der Nationalsozialistischen "Wehrwirtschaft" 1933 bis 1936', *Francia* 5 (1977), pp. 513–38.

29. D. Petzina, *Autarkiepolitik im Dritten Reich: der ns Vierjahresplan* (Stuttgart, 1968), p. 183.

30. See J. Gillingham, 'The "Deproletarianization" of German Society: Vocational Training in the Third Reich', *Journal of Social History* 19 (1985–6), pp. 427–8.

31. Maddison, *Capitalist Development*, pp. 97–8, 117–20; L. Rostas, 'Industrial Production, Productivity and Distribution in Britain, Germany and the United States', *Economic Journal* 53 (1943).

32. On the war economy see W. Abelshauser, 'Germany: Guns, Butter, and Economic Miracles', in M. Harrison, ed., *The Economics of World War II: Six Great Powers in International Comparison* (Cambridge, 1998), pp. 122–70; on resource mobilization see R.J. Overy, *War and Economy in the Third Reich* (Oxford, 1994), chs 9, 11; on financing war see W. Boelcke, *Die Kosten von Hitlers Krieg* (Paderborn, 1985).

33. 'V', 'The Destruction of Capitalism in Germany', *Foreign Affairs* 15 (1937), pp. 596, 606.

34. S. Andic and J. Veverka, 'The Growth of Government Expenditure in Germany', *Finanzarchiv* 25 (1964), pp. 242–5, 247, 260–1.

35. J.P. Cullity, 'The Growth of Governmental Employment in Germany, 1882–1950', *Zeitschrift für die gesamte Staatswissenschaft* 123 (1967), pp. 202–4; figures on local government from *Statistisches Jahrbuch*, 1935, p. 453, and 1940, pp. 528–9. On wartime administration see Imperial War Museum, FD 3056/49, statistical material on the German manpower position during the war, FIAT report, 3 July 1945.

36. Andic and Veverka, 'Government Expenditure', pp. 247, 258–9.

37. G. Ambrosius, *Der Staat als Unternehmer: öffentliche Wirtschaft und Kapitalismus seit dem 19. Jahrhundert* (Göttingen, 1984), pp. 64, 79.

38. Bundesarchiv Koblenz, BAK R7/992, Economics Ministry, 'Schulden der staatlichen Unternehmungen 1933–1945'; National Archives, Washington, Microcopy T83, Roll 74, Reichswerke files, frames 3445183–98, 'Der Zuwachs an staatlichen Unternehmungen in Privatrechtsform'.

39. Hardach, 'Banking and Industry', pp. 94–7. In general see C. Kopper, *Zwischen Marktwirtschaft und Dirigismus: Bankenpolitik im 'Dritten Reich', 1933–1939* (Bonn, 1995).

40. S. Reich, *The Fruits of Fascism: Postwar Prosperity in Historical Perspective* (Ithaca, NY, 1990), pp. 147–60, 192–4; see too H. Mommsen, *Das Volkswagenwerk und seine Arbeiter im Dritten Reich* (Dusseldorf, 1996), chs 2–5.

41. *Walther Rathenau: gesammelte Reden* (Berlin, 1924), pp. 161–2 'Der Hohepunkt des Kapitalismus. Vortrag am 27 April 1921'.

42. See, for example, W. Sombart, 'Weltanschauung, Wissenschaft und Wirtschaft', in *Probleme des deutschen Wirtschaftslebens* (see n. 26), pp. 768–89. Sombart approved of economic discourse that considered 'the *Volk* (the "whole") as the centre-point' and realized that 'all economy is "political"'.

43. W. Treue, 'Der Denkschrift Hitlers über die Aufgaben eines Vierjahresplans', *Vierteljahreshefte für Zeitgeschichte* 3 (1954), p. 206. See too the discussion of Hitler's economic and social ideas in R. Zitelmann, *Hitler. Selbstverständnis eines Revolutionärs* (Hamburg, 1989), pp. 195–215, 221–41.

44. See particularly H. Woll, *Die Wirtschaftslehre des deutschen Faschismus* (Munich, 1988); W. Krause and G. Rudolph, *Grundlinien des ökonomischen Denkens in Deutschland, 1848 bis 1945* (Berlin, 1980), pp. 433–69; H. Janssen, *Nationalökonomie und Nationalsozialismus* (Marburg, 1998).

45. See esp. A. Barkai, *Nazi Economics: Ideology, Theory and Policy* (Oxford, 1990), ch. 3, for the arguments surrounding the establishment of 'corporativist' institutions.

46. The literature is now vast on the connections between economic and military expansion and the radicalization of German race policy. See particularly G. Aly, *The Final Solution* (London, 1998); R.-D. Müller, *Hitlers Ostkrieg und die deutsche Siedlungspolitik. Die Zusammenarbeit von Wehrmacht, Wirtschaft und SS* (Frankfurt/Main, 1991).

47. BAK R7/2149, Otto Ohlendorf manuscript, 'Grundsätze der Volkswirtschaftspolitik', n.d. [ca. Sept 1936], p. 9; 'Unsere Wirtschaftsauffassung. Das Programm der NSDAP', n.d., p. 9. On the idea of the 'managed economy' see W. Krause, *Wirtschaftstheorie unter dem Hakenkreuz* (Berlin, 1969), pp. 140–5.

48. 'Freie Wirtschaft und Planwirtschaft', *Die Neue Zeitung* 14 (Oct 1946), reproduced in L. Erhard, *Deutsche Wirtschaftspolitik. Der Weg der sozialen Marktwirtschaft* (Düsseldorf, 1962), pp. 20–1.

49. R. Berthold, ed., *Produktivkräfte in Deutschland, 1917/18 bis 1945* (Berlin, 1988), p. 347.

50. F. Blaich, 'Why Did the Pioneer Fall Behind? Motorisation in Germany Between the Wars', in T. Barker, ed., *The Economic and Social Effects of the Spread of Motor Vehicles* (London, 1987), pp. 148–60.

51. E. Grunberg, 'The Mobilization of Capacity and Resources of Small-scale Industry in Germany', *Journal of Business* 64 (1941), p. 329.

52. R. Liefmann, *Cartels, Concerns and Trusts* (London, 1932), pp. 30–1.

53. C.W. Guillebaud, *The Economic Recovery of Germany, 1933–1938* (London, 1939), pp. 55–6, 166–80.

54. W. Feldenkirchen, 'Big Business in Interwar Germany: Organizational Innovation at Vereinigte Stahlwerke, IG Farben, and Siemens', *Business History Review* 61 (1987), pp. 421–7, 432–40, 447–9. See also H. Levy, *Industrial Germany: A Study of its Monopoly Organisations and Their Control by the State* (London, 1935), pp. 164–86.

55. Details in E. Hexner, *International Cartels* (London, 1946).

56. On VS and the Reichswerke see G. Mollin, *Montankonzerne und 'Dritten Reich': Der Gegensatz zwischen Monopolindustrie und Befehlswirtschaft in der deutschen Rüstung und Expansion* (Göttingen, 1988); on IG Farben see P. Hayes, *Industry and Ideology: IG Farben in the Nazi Era* (Cambridge, 1987).

57. See V. Berghahn, *The Americanization of West German Industry, 1945–1973* (Leamington Spa, 1986), esp. pp. 84–110, 155–81 on decartelization and cartel legislation. A good case study is R.G. Stokes, *Divide and Prosper: The Heirs of IG Farben under Allied Authority, 1945–51* (Berkeley, CA, 1989), pp. 203–9.

58. There is a vast literature on industry in the Weimar Republic. See in particular G. Feldman, *Iron and Steel in the German Inflation, 1916–1923* (Princeton, NJ, 1977); B. Weisbrod, *Schwerindustrie in der Weimarer Republik. Interessenpolitik zwischen Stabilisierung und Krise* (Wuppertal, 1978); D. Abraham, *The Collapse of the Weimar Republic: Political Economy and Crisis* (Princeton, NJ, 1981).

59. See esp. H.A. Turner, *German Big Business and the Rise of Hitler* (Oxford, 1985). On the attraction of small business to Nazism see C. Szejnmann, *Nazism in Central Germany: The Brownshirts in 'Red Saxony'* (Oxford, 1999), pp. 149–51, 176–82.

60. Krupp's views in Overy, *War and Economy*, pp. 119–23. In general on German business see P. Hayes, 'Industrial Factionalism in Modern German History', *Central European History* 27 (1991), pp. 122–31; V. Berghahn, 'Big Business in the Third Reich', *European History Quarterly* 21 (1991), pp. 97–108; J. Gillingham, *Industry and Politics in the Third Reich* (London, 1985); L. Gall and M. Pohl, eds, *Unternehmen im Nationalsozialismus* (Munich, 1998).

61. Details in F. Thyssen, *I Paid Hitler* (London, 1941), pp. 48–9.

62. See W.E. Mosse, *Jews in the German Economy: The German–Jewish Economic Elite, 1820–1935* (Oxford, 1987), pp. 362–4, 373–9.

63. Details in A. Barkai, *From Boycott to Annihilation: The Economic Struggle of German Jews, 1933–1943* (Hanover, NH, 1989), pp. 113–14, 154–5. See too Mosse,

Jews in the German Economy, pp. 374–9; A. Fischer, *Hjalmar Schacht und Deutschlands 'Judenfrage'* (Cologne, 1995), pp. 205–22; L.M. Stallbaumer, 'Big Business and the Persecution of the Jews: The Flick Concern and the "Aryanization" of Jewish Property Before the War', *Holocaust and Genocide Studies* 13 (1999), pp. 1–15.

64. Barkai, *From Boycott to Annihilation*, p. 177.

65. *Nazi Gold: The London Conference 2–4 December 1997* (HMSO, London, 1998), pp. 45–58, 513–26, 545–6.

66. On foreign labour see U. Herbert, *Fremdarbeiter: Politik und Praxis des 'Ausländer-Einsatzes' in der Kriegswirtschaft des Dritten Reiches* (Berlin, 1985); C. Bermani, S. Bologna and B. Mantelli, *Proletarier der 'Achse': Sozialgeschichte der italienischen Fremdarbeit in NS-Deutschland, 1937 bis 1943* (Berlin, 1997). On the camps see W. Sofsky, *The Order of Terror: The Concentration Camp* (Princeton, NJ, 1997), pp. 34–43. On the behaviour of one German firm see N. Gregor, *Daimler-Benz in the Third Reich* (New Haven, CN, 1998), pp. 175–217.

67. Berthold, *Produktivkrafte*, pp. 346–7.

68. On the growth of female industrial employment see A. Tröger, 'Die Planung des Rationalisationsproletariats: Zur Entwicklung der geschlechtsspezifischen Arbeitsteilung und das weibliche Arbeitsmarkt im Nationalsozialismus', in A. Kuhn and J. Rüsen, eds, *Frauen in der Geschichte: Band II* (Düsseldorf, 1982), pp. 259–62; on female employment during the war see E. Hancock, 'Employment in Wartime: The Experience of German Women During the Second World War', *War and Society* 12 (1994), pp. 43–60.

69. See particularly the two case studies B.P. Mellon, *Mercedes in Peace and War: German Automobile Workers, 1903–1945* (New York, 1990), chs 6, 7; H. Homberg, *Rationalisierung und Industriearbeit: Arbeitsmarkt – Management – Arbeiterschaft im Siemens-Konzern Berlin, 1900–1939* (Berlin, 1991).

70. See R. Hachtmann, *Industriearbeit im 'Dritten Reich'* (Göttingen, 1989), pp. 207–23. On wage policy in general see T. Siegel, 'Wage Policy in Nazi Germany', *Politics and Society* 14 (1985), pp. 5–37.

71. Figures in C.D. Long, *The Labor Force under Changing Income and Employment* (Princeton, NJ, 1958), p. 369; I. Svennilson, *Growth and Stagnation in the European Economy* (London, 1954), p. 235.

72. Siegel, 'Wage Policy', pp. 27–32; on saving see Overy, *War and Economy*, pp. 272–3. On labour participation in the DAF see for example W. Zöllitsch, 'Die Vertrauensratswahlen von 1934 und 1935: zum Stellenwert von Abstimmungen im "Dritten Reich" am Beispiel Krupp', *Geschichte und Gesellschaft* 15 (1989), pp. 361–81. On labour policy see T.W. Mason, *Social Policy in the Third Reich* (Oxford, 1993), ch. 6. On the limits of labour resistance and participation see the essays in C. Sachse *et al.*, *Angst, Belohnung, Zucht und Ordnung: Herrschaftsmechanismen im Nationalsozialismus* (Düsseldorf, 1982).

73. Memorandum by Col. Hossbach, 10 Nov 1937, Minutes of the conference in the Reich Chancellery, 5 Nov 1937, in *Documents on German Foreign Policy*, ser. D, vol. 1, pp. 29–39.

74. Cited in G. Stoakes, *Hitler and the Quest for World Dominion* (Leamington Spa, 1986), pp. 39–40.

75. On the link between ideas on territory and power see A.A. Kallis, 'Expansionism in Italy and Germany between Unification and the First World War: On the Ideological and Political Origins of Fascist Expansionism', *European History Quarterly* 28 (1998), pp. 435–60. The instrumental use of ideas on territoriality are explored in G.H. Herb, *Under the Map of Germany: Nationalism and Propaganda, 1918–1945* (London, 1997), ch. 6.

76. Sommariva and Tullio, *Macroeconomic History*, pp. 226–7; Maddison, *Capitalist Development*, pp. 250–2. On the preference for trade over FDI see for example V. Schröter, 'The IG Farbenindustrie AG in Central and South-Eastern Europe, 1926–38', in A. Teichova and P. Cottrell, eds, *International Business in Central Europe, 1919–1939* (Leicester, 1983), pp. 139–62.

77. Schuker, *American 'Reparations'*, pp. 115–19. In general see B. Kent, *The Spoils of War: The Politics, Economics and Diplomacy of Reparations, 1918–1932* (Oxford, 1989).

78. For a contemporary description see K. Krüger, *Deutsche Grossraumwirtschaft* (Marburg, 1932); H. Kremmler, *Autarkie in der organischen Wirtschaft* (Dresden, 1940). See in general E. Teichert, *Autarkie und Grossraumwirtschaft in Deutschland, 1930–1939* (Munich, 1984).

79. Figures in L. Zumpe, *Wirtschaft und Staat in Deutschland, 1933 bis 1945* (Berlin, 1979), p. 221; H.-E. Volkmann, 'Die NS-Wirtschaft in Vorbereitung des Krieges', in W. Deist *et al.*, *Das Deutsche Reich und der Zweite Weltkrieg: Band I* (Stuttgart, 1979), p. 262.

80. B.-J. Wendt, *Grossdeutschland: Aussenpolitik und Kriegsvorbereitung des Hitler-Regimes* (Munich, 1987), ch. 4; H. Kahrs, 'Von der "Grossraumwirtschaft" zur "Neuen Ordnung"', in H. Kahrs *et al.*, *Modelle für ein deutsches Europa: Ökonomie und Herrschaft im Grosswirtschaftsraum* (Berlin, 1992), pp. 9–26.

81. On central and eastern Europe see M. Broszat, 'Deutschland–Ungarn–Rumänien: Entwicklung und Grundfaktoren nationalsozialistischer Hegemonial- und Bündnispolitik, 1938–1941', *Historische Zeitschrift* 206 (1968), pp. 45–96; D. Kaiser, *Economic Diplomacy and the Origins of the Second World War* (Princeton, NJ, 1980), chs 9–10. On German–Soviet economic relations see H. Schwendemann, *Die wirtschaftliche Zusammenarbeit zwischen dem Deutschen Reich und der Sowjetunion von 1939 bis 1941* (Berlin, 1993).

82. See J. ten Cate, G. Otto and R.J. Overy, eds, *Die 'Neuordnung' Europas: NS-Wirtschaftspolitik in den besetzten Gebieten* (Berlin, 1997); on the USSR see

R.-D. Müller, 'Von der Wirtschaftsallianz zum kolonialen Ausbeutungskrieg', in J. Förster *et al.*, *Das Deutsche Reich und der Zweite Weltkrieg: Band 4* (Stuttgart, 1983), pp. 98–189.

83. Public Record Office, London, T160/995, Memorandum of Mr Keynes, 'Proposals to counter the German "New Order", 1 Dec 1940'. Keynes said Britain should propose the same kind of system of closed economy as Germany only 'better and more honestly'.

CHAPTER THREE

Did Hitler create a new society?
Continuity and change in German social
history before and after 1933

HARTMUT BERGHOFF

There can be no doubt that the Nazi Party (NSDAP) claimed to be a revolutionary movement and promised to create a totally new type of society. There is, however, considerable uncertainty about what kind of changes in the texture of German society were actually intended; and even more difficult to discern is the extent to which these plans were made reality by the Nazi leadership. Their various statements and proclamations were highly contradictory and in most cases did not conform to the policies implemented. Moreover, it is impossible to disentangle romantic and technocratic, egalitarian and elitist aspects of the Nazi programme. Hitler's political manifesto, *Mein Kampf*, essentially amounts to an evil concoction of resentment. The self-appointed Führer despised the Habsburg and Hohenzollern monarchies, the aristocracy and the bourgeoisie, intellectuals and capitalists, the working classes and the petite bourgeoisie, state officials and bureaucrats, and most of all Jews and Slavs. Hatred was the key to his conception of the world and destruction his ultimate goal.

On the other hand, Hitler indulged in megalomaniacal visions of modernity such as gigantic railway and motorway systems as well as monumental public buildings and colossal cities. He admired the USA for its technological and industrial potential just as much as he detested it for its economic order, social structure, and, most of all, for its multiracial population.[1] He further propagated equal opportunities for all Germans regardless of their parents' position. Nazi ideology claimed that within the 'Third Reich' all traditional privileges of class and status would disappear and individual performance and merit would become the only criteria for advancement. The NSDAP's party programme of 1920 demanded the opening up of all careers to talent and achievement. This emphasis on equal opportunities did, however, exclude Jews and other 'racially inferior' groups as well as political dissenters. The Aryan *Volksgemeinschaft*, i.e. the community of 'racially pure' and politically reliable Germans, would constitute a truly classless society without barriers of wealth, birth, religion or ideology, which had sharply sectionalized the societies of Imperial and Weimar Germany.

The turbulent years between 1918 and 1933 had seen a deepening rather than a lessening of social divisions. The upheaval of the Great War and the humiliating experience of defeat, the insecurity and bitterness following the end of the monarchy and the trauma of hyper-inflation and impoverishment, the acceleration of cultural change in the short 'golden twenties' as well as depression and mass unemployment had increased social tensions and endangered the cohesion of German society. This constellation was reflected by the existence of several large parties, each representing certain milieux, and a flourishing scene of splinter parties speaking for a variety of special-interest groups.[2]

Thus, the integrative ideology of a classless *Volksgemeinschaft* was the answer to Weimar's rising social antagonism and its highly polarized political landscape. The *Volksgemeinschaft* concept, however, did not entail an egalitarian society at all. On the contrary, the new Germany was to be clearly structured by the *Führerprinzip*, the leader principle. An unambiguous hierarchy reaching from the Führer down to the rank and file of his party was to create a rigorous structure of command and subordination. The top positions were to be filled by *homini novi* imbued with superior qualities, i.e. charismatic *Führergestalten* born to rule. Hitler believed in the social Darwinist concept of the survival of the fittest. For this universal competition to take place, equal chances for all members of the nation were a prerequisite. Thus he repeatedly announced that talented working-class youth should be given the opportunity to enter further and higher education at the taxpayers' expense.[3]

The *Volksgemeinschaft* ideology also had its tactical side. The NSDAP's propaganda pursued a catch-all strategy promising something for everyone. Each social group was addressed separately and offered some specific gains in order to lure its members into the clutches of the party: jobs for the unemployed, guaranteed incomes and writing off of mortgages for farmers, shelter from market pressures for shopkeepers, artisans and small business-men, security for the elderly, career prospects for the young, orders for industry, and so on. Lawyers, doctors, teachers, farmers, workers, clerks, small businessmen, students, women and juveniles had their separate organizations within the party. Admittedly the NSDAP's membership was not an exact mirror of German society but it covered a wide spectrum ranging, by 1930, from the subproletariat to the aristocracy. Blue- and white-collar employees, however, were the largest groups, representing more than half of all members. Compared with the overall population, workers were significantly under- and clerks significantly over-represented. Farmers, artisans, profes-sionals, low-ranking bureaucrats, small businessmen, university graduates and Protestants also counted disproportionally high quotas among the NSDAP's members, while workers, aristocrats, Catholics and women displayed dis-proportionally low quotas. In the last years of the Weimar Republic, the NSDAP was – apart from the catholic *Zentrum* – the only integrative people's party recruiting members from all strata of society. The most striking feature of this ultra-nationalistic, anti-Marxist and anti-Semitic party was its rela-tive youthfulness. In 1930 36.8 per cent of the NSDAP's members and 26.2 per cent of its functionaries were younger than 30 years of age. Its radical dynamism appealed most to those who, in the early 1930s, perceived them-selves to be deprived of their future by a selfish and lethargic older generation. The NSDAP's aggressive slogan *Macht Platz ihr Alten* ('get out of the way you oldies') promised radical solutions for an agonizing generational conflict intensified by economic crisis.[4]

Before comparing the NSDAP's promises with the reality of Nazi rule along class lines, it has to be emphasized that the NSDAP's revolutionary drive was stifled immediately after Hitler gained power. In the words of David Schoenbaum, the NSDAP 'found itself in the position of stowaways suddenly in control of an ocean liner. The resources at hand were suitable . . . for seizing the bridge. But . . . the available personnel was of rather less use in maintaining the engines or the course.' A 'rapprochement with the representatives of the old order' became necessary 'to keep the ship afloat'.[5] Therefore, compromises with the traditional elites marked the beginning of Hitler's reign. As he was not able to run the country and, more importantly, prepare for war without them, he had to come to arrangements with them.

As early as June 1933 Hitler warned the *Reichsstatthalter*, the highest representatives of the Berlin administration in the federal states, that the Nazi revolution should come to an end and be replaced by an evolutionary course: 'It is not permissible to dismiss a business leader when he is a good business leader but not a National Socialist, and particularly when the National Socialist appointed to his place has no idea of business.'[6] Such developments did actually occur during the first few months after Hitler's appointment, when the left wing of the NSDAP tried to claim the spoils of their fight against the Republic. As Hitler aimed at integrating rather than replacing the old elites, at least in the short run, unauthorized violations of private property rights by Nazi activists were firmly stopped. One part of the pent-up revolutionary energy, however, was channelled into brutal riots against political enemies and helpless minorities such as the Jews. In June 1934 the NSDAP's left wing was finally pruned by the murder of Strasser and other leading SA functionaries. In September 1934 Hitler again pro-claimed the end of the National Socialist revolution. This was a pragmatic decision against any social experiments in favour of the dynamics of a modern industrial society urgently needing to prepare for war. A return to pre-industrial conditions was out of the question. Those who had such aspirations were eliminated or marginalized within the first year of the takeover.

As far as social structures were concerned, the Nazi regime was definitely not revolutionary in its formative years. But did it have long-term effects on the texture of German society? An aggressive as well as comprehensive system like Hitler's dictatorship must have had a significant impact. The exact effect of his rule must be analysed in more detail. Therefore this article will deal with the main social groups separately and discuss the complicated mixture of continuities and politically induced changes. It will then move on to the question of social mobility in general and the recruitment of elites in particular. By taking this approach it will look at some central institutions that either bestowed power on their personnel – such as the military or the administration – or that heavily increased chances of social climbing – such as the educational system. One of the key questions is whether chances of upward mobility grew under the dictatorship, or whether traditional social divisions were retained.[7] Did 1933 mark a caesura in German social history, or did the structures inherited from the Weimar Republic remain largely intact? These questions will also be related to the highly controversial debate over whether the 'Third Reich' had a modernizing or reactionary impact on German society. Did Hitler turn back the clock, or did he accelerate change towards a more fluid and open society that put achievement before status and whose degree of urbanization, industrialization, professionalization and division of labour was increasing?[8]

The largest social groups in Germany

The peasantry

German agriculture had been crisis-ridden ever since the globalization of the world's food markets in the second half of the nineteenth century. By and large it was characterized by overproduction, shrinking incomes, labour shortage, indebtedness, compulsory auctions and foreclosures. These problems were aggravated by protectionist politics that artificially slowed down inevitable structural change, i.e. the transfer of capital and people from agriculture into the industrial and service sectors. Thus in the Weimar Republic German agriculture was overpopulated and undercapitalized, inefficient and uncompetitive and, therefore, increasingly dependent on state subsidies. Long-term structural problems such as the predominance of small farms worsened after 1918. In view of this remarkable concentration of problems, it comes as no surprise that agriculture was particularly hard hit by the depression and that farmers were only too eager to support a party that promised them preferential treatment and addressed them as the 'nation's life-source' or even as the 'fountainhead of the Nordic race'. The NSDAP managed to convince many farmers that Hitler would solve their problems and reverse secular trends such as continuing industrialization and urbanization, globalization and commercialization. All these processes had in fact contributed to agriculture's overall loss of importance, which the NSDAP promised to reverse. Thus, the peasantry entered the 'Third Reich' as the 'ideological darling'[9] of the regime. But what happened between the Nazis and farmers after the initial honeymoon period?

At first the regime kept its word and delivered on many of the promises it had made before 1933 because agriculture was to play a crucial role in making Germany self-sufficient. The experience of virtual starvation due to the Allied blockade in the First World War had not been forgotten and served as a constant reminder to treat farmers with great care. Moreover, the regime's agricultural policy was not only tactically motivated. Many leading National Socialists also believed in the superior virtues of rural life and had romantic visions of a return to the land. From their point of view, farmers guaranteed racial purity and strength. *Wehrbauern*, or peasant militias, were to act as the backbone of Hitler's boundless colonization scheme in the East.

The regime viewed the small family farm as the ideal model of agrarian life. As it was endangered particularly by indebtedness and fragmentation, credit provisions to bail farmers out of their debts were forthcoming. Moreover, in 1933 small and middle-sized properties were covered by the *Erbhofgesetz*, the law on hereditary farm entailment, which made it illegal to sell, foreclose, subdivide or mortgage such farms. Inheritance was restricted to a sole heir and the male line, stressing again the party's anti-feminism. Although this measure was intended to strengthen the family farm, it did in fact weaken it. By taking it out of the regular property market, it was cut off from the credit facilities it badly needed for modernization. It also drove away relatives who had formerly supported the family farm without pay because they had expected to inherit part of the property. Even compensating disinherited sons financially became more difficult. The *Erbhofgesetz* was therefore extremely unpopular with those for whom it was designed. It also had little or no impact on the overall pattern of landholding in Germany.[10]

This law further hastened migration to urban centres, whose growth – notwithstanding all hazy pipe dreams of returning to the land – continued after 1933. Apart from the unfavourable position of disinherited children, relatively high wages in booming industry led to a sharp decline in agricultural employment. The resettlement programme, which was drawn up to counter this movement and to create new peasant holdings especially in underpopulated eastern Germany, turned out to be a complete failure. The quantity of new farms created during the Nazi period was lower than the corresponding Weimar figure. From 1934 onwards their numbers were decreasing, again in blatant contrast to the years before the 'seizure of power'. One of the main problems was the lack of available land and funds. The regime's unwillingness to adopt far-reaching structural reforms, such as the nationalization or redistribution of the large East Elbian estates, played a large role in ruling out any real increase in the size and vigour of the German peasantry.[11]

A fundamental land reform, the reparcelling of dispersed smallholdings, thorough mechanization or the propagation of machine co-operatives and other measures that could have really modernized German agriculture would all have been well within the reach of an authoritarian regime like Hitler's. However, the romantic view of farming and the lack of funds as well as sheer incompetence prevented any decisive rise in agricultural productivity. Modest gains were mainly due to the intensified use of artificial fertilizers which were highly subsidized. Thus the Nazi regime never even approached its self-postulated aim of full autarky. For the farmers the incentive to invest remained low. This was not only a consequence of the *Erbhofgesetz*, but also of the monopolistic system of marketing created by the *Reichsnährstand*, the compulsory organization comprising all producers, wholesalers and retailers of food as well as some processing industries. It regulated production, prices and sales in a highly bureaucratic way. From 1933 to 1935 this system helped farmers to recover from depression, as prices rose faster than wages. After 1935, despite buoyant demand, agricultural prices increased only very slowly and were still below the level of the 1920s. The *Reichsnährstand* thus prevented farmers from cashing in on the pre-war economic boom.

By banishing the law of supply and demand from the German food market and replacing it with a complicated system of guaranteed incomes and quotas, modernizing farms simply did not pay. The *Reichsnährstand* further taught farmers not to act on their own initiative but to rely on the state. It also found no way to stop the drain of manpower from the country into the towns, which further weakened agriculture. The small family farm kept on being an endangered species. Despite all the subsidies, compulsory auctions continued, and the mundane reality was one of inefficient production, overworked families and meagre returns. Notwithstanding all ideological convictions and propagandistic flattery, agriculture remained a shrinking and by and large needy sector of the German economy. Not one of its core problems had been solved by the Nazi regime.[12] It had essentially proved itself unable to reverse long-term trends such as urbanization and industrialization because the economic costs would have been disastrous for a regime hoping to wage an industrial war all over Europe.

The fact that post-1945 German agriculture had a very different pattern of landholding was only indirectly the result of Nazi policies. The immediate cause of this fundamental change was Germany's total defeat in 1945. The flight and expulsion from East Germany plus the Soviet land reform in what was to become the German Democratic Republic broke up the power of the East Elbian junkers. With their economic base destroyed, any claim to social and political leadership finally disappeared. Thus postwar Germany was spared Weimar's fatal problem of a moribund upper class trying to stop its economic decline by blocking democratization.[13]

Apart from this far-reaching historic caesura, continuities prevailed, at least in West Germany. The Federal Republic too was confronted with the structural problem of an uncompetitive peasantry, which was increasingly marginalized within an essentially non-agrarian society. The response the democratic state found to this challenge resembled, in many ways, the answers of the Nazi regime. Even if the system of the *Reichsnährstand* was stripped of its ideological framework, its regulations were essentially reinstated and later even extended to the European Economic Community. Protection from market forces, bureaucratic regulation and heavy subsidies did not, however, succeed in producing a healthier agricultural structure but rather prolonged the crisis, especially of family farming, at horrendous expense to consumers and taxpayers alike.

The old *Mittelstand*

Mittelstand is a vague, collective term for very different social groups ranging from shopkeepers to clerks and from artisans to owners of, sometimes large, family businesses. Their only common denominator was the fact that they shared the fear of being crushed between society's two mighty power blocs, big business on the one hand and the well-organized labour movement on the other. Indeed, the *Mittelstand* was neither wealthy nor politically influential but, above all, it was on the defensive. Moreover, the old *Mittelstand*, i.e. artisans and shopkeepers, as opposed to the new *Mittelstand* of white-collar employees, felt themselves to be victims of industrial modernity. Apparently unable to meet the challenge of competition from factories or department stores, these small businessmen anticipated a bleak future. The feeling of impending doom was further intensified by the economic crisis of the 1920s and the fact that many of the unemployed searching for some kind of alternative became self-employed, thus swelling the already overpopulated ranks of the old *Mittelstand*. The influx of new competitors with the potential of undercutting prices and spoiling professional standards, the rise of new and more efficient retail organizations such as department or chain stores, and the proliferation of publicly owned firms (*Regiebetriebe*) in many artisan trades prepared a fertile soil for antimodernistic and anti-capitalistic resentment, which was inseparably linked with latent or open anti-Semitism. Frustration grew further because the *Mittelstand* perceived themselves to be society's golden middle, guarantors of social stability capable of bridging the widening gulf between capital and labour. From this self-image the *Mittelstand* derived its claim for privileges granted by the state. As the Weimar crisis mounted, the *Mittelstand*'s demands for protection grew louder and desperation about government inaction reached unprecedented heights. Therefore, substantial parts of the *Mittelstand* became easy game for the NSDAP who succeeded in appealing to their anticapitalistic yearning and convincingly promised social stability and economic protection. To what degree, however, did the Nazi regime deliver?

For artisans the abolition of the freedom to trade was the main change that they hoped would solve the problems of overcrowding and undercutting. Indeed, the regime fulfilled this long-standing demand of artisan pressure groups. In 1935 the passing of the master's exam (*Meisterbrief*) became the prerequisite for the right to set up a new shop. Until then the *Meisterbrief* was only optional, and most owners of artisan enterprises did not have it. Thus the exam could be used as a safety valve to regulate entry into a particular trade and thereby limit the degree of competition. In 1934 obligatory trade guilds were introduced in order to implement strict discipline and to bring all artisans under the authorities' rule. As the guilds themselves held the decisive master's exams and were entitled to recommend prices, the artisans received what they had campaigned for so eagerly since the middle of the nineteenth century, namely direct control of entry into their trades and restrictions on price competition. To be in command of these instruments must not be mixed up with a complete solution of all problems of the artisan trades. The immediate effects of Nazi legislation remained limited. Most owners of artisan enterprises without the *Meisterbrief* – 70 per cent of all self-employed artisans in 1936 – were allowed to stay in business. Only newcomers could effectively be excluded. The advantages of uniform and comprehensive professional organizations were outweighed in the end by their political instrumentalization. Artisans as well as other professional groups particularly disliked the Nazis' inclination to constant spoon-feeding in the form of proliferating red tape, and the obligation to pay high compulsory contributions, for the purpose of financing their own monitoring.[14]

Artisans no doubt benefited from the rearmament boom, although industry received the lion's share of the state's massive orders. Besides, other groups witnessed much faster income increases, and in many trades poverty remained a feature of artisan life. Thus, no preferential treatment was systematically bestowed upon artisans, as had been promised, even if their incomes rose and many of their old demands were met. The longer the Nazi reign lasted, the more artisans were disadvantaged by a state that concentrated on industry to feed the insatiable appetite of total warfare. Artisans lost the monopoly to train apprentices, who from 1937 could also be educated by industrial firms. After 1935 an open competition for quali-fied workers between industrial and artisan enterprises developed, in which the latter overwhelmingly lost out. From 1939 onwards artisans could be forced to close their shops without compensation in order to set free man-power for the armed forces or the armaments industry. In the second half of 1939 alone, almost 200,000 shops had to shut up. From then on, the competition for scarce resources such as materials and labour became fiercer, and artisans increasingly came off worst.[15]

What were the long-term effects of Nazi policies on German artisans? Some of the measures introduced between 1933 and 1945 no doubt had a modernizing impact. Professional training for artisans improved due to the foundation of several technical colleges. In 1937 book-keeping was made compulsory for artisans for the first time; this taught them to observe the basic principles of economics. Involuntary closures hit small and inefficient shops most heavily; therefore, the overall productivity of the whole sector increased without solving the problem of marginal shops and impoverished masters.[16] In the Federal Republic artisans managed to regain the legal privileges granted in 1934 and 1935, together with the trade guilds and the ban on opening shops without a *Meisterbrief*. In contrast to the Nazi period, these measures now succeeded in effectively limiting competition and keep-ing up prices. Together with the favourable circumstances of West Germany's 'economic miracle', these anticapitalistic regulations helped artisans to survive in a market economy and to improve their living standards substantially. In the long run, however, it was not the small, marginal shops, whose owners had so vehemently demanded help in the 1920s and early 1930s, that survived. On the contrary, many of them had to give up due to economic pressures before and after 1945 or due to administrative intervention during the war. The long-term trend did not favour the small shop run by a sole master, but the larger establishment with ten or more employees. This trend continued and even accelerated during the Nazi regime.

Shopkeepers, the second pillar of the old *Mittelstand*, campaigned for the closure of all large-scale competitors, especially department and chain stores, consumer cooperatives, five-and-ten stores (*Einheitspreisgeschäfte*), mail-order businesses and vending machines as well as for the elimination of 'unfair com-petition', especially price-cutting. In the first few months after Hitler's take-over it appeared that these demands would be fulfilled. The creation of new department stores and the expansion of existing premises was prohibited. Price rebates were restricted to a maximum of 3 per cent. The aggressive *NS-Kampfbund für den gewerblichen Mittelstand* (the Small Business Combat League) not only incorporated and unified all organizations of retailers and artisans but also dedicated its energy to intimidation, for example attacks on and boycotts of department stores and Jewish shops. In some cases they smashed windows, stormed the premises and dismissed the branch managers without authorization. As early as the summer of 1933 such chaotic action was stopped, when the new government proclaimed the end of the revolutionary phase. The *Kampfbund* was suspended and all unauthorized measures strictly forbidden. The tide had already turned in favour of stability. Even the ailing Hertie concern, a department store chain owned by the Jewish Tietz family, was rescued from impending collapse, mainly to save the 14,000 jobs at risk.[17]

From then on the Nazi regime generally tolerated large-scale retailers but disadvantaged them in many ways. They were excluded from public orders and from the lucrative business with the state's marriage credits. Various NSDAP organizations temporarily boycotted department stores. In some states a surtax was levied on their turnover. Consumer cooperatives fared worst mainly because of their former affiliation with the labour movement. They suffered not only incorporation into the Nazi Labour Front but also a drastic decline in membership and turnover. Nevertheless, on the whole large-scale retailing remained an essential part of the economy and continued to worry the small shopkeeper across the street. The government did not dare to reorganize retailing in any radical way because of the large units' substantial employment and their superior efficiency in supplying millions of Germans with cheap merchandise. It did not shy away, though, from massive intrusion upon property rights when Jewish citizens or trade unions were concerned. This success in implementing racial and political hatred must, however, not be confused with a victory of *Mittelstand* ideology. Even an Aryanized, that is, de facto confiscated department store, kept on being a department store threatening the existence of the small corner shop. Moreover, the Aryanization speeded up capital concentration in German retailing. In other words, it increased rather then eased competitive pressures on the *Mittelstand*. Vending machines and mail-order businesses were subject to certain restrictions which did not, however, do them a great deal of harm. Other measures of the Nazi regime such as the regulation of prices could only be initially interpreted as protection from price-cutting and unfair competition. In the long run the price freeze acted against the retailers' interests, making it difficult to improve their returns. Attempts to impose a *numerus clausus* by preventing the opening of new shops and demanding a formal qualification of competence (*Sachkundenachweis*) were cautiously made but never put through rigorously.[18]

During the war small units generally were among the first victims of emergency measures. Shopkeepers shared the experience of artisans in that their shops were the first to be closed, their staff the first to be drafted and their representatives the last to be consulted and to be appointed to influential posts within war economy organizations. Rising numbers of unpaid family members as opposed to falling figures of regular employees signalled even before 1939 that shops were not able to compete with larger units as far as salaries and perks were concerned. Their decline went on, notwithstanding the regime's *Mittelstand* rhetoric. All in all, no modernization drive took place. The large and more modern forms of retailing were ideologically suspect and disadvantaged rather than promoted, even if their existence was never really endangered. Inconsistency and half-heartedness were the main features of NSDAP *Mittelstand* policy that neither destroyed the modern forms of mass distribution nor efficiently supported the traditional shopkeeper. The structural problem of German retailing, namely the continued predominance of small shops, undercapitalized, hardly earning the owner a living, and extremely vulnerable to more efficient competitors, was not solved in the 'Third Reich'. Drastic structural change had to wait until the late 1950s and the 1960s when the triumph of supermarkets, mail-order businesses and department stores led to a massive shake-out. Fortunately, former shopkeepers and their employees were easily absorbed then by an almost empty labour market.

The new *Mittelstand*

The new *Mittelstand*, comprising mainly *Angestellten* (salaried employees), was in no way linked to the pre-industrial world but was an integral and fast growing part of modern society. Therefore its political targets were hardly determined by outright anticapitalism. Instead traditional privileges within the industrial labour market played a paramount role in shaping the political objectives of the *Angestellten*. Due to a special legal status, their jobs were more secure than those of manual workers, even if incomes in many cases converged. They received salaries instead of wages, and enjoyed their own social security system, which granted much better benefits. Nothing was so important to them as a sharp delineation from the proletariat, in legal as well as socio-cultural terms. Although the new *Mittelstand* was not as hard hit by the depression as the old *Mittelstand* or industrial workers, their self-perception of being efficiently insulated against economic fluctuations received a fatal blow. The feeling of being akin to *Beamten*, that is, state officials in permanent employment, was shattered, and fear of being proletarianized spread among *Angestellten*.

The demands of the *Angestellten* were aimed at preserving their legal privileges and at regulating their particular segment of the labour market by a strict control of entry. Obligatory exams and comprehensive organization should keep down the numbers admitted in order to create conditions of scarcity. The regime translated none of these plans into reality, apart from the fact that it united all *Angestellten* unions by force. The new, compulsory organization, however, was incorporated into the Labour Front, a procedure in complete disregard of the salaried employees' desire to remain dissociated from the despised manual labour force. To make things worse, in 1935 even the separate *Angestellten* branch within the Labour Front was dissolved, and from now on all *Angestellten* were organized together with workers. The firm became the Labour Front's smallest recruitment unit irrespective of the members' legal status. This blurring of traditional status lines corresponded very much with the *Volksgemeinschaft* ideology and the attempts of the Labour Front's left wing to remove all legal privileges from the *Angestellten*. *Arbeiter der Faust und der Stirn*, that is, workers of the hand and the head, were to be treated alike. These in many ways very modern concepts, which would have destroyed a rather awkward, old-fashioned and dysfunctional status differentiation, did not get very far, though, because the higher bureaucracy opposed them obstinately and the government did not support them strongly enough.[19]

The regime did virtually nothing to limit the number of white-collar employees. It did not impose a *numerus clausus* or any other form of admission control such as compulsory examinations. Any attempt to erect an extra status barrier would have been economically counterproductive and would have violated the employers' freedom of contract. Thus it was still up to them to employ someone as worker or as *Angestellte*. Improvements for manual workers often amounted to narrowing the gap between them and the *Angestellten*, without compensating the latter. Thus *Angestellten* suffered from relative deprivation. During the war the experience of absolute deprivation and even dreaded proletarianization was added. Many clerks found themselves forced to work on the shopfloor to stand in for drafted manual labourers, a kick in the teeth for every status-conscious *Angestellte*.

Their particularism was never really eradicated by the Nazi regime, and it re-emerged with a vengeance after 1945. Almost all limited measures of the regime in levelling off the differences between wage and salary earners were soon withdrawn, despite the resistance of the Allies. *Angestellten* ardently and successfully fought for their traditional legal status and for their own, exclusive trade unions and social security institutions. Even in the relatively open West German society, the collar line remained a significant badge of social distinction between groups whose income was often very similar.

Therefore it is hard to see Nazi politics as a modernizing factor in this part of German social history.[20]

Professionals

Professionalization is essential to modernization. It increases the division of labour and the overall level of productivity. Highly qualified, full-time experts replace the amateur generalist and secure a market monopoly by excluding non-professionals from their respective occupations. They form associations which exercise functions of collective self-control and watch over professional standards and codes of honour as well as over the training and admission of junior members. Based on their specific competence they claim a high degree of autonomy, especially freedom from control by laymen.[21]

Did the Nazi regime support the rise of professionalism, or did it prevent the proliferation of professional principles? In many fields a clear tendency of deprofessionalization can be observed. Hitler hated intellectuals as well as specialists and often entrusted politically loyal laymen with special tasks. The status of students and graduates did not generally improve. On the contrary, there was a strong tendency to downgrade them to *Arbeiter der Stirn*, in other words to stress the equality of all citizens within the *Volksgemeinschaft*. Racial and political purges thinned the ranks of many academic subjects. In some cases, as for example in nuclear physics, persecution led to a brain drain which ousted the best scientists. Ideological interference and a strong emphasis on applied sciences lowered the quality of German universities and institutes and in some instances produced unscientific research. German academia's links to the world's scientific community were weakened, and its once excellent reputation rapidly declined. The budget for education did not reach the level of 1928 under the Nazis. German universities not only lost their international standing but also a considerable number of students. Their number decreased drastically during the 'Third Reich', from 138,010 in 1931 to 40,968 in 1941 and 61,066 in 1943. The duration of school and college courses was considerably shortened due to mounting pressures from the armed forces and the labour market. Whereas undergraduates traditionally spent nine years at grammar school (*Gymnasium*) before being accepted by a university, courses were shortened to seven and a half years and, for war participants, to a mere six years.[22]

Classes grew larger, and teaching was heavily politicized. Academic standards declined as exams became easier and dropouts rarer. The 'Germanization' of research and teaching at all levels enforced the predominance of ideology at the expense of academic standards. Physical fitness, political reliability, 'racial purity' and 'sound character' were more highly esteemed than intellectual capabilities. Compulsory labour service and the draft, Nazi organizations from the Hitler Youth to the Student Unions, as well as the obligation to help out farmers during the harvest and to work in factories, took away an enormous amount of time from education.[23]

Nazi higher education policy turned out to be a fiasco. In the first few years student numbers were cut and women especially discouraged from enrolling. By 1936, however, Germany faced a growing shortage of graduates, which led to a hasty recruitment drive and a shortening of grammar school courses by one year to overcome the self-inflicted deficit of academic manpower. Even core ideological principles like the NSDAP's deeply rooted anti-feminism were temporarily suspended as the regime encouraged women to study and to stand in for absent male colleagues as doctors and teachers. In spite of Hitler's pre-1933 promises and all the hollow *Volksgemeinschaft* rhetoric, access to universities narrowed in social terms during the Nazi years. The universities remained firmly in the hands of the upper middle classes. The percentage of freshmen with parents from the *Bildungsbürgertum* who had themselves been to university grew from 22 per cent in 1933 to 28 per cent in 1939. Children from the other upper middle-class groups sent 11 and 13 per cent respectively. The middle and lower middle classes accounted for about half of all new students. Children of workers, however, only represented a meagre 4 per cent in 1933, and even this tiny share fell to 3 per cent in 1939.[24]

Professional associations lost their independence and fell victim to moral corruption. There was hardly any resistance against the persecution of some of their long-standing members for racial and political reasons. German professionals typically reacted to the 'seizure of power' by opportunism and 'quick, voluntary collaboration'.[25] By opening themselves to non-expert interference, they lost not only their professional autonomy but also their ethos and impartiality, both core qualities of professionalism. Judges and bureaucrats for example became willing administrators of injustice and perverters of law. Many doctors ignored their Hippocratic oath. Instead of healing their patients, they became harbingers of pain and death. Engineers dedicated their creativity to designing technology for mass killing and maiming. Teachers lent themselves to indoctrinating and spying on their students.

These obvious deprofessionalization processes coincided with tendencies that pointed in the opposite direction. The Nazi regime, after all, advanced professionalism in a number of ways. With the active support of the Nazi government relatively new academic subjects, such as sociology and psychology, established themselves firmly within universities. For obvious reasons, engineers and technicians benefited from the rearmament boom. They acquired an enormous increase in influence and social esteem. Hitler entrusted young engineers such as Todt and Speer with crucial tasks like constructing the motorways or reorganizing the war economy.

The regime was obsessed with forcing virtually all occupational groups into official corporations. This organizational fetishism coupled with the principle of compulsory membership did not only straitjacket the occupations concerned but at the same time created opportunities to build up new professional associations. These were hybrid bodies, official corporations of the state and professional organizations with a limited but not inconsiderable amount of autonomy. Especially in atomistic occupations with no or only small, inefficient associations in Weimar Germany, the Nazi *Gleichschaltung* did hasten professionalism in both the short and the long run. To be precise, these associations were dissolved in 1945. Informally, however, successor organizations relying on the old functionaries and membership files grew out of these bodies.

A good example is the advertising industry,[26] which suffered before 1933 from a low level of organization and the absence of professional standards from controls on entry to technical and commercial norms. Advertising was basically open to anyone, and cut-throat competition was the norm. The Nazi regime introduced compulsory corporations for everyone in the industry, set up arbitration bodies, founded the Imperial College for Advertising (the *Reichswerbefachschule*), and issued strict regulations concerning prices and technical norms as well as ideological and cultural guidelines. Many of these regulations and organizations survived the end of the Nazi dictatorship under new names. Therefore, in the Federal Republic of the 1970s and 1980s leading advertising men were able to condemn the political aims and methods of the regime and at the same time praise its ability to bestow a 'healthy order on a chaotic trade' and to create 'fair rules for everyone'.[27]

Other occupational groups had the same experience of, on the one hand, winning greater professional unity, and, on the other, of being used and monitored for political purposes. Obligatory curricula for professional training, often drafted by the new corporations themselves, the foundation of colleges, and compulsory vocational exams were introduced for several occupations. In this way the responsibilities of particular vocations were delineated and their markets fenced off against competing rivals. For example, the regime advanced the professionalization of non-medical practitioners, psychotherapists, accountants and pharmacists.[28] All in all, professionalization and deprofessionalization took place side by side. The dictatorship therefore simultaneously acted as a modernizing and a retarding force.

Workers

Workers, as the largest group of the German society and electorate, received Hitler's special attention for a number of reasons. He knew very well that without a minimum of support from the working classes his regime would soon crumble and all rearmament plans fail. Above all, he never forgot that workers had brought down the Empire in 1918 by strikes and protests, a fact which not only he interpreted as a 'stab in the back' of the German army. Therefore, he was anxious to prevent a repetition of this alleged 'betrayal'. In fact, during the Second World War the home front remained largely intact until the very end.

In dealing with the working classes the regime employed a double strategy of terror and enticement. The former meant that all proletarian mass organizations, especially the independent trade unions as well as the Social Democratic and the Communist parties, were forcibly dissolved and their functionaries expelled, arrested, locked up or killed. Almost all workers were integrated into the NSDAP's Labour Front, which controlled rather than represented them. On the positive side, the *Volksgemeinschaft* propaganda promised workers more prestige, a higher standard of living and an end to all forms of social disadvantage and disparagement. 'Arbeit adelt' ('work ennobles') was an alluring, albeit sometimes ridiculed slogan. Workers as well as farmers became a favoured motif of the regime's official art. After all, the NSDAP was a 'workers' party'. The contradictory policy towards the workers was to serve two ends, namely to emasculate them politically and to motivate them economically. The regime wanted their full ideological commitment as *Volksgenossen* and their best performance in the factories.

As far as the workers' standard of living is concerned, the results of Nazi policies were highly ambiguous. Under Weimar workers had successfully secured for themselves a larger part of the national income than they had been able to prior to the First World War. The acceptance of collective bargaining following the revolution of 1918, the relative strength of trade unions and state intervention on behalf of workers (including compulsory arbitration) had shifted the balance in their favour. This trend was sharply reversed in the depression and continued throughout the 'Third Reich'. The share of wages in the national income declined continuously after 1932. Not until 1937 did real wages reach pre-depression levels (1928); in contrast the National Product had substantially increased. The winners were the employers. Their real incomes rose between 1933 and 1939 by 130 per cent. Their staff, by comparison, took home increases of only 49 per cent on average. Contrary to their propaganda, the Nazis deprived workers of the modest relative gains for which they had fought hard during the Weimar years. The balance in the labour market was moved back in favour of the employers. The main reason for this U-turn was the abolition of collective bargaining and the introduction of authoritarian wage decrees in 1933–4.[29]

Why did workers accept a development that so blatantly violated their interests? Six reasons explain why, by and large, they remained silent, although protest and even local strikes did occur occasionally. First, the Nazi terror had a deterrent effect, which led to depolitisization and to a retreat into the private sphere. Second, most people compared their situation with the misery of depression, not with Weimar's good years. Seen in this light, the Nazi government had delivered impressive as well as substantial improvements. Full employment was reached by 1936, which also meant more earners per family and increased chances of working overtime. Besides, there were additional premiums and perks, many of which did not show up in the official statistics. People now had an apparently secure long-term future in their professional and private lives. This fundamental experience of regained stability was obvious for everyone. The shrinking proportion of wages in the national income, that is the relative deterioration of the workers' position vis à vis their bosses, was not, however, widely known. Third, there was no organizational framework for large-scale protests any more. Individuals who could have acted as the workers' authentic representatives had been removed from their positions or left the country.[30]

Fourth, social standards within the factories were raised by initiatives of the Labour Front and its sub-organization *Schönheit der Arbeit* (Beauty of Labour). Although many of their initiatives amounted to propagandistic ballyhoo, there were also a number of tangible improvements. Showers and changing rooms, refectories and crèches were built, factory journals and outings introduced, and stricter health and safety regulations imposed. These measures, even if they may seem too basic to be of any real importance, had a definite impact on workers' everyday lives. No doubt they were part of a calculated rationalization drive and were sometimes wrapped up in ideological glorification bordering on the absurd. Nevertheless, these reforms were substantial and overwhelmingly acknowledged by the workers. Moreover, it cannot be denied that, with regard to industrial social work, the regime set new standards for the postwar era, thus exerting an enormous modernization impact in these areas.[31]

Fifth, the virtual wage freeze was alleviated by several compensatory concessions. The social security system, which was taken over from Weimar, was never fundamentally reformed. Instead a number of new or improved benefits were introduced, especially better provisions for mothers, children and widows. Additionally, the average duration of paid holidays was doubled from three to six days per year. Some workers even had their holiday period extended to twelve days. The regime promoted subsidized mass tourism and cultural events. It further promised new mass consumer products by promoting the legendary Volkswagen beetle, refrigerators and other electric appliances as well as houses for everyone. The Nazi government created desires for new consumer items. Even if it fulfilled very few of them, the decisive fact for the regime's stability was that propaganda made these modern products appear to be within everybody's reach for the first time. For Tim Mason the 'Third Reich' looked like a 'synthesis of work house and supermarket' forcing upon the workers a 'dissociated consciousness', namely the ability to separate the negative from the attractive aspects of the regime and to manipulate them into forgetting about the former and enjoying or at least anticipating the latter.[32]

Sixth, changes on the shop floor also weakened workers' ability to act collectively. Under the combined pressures of the state's massive requests for arms deliveries and increasing manpower shortages, many large firms rationalized their production. Work intensification, longer working hours and more shift work confronted staff with rising demands on their physical and mental energies. Traditional group work was replaced by the assembly belt, which made possible the massive influx of unskilled labour. Their employment often destroyed the traditional culture of craft-based industries and broke up departments or crews that had worked together for years. In a regime that relied heavily on informers, every unknown person could switch off open communication. Individualistic, performance-related payment schemes, especially piece rates and premiums, replaced shop-floor collectivism by competition and isolation. A widening of wage differentials was another consequence that undermined proletarian solidarity.[33]

These processes of Taylorization and individualization corresponded to the internal logic of industrial development and, beyond doubt, contributed to the modernization of German industry, although they were promoted for ideological reasons that were extremely antimodernist and inhumane. The ugly framework of this purely organizational and technological modernization was characterized by political suppression, terror and the deprivation of all democratic rights from the vote to the representation by independent trade unions. The freedom to move from one job to another was abolished from 1935 onwards in more and more branches of industry. In 1938 open militarization of the labour market began with the introduction of a draft for what was considered essential work. During the war the unscrupulous and horrific exploitation of millions of foreign workers, many of them prisoners of war, abducted civilians and concentration camp inmates, revealed the true face of industrial relations under National Socialism.

Still, the long-term effects of these transformations were modernizing in the sense of increasing economic efficiency. Taylorization was accompanied by the promotion of vocational competitions and training. The employment of unskilled and foreign labour played a large role in opening up new opportunities for social mobility within one's class for regular staff, i.e. to climb the ladder from unskilled to semi-skilled status or to take over supervisory functions. In some cases even the attractive status of *Angestellte* could be reached. This was social mobility virtually on the back of millions of foreign workers. Despite this reprehensible context, the overall qualification level of the German workforce increased during the 'Third Reich'. In the impersonal language of economics, Germany experienced a lasting improvement of her human capital, which was one of the key factors for rapid postwar reconstruction.[34]

In the Federal Republic the industrial workforce looked very different from Weimar's working class. It was not only generally better qualified but also more strongly orientated towards individual achievement, consumption and advancement as well as less politicized and class-conscious. The former proletarian milieu with its distinct subculture had not survived the Nazis' persecution. This social–cultural homogenization process has been described by several different labels, from 'the end of proletarianism' to 'embourgeoisement' or the integration of workers into a levelled-off middle-class society.[35] At all events, the result of the Nazis' reign was individualization and deproletarianization. Even without the 'Third Reich' both processes would have taken place because closed milieux have no place in a modern industrial society. Therefore, the regime's main impact seems to have been to speed up a development already under way in the Weimar Republic.[36]

Social mobility and elite recruitment

As far as incomes were concerned, German society's internal cleavages did not close under Hitler. In fact they widened. In this sense the *Volksgemeinschaft* clearly failed. But did this ideology at least make it easier to overcome the social barriers and to move from one stratum to the next? Did it offer individuals better chances of moving into careers that had formerly been closed to them because of their backgrounds? Did the recruitment base for the state's top positions widen? Did Hitler keep his promise of creating a more open and more achievement-orientated society?

Before answering these questions, mainly in the negative, we have to recall that the formation of Hitler's dictatorship would not have been successful without the active support of existing elites. By promising them not to tamper with their status and offering an authoritarian solution to Weimar's political crisis, Hitler had no difficulty in winning their loyalty. The first months of Hitler's dictatorship were marked by two related phenomena that stabilized the new regime. On the one hand, there was a rush of Germans from all social groups, especially from the middle classes, to join the party. This rush to jump on the bandwagon was so intense that admission of new members had to be suspended in May 1933. Between 30 January, when Hitler was appointed Chancellor, and May, 1.6 million people had joined, thus doubling the membership. On the other hand, the process of *Gleichschaltung* (coordination), that is, bringing German society into line, proceeded with unexpected speed and without serious opposition, which surprised even the most optimistic Nazis. With a mixture of promises and threats, terror and enticement, the regime managed to secure loyalty across a wide social and political spectrum. Where this was impossible, as in the case of most Communists and many Social Democrats, any manifest resistance was crushed by force. Most organizations, however, did everything to vow allegiance to the new government in order to survive. Even the trade unions tried – albeit unsuccessfully – to come to terms with the new regime. From the lower middle classes upwards zealous protestations of loyalty and more or less voluntary promises of collaboration were the typical way of dealing with the Nazi government.

As early as March 1933 the influential Lawyers' Association welcomed 'the strengthening of national thought and will' and vowed 'to concentrate its energy on serving the recovery of the nation and the empire, on making the state secure and on unifying the people across classes and occupations'.[37] Where self-coordination did not proceed smoothly, pressure from the regime, often quite subtle, helped to overcome all reservations or resistance. Admiration for Hitler, belief in his promises, national pride, sheer opportunism, fear and cowardice or a mixture of all of these factors paved the way to a relatively smooth self-coordination of German society. Thus Hitler was able to rely on a broad base of people who either admired him or were at least prepared to accommodate themselves to the new circumstances.

This political constellation explains why there was so little immediate social change in 1933, no Soviet-style expropriations or oustings, no complete exchange of political, economic or administrative elites. It also sheds light on the fact that many *Alte Kämpfer*, hardened Nazis of long standing, found themselves increasingly isolated within their own party as well as within the new state. Their expectation of sharing out spoils for their own benefit, in terms of influential positions, was often frustrated. Instead of satisfying the ambitions of all those who had fought for him before 1933, Hitler strove to preserve much of the existing social structure in order not to weaken the efficiency of a complex industrial society and not to endanger his aggressive expansionism. Admittedly, in the long run he planned to substitute the old elites with a new, 'racially superior' and efficient cadre of thorough National Socialists, who would have been indoctrinated from their earliest childhood. But in view of his revanchist plans to redraw the map of Europe as soon as possible, the far-reaching reconfiguration of social structures had to be suspended until after the war. This constellation did not prevent Hitler from dismissing individual representatives of the old elites like Schacht or von Neurath, who had initially lent the regime their expertise as well as an air of respectability but became too sceptical to be of further use.

Nevertheless, traditional screening devices for social selection displayed a remarkable inertia. Educational qualifications like the *Abitur* or university degrees remained the key to social advancement and the basic prerequisite for entering the higher ranks of the administration, professions and armed forces. Any really egalitarian policy would thus have had the effect of lowering the social barriers within the educational system. Instead of creating new channels for talented youths with humble origins into secondary schools and universities, both systems remained fee-paying and therefore effectively locked out sons and daughters of workers. As we have already seen, the social structure of the undergraduate population witnessed a strengthening of existing middle-class preponderance. Overall numbers of students passing the *Abitur* stagnated, although the school leaving age and academic requirements were lowered considerably. Several grants and schemes to enter universities without the *Abitur* were introduced but only touched very few people. Female graduates, whose numbers had risen considerably in the 1920s, declined in the 1930s under the combined effects of the depression and political discrimination by the Nazi regime. Only during the war was this trend reversed, with the female quota reaching unprecedented heights. This breakthrough, however, was not welcomed by the regime, but rather grudgingly tolerated under wartime conditions.[38] All in all, the Nazi regime adopted an extremely reactionary educational policy, reinforcing traditional patterns of social and sexual discrimination. Despite this antimodernist stance, the number of female graduates increased significantly after 1941. A type of modernization took place, even if it was not intentionally promoted by the regime but rather brought about by external pressures.

The situation in the armed forces was, in a sense, similar. Their size increased from a mere 115,000 men (the maximum permitted under the Versailles treaty) to 3 million in 1939 and 9.5 million in 1943. The number of army officers grew from 3,858 in 1933 to 89,075 in 1939 and 248,537 in 1943.[39] Despite this enormous expansion no radical renunciation of traditional recruitment principles for the military elite took place. Although the speed of promotion and chances for young men increased dramatically, well-established criteria remained in force such as the *Abitur*, ancient rituals like the cooptation by the incumbent officer corps, equality of birth (meaning at least middle-class origin), a socially adequate marriage, and the observation of a strict code of honour including feudal relics. In an atmosphere of widespread admiration for the military, there was no shortage of suitable young men. Therefore, the social structure of the German officer corps by

1941 was dominated by soldiers who would have been *offiziersfähig* (that is, fit to be commissioned) before 1914. In other words, the fathers of most officers had been officers themselves, civil servants, graduates, landowners or, though with declining frequency, aristocrats. Promotion was not granted by individual achievement or qualification but exclusively by length of service. Internal honour courts watched over the corps' ethos.

It goes without saying that the result was a highly status-conscious officer caste that was not always up to technical warfare. The retention of its social homogeneity and core elements of traditional military culture can be seen as concessions for the army's abstention from politics. A real U-turn, however, which abolished antiquated recruitment principles and promotion criteria, took place in 1941–2. This change did not happen as a consequence of any deliberate modernization policy but was entirely due to bare necessity, namely the military crisis of the winter of 1941–2. Under the threat of impending defeat and a mounting death toll, all considerations for the traditional identity of the officer corps were dropped. Something had to be done to avert the fiasco. Under these circumstances the *Volksgemeinschaft* ideology helped to justify the crushing of the officers' caste spirit, but it had not caused this step in the first place.

In the second half of the war the social recruitment base was widened and the *Abitur* no longer demanded as a basic entry qualification. The ancient cooptation rules, marriage requirements and honour courts were abolished. Military efficiency, which now increasingly meant fanatical powers of endurance and blind obedience, became the dominant promotion criterion. The antiquated rules of a secular order of knights had eventually been replaced by the selection principles of the industrial world. The result was a considerable rejuvenation and social heterogenization of Germany's military leadership. Ironically, the army that surrendered unconditionally in May 1945 possessed a more professional and modern officer corps than the victorious army of 1939–40. The lasting effect of this profound change was the final destruction of the officer caste as a distinct social rank. When the Federal Republic set up a new German army in the 1950s, the officer corps became a professional body rather than a closed shop separated from the rest of society by a set of specific values, symbols and rules.[40]

Looking at the social composition of other functional elites in the 'Third Reich', the dominant feature is relative continuity from Weimar to the Federal Republic. The Nazi regime needed the skills and expertise of the old elites and had, by and large, to rely on their traditional methods of training and recruitment. In dealing with them subversion, indoctrination and collaboration, not large-scale purges and the imposition of counter-elites, were characteristic of Hitler's tactics. When senior personnel were removed for political or racial reasons, they were in most cases replaced by people with similar social and qualificational backgrounds. Exceptions did occur when hardened Nazis had to be catered for or ideologically trustworthy persons brought into key positions. In such cases the normal educational requirements and professional standards could be suspended, but these cases remained rare, especially in the traditional parts of the administration.

The most spectacular exception to this rule was Hitler himself. With his breathtaking career from unemployed artist who had once lived in a shelter for the homeless to head of the government, he found himself in a minority position even within his own cabinet. Out of 31 ministers in office between 1933 and 1945 only two, Hitler and Kerrl, were of lower middle-class origin. The NSDAP did not manage to give a single ministerial seat to a former industrial or agricultural worker. Not a very impressive result for a 'workers' party'! Instead the Nazis went for high civil servants and distinguished professionals. Hitler's cabinets even included five aristocrats.[41]

Most Berlin ministries experienced a similar continuity in terms of the background of their senior employees. Neither the Foreign Office nor the Interior Ministry were flooded with hardened Nazis because they lacked the formal qualifications traditionally required.[42] A slightly different situation prevailed in the ever growing number of ministries or special authorities that were newly created by the regime. The same goes for the NSDAP's own political cadre. *Gauleiter* and *Kreisleiter*, that is, the NSDAP's district and regional leaders, were of lower social origins and possessed fewer qualifications than their counterparts in the states' administrations, the *Ministerpräsidenten* and *Landräte*.[43] Within the party and within new official bodies no reservations of long-serving bureaucrats had to be overcome, and recruitment and promotion rules were significantly more lax. Nevertheless, there was no shortage of young graduates, who were only too happy to fill these new posts and to serve the regime willingly. Himmler's SS had no difficulty in recruiting large numbers of lawyers and doctors. In 1938 the SS, far from being a bunch of brainless fanatics and social desperadoes, employed 12,000 university-trained staff, among them 3,000 lawyers and 3,000 doctors.[44] Besides, the SS offered considerably more chances for social advancement than institutions such as the army or the traditional bureaucracy that had been taken over from Weimar. The main common characteristic of top personnel in the SS and other genuine Nazi institutions was their relative youth.[45] The enormous proliferation of new administrative bodies, most of them competing with the traditional civil service as well as with each other, opened up new opportunities, above all for young graduates rather than for hardened Nazis or the hitherto underprivileged.

Zapf's study of the regime's senior personnel revealed on average a certain lowering of the level of formal qualifications and social origins compared with Weimar. On closer inspection it turns out that this change was largely confined to party functionaries who had frequently left school or college without completing their courses. Apart from this, continuity prevailed in social and qualificational profiles. The common denominator of the Third Reich's elite was their relative youth and their ability to corrupt, inflate, atomize and finally dissolve the state.[46]

The regime tampered continuously with the bureaucratic infrastructure and in the end caused administrative chaos. By splitting existing, and setting up new and competing, authorities with overlapping areas of responsibility, the traditional bureaucratic order disintegrated, even if the façade remained intact. With the *Waffen-SS* a second army was set up. If the modern state is defined by a certain degree of rationality and unity, predictability and stability, the Nazi dictatorship was antimodernist in the extreme. Geared to Hitler's charismatic leadership, a personalized, quasi-feudal structure of authority with highly arbitrary and atavistic characteristics progressively asserted itself against the remnants of traditional governmental and administrative principles. Ultimately Hitler's will represented the only relevant criterion. This erratic variable was to act as the constitution and to unify a complex industrial society with millions of people. The essence of charismatic leadership is its capacity for solving crises. 'Nazism was rooted in crisis, and its whole system of politics was geared, in effect, to the maintenance of crisis as a permanent state.'[47]

Nazism's irrational, deeply antimodernist characteristics expressed themselves in its inability to settle down to 'normality', to control constructive energy and build up permanent structures. The modern state basically exists independent of individuals. A constitution guarantees continuity. The 'Third Reich' had neither a constitution nor any provisions for the time after Hitler's death. Within the top echelons of the NSDAP no normal elite circulation took place, no regular patterns of entry and retirement, recruitment and succession existed. Death or expulsion were the only ways of leaving the party executive committee. The only way in was appointment by the Führer himself. According to Zapf, no other elite in twentieth-century German society was more closed and petrified than the NSDAP executive committee. The party did not have any rational or at least reliable rule for elite recruitment or even for the selection of minor functionaries. Instead a maze of personal connections, a mess of strings to be pulled as well as political loyalty and racial criteria replaced 'normal' selection procedures. The 'Third Reich' developed the traits of quasi-feudal structures, replacing official channels by personal allegiance. Not surprisingly, it was not the modern criteria of talent and merit, but rather ideological and personal loyalties, and above all opportunism, that became core structural elements of the regime. It fostered conformity and corruption, qualities diametrically opposed to rationality and modernity. The same applies to the arbitrary persecution, expulsion and extermination of certain groups for alleged racial defects.

All in all, the Nazi regime did not take decisive steps towards creating a new society and towards guaranteeing more equal opportunities. It must, however, be borne in mind that

> Nazism was defeated in war before it had the chance to implement its full programme and, therefore, it can never be finally determined how revolutionary the movement and regime really were. . . . During the pre-war years, the Nazis were limited in their action by a number of factors – the need to accommodate the existing élites, limited economic resources, public opinion at home and . . . abroad, . . . some of which would have been removed . . . had the Nazis been victorious. The war itself removed some of these obstacles, producing a significant radicalisation . . . Hitler's more far-reaching plans should not simply be regarded as fantasies.[48]

Still, how society might have been structured after a 'final victory' remains pure speculation. Some outlines emerged during the war, especially in the occupied areas in the East. A racist hierarchy would have decided on the right to exist and the conditions of life. Underneath the Aryan community several layers of enslaved pariahs would have had to serve their masters. It seems likely that a new, genuine National Socialist elite would have sprung up, and that the foundations of the state and traditional social structures would have been crushed. In this new *Germania* the SS would have played a central role. By the end of the war Himmler commanded his own army, bureaucracy, secret service, police, the regime's colossal apparatus of terror as well as a substantial economic empire. Fortunately, the regime never had the chance to push further ahead with its destructive dynamism, and the world was spared the experience of yet another escalation of monstrosities.

Conclusion

The Nazi regime had a complex as well as a contradictory impact on the course of German social history. In some areas the Janus-faced dictatorship accelerated modernizing trends already under way, but it generated very few that would not have sprung up without Nazism. Good examples are the workers' deproletarianization or the partial strengthening of professionalism. In other areas the regime sharply reversed social changes that corresponded to the logic of the industrial world. This can be seen most clearly in the case of anti-market regulations on behalf of peasants and artisans.

The overall result was a blurred picture combining elements of both change and continuity, with the latter prevailing. The regime fundamentally altered neither the composition of elites nor the distribution of wealth. Class barriers remained fairly rigid especially in the decisive educational sector. Upward social mobility did not increase to any considerable degree. Although the regime created many new opportunities, especially for the younger generation, traditional selection mechanisms basically remained intact. If they were suspended, it was not primarily in the interest of overcoming social divisions but for reasons of political patronage or, as in the officer corps after 1941, out of sheer necessity. In these cases class divisions were not torn down but rather bypassed. Therefore, the partial relaxation of existing career patterns must not be confused with a stringent modernization policy trying to create a meritocratic society. In fact the disregard for achievement as such, for academic and professional standards, and the excessive attention given to irrational criteria such as race, opportunism and personal connections amounted rather to an aberration from modernization. All in all, incoherence and inconsistency were the main characteristics of the regime's approach to social policy. As long as it was unable to produce any alternative of its own, the dictatorship parasitically made use of existing social structures.

The NSDAP's shortage of qualified people forced the regime to turn existing elites into accomplices or at least into collaborators by a double strategy of intimidation and enticement – not a good starting point for reshuffling social structures. During the run-up to the war and during the war itself no scope was left for any initiative to bring about fundamental social change. Hitler knew very well that it was impossible to keep an engine running at full throttle while attempting to rebuild it. In the interests of the war effort, root-and-branch intervention into the fabric of society was either pursued half-heartedly or postponed until 'final victory'. This rationale did not, however, apply to Jews and other victims of racism who were persecuted and murdered without consideration of the economic and social consequences. The Holocaust demonstrated in a horrific way the degree of destructive energy inherent in National Socialism, which had no constructive counterpart whatsoever.

The fact that the social structures of the two Germanies succeeding the 'Third Reich' looked very different from what German society had been in 1933 or 1939 was mainly due to the upheaval of war. Though there can be no doubt that this war was started by the Nazi regime, the course of the war did not correspond to Hitler's plans. He lost the strategic initiative in 1942. The profound social change that took place from then on until the immediate aftermath of war can only indirectly be attributed to him. Total warfare and the mobilization of the last reserves, millions of dead and maimed, massive destruction of German towns, large-scale population movements, the disintegration of families, the eviction and expropriation of millions of East Germans, the demise of the East Elbian junkers, who lost their economic base and with it their political influence, and the bankruptcy of Prusso-German militarism had a lasting impact on the texture of German society. These were the forces that most dramatically remoulded Germany and relentlessly crushed many obstacles to modernization. Consequently, the remarkable staying power of the German aristocracy was finally wiped out and no longer obstructed democratization. The military never regained its grip on society. Millions of uprooted people had to start all over again, a fact that increased the overall level of mobility and diligence. Since old values had been discredited, new models had to be sought out. Thus, in the Federal Republic many elements of Western, capitalistic culture were accepted for the first time. In this way the Second World War possessed its own momentum for rapid as well as lasting modernization. For historical analysis it is crucial, however, to differentiate between social changes intentionally designed by the regime and those indirectly and unwittingly caused by Nazism.

Notes

1. Rainer Zitelmann, *Hitler: Selbstverständnis eines Revolutionärs* (Stuttgart, 1990), esp. pp. 349–65. Zitelmann's book has caused much controversy and can be (mis)understood as a partial apology for Hitler. See also Michael Prinz, 'Die soziale Funktion moderner Elemente in der Gesellschaftspolitik des Nationalsozialismus', in *idem* and Rainer Zitelmann, eds, *Nationalsozialismus und Modernisierung* (Darmstadt, 1991), pp. 320–1.

2. Detlev J.K. Peukert, *Die Weimarer Republik: Krisenjahre der klassischen Moderne* (Frankfurt/M., 1987), esp. pp. 61–111 and 149–63; Heinrich-August Winkler, *Weimar, 1918–1933: Die Geschichte der ersten deutschen Demokratie* (Munich, 1993), pp. 285–305.

3. Zitelmann, *Hitler*, pp. 120–45.

4. Jürgen W. Falter, *Hitlers Wähler* (Munich, 1991); Hans-Ulrich Thamer, *Verführung und Gewalt: Deutschland, 1933–1945* (Berlin, 1994), pp. 172–83; David Schoenbaum, *Hitler's Social Revolution: Class and Status in Nazi Germany, 1933–1939* (New York, 1966), p. 47.

5. Quoted in ibid., p. 53. See also Ian Kershaw, *The Nazi Dictatorship: Problems and Perspectives of Interpretation* (London, 1985), pp. 50–60.

6. Quoted by Schoenbaum, *Revolution*, p. 53.

7. Similar questions are asked by Volker Hentschel, 'Wirtschafts- und sozialhistorische Brüche und Kontinuitäten zwischen Weimarer Republik und Drittem Reich', *Zeitschrift für Unternehmensgeschichte* 28 (1983), pp. 39–80; John Hiden and John Farquharson, *Explaining Hitler's Germany. Historians and the Third Reich* (London, 1983), pp. 83–109; Jens Alber, 'Nationalsozialismus und Modernisierung', *Kölner Zeitschrift für Soziologie und Sozialpsychologie* 41 (1989), pp. 346–65; William Janner, 'National Socialists and Social Mobility', *Journal of Social History* 9 (1976), pp. 339–66; Jeremy Noakes, 'Nazism and Revolution', in Noel O'Sullivan, ed., *Revolutionary Theory and Political Reality* (Brighton, 1983), pp. 73–100.

8. The discussion was started by Ralf Dahrendorf, *Gesellschaft und Demokratie in Deutschland* (Munich, 1965) and Schoenbaum, *Revolution*, and taken up by Prinz and Zitelmann, *Nationalsozialismus und Modernisierung*. The main critic of the modernization thesis is Hans Mommsen, 'Nationalsozialismus als vorgetäuschte Modernisierung', in *idem, Der Nationalsozialismus und die deutsche Gesellschaft* (Reinbek, 1991), pp. 405–27; *idem*, 'Noch einmal: Nationalsozialismus und Modernisierung', *Geschichte und Gesellschaft* 21 (1995), pp. 391–402. Further critics are Noakes, 'Nazism'; Alber, 'Nationalsozialismus'; Norbert Frei, 'Wie modern war der Nationalsozialismus?', *Geschichte und Gesellschaft* 19 (1993), pp. 367–87. Still a useful introduction to the concept of modernization is Hans-Ulrich Wehler, *Modernisierungstheorie und Geschichte* (Göttingen, 1975).

9. Schoenbaum, *Revolution*, p. 160. See also John E. Farquharson, 'The Agrarian Policy of National Socialist Germany', in R.G. Moeller, ed., *Peasants and Lords in Modern Germany: Recent Studies in Agricultural History* (Boston, 1986), pp. 233–59; *idem, Hitler and the Peasants: Agrarian Policy of the Third Reich, 1930–1939* (New York, 1990), pp. 1–42.

10. John E. Farquharson, *The Plough and the Swastika: The NSDAP and Agriculture in Germany, 1928–45* (London, 1976), pp. 107–40; Gustavo Corni, *Hitler and the Peasants: Agrarian Policy of the Third Reich, 1930–1939* (New York, 1990), pp. 143–52; Daniela Münkel, 'Bäuerliche Interessen versus NS Ideologie: Das Reichserbhofgesetz in der Praxis', *Vierteljahrshefte für Zeitgeschichte* 44 (1996), pp. 549–80.

11. Schoenbaum, *Revolution*, pp. 167–8.

12. Hentschel, 'Brüche', pp. 52–3, 72–4; Schoenbaum, *Revolution*, pp. 159–86; Farquarson, *Plough*, pp. 57–106; Corni, *Hitler*, pp. 66–115; Corni and Horst Gies, *Blut und Boden: Rassenideologie und Agrarpolitik im Staat Hitlers* (Idstein, 1994).

13. Hartmut Berghoff, 'Population Change and its Repercussions on the Social History of the Federal Republic', in Klaus Larres and Panikos Panayi, eds, *The Federal Republic of Germany Since 1949: Politics, Society and Economy Before and After Unification* (London, 1996), pp. 36–51.

14. Hans-Peter Ullmann, *Interessenverbände in Deutschland* (Frankfurt/M., 1988), pp. 154–63, 210–18; Friedrich Lenger, *Sozialgeschichte der deutschen Handwerker*

seit 1800 (Frankfurt/M., 1988), pp. 166–202; Adelheid von Saldern, *Mittelstand im 'Dritten Reich': Handwerker – Einzelhändler – Bauern* (Frankfurt/M., 1979), pp. 31–58, 95–112.

15. Lenger, *Sozialgeschichte*, pp. 195–202.

16. See the controversy between Heinrich-August Winkler, 'Der entbehrliche Stand', *Archiv für Sozialgeschichte* 17 (1977), pp. 1–38 and Adelheid von Saldern, '"Alter Mittelstand" im "Dritten Reich": Anmerkungen zu einer Kontroverse', *Geschichte und Gesellschaft* 12 (1986), pp. 235–43.

17. Schoenbaum, *Revolution*, pp. 136–41.

18. A.R.L. Gurland *et al.*, *The Fate of Small Business in Nazi Germany* (New York, 1975, first published 1943), pp. 50–70; Heinrich Uhlig, *Die Warenhäuser im Dritten Reich* (Cologne, 1956); Saldern, *Mittelstand im 'Dritten Reich'*, pp. 58–67, 105–12.

19. Michael Prinz, *Vom neuen Mittelstand zum Volksgenossen: Die Entwicklung des sozialen Status der Angestellten von der Weimarer Republik bis zum Ende der NS-Zeit* (Munich, 1986), pp. 92–328; Schoenbaum, *Revolution*, pp. 6–11, 71–2, 114–16.

20. For a different interpretation see Prinz, *Mittelstand*, pp. 328–36.

21. As a survey, see Heinz-Elmar Tenorth, 'Professionen und Professionalisierung: Ein Bezugsrahmen zur historischen Analyse des Lehrers und seiner Organisationen', in Manfred Heinemann, ed., *Der Lehrer und seine Organisation* (Stuttgart, 1977), pp. 457–63; Konrad H. Jarausch, *The Unfree Professions: German Lawyers, Teachers, and Engineers, 1900–1950* (New York, 1990), pp. 3–24.

22. Michael Grüttner, *Studenten im Dritten Reich* (Paderborn, 1995), p. 487; Jarausch, *Professions*, p. 176; Hartmut Kaelble, *Soziale Mobilität und Chancengleichheit im 19. und 20. Jahrhundert* (Göttingen, 1983), pp. 141–5.

23. Jarausch, *Professions*, pp. 156–76; Grüttner, *Studenten*, pp. 317–56.

24. Grüttner, *Studenten*, pp. 493, 101–26.

25. Jarausch, *Professions*, p. 3.

26. Hartmut Berghoff, 'Von der "Reklame" zur Verbrauchslenkung: Werbung im nationalsozialistischen Deutschland', in *idem*, ed., *Konsumpolitik: Die Regulierung des privaten Verbrauchs im 20. Jahrhundert* (Göttingen, 1999), pp. 77–112.

27. Hubert Strauf, 'Werbung im Wandel seit 1945 als Standort für den Ausblick', in Carl Hundhausen, ed., *Werbung im Wandel, 1945–1995: Eine Sammlung von werbefachlichen Texten* (Essen, 1972), p. 4; Harry Damrow, *Ich war kein geheimer Verführer* (Rheinzabern, 1981), p. 47 (my translations).

28. Prinz, 'Elemente', pp. 309–10.

29. Ludolf Herbst, *Das nationalsozialistische Deutschland, 1933–1945* (Frankfurt/M., 1996), p. 238; Dietmar Petzina *et al.*, *Sozialgeschichtliches Arbeitsbuch III: Materialien zur Statistik des Deutschen Reiches, 1914–1945* (Munich, 1978), pp. 89–94, 106;

Mark Spoerer, *Von Scheingewinnen zum Rüstungsboom: Die Eigenkapitalrendite der deutschen Industrieaktiengesellschaften, 1925–1941* (Stuttgart, 1995).

30. Wolfgang Zollitsch, *Arbeiter zwischen Weltwirtschaftskrise und Nationalsozialismus: Ein Beitrag zur Sozialgeschichte der Jahre 1928–1936* (Göttingen, 1990), esp. pp. 238–45.

31. Matthias Frese, *Betriebspolitik im 'Dritten Reich': Deutsche Arbeitsfront, Unternehmer und Staatsbürokratie in der westdeutschen Großindustrie* (Paderborn, 1991); Gunther Mai, 'Warum steht der deutsche Arbeiter zu Hitler? Zur Rolle der Deutschen Arbeitsfront im Herrschaftssystem des Dritten Reiches', *Geschichte und Gesellschaft* 12 (1986), pp. 212–34; Martin H. Geyer, 'Soziale Sicherheit und wirtschaftlicher Fortschritt: Überlegungen zum Verhältnis von Arbeitsideologie und Sozialpolitik im "Dritten Reich"', *Geschichte und Gesellschaft* 15 (1989), pp. 382–406; Hartmut Berghoff, *Zwischen Kleinstadt und Weltmarkt: Hohner und die Harmonika 1857 bis 1961: Unternehmensgeschichte als Gesellschaftsgeschichte* (Paderborn, 1997), pp. 453–63.

32. Timothy W. Mason, 'Die Bändigung der Arbeiterklasse im nationalsozialistischen Deutschland: Eine Einleitung', in Carola Sachse *et al.*, *Belohnung, Zucht und Ordnung: Herrschaftsmechanismen im Nationalsozialismus* (Opladen, 1982), pp. 46–7.

33. Rüdiger Hachtmann, *Industriearbeit im 'Dritten Reich': Untersuchungen zu den Lohn- und Arbeitsbedingungen in Deutschland, 1933–1945* (Göttingen, 1989).

34. This effect was greatly intensified in West Germany by the steady influx of expellees and refugees from East Germany. See Werner Abelshauser, *Wirtschaftsgeschichte der Bundesrepublik Deutschland, 1945–1980* (Frankfurt/M., 1983), p. 24; Berghoff, 'Population', pp. 36–51.

35. Josef Mooser, *Arbeiterleben in Deutschland, 1900–1970* (Frankfurt/M., 1984), pp. 213–16, 235; Hans Braun, 'Helmut Schelskys Konzept der nivellierten Mittelstandsgesellschaft und die Bundesrepublik der 50er Jahre', *Archiv für Sozialgeschichte* 29 (1989), pp. 199–233.

36. Peukert, *Republik*, pp. 150–7.

37. Quoted by Jarausch, *Professions*, p. 1.

38. Grüttner, *Studenten*, pp. 136–54, 109–26.

39. Jost Dülffer, 'Vom Bündnispartner zum Erfüllungsgehilfen im totalen Krieg: Militär und Gesellschaft in Deutschland 1933–1945', in Wolfgang Michalka, ed., *Der Zweite Weltkrieg: Analysen, Grundzüge, Forschungsbilanz* (Munich, 1989), pp. 286–7.

40. See ibid.; Bernhard R. Kroener, 'Strukturelle Veränderungen in der militärischen Gesellschaft des Dritten Reiches', in Prinz and Zitelmann, *Nationalsozialismus*, pp. 267–96.

41. Schoenbaum, *Revolution*, p. 258.

42. Hans Mommsen, *Beamtentum im Dritten Reich* (Stuttgart, 1966); Kaelble, *Mobilität*, pp. 83, 87; Jane Caplan, *Government without Administration: State and Civil Service in Weimar and Nazi Germany* (Oxford, 1988), pp. 102–338; Michael Ruck, 'Administrative Eliten in Demokratie und Diktatur: Beamtenkarrieren in Baden und Württemberg von den zwanziger Jahren bis in die Nachkriegszeit', in Cornelia Rauh-Kühne and Michael Ruck, eds, *Regionale Eliten zwischen Diktatur und Demokratie: Baden und Württemberg, 1930–1952* (Munich, 1993), pp. 37–69.

43. Ronald Rogowski, 'The Gauleiter and the Social Origins of Fascism', *Comparative Studies in Society and History* 19 (1977), pp. 399–430; Peter Hüttenberger, *Die Gauleiter: Studie zum Wandel des Machtgefüges in der NSDAP* (Stuttgart, 1969).

44. Schoenbaum, *Revolution*, p. 239.

45. Ruth Bettina Birn, 'Himmlers Statthalter: Die Höheren SS- und Polizeiführer als Nationalsozialistsiche Führungselite', in Michalka, *Zweite Weltkrieg*, p. 278; Ulrich Herbert, *Best: Biographische Studien über Radikalismus, Weltanschauung und Vernunft, 1903–1989* (Bonn, 1996), pp. 191–6.

46. Wolfgang Zapf, *Wandlungen der deutschen Elite: Ein Zirkulationsmodell Deutscher Führungsgruppen* (Munich, 1966), pp. 169–77, 141; Daniel Lerner, *The Nazi Elite* (Stanford, 1951), pp. 77–93; Noakes, 'Nazism', pp. 94–6. For an exemplary case study see Hartmut Berghoff and Cornelia Rauh-Kühne, *Fritz K. Ein deutsches Leben im 20. Jahrhundert* (Stuttgart, 2000), esp. pp. 102–54.

47. Noakes, 'Nazism', p. 95.

48. Ibid., p. 92.

CHAPTER FOUR

The transition from Weimar to the Third Reich: the political dimension

EDGAR FEUCHTWANGER

Revolution and restoration in the establishment of the Nazi dictatorship

Revolutions of a sort, suggesting discontinuity, began and ended the Weimar Republic. The history books pin the label 'revolution' onto the events of 1918, principally because the fall of the German monarchies, as a result of pressure from the streets, could hardly merit a lesser title. Most historians are, however, critical of the failure to turn this political revolution into a broader social and economic transformation. On 30 January 1933 there was no revolution, not even to the extent there was in November 1918. Hitler's appointment as chancellor was called, mostly after the event, the *Machtergreifung*, for which 'seizure of power' is the normal translation. This is misleading, for there was no suggestion of illegality in the appointment itself, nor any direct pressure from the streets. The break with constitutional legality began immediately after Hitler's appointment and became progressively more marked. After the Reichstag elections of 5 March 1933 the process can appropriately be called a *Machteroberung*, a conquest of power, and its revolutionary nature became more evident. The incidence of violence was arguably greater in March 1933 than it was in November 1918. Hitler regarded himself as the greatest of revolutionaries, but much effort was devoted by him and his associates to disguising the revolutionary nature of their undertaking. This was for the benefit of those large sections of German society who expected from the Nazis above all a restoration of stability. The term *Nationale Erhebung*, national renaissance, churned out by the newly installed Goebbels propaganda machine, was characteristic of this attempt to cloak the Nazi take-over with the language of restoration, tradition and continuity, reaching back beyond 1918. Posters depicted Hitler in a line of German heroes stretching from Frederick the Great through Bismarck and Hindenburg. On the day of Potsdam, 21 March 1933, Hitler, dressed in top hat and morning suit, bowed deep before Hindenburg, who was wearing the uniform of an Imperial field-marshal. A seat was left vacant for the Kaiser. It was the ceremonial opening of the Reichstag which was two days later to surrender its functions by passing the Enabling Act.[1]

The Nazi take-over thus encompassed both continuity and revolution, with the conflict between these two elements disguised by deliberate propagandistic deception and ideological sleight of hand. The trajectory of the Third Reich during the twelve years of its existence can be plotted in terms of the progressive supersession of continuity by radical transformation. Another perspective on this development is to see it as a gradual process by which an alliance between many of the elites in German society – army, bureaucracy, business – was replaced by the charismatic leadership of the dictator as the main factor of control and integration. The trajectory of the Third Reich can also be examined in terms of a drift from a state governed by the rule of law to one subject to the arbitrary exercise of power, or from a state based on normative law to one subject to a perpetual state of emergency. It can be regarded as a process of creeping revolution ending in self-destructive radicalization. From this the further question arises, a problem that has spawned divergent interpretations among historians, as to what extent these developments were the result of the Nazi ideology or Hitler's personal intentions, or whether they were primarily the outcome of self-generating factors inherent in the dynamic unleashed by the charismatic rule of the dictator. This debate between 'intentionalists' and 'functionalists' is also relevant to the theme of continuity between Weimar and the Third Reich.[2]

The conceptual framework of a polarity between continuity and a revolutionary transformation is useful for examining the political events that led from Weimar to the Third Reich. The change from democracy to dictatorship took place predominantly in the specific sphere of politics. Other spheres, the economy or social structures, were much more slowly and gradually affected and mostly in consequence of political events or decisions. The Nazi *Machtergreifung* is thus a clear case of the primacy of politics. Even before 1933 it was a central feature of the mass mobilization achieved by the NSDAP that the party managed simultaneously to satisfy the deep-seated pressure for systemic transformation and the profound yearning for the recovery of an allegedly stable and glorious past. Such conflicting pressures had been strong in German society since war had ended in defeat and were powerfully reinforced by the economic slump after 1929. Hitler's style of leadership, and the way he had institutionalized it in the

106

NSDAP after its re-establishment in 1925, proved particularly well adapted to this task of simultaneously satisfying revolutionary and restorative aspirations.[3] The mythical concept of a Third Reich under a strong leader, an image conjured up by the Nazi propaganda machine in place of a detailed programme, could carry both revolutionary and stabilizing connotations.[4]

Hitler's use of legality as a tactical device

An important part of this Janus-faced character of National Socialism was the tactic of legality employed by Hitler during the years up to 1933, when he had become a serious contender for power. The failure of his putsch of 1923, but probably other events as well, such as the course of revolution in 1918 and Mussolini's seizure of power in Italy, had convinced him that revolutions in highly developed modern societies could not be made at the barricades, nor against the forces of law and order. Democracy could only be defeated by its own methods, namely through the ballot box. This was an insight which he relentlessly asserted against the impatience and dedication to revolutionary violence of many of his followers, and which he at the same time regarded as one of his most important and to him most congenial assets. His clearest public statement of the legality tactics came when he was called as a witness at the trial, in the autumn of 1930, of three young army officers stationed at Ulm, who were accused of illegal, pro-Nazi activities in the *Reichswehr*. In his testimony under oath Hitler disavowed any unconstitutional or illegal activity by his movement, but he pulled no punches in explaining his intention of eliminating all opposition once he had attained power. Heads would roll, he declared.[5] His appearance at the trial in Leipzig was given added weight by the stunning electoral breakthrough the NSDAP had won only ten days earlier. No one should therefore have been under any illusions about what would be the consequences if Hitler and his movement should come to power.

Even this limited commitment to legality was difficult to maintain in the face of the rapidly accumulating revolutionary potential in the enormously expanding Nazi following. It was especially marked in the SA (*Sturmabteilung*), and Hitler had to face down several revolts among his impatient storm troopers.[6] The most notable of these revolts occurred in the Berlin SA under the leadership of Walter Stennes. In order to contain these pressures, but at the same time to reassure the leaders of the *Reichswehr*, Hitler recalled Ernst Röhm as chief of staff of the SA in 1931. Hitler's ability to keep to the legality tactics while utilizing the revolutionary potential of his movement shows the vital role played by his form of charismatic leadership even before his attainment of power. Walking the tightrope between maintaining the revolutionary dynamic, and reassuring the elites and the middle-class voters that National Socialism in power meant a return to stability and to the traditional values undermined since 1918, continued to be a difficult feat right up to 30 January 1933.

The formation of presidential cabinets from 1930

Hitler's tightrope act between legality and violence unfolded against the background of the shift to presidential cabinets, which occurred in 1930. By that time dissatisfaction with the weak, multi-party state of Weimar was widespread. Calls for a tighter ship, a more authoritarian form of rule, a charismatic leader, were ubiquitous. The immediate problem at the end of 1929 was that, under the pressure of the economic downturn, the great coalition formed in 1928 under the SPD chancellor Hermann Müller was threatening to fall apart. The SPD on the left and the DVP on the right could not agree on how to balance the budget. A way out was to form a government that would pass the necessary legislation under the decree-making powers of the Reich president under article 48 of the Weimar Constitution. This article gave the president power to issue decrees with the force of law in an emergency. The Reichstag could render such decrees invalid by voting against them. Article 48 had been used under the first president of the Republic, the SPD leader Friedrich Ebert, in particular to deal with the introduction of a new currency after the great inflation of 1923. In Ebert's day the use of article 48 had been a genuine emergency measure, to tide the country over until normal parliamentary procedures could function again. Hindenburg's intentions were different. He and his advisers wanted to use article 48 to bring about a permanent shift towards a stronger executive centred on the president, a step that was being widely advocated. The most influential of Hindenburg's entourage at this time was General Kurt von Schleicher, chief of the *Ministeramt* in the Defence Ministry, and as such the political adviser of the defence minister, General Wilhelm Groener. Hindenburg, Schleicher, Groener and others wanted a strong, non-socialist government that would be able to master the problems of the economic slump and would meet the requirements of the *Reichswehr*. These requirements included due regard for the budgetary needs of the armed forces and a more assertive foreign policy than had been pursued under the recently deceased Gustav Stresemann, the foreign minister since 1923. The *Reichswehr* generals wanted strong pressure to be mounted for a revision of the disarmament clauses of the Versailles treaty. In anticipation of the collapse of the Müller coalition Heinrich Brüning, the chairman of the Catholic Centre Party's Reichstag representation, was being groomed as the next chancellor, who would be allowed, if necessary, to use the presidential powers under article 48. When Müller resigned in March 1930, Brüning succeeded him as head of a minority government. He at first tried to get a majority for the measures he considered necessary to cope with the economic situation, but when he failed, they were re-enacted by the president under article 48. The Reichstag again rejected them, but Hindenburg then, in July 1930, allowed Brüning to dissolve the Reichstag. This was stretching the Constitution to its limits. The result was the disastrous Nazi electoral breakthrough in September 1930, which made Hitler's party the second largest after the SPD. Brüning could thereafter only carry on ruling by decree as long as the SPD did not join the other parties, the NSDAP and Nationalists on the right and Communists on the left, in rejecting the decrees. This policy of toleration by the SPD for measures exceedingly repugnant to its supporters, such as cuts in welfare payments, led to a steady electoral decline of the party. The alternative seemed, however, to be a right-wing dictatorship dominated by the Nazis. The SPD after 1930 was truly in a no-win position.

Historians have debated whether the switch to presidential cabinets using article 48 was already the end of Weimar, or whether it was a last-ditch attempt to save the remaining vestiges of parliamentary government and the rule of law. During the Brüning regime, until the dismissal of this chancellor by Hindenburg on 30 May 1932, the second interpretation had some validity. Brüning claimed later, in exile, that his long-term aim had been the introduction of a British-style parliamentary monarchy, with a stable executive government, but at the time he seemed to be doing little more than holding on, while his deflationary policies were radicalizing the electorate by the day. He was entirely dependent on Hindenburg's willingness to sustain him and the only countervailing force was his dependence on the toleration of the SPD. Together with Brüning's own Centre Party, the SPD was still the leading partner in the Prussian coalition government, which controlled the police forces in two-thirds of Germany. After Brüning's departure the chances of avoiding a Nazi dictatorship were further reduced. Neither of the two subsequent chancellors, Franz von Papen and Schleicher himself, had even the slender foothold in parliamentary legitimacy that Brüning had managed to retain. The Prussian government lost its majority in the *Landtag* elections of 24 April 1932 and was removed from office by Papen three months later, on 20 July. After the Reichstag elections of 31 July, the Nazis became much the largest party, with over 37 per cent of votes, and Hitler stood on the threshold of power. But Hindenburg and his advisers were still unwilling to hand him uncontrolled power, the probable result if his demand that he be appointed chancellor of a presidential cabinet had been met. What the president and the various elites influential in decision-making wanted was a Nazi participation in government, so that the NSDAP's enormous electoral strength could be harnessed and the party forced to share the responsibility for unpopular measures. They were not yet willing to risk a fully fledged Nazi dictatorship: they wanted Hitler 'tamed'.[7]

When Hindenburg refused to appoint Hitler chancellor after his great election triumph of 31 July, the Führer's legality tactics seemed to have failed spectacularly. The revolutionaries in the ranks of the SA were deeply disappointed and they began to drift away. In the next few months Hitler's attempt to obtain power by a combination of constitutional pressure with the threat of violence was looking threadbare. When in November 1932 the Nazi electoral setback, with support down to 33 per cent, broke the dynamic of irresistibility, Hitler faced the danger of erosion in his movement. Paradoxically, it was just these signs of weakening electoral and revolutionary momentum that made Hitler more palatable to the power-brokers among the various elites. The policy of 'taming' the Nazis, so long pursued by Schleicher, Papen and many others, now seemed to have a realistic chance of success. Through the shift to presidential cabinets a spectrum of continuity had been established that led, though not inevitably, by stages from democracy to dictatorship.

The *Reichswehr* as a factor of continuity between Weimar and the Third Reich

It has become a commonplace of historical interpretation to analyse the formation of the Hitler cabinet in January 1933 in terms of an alliance between the various elites in German society and a mass movement which they sought to use for their own purposes, and to point out that the elites were guilty of one of the great illusions of history.[8] There are many complexities about such an interpretation: the inbuilt lack of coherence among groups such as industrialists, the importance of individuals such as Papen, who were playing their own game rather than acting as representatives for any group. The alliance interpretation can be most clearly substantiated in the case of the *Reichswehr*.[9] Its senior officers constituted by definition a reasonably coherent group, though even among them there were divergencies of outlook and of interest. The leading figures in the *Reichswehr*, for most of the time even Schleicher, had taken Hitler's professions of legality at face value, because it suited them. If there was any substance to Hitler's professions they were most relevant in relation to the *Reichswehr*. The Nazi movement for all its numerical strength was in no condition to take on the *Reichswehr* and risk a rerun of 1923. The last thing Groener, Schleicher and other senior officers wanted, for their part, was a confrontation with the valuable, militantly nationalist manpower reservoir of the SA.

Many other considerations made the *Reichswehr* arguably the most important factor of continuity between Weimar and the Third Reich. At the very moment of defeat in 1918 a man like Groener, a progressive and forward-looking figure among the military leaders of the time, was already thinking about how the German great-power position might be revived and the role the army might play in restoring it. This problem continued to preoccupy the military leaders throughout the 1920s and shaped their attitude to the Republic. They were acutely aware of the tensions between the military and society that had contributed to the defeat of 1918. The old Prussian junker view of a military elite had come into conflict with the need to mobilize the whole of society for the purposes of total war.[10] The *Reichswehr* of the 1920s, because of the limitations imposed by Versailles, had an officer corps still predominantly drawn from the Prussian aristocracy, yet this was hardly a satisfactory basis for fighting a future war. The *Reichswehr* leaders considered themselves, rather than the republican politicians, to be the true trustees of the continuity of the German state, but they felt uneasy about the ambiguous relationship between themselves and the Social Democratic labour movement, the most representative organization of Weimar repub-licanism. Among the younger officers there was dissatisfaction with the exclusive view of the army's place in society as advocated by von Seeckt, commander-in-chief from 1920 to 1926. It is not difficult to see why the Nazi movement, when it became a major player after 1929, seemed the answer to the generals' prayer, if only it could be harnessed appropriately. It could become a powerful instrument towards the total mobilization of society, both materially and ideologically. It would meet the requirement that had become evident in the First World War, but which organizations like the Fatherland Party of 1917 and 1918, even though it had character-istics foreshadowing National Socialism, had not been able to fill adequately.

Hindenburg's *sine qua non* in giving his reluctant consent to a Hitler chancellorship in January 1933 was to safeguard the *Reichswehr*, but even in the military sphere the formation of the Hitler cabinet had elements of discontinuity. It marked the end of the Schleicher regime, though Schleicher himself seems to have expected in those last January days that he might retain the defence portfolio in a government headed by Hitler.[11] Schleicher fell, not because his concept of 'taming' the Nazis was considered mistaken, but because he had failed to put it into practice successfully. His endless manoeuvres and intrigues had finally cost him the confidence of Hindenburg and alienated groups like the industrialists. Some of his colleagues in the army had fallen foul of him personally, for example Blomberg, who replaced him. A majority of senior officers had grown tired of the high political profile of the *Reichswehr* under the Schleicher regime. Like so many members of the conservative German establishment the generals thought themselves above politics, but Schleicher had dragged them right into it. They wanted a government that would enable the *Reichswehr* to withdraw from an overtly political role, that in foreign policy would work rapidly towards dismantling what remained of the Versailles system and that domestically would provide an environment favourable to the remilitarization (*Wiederwehrhaftmachung*) of society as a whole.[12]

Hindenburg was persuaded that the appointment of Blomberg as defence minister in place of Schleicher, who had held the portfolio in Papen's and in his own cabinet, would safeguard continuity for the *Reichswehr*. In many of the minor constitutional infringements that would soon mount up to a revolution, Blomberg was sworn in ahead of other members of the Hitler cabinet, in order to forestall any countermove by the Schleicher faction, a rumoured plot for which there has never been any concrete evidence. Hindenburg was probably not aware of the extent to which Blomberg had become a Nazi sympathizer, partly through the influence of Ludwig Müller, chaplain to the East Prussian Military District headed by Blomberg, a leading German Christian and soon to become *Reichsbischof*. This was precisely what made Blomberg acceptable to Hitler, who at some stage in the intrigues of January 1933 had wanted a Nazi in the post of defence minister. The other contenders for the post, which included von Fritsch, later commander-in-chief of the army, would probably have been no less sympathetic to the inclusion of Nazis in government and would have regarded it as a development favourable to the concerns of the *Reichswehr*. Blomberg appointed his chief of staff in East Prussia, Colonel Walther von Reichenau, as chief of the Ministerial Office (*Ministeramt*), in place of von Bredow, who had held this office under Schleicher, who in turn had held it under Groener.[13] Blomberg was a man of limited ability, whose gentlemanly veneer had probably commended him to Hindenburg. He became known as a *Gummilöwe* (rubber lion) and was soon under the sway of Hitler's personality. Reichenau was made of sterner stuff: he was an ambitious man of power, with a sharp intelligence and few scruples. Within days of his appointment the new chancellor seized an opportunity to address the leading generals of the *Reichswehr*. The occasion was a party held in the flat of the commander-in-chief of the army, von Hammerstein, to celebrate the 60th birthday of the foreign minister, von Neurath, a survivor from the Papen and Schleicher cabinets and as a career diplomat another token of continuity. Hitler's speech, as reported in the notes taken by one of those present, shows a remarkable similarity of thought with a memorandum composed under very different circumstances in March 1926 by Joachim von Stülpnagel, then a section head in the *Truppenamt*, the thinly disguised general staff.[14] Both Hitler and Stülpnagel projected a revision of Versailles, of which a lot less was left in 1933 than in 1926, the recovery of full German sovereignty and of the lost territories, the *Anschluss* of Austria, and the rebuilding of German hegemony in Europe as a prelude to becoming once more a world power, what historians later called a *Stufenplan*. Military power was essential for the achievement of these aims and for both Stülpnagel and Hitler force was the essential arbiter between nations. Hitler, from his perspective, added that his government would ruthlessly extirpate Marxism and pacifism from the German body politic and restore the military will and capacity of the *Volk*. Hitler was a past master at telling his audiences what they wanted to hear and this was precisely tailored to the outlook of the officers present. They had no difficulty in going along with the new government.

Stages in the transition from democracy to dictatorship

The military side of Hitler's initial take-over is therefore paradigmatic for the interplay between continuity and radical change that marked the transition from Weimar to the Nazi dictatorship and the subsequent evolution of the Third Reich. It also shows how the close location of conservative–nationalist ideologies to National Socialism, with its deliberate vagueness, eased the path of many into the Third Reich.[15] An essential feature of the transition was that the pretence of constitutional continuity was maintained. Hitler's arrival in the chancellery was itself the product of the refusal of Hindenburg and his advisers to risk a formal breach of the Weimar Constitution. Schleicher had asked the president to set aside the requirement in the constitution that new elections to the Reichstag must be held within 60 days of a dissolution. Since this procedure had already been followed twice since the previous June without resulting in a viable government, it seemed reasonable to claim that a state of emergency existed justifying the postponement of elections beyond the 60 days. Schleicher was undoubtedly in a weak position in asking Hindenburg to bend the constitution in this way, since it was only eight weeks earlier that he had advised the president to accept Papen's resignation rather than grant a dissolution on similar grounds. Schleicher's fate was finally sealed when on 28 January Hindenburg refused him a dissolution and a postponement of elections. There were many other factors in Schleicher's fall and in Hitler's accession, notably the feverish intrigues and negotiations that went on throughout January, but Hindenburg's eventual reluctant appointment of Hitler in preference to risking a formal breach of the constitution clinched the matter.[16]

For Hindenburg a formal breach of the Weimar Constitution was risky, for it might have exposed him to judicial proceedings at a moment when he and his family were touched by scandal. For Hitler the maintenance of formal constitutional propriety was vital to ensure a smooth transition to dictatorship. Hitler therefore broke or bent the Weimar Constitution in carefully graduated doses and never actually abolished it. One of his first steps on becoming chancellor was to engineer the dissolution of the Reichstag that had just been refused to Schleicher. There is little doubt that Hindenburg, in appointing Hitler, was under the impression that he would not be a presidential chancellor, but would seek parliamentary backing. Hitler therefore engaged in the charade of abortive negotiations with the Centre Party, to show that he needed yet another dissolution of the Reichstag. The dissolution of the Prussian *Landtag* a few days later, so that elections could take place simultaneously with the Reichstag elections on 5 March, involved procedures beyond strict constitutionality. Göring's police measures as Commissarial Prussian Minister of the Interior broke the spirit of the rule of law, and so did the measures to suppress oppositional meetings and newspapers. The presidential decrees issued on the day after the Reichstag fire suspended civil liberties normal in an open society, but in form they did not differ from the many decrees issued under article 48 of the Weimar Constitution since 1930 and even in the days of Ebert's presidency. They remained cornerstones of the police state that the Third Reich was to become.

After 5 March the process of *Machteroberung* started in earnest. The revolutionary dynamic of the SA was given full reign and opponents felt the full fury of the Nazi terror. Concentration camps, mostly of the wild variety, began to appear, but Himmler's assumption of the office of Police President in Munich led to the establishment of the first official concentration camp at Dachau. The forceful eviction of the Bavarian government, still controlled by the Bavarian People's Party, from office on 8 and 9 March was the most important of the local Nazi take-overs during this phase. The coping stone to this process of graduated erosion of the Weimar Republic was the passage of the Enabling Act on 23 March. The legal positivism of German jurisprudence has often been cited as an important factor in making such erosion possible, but it was also the case that Hitler avoided any single step that would have amounted to a major open breach of the constitution. After the passage of the Enabling Act such caution was no longer necessary. There was no longer any possibility of a constitutional interposition by Hindenburg, though there was no sign that he had any intention of using what powers remained to him to put a brake on the Nazi revolution. Only a week after the passage of the Enabling Act a law for the *Gleichschaltung* of the *Länder* imposed an unprecedented departure from the federalism that was one of the great continuities of German history. *Land* parliaments and other organs of local self-government could be dissolved and reconstituted according to the party strengths emerging from the national elections of 5 March. A new office of *Reichsstatthalter*, Commissar for the Reich, was created, empowered to appoint governments in the *Länder* without parliamentary sanction. In most cases those assuming the office of *Reichsstatthalter* were the Gauleiters of the NSDAP in the region. Thus only two months after his appointment Hitler controlled these officials by virtue of his office as Reich Chancellor, but they also owed him personal, quasi-feudal loyalty as the Führer of the party. A Reich that for centuries had been a federation was subjected to a degree of centralization never before experienced.

The bureaucracy as a factor of continuity

The acquiescence of the vast German civil service machine was no less important to the Nazi take-over than that of the army. Like the army, the old Prussian civil service had considered itself as having a special relationship to the state and to be above politics.[17] This elitist concept had been difficult to maintain even in Imperial Germany, when the growth of a modern industrial state required an enormous expansion of bureaucracy. There was even then a danger that the lower reaches of the bureaucratic machine might be infiltrated by elements and attitudes that were not *staatserhaltend*, that is, not dedicated to the concept of a state separate and superior to civil society. Hence the fear that sections of the state bureaucracy, which included large sections of railway or postal workers, might be taken over by adherents of social democracy or members of trade unions. It was the same fear that made the largely Prussian junker military elite reluctant to expand the army to the point where it might become unreliable as a factor in internal politics.

The uncertainties and ambivalences surrounding the civil service were greatly aggravated by the Revolution of 1918 and the advent of the Weimar Republic. The republican constitution contained special safeguards for civil servants and their status, yet the bureaucracy's cooperation with republican governments was rarely wholehearted. It was only by a narrow margin that the top civil servants remained loyal to the Republic in the Kapp Putsch of 1920, and their posture was not dissimilar to the waiting attitude displayed by the leaders of the army during these events. After this experience the Prussian government, until 1932 a stronghold of republicanism, began to take steps to replace civil servants of doubtful loyalty with persons with assured republican credentials. There were strict limits to what could be done in this direction, because of the stringent safeguards enshrined in the Weimar Constitution for the security of tenure of civil servants and their immunity from political interference. It is one example of the way the Republic had to defend itself against its enemies with its hands tied behind its back. In spite of the all too limited scope of political appointments in the Weimar era it became an article of faith on the right, mainly represented by the DNVP and not yet by National Socialism, that republican governments were undermining the non-political nature of the civil service and its status above politics. The reluctant allegiance of civil servants, as of other middle-class groups, to the Republic was further weakened by the experience of inflation, the reduction in numbers at the beginning of stabilization in 1924 and by the relative loss of economic status. Big salary rises in 1927, seen by some as a major factor in the weak state of German public finances at the onset of the great depression, could not assuage the sense of grievance among civil servants.

The presidential regimes from 1930 in one way enhanced the self-esteem of civil servants, for they signalled a reversion to the older, elitist, non-political status. Civil servants could make and implement policy undisturbed by the unpredictable interference of parliaments and parties. On the other hand the stringent salary reductions imposed by Brüning, made unnecessarily severe by his dour, hair-shirt attitudes, inflicted further psychological damage. It is not surprising therefore that civil servants voted Nazi in numbers above average after 1929, though few of them defied the ban on political affiliation enforced in Prussia and elsewhere. The overwhelming majority of civil servants were therefore prepared to accept at face value the legality of the Nazi take-over in 1933 and to participate without reserve in the euphoria, the *Aufbruchsstimmung*, that took hold of much of German public opinion in the spring of 1933. Thus the Nazi revolution was able to take advantage of a continuity in the administrative sphere no less important than the smooth change-over in the military sphere.

After the Papen coup in Prussia in July 1932 there had already taken place a purge of officials considered to be republican sympathizers. One of the first laws passed under the Enabling Act of March 1933 was the Law for the Restoration of a Professional Civil Service (*Berufsbeamtentum*) of 7 April 1933.[18] The title itself was a typically Nazi perversion of language. It was in fact a law for purging the civil service of politically and racially unreliable elements, but its name perpetuated the myth that the republican governments had politicized the service and that it was now necessary to restore its non-political status. This was a major breach with the principle of security of tenure which had always been fully maintained in the Weimar era. Since the law's victims were the comparatively small number of republican sympathizers and non-Aryan civil servants, here for the first time legally discriminated against, it did not lead to any resistance against the new masters on the part of the overwhelming majority of civil servants. To some extent the law was a legalization after the event of the dismissal of officials, particularly on the communal level, which had often been brought about by violence and terror by the SA. It was particularly at the communal level that Nazi 'old fighters' had forced out established officials at the point of a gun. The turnover of personnel, either by direct pressure or by quasi-legal means, remained within fairly narrow limits, for the regime could not have done without the professional expertise of the civil service at all levels. Acceptance by the bureaucracy, as by the army, was therefore one of the fundamental continuities that made the establishment of the essentially revolutionary Nazi regime possible.

The ease with which the regime bent the bureaucracy, and the subsection of it that constituted the judiciary, to its purposes cannot obscure the fact that there remained an underlying and never resolved tension between the dynamic of National Socialism and the principles upon which both bureaucracy and judiciary had to operate. They were part of the normative state against which National Socialists, dedicated to unleashing the vital forces of the *Volk*, had always pitted themselves. Hitler in his personal views was always deeply antagonistic towards and suspicious of lawyers and bureaucrats, whom he saw as strangling the vital forces of the race. In his table talk during the war, when he was the supreme overlord of huge civil and military machines, he still expressed the same opinions.[19] As the Third Reich was consolidated and progressed a vast amount of effort went into setting out what claimed to be a specifically National Socialist concept of administration and law. Wilhelm Frick, long-serving party member and Reich Minister of the Interior, was the most prominent of those who sought to give the Third Reich a constitutional framework, but in the end he always came up against Hitler's reluctance to proceed down this road. The Third Reich thus became the 'organized chaos' that makes the analysis of its structure such a headache to historians to this day. This chaos cannot be simply classified as clashes between established organizations, staffed by civil servants with a traditional ethos, and National Socialist organizations, such as the party and its sub-organizations, or the SS and its ramifying empire.[20] Party or SS and *Sicherheitsdienst*, or new ministries like Goebbels's Propaganda Ministry, were themselves bureaucracies, at least in part staffed by civil servants taken over from older organizations. Their new recruits were often men who in pre-Nazi days would have joined the civil service through its regular recruitment procedures, but who now saw an easier and quicker way into positions of influence through membership of the party. There was constant pressure to relax the conditions of entry into the civil service for those who could prove loyal adherence to sound National Socialist principles. On the other hand established bodies like the Foreign Ministry or the chancellery were staffed by men who assumed SS or other party ranks. There was a process of interpenetration, an inextricable linking of continuity and transformation, with the final goal of complete Nazification to be attained after final victory. Hitler himself, for all his suspicion of civil servants and lawyers and his reluctance to bind himself constitutionally, was wary of anything that might seriously antagonize opinion or, once the war had started, interfere with the war effort.

Deception and ideological confusion in the establishment of dictatorship

Army and bureaucracy were the sections of the traditional German elites whose cooperation was most crucial to the consolidation of Nazi rule and to the further development of the Third Reich. The ease with which they, in common with most other sectors of German society, adapted to the regime owes much to the masterly deception staged by Hitler and Goebbels under the slogan *Nationale Erhebung*. This deception was greatly facilitated by the ideological continuity and overlap that existed between German nationalism in its various manifestations and National Socialism. This continuity, as well as the many confusions it gave rise to, can be seen at work in countless individual cases. General Ludwig Beck and Fritz-Dietlof von der Schulenburg were typical representatives of their respective organizations, army and civil service. Both became active resisters later on, but were enthusiastic supporters of the Nazi take-over. Beck had celebrated the Nazi electoral breakthrough in 1930 and had strongly defended his young officers accused of collaboration with the Nazis in the trial of 1930.[21] Schulenburg, a *Regierungsrat* in Königsberg, had been a member of the NSDAP since 1931. He wrote in a memorandum in April 1933 how the coming recruits to the civil service, 'which at its height comprised the best biological components of the *Volk*', might be permeated with the National Socialist idea of the state.[22] Men like General Werner von Fritsch, soon to become commander-in-chief of the army, clung to the notion of remaining 'non-political', while sharing much of the stock-in-trade of Nazi mythology, such as the view of the revolution of 1918 as a stab in the back by a Jewish–Bolshevik world conspiracy.[23] He still expressed such opinions after he had fallen victim to Hitler's and Himmler's blackmail in February 1938 in a crisis that marked a milestone in the progress of the Third Reich from continuity to revolution. Such predispositions and confusions were the rule among all except the firmly liberal and left-wing sections of the German population and they were clearly in a minority by 1933. Unfortunately even the Left fell victim to the confusions deliberately fostered by the Nazis. In the SPD and even more markedly in the trade unions there was a widespread belief, after 30 January 1933, that strict adherence to legality, emphasized in many statements intended to propitiate the new masters, could save their organizations. The historical example of survival during Bismarck's proscription of the SPD after 1879 was constantly invoked. If Bismarck had failed to annihilate the socialist movement, so it was argued, how much less likely was it that a mere Austrian house-painter could succeed.[24] Marxist determinism was strong and alive in the SPD and the free unions. It reached suicidal proportions in the KPD.

The SA and a 'Second Revolution'

The ideological confusion of so many is perhaps the most depressing aspect of the Nazi seizure of power. The victors were, however, not immune themselves to the disorientation wrought by the simultaneous claim to restoration and revolution. It was their confusion that produced the first great crisis of the regime, the Night of the Long Knives, 30 June 1934. This crisis was also a turning point on the path from continuity to radicalization and, as with the *Machtergreifung* itself, deception and confusion were central to the outcome. By the summer the political transformation of Germany had been taken as far as it could be for the moment without endangering the process of consolidation that was vital for the survival of the regime. This left the SA, the force that had supplied the revolutionary element of violence and terror essential to the Nazi take-over, without a clear purpose. It was a part-time army by now 2 million strong and still expanding, while a block on party membership had been in operation since May 1933. The SA comprised much of the *sans-culotte* element in National Socialism, but it had also, even before 1933, attracted recruits from the elites, from Prince August Wilhelm, a son of the Kaiser known as Auwi, downwards.[25] From its beginnings in the early 1920s there had been the lack of a clear demarcation line between the SA and the party itself. It played its part in the failure of the Beer Hall Putsch, to some extent an example of the paramilitary tail wagging the political dog. It had led to a divergence between Hitler and Röhm when the party was refounded in 1925 and eventually to the latter's withdrawal to Bolivia as a military instructor. Röhm had been Hitler's advocate with the army in his early days in Munich and when relations with the *Reichswehr* became vital again after 1930, Hitler recalled him. Hitler's concept for the SA was essentially a political rather than a military one. It was an instrument for using violence and terror propagandistically, to attract attention, to show domination to both friend and foe. Röhm, the archetype of the perpetual soldier, who had nothing like Hitler's political sophistication, saw his force as a revolutionary army. The policy-makers of the *Reichswehr*, with Schleicher and Groener in the lead, equally saw it as a valuable reservoir of nationally minded recruits. They envisaged that the expansion of the army would require the creation of a militia to provide reserves and for this the manpower assembled in the SA would be vital.

In the summer of 1933 the question of the future role of the SA was made acute by the fact that the immediate expectations of its core of 'old fighters' were bound to be disappointed. For them the process of *Machtergreifung* had satisfied some of their revolutionary instincts. They had been able to settle old scores and find an outlet for their brutality in humiliating their opponents. The age-old motive of *enrichissez-vous*, always present in revolutions, was less easy to satisfy. Jobs had been found for many 'old fighters', particularly in *Länder* and local administration, but they were mostly low-level ones. A system of 'special commissars' had flourished. Many businesses and commercial enterprises had been forced to take on or to promote 'old fighters', but this had to be kept within limits, given the lack of expertise of most of them and the need to safeguard the possibility of economic recovery. Most, and sometimes even more, of what could be done for 'old fighters' had been done by the summer of 1933; hence Hitler's determined efforts to declare a halt to 'revolution'. At this stage he was concerned to emphasize the integrity of the state, its officials and organs against both party and SA, for both domestically and in foreign affairs a period of consolidation was essential. He had no alternative but to adhere to the understanding that had been part of the deal when he formed his cabinet, namely that the army should remain exempt from *Gleichschaltung*. He talked of a 'two pillar' theory of the National Socialist state, the party and the army. Against this the intentions of Röhm and his associates remained nebulous. In an article in June 1933, entitled 'SA and German Revolution', Röhm attacked the petit-bourgeois philistines who had been *gleichgeschaltet*, now called themselves National Socialists but were in fact traitors to the revolution. He was determined to maintain the SA as a separate centre of power in the Nazi regime and his ambitions focused increasingly on its military function. It would eventually become a people's army that would absorb the *Reichswehr* into its ranks. There was much loose talk from the SA against other Nazi bigwigs, against the hidebound officer corps and even against Hitler himself. Thus Röhm and his associates collected ill-will in high places in addition to the unpopularity and fear their unruly and greedy behaviour aroused in the general population.[26]

Hitler himself played his cards close to his chest and was double-tongued in his dealings with Röhm, the only major figure permitted to call him *du*. He displayed what became the enduring characteristics of his leadership style, distancing himself from conflicts and hovering above them in an apparent posture of moderation. Even at this stage, when his position as leader was by no means fully formed, he was not acting from weakness. All parties to the conflict were competing for his favours: the *Reichswehr* generals, with Blomberg and Reichenau in the van, Göring and Frick, trying to build up their own power bases by safeguarding normal state procedures, Himmler, nominally subordinate to Röhm, but getting a grip, step by step, on the political police and security apparatus in one locality after another, Goebbels, sticking close to his Führer but already playing an essential role in building up the Hitler myth. Blomberg and Reichenau went out of their way to demonstrate loyalty by adopting the swastika for army insignia and, shamefully, the 'Aryan paragraph' for the officer corps.[27]

The Night of the Long Knives, 30 June 1934

It is difficult even now to know at what point precisely Hitler decided to cut the Gordian knot by force, though it is clear that throughout the early months of 1934 Himmler, Göring and Reichenau were preparing for a showdown. The growing crisis was aggravated by popular discontent and fuelled by the relatively slow progress of economic improvement. The likelihood of Hindenburg's early death meant that Hitler had to pre-empt any attempt, such as the restoration of the monarchy, to put a limit on his power. His erstwhile national–conservative partners had signally failed to put their initial concept of 'taming' the Nazis into effect and the link between Papen and Hindenburg was virtually the only card left to them. When Papen's entourage, in particular Edgar Jung, finally screwed up the courage of their master to speak out against Nazi excesses and demand a return to the rule of law, in the speech at Marburg University on 17 June 1934, Hitler must have realized that it was high time to hit out ruthlessly against the threats encircling him. That he was reluctant to act against the SA and to follow the self-interested advice fed to him by Göring, Himmler and Reichenau is hardly surprising. The men assembled in the SA were just the kind of 'human material' most valuable to his revolution: the more dubious their private morality, the more committed they were to him and to the cause. The homosexuality which loomed so large in the indictment of Röhm and his associates after their murder had never disturbed Hitler in the past and could be used as a means of manipulation. The last thing Hitler wanted was to make himself a prisoner of the generals and other conservative forces, however indispensable they were for the moment. In the bunker, in March 1945, Hitler and Goebbels were still regretting that they had been compelled to act against the SA rather than against the generals who had betrayed them.

In retrospect, the Night of the Long Knives looks like a major milestone in the Third Reich's evolution from continuity to radicalization, but at the time it seemed to most Germans to have the opposite effect.[28] Even if the interpretation of Hitler's appointment as chancellor as an alliance between the Nazi mass movement and various elites in German society is not fully satisfactory, there can be little dispute that most of the elites adapted rapidly to the Nazi take-over and found it on the whole acceptable. The sense that National Socialism formed a seamless web with the more positive aspects of the German past, in which the Weimar Republic was an inglorious interlude, was widespread. If there were doubts about the adventure upon which Germany had embarked, they came mainly from the potentiality for violence and terror that was stored up in the Nazi movement, most obviously in the SA. Usually these doubts were dismissed by reflections along the lines of 'you can't make an omelette without breaking eggs'. From this perspective the events of 30 June 1934 evoked a great collective sigh of relief. The leaders of the *Reichswehr*, who had made a direct contribution to the purges, appeared to have most cause for rejoicing and did not allow themselves to be disturbed by the murder of two of their senior colleagues, Schleicher and Bredow. They repaid the debt they thought they owed Hitler by smoothing his succession to Hindenburg at the beginning of August 1934 and by themselves suggesting the wording of the oath that tied the armed forces to their new supreme commander. The gains for the *Reichswehr* seemed to be clear and palpable, but most of the German population thought they could now settle down to a comfortable relationship with the regime. This feeling did not stop at the working population, who might be thought the most obvious losers from the events of the previous eighteen months. This acceptance by the working classes of the new dispensation was enhanced by the Röhm purge and emerges clearly from the Sopade reports, published by the SPD organization in exile. It was only now that it dawned on the exiled SPD leaders that they might be in for a very long haul. There has been a historical debate about the extent to which there was a social revolution in the Third Reich. To contemporaries it could seem that such social revolution as there was had been stopped in 1934. Thereafter it was the rhetoric of *Volksgemeinschaft* rather than substantive changes in the hierarchical nature of society that seemed to characterize the state of affairs. Even for the short period of relative stability until 1938 the picture drawn by Nazi propaganda of greater social mobility was not entirely illusory, but it was the apparent economic improvement achieved by the regime, as well as the foreign policy successes, that was above all responsible for keeping the masses relatively contented, rather than a sense of greater social justice.

The prevailing sentiment among the majority of the German public was therefore that continuity and underlying permanent realities had reasserted themselves after 30 June 1934. If the Third Reich ever achieved a temporary plateau of stabilization, it did so in the next three or four years. For contemporaries, and also to foreign observers, it could now seem plausible that what had taken place was essentially a restoration rather than a revolution. The *Reichswehr*, soon to become the greatly expanded *Wehrmacht*, and civil service could continue their task of sustaining the state without qualms. Soon both organizations were to undergo further interlacing of traditional and new elites. It was most obvious in the *Wehrmacht*, where the enormous expansion of the officer corps made it increasingly futile to keep it free of National Socialist influence, something that Fritsch was still inclined to attempt. Neither he nor any of the other leading military figures had been backward in demanding the expansion and rearmament of the forces and up to 1935 Hitler, encouraged in this respect by the career diplomats of the Foreign Office, had often been more cautious than they were. For example, Germany's departure from the League of Nations in October 1933 was spearheaded by the *Reichswehr* leaders, who were anxious to clear the way for rapid rearmament. Hitler's early foreign policy successes strengthened the willingness of the elites to play their part in the Third Reich. The reintroduction of conscription in March 1935 and the remilitarization of the Rhineland in March 1936 were precisely the steps that had long been part of every German nationalist agenda, and their successful achievement could only reinforce the view that the legitimate aims of German nationalism and those of Hitler were identical, and that the Führer was a man who could be trusted, like no one before, to implement them with energy and skill.

The Hitler myth and the Führer-State

All this was an illusion and the view of observers, mostly outside Germany, that the Night of the Long Knives showed the dangerously revolutionary character of the regime was correct. The German man in the street, as well as the elites, thought that a moderate Hitler had cut down the lawless and violent elements in the Nazi movement. This perception gave a powerful boost to the rise of the Hitler myth, which became the integrating factor in the Third Reich.[29] The burgeoning effectiveness of the myth, combined with Hitler's apparent successes at home and abroad, made the dictator increasingly irresistible and underpinned his charismatic leadership. Under this umbrella there developed the many sub-empires of the Nazi state which progressively, but never totally, disintegrated the cohesive normative state inherited from the Weimar period. Many of the features characteristic of Hitler's style of governing now emerged. The dictator largely withdrew from continuous contact with the machinery of government, by the simple device of withdrawing physically, much of the time, to his mountain retreat in Berchtesgaden, where only those he wanted to see could contact him personally.[30] He was not a weak, but a fitful dictator, who concentrated on those areas central to his purpose and necessary to the maintenance and enhancement of his power. He relied on the quasi-feudal ties of loyalty of his subordinate leaders, nationally his inner circle, regionally the Gauleiters, many of them doubling as *Reichstatthalter*, to carry out his intentions. The absence of constitutional definitions of his power made it possible through various types of orders emanating from the Führer to equip subordinate leaders like Himmler with far-reaching powers that cut through the network of normal law. The method by which the killings of 30 June 1934 had been carried out and were subsequently legalized shows how the normative law could be undermined and disintegrated. When Schleicher and his wife were killed by a hit squad in their villa in a leafy suburb of Berlin, the normal machinery of legal investigation through the local police was activated. It was halted in its tracks by direct intervention from the Reich Ministry of Justice, still headed by Franz Gürtner.[31] He was an inheritance from the previous governments of Papen and Schleicher, a long-serving Bavarian minister of justice and a member of the DNVP. He and others like him spent their time saving vestiges of the rule of law while accepting that law in the Third Reich had the overriding purpose of serving the needs of the *Volk* and had to be guided by the 'healthy instincts of the people' (*das gesunde Volksempfinden*). Subsequently the proceedings of 30 June 1934 were legalized by Hitler's claim that he had to act as 'the supreme justiciar of the German people'. For good measure Carl Schmitt, leading constitutional theorist, who at a previous stage had provided the philosophical underpinning for the widely desired modification of the Weimar Constitution after 1930, now published the theoretical justification for this further disintegration of the liberal state in an article entitled 'The Führer protects the Law'.[32] The illusion that the Nazi revolution could be controlled and canalized by legal means had already motivated some of those, like the deputies of the Centre Party, who had voted for the Enabling Law in March 1933. When in

September 1935 the Nuremberg Laws were hurriedly drafted, some of the civil servants involved subsequently claimed that their efforts had helped to canalize the impulse to pogrom among the Nazi rank and file into more orderly and predictable channels. It was an opinion shared even by some of the victims at the time. Racial persecution was no longer at the mercy of street violence, so it was claimed, but was subdued by due process.

Remaining factors of continuity

Illusion, deception, adaptation, lamentable as they were, should not obscure the fact that there were still elements of continuity. Without this continuity the Third Reich could not have gone along its trajectory, until 1941 stunningly successful, thereafter true to its inherent self-destructiveness. This is again most clearly demonstrated by the situation of the *Wehrmacht*. It continued to be, no less than Hitler himself, the driving force behind the headlong rush towards rearmament. Attempts by Schacht to impose a more sustainable pace came to grief not only on Hitler, but on the demands of the generals. Hitler's secret four-year plan memorandum of August 1936, requiring war readiness by 1940, had already been anticipated in a memorandum, by the Chief of the General Staff Beck, of December 1935.[33] Naturally there were doubts voiced from among the military planners about the feasibility of such a timetable and the risks it implied. Occasions such as the famous meeting of 5 November 1937, recorded by Colonel Hossbach, made the heads of the armed services aware of how Hitler intended to transcend the contradictions inherent in their own as well as his policies by a relentless push forward, aptly described in German as a *Flucht nach vorn* (flight forward).[34] It set alarm bells ringing among the military commanders and through Neurath in the Foreign Office. In turn it fed the Führer's suspicions that he had not yet fully succeeded in reducing the military or civilian bureaucracies into instruments of his intentions. The great personnel upheavals of February 1938 were, like many of Hitler's coups, improvised rather than planned, but at this stage he was, incipient signs of megalomania notwithstanding, still a past master at keeping his potential adversaries off balance and exploiting opportunities to his advantage. The most crucial difference between continuity and revolution in the transition from previous regimes to the Third Reich had always been implicit in totally divergent perceptions of Germany's place in the world. Hitler's vision of a racially based Greater German Reich with the potential for world domination was qualitatively different from even the most extreme previous versions of the German destiny. The realization of this vision became therefore the key to the revolutionary transformation of society along National

Socialist lines. The internal and external requirements for realizing the vision were linked. Ideological wars of racial conquest could only succeed if German society had reached a degree of material and psychological mobilization for them, but the total transformation of society into the National Socialist ideal could only come after final victory. For this reason, as well as for others, Hitler felt pressed for time.

Hitler's remark after the remilitarization of the Rhineland, that he was going on the way Providence had marked out for him with the certainty of a sleepwalker, shows a dangerous inclination to believe in his own myth as the greatest revolutionary the world had ever seen. But at this stage he could still combine the instincts of the gambler with a degree of salutary caution. He knew when his radicalism had to be tempered with due regard for the prejudices of a conservative society and of conservative nationalist elites with whose services he could not dispense. His policy towards the protestant churches is a good example of this. Before 1933 he had done all he could to exploit the attraction his movement had for Lutherans. SA formations were often ordered to attend Lutheran services as a body and in uniform. This did not fail to impress many church-going Lutherans, who were thoroughly alienated from Weimar and all the manifestations of modernity that clustered around it. National Socialism promised them a return to the healthy, clean-living, hierarchical, patriotic and Christian society they had lost in 1918.[35] Even before 1933 the German Christians who wanted a racially sound Christianity cleansed of its Jewish accretions made remarkable headway in synodal elections. This led Hitler, who knew little about the Lutheran churches, to believe that, swept up as they were into the euphoria of the Nazi take-over, they could be *gleichgeschaltet* without difficulty. The regime put its weight behind the German Christians and Ludwig Müller, a relative moderate within that sect. The result was resistance and the foundation of the Confessing Church (*Bekennende Kirche*).[36] To be sure, the Confessing Church was never a real threat to the regime and its opposition to National Socialism was confined to a narrow range of issues. But it showed the limits beyond which revolutionary totalitarianism could not, for the time being, penetrate. Hitler regarded these limits as temporary, not likely to last beyond final victory, but he thought it wiser not to pursue this particular conflict to its logical conclusion, something that came hard to him. After 1935 the assault on recalcitrant Lutheran pastors was resumed, under the aegis of Hans Kerrl, appointed Reich Minister for Church Affairs, but Hitler always in the end shied away from carrying it too far. It was an area in which the conservative–nationalist elites, who in other respects had allowed themselves to become executants of Hitler's increasingly radical policies, showed some courage in protecting churchmen who became victims of persecution.

Legally the Führer-State was complete by 1935, but in practice there were still limits to the way in which the Führer's power could operate. The terms of the original alliance with the traditional elites could not be entirely ignored. The other major factor that continued to inhibit radicalization was the need to pay attention to the opinions and the moods of the population in general. To put a brake on the radical dynamic of the regime would have required elites and public opinion at large to move in step. This occurred only in a few instances, the temporary stop imposed on the euthanasia campaign as late as 1941 being the most obvious example. The resisters in the army were frequently baulked in obtaining the collaboration of their fellow officers by the fact that those senior officers felt it was not for them to oppose the Führer when he so patently had the support of the people. Because effective resistance was difficult as long as the regime enjoyed popular support, therefore it had constantly to make sure that it had that support. The best way of ensuring it was to pile one sensational foreign policy success upon another, while maintaining the sense of economic improvement. For the man or woman in the street it was always the Führer to whom the credit was almost exclusively due. His personal position became therefore virtually impregnable. Yet Hitler was haunted by fear of a collapse of the home front, which he regarded as the prime cause for the defeat of 1918. The repercussions of this on the whole range of military and economic preparations for war is well known. For all its sensational successes and ceaseless triumphalism the regime was nervous and given to taking its own temperature. The reports of the security services that are now so valuable to historians were a product of this nervousness.[37] The enormity of the National Socialist revolution required, in the minds of Hitler and his inner circle, continued caution and dissembling. Many of the decisions already taken and programmes set in train, particularly in the areas of rearmament and economic policy, ensured that the situation could not remain on a plateau. In these decisions Hitler himself had played an important, some-times decisive, role, but he was by no means the sole actor. The unco-ordinated, chaotic situation which, under the umbrella of his charismatic leadership, he had, by calculation and even more by instinct, allowed to arise, ensured that matters had to move forward if they were not to slip back into crisis. Yet there was a sense almost of panic around the dictator and his inner circle that the forces of continuity and inertia might after all reassert themselves. Hitler would then figure in history not as the greatest revolutionary of all time, but merely as the figurehead of a traditional authoritarian, conservative–nationalist regime. In a worst-case scenario the Third Reich would founder on its own inner contradictions and on the incompatibility of its policies, particularly in economic affairs. Hitler's impatience before 'the great leap forward' is palpable and shows in his speeches and in a testing of the waters, as on 5 November 1937. The continuing caution shows in his reluctance to let Schacht finally go and even in the handling of the first territorial expansion, the *Anschluss* of March 1938. It was only after this that caution was almost completely thrown to the winds in the quest for speed and irresistible momentum. Hitler's revised directive to his armed forces about the treatment of Czechoslovakia, 'Case Green', of 30 May 1938, may be seen as the point where this occurs, after the partial mobilization of the Czech forces ten days earlier had appeared for the moment to check the forward momentum. It was now no longer a matter of awaiting a suitable political opportunity for action, it was 'my unalterable decision to smash Czechoslovakia by military action within a foreseeable time'. There are indications that even within Hitler's inner circle there were doubts. A man as close to him in mentality as Goebbels confided these doubts to his diary, but tried to drown them by asserting his belief in the Führer's genius.[38]

War as an instrument of radicalization

Territorial expansion and war were therefore the most potent agents of the revolutionary dynamic inherent in National Socialism and the most powerful antidote to continuity and inertia. Hitler had activated these agents of radicalization and revolutionary transformation by increasingly detaching himself from all organs of government and concentrating the key decisions in his own hands. This does not mean that one has to subscribe to an over-personalized or excessively Hitler-centric view of events. The 'functionalists' have a point when they emphasize the importance of self-generating radicalization in a system such as the German Führer-State, in which only the charismatic leadership of a messiah figure provided psychological integration and minimal coordination. It was a system, or lack of system, that ensured not only radicalization but also ultimate failure. All the many components of high-level decision-making were in fact not coordinated. Hitler's total dynamism did not take into account the pace of economic preparation, the balance of armaments and of risks, the possible strategic options. It relied on sheer momentum for success. Even the *Blitzkrieg* strategy was by no means a fully fashioned operational concept and was full of inbuilt contradictions.[39]

Even under these conditions the factors of continuity should not be underestimated. War and the early military successes as well as the later mobilization associated with Speer were only possible because so much of the long-established and relatively efficient military and civil structures of the German state had survived. The elites whose cooperation had been so vital all along continued to cooperate. The big diplomatic and military decisions of the years 1938–41 were taken by Hitler, and input from previous power centres like the Foreign Ministry and the army high command was greatly reduced. These organizations had been emasculated in their capacity to offer independent advice by being put in charge of personalities almost entirely subservient to Hitler, men like Ribbentrop, Keitel or Brauchitsch. Yet particularly in the actual conduct of war the Führer could not act without the preparation, planning and execution of the military staffs. The campaign against France in May 1940, which brought Hitler to the peak of his power, was the work of the military staffs and its success was the result of German military efficiency pitted against French military inadequacy. Hitler was able to press for early action and he could choose between different plans submitted to him. The generals were the executants of his policy, but the manner of execution remained decisive. If anything the war itself and the successes up to at least 1942 made the cooperation of the elites more unconditional than it had been. For them, as for the population at large, it had become the great patriotic war. The military plotting against Hitler was on the back-burner. The cooperation of industrial and diplomatic bureaucracies in the exploitation of Hitler's conquests was willing. The generals did not hang back when it came to the preparation of ideological war against Soviet Russia.[40] The fighting of this war as a battle of annihilation was not just a matter for the SS.

The population as a whole entered the war without enthusiasm, and Hitler might bewail the fact, as in his speech of 10 November 1938, that he had been compelled to talk the language of peace for so long that the German people were not prepared for the war he had always envisaged. It was no coincidence that he gave the speech on the morning after the *Kristallnacht*, an anti-Jewish pogrom carried out openly and violently, a clear indicator that the Nazi revolutionary design need no longer be concealed. The 'old fighters' of the emasculated SA could be allowed to cool their ardour by smashing Jewish shop-windows and burning synagogues. The true nature of the Third Reich had no longer to be disguised and triumphalism knew no bounds. Dedicated National Socialists were even by 1939 still a minority of the population as a whole, though a large and growing one. Outside the ranks of committed Nazis there was unease about *Kristallnacht* and even more of a sinking feeling when war was declared. Yet there was no resistance to the war nor any hesitation in fighting it. All the evidence supports the view that when at last a section of the elites struck against the dictator on 20 July 1944 they could count on little popular support. No doubt this was largely due to the fact that any political alternatives to the Third Reich had been effectively eliminated and that there appeared to be no continuity left with the previous German political structure. Hitler's secondary purpose in promoting genocide, holocaust and ideological war of annihilation was to turn the German population into his accomplices, for whom all exits would be barred because of the heinous nature of the crimes committed in their name.

The concept of zero hour (*Stunde Null*) is nevertheless impressionistic rather than realistic. It is something that Hitler, the failed world revolutionary, would have liked to bring about at the very end with his scorched earth order, *Nerobefehl*, but it was not only Speer's refusal to carry this out that rendered it inoperative. There was always a significant number of Germans who did not share the vision of a thousand-year Reich. All those members of the Weimar political, intellectual and artistic establishments who had been forced into exile had never shared it. Resistance (*Resistenz*) and inner exile inside Germany accounted for a further, numerically small, but significant minority who remained unconvinced. Even sections of the outwardly cooperating elites, for example industrialists, began quietly to prepare for the future when they saw defeat coming. After May 1945 there was soon a revival of political activity. The torch was picked up where it had been dropped in 1933. History knows no zero hours, only continuities.

Notes

1. K.D. Bracher, W. Sauer and G. Schulz, *Die nationalsozialistische Machtergreifung: Studien zur Errichtung des totalitären Herrschaftssystems in Deutschland 1933/34* (Köln and Opladen, 1962) remains indispensable for this phase of the Nazi dictatorship.

2. This debate is summarized in I. Kershaw, *The Nazi Dictatorship: Problems and Perspectives of Interpretation* (London, 1985), ch. 4.

3. D. Orlow, *History of the Nazi Party*, vol. I: *1919–1933* (Newton Abbot, 1971).

4. K.D. Bracher, *The German Dictatorship* (London, 1973), pp. 44ff.; J. Hiden and J. Farqharson, *Explaining Nazi Germany: Historians and the Third Reich* (London, 1983), ch. 2; E. Jäckel, *Hitler's World View: A Blueprint for Power* (Cambridge, MA, 1981).

5. P. Bucher, *Der Reichswehrprozess: Der Hochverrat der Ulmer Reichswehroffiziere 1929/30* (Boppard, 1967).

6. R. Bessel, *Political Violence and the Rise of Nazism: The Storm Troopers in Eastern Germany* (New Haven, CN, 1984); C.J. Fischer, *Storm Troopers: A Social, Economic and Ideological Analysis* (London, 1983).

7. The classic account of the disintegration of the Weimar Republic is still K.D. Bracher, *Die Auflösung der Weimarer Republik: Eine Studie zum Problem des Machtverfalls in der Demokratie*, 2nd edn (Stuttgart, 1957). For shorter accounts in English, see E.J. Feuchtwanger, *From Weimar to Hitler: Germany, 1918–33*, 2nd edn (London and Basingstoke, 1995), ch. 4; I. Kershaw, ed., *Weimar: Why Did German Democracy Fail?* (London, 1990); M. Broszat, *Hitler and the Collapse of Weimar Germany* (Oxford/New York, 1987).

8. H.A. Turner, Jr, *German Big Business and the Rise of Hitler* (New York, 1985); R. Neebe, *Grossindustrie, Staat und NSDAP, 1930–1933: Paul Silverberg und der Reichsverband der Deutschen Industrie in der Krise der Weimarer Republik* (Göttingen, 1981); Dick Geary, 'The Industrial Elite and the Nazis in the Weimar Republic', in P. Stachura, *The Nazi Machtergreifung* (London, 1983), pp. 85–100; T. Eschenburg, 'Die Rolle der Persönlichkeit in der Krise der Weimarer Republik: Hindenburg, Brüning, Groener, Schleicher', *Vierteljahrhefte für Zeitgeschichte* 9 (1961), pp. 1–29; H.A. Turner, Jr, '"Alliance of Elites" as a Cause of Weimar's Collapse and Hitler's Triumph?', in H.A. Winkler, ed., *Die deutsche Staatskrise, 1930–1933* (Munich, 1992), pp. 205–14.

9. F.L. Carsten, *Reichswehr and Politics* (Oxford, 1966); M. Geyer, *Aufrüstung oder Sicherheit: Die Reichswehr in der Krise der Machtpolitik, 1924–1936* (Wiesbaden, 1980).

10. M. Geyer, 'Professionals and Junkers: German Rearmament and Politics in the Weimar Republic', in R. Bessel and E.J. Feuchtwanger, eds, *Social Change and Political Development in Weimar Germany* (London, 1981), pp. 77–133.

11. V. Hentschel, *Weimars letzte Monate: Hitler und der Untergang der Republik* (Düsseldorf, 1978); H.A. Turner, Jr, *Hitler's Thirty Days to Power: January 1933* (London, 1996); Feuchtwanger, *From Weimar to Hitler*, pp. 299–315; E. Jäckel, 'Der Machtantritt Hitlers – Versuch einer geschichtlichen Erklärung', in V. Rittberger, ed., *1933: Wie die Republik der Diktatur erlag* (Stuttgart, 1983), pp. 123–39.

12. K.-J. Müller, *Das Heer und Hitler* (Stuttgart, 1969); P. Hayes, '"A Question Mark with Epaulettes"? Kurt von Schleicher and Weimar Politics', *Journal of Modern History* 52 (1980), pp. 35–65.

13. Bracher, Sauer, Schulz, *Machtergreifung*, pp. 684ff.

14. For Stülpnagel's memorandum, see Geyer, *Aufrüstung*, p. 126; for Hitler's speech, see Bracher, Sauer, Schulz, *Machtergreifung*, p. 719.

15. M. Broszat, 'Der Zweite Weltkrieg: Ein Krieg der "alten" Eliten, der Nationalsozialisten oder der Krieg Hitlers?', in M. Broszat and K. Schwalbe, eds, *Die deutschen Eliten und der Weg in den Zweiten Weltkrieg* (Munich, 1989), pp. 32ff.

16. M. Broszat, *Der Staat Hitlers* (Munich, 1969), ch. 3.

17. J. Caplan, *Government Without Administration* (Oxford, 1988), chs 1–4.

18. H. Mommsen, *Beamtentum im Dritten Reich* (Stuttgart, 1966), ch. 3.

19. H. Trevor-Roper, ed., *Hitler's Table Talk, 1941–44* (London, 1973), pp. 103–6, 373–7.

20. Caplan, *Government Without Administration*, p. 325; Broszat, *Staat Hitlers*, ch. 7.

21. K.-J. Müller, 'Staat und Politik im Denken Ludwig Becks', *Historische Zeitschrift* 215 (1972), pp. 607–31.

22. Mommsen, *Beamtentum*, p. 137.

23. M. Messerschmidt, 'Die Wehrmacht im NS-Staat', in K.D. Bracher, M. Funke and H.A. Jacobsen, eds, *Deutschland, 1933–1945: Neue Studien zur nationalsozialistischen Herrschaft* (Düsseldorf, 1992), p. 384.

24. K. Schönhoven, 'Der demokratische Sozialismus im Dilemma: Die Sozialdemokratie und der Untergang der Weimarer Republik', in W. Michalka, ed., *Die nationalsozialistische Machtergreifung* (Paderborn, 1984), pp. 74–84; H.A. Winkler, *Der Weg in die Katastrophe: Arbeiter und Arbeiterbewegung in der Weimarer Republik, 1930 bis 1933* (Berlin and Bonn, 1987), ch. 5.

25. P. Longerich, *Die braunen Bataillone: Geschichte der SA* (Munich, 1989).

26. M. Gallo, *Der schwarze Freitag der SA: Die Vernichtung des revolutionären Flügels der NSDAP durch Hitlers SS im Juni 1934* (Munich, 1972); H. Höhne, *Mordsache Röhm: Hitlers Durchbruch zur Alleinherrschaft, 1933–34* (Reinbek, 1984); Bracher, Sauer, Schulz, *Machtergreifung*, pp. 897ff.

27   Messerschmidt, 'Die Wehrmacht im NS-Staat', p. 386.

28. M. Jasmin, 'Das Ende der "Machtergreifung": Der 30. Juni 1934 und seine Wahrnehmung in der Bevölkerung', in Michalka, ed., *Machtergreifung*, pp. 207–19.

29. I. Kershaw, *The 'Hitler Myth': Image and Reality in the Third Reich* (Oxford, 1987).

30. Broszat, *Staat Hitlers*, pp. 353ff.; N. Frei, *National Socialist Rule in Germany: The Führer State, 1933–1945* (Oxford, 1993).

31. L. Gruchmann, *Justiz im Dritten Reich, 1933–1940: Anpassung und Unterwerfung in der Ära Gürtner*, 2nd edn (Munich, 1990).

32. J.W. Bendersky, *Carl Schmitt: Theorist for the Reich* (Princeton, NJ, 1983), p. 216.

33. W. Deist, 'Aufrüstung der Wehrmacht', in W. Deist, M. Messerschmidt, H.-E. Volkmann and W. Wette, *Ursachen und Voraussetzungen der deutschen Kriegspolitik*, vol. I of *Das Deutsche Reich und der Zweite Weltkrieg* (Stuttgart, 1979), p. 429.

34. Ibid., Messerschmidt, 'Aussenpolitik und Kriegsvorbereitung', pp. 623ff.

35. J.R.C. Wright, *Above Parties: The Political Attitudes of the German Protestant Church Leadership, 1918–1933* (Oxford, 1974).

36. U. von Hehl, 'Die Kirchen in der NS-Diktatur: Zwischen Anpassung, Selbstbehauptung und Widerstand', in Bracher, Funke and Jacobsen, eds, *Deutschland, 1933–1945*, pp. 160ff.

37. K.-M. Mallmann and G. Paul, 'Omniscient, Omnipotent, Omnipresent? Gestapo, Society and Resistance', in D.F. Crew, ed., *Nazism and German Society, 1933–1945* (London, 1994), pp. 166–96.

38. Broszat, 'Der Zweite Weltkrieg', in Broszat and Schwalbe, eds, *Die deutschen Eliten*, pp. 49–61; for the interpretation of Hitler's role, see G. Schreiber, *Hitler: Interpretationen, Ergebnisse, Methoden und Probleme der Forschung*, 2nd edn (Darmstadt, 1988); also R. Zitelmann, *Hitler: Selbstverständnis eines Revolutionärs* (Stuttgart, 1990).

39. D.C. Watt, *How War Came* (London, 1989), ch. 3; K.J. Müller, 'Deutsche Militär-Elite in der Vorgeschichte des Zweiten Weltkriegs', in Broszat and Schwalbe, eds, *Die deutschen Eliten*, pp. 271–90; D. Rebentisch, *Führerstaat und Verwaltung im Zweiten Weltkrieg, 1939–1945* (Stuttgart, 1989).

40. O. Bartov, *The Eastern Front, 1941–45* (London, 1985); also O. Bartov, 'Savage War', ch. VIII in M. Burleigh, ed., *Confronting the Nazi Past: New Debates on Modern German History* (London, 1996), pp. 125–39.

CHAPTER FIVE

German foreign policy in the Weimar Republic and the Third Reich, 1919–1945

IMANUEL GEISS

The historical background before 1918

It is a commonplace that the foreign policy of the Weimar Republic and the Third Reich has to be seen against the background of the Second German Empire.[1] Yet even the most obvious truism remains true, and most pedestrian commonplaces may offer common ground for historical analysis. After all, Germany in its three major formations between 1871 and 1945 – the Second and Third Reichs, with the Weimar Republic as an uneasy interregnum in between – has one great common denominator: the German Empire was a European Great Power, despite all its fluctuations in shape and strength, even the biggest power centre on the continent, even in the interlude of the Weimar Republic.

Germany: from power vacuum to power centre, 1198–1871

In historical perspective of power structures of the *longue durée*, the epoch of Germany as a first-class power centre was preceded by a much longer period as a relative power vacuum, from the beginning of the dynastic strife or civil war between the rival dynasties of the Welfs and Staufers in 1198 until 1871.[2] Before these almost 700 years of existence as a great power vacuum, the First German Roman Empire had started with its victory over the Hungarians near Augsburg in 955 and the Imperial coronation in Rome in 962 as the first power centre in western Europe of Roman–Latin persuasion and cultural affiliation. After 1198, Germany, without an effective central government and 'national' army, gradually became the battlefield for foreign powers, from the religious wars of 1545–1648 to the French Revolutionary and Napoleonic Wars of 1792–1815. Foreign powers had a powerful influence on shaping the destinies of the German power vacuum, ratified by international law through the peace instruments of Westphalia (1648) and Vienna (1815).

The First German (Holy Roman) Empire eroded into a kind of confederation (after 1648) of sovereign political entities, small and great, albeit with a formal head of state (the emperor), contrary to the theory of constitutional and international law. Yet after the Napoleonic intermezzo, which had ended the Old German Empire in 1806 in favour of the modern First French Empire, the German Confederation (*Deutscher Bund*) of 1815 carried on the tradition of the Old Reich in one respect: it was a loose confederation of sovereign states, now really without a common head of state and government, but in times of crisis theoretically with a federal army.

Yet the German power vacuum contained two Great Powers, Austria and Prussia, which cancelled each other out by internal rivalry for hegemony in Germany (the German 'dualism', 1740–1866) and, in the last analysis, also over Europe. After Napoleon's fall in 1814–15, the foreign Great Powers, in their turn, had blocked in horror demands of old-fashioned German Imperial patriots like Stein and Arndt to restore a new German Empire after victory over the French Napoleonic Empire: England, Russia and France saw that a newly united German Empire, fired by the revolutionary idea of modern nationalism, would emerge as a superpower in the centre of Europe.

In the long run, however, German unification became an elementary process and acquired an irresistible momentum of its own: in the age of industrial and national revolution, both converged in the making of 'national' markets and economies. Among the national questions erupting after 1789, the Germans constituted the biggest in terms of quantity (size of territory and population) and quality (education, economic power, modern infrastructures). In all innocence, they claimed their 'natural right' to have their own sovereign national state. The world after 1815 had not yet seen the explosive results – two world wars – which proved what could have been only vaguely feared before the actual experiences took place – that German unification would destroy any balance of power on the continent.

Structurally, German unity, despite obstacles erected by the Vienna settlement in constitutional and international law, proved irresistible. The logic of industrialization demanded wider, that is, national, markets and favoured nationalism, harping back to a 'glorious' Imperial past. Both conspired to negotiate any hurdles in a complex race for national unity and Imperial power: the German Customs Union (1834), the confused German Revolution of 1848–9, the three wars for founding the German Empire

(1864–71) were key stages in the progression from the German Confederation (1815) to the Second German Empire (1871).

The *großdeutsch–kleindeutsch* Dilemma

The options of 1848, however muddled at the time, become especially instructive in the light of history: the Frankfurt Paulskirche of 1848–9, in its first attempt to establish parliamentary government, foundered on several dilemmas that were insoluble by political (that is, peaceful) means. They remained as internal apriories of German policy, foreign and domestic: the dialectics of the rival concepts of the Greater and Lesser German solution (*großdeutsch–kleindeutsch*)[3] went much further than just answering the question of who would unite and lead Germany – Austria, the older, more cultured and more prestigious Imperial power, still with a sovereign titled Emperor, or the younger upstart, Prussia, more austere and militarily efficient, more dynamic and modern in economic terms thanks to the Rhineland, acquired in 1815.

Austrian leadership would have been more subtle internally, but with the instantly wider geographical impact of an Austrian Greater Germany on Europe. Prussian leadership, which carried the day in 1866 under Bismarck, would be, apparently, more modest in geographical terms, but more centralizing and compact internally. In the end, the dynamics of even Lesser Germany spilled over into Hitler's Greater Germany: as an Austria-born German he used the Lesser German Empire as a springboard to the Greater German Empire, fulfilling his own daydreams and those of millions of his compatriots.

After 1945 German democrats, bent on peace after the horrible experience of two world wars starting from Germany, fostered an illusion – that democracy and parliamentary government *per se* would have made for peace as a viable alternative to the volatile 'course of German history' (A.J.P. Taylor), from Vienna 1815 to Berlin 1945. 'Democrats', in the parlance of 1848–9 the most extreme partisans of the French Revolution, wanted to overthrow princes in Germany and replace them by a centralist unitarian republic on French Jacobin lines of the '*nation une et indivisible*'. The consequences would have been just as disastrous: internally, they would have produced a repressively assimilationist power structure, only in the name of progress and democracy; externally, German democrats from 1848–9 were, as a matter of course, Greater German in their outlook: Ferdinand Lasalle hoped that battalions of German workers in Constantinople would hoist the flag of Progress and Enlightenment to teach the Balkan peoples Civilization – *German* civilization.[4]

The net result of a victory for the German democrats in 1848–9 would have been the great final war with Tsarist Russia to liberate oppressed

Poland. Here they were in *unisono* with Mazzini and most liberals of the time, at least on the continent. During the Bulgarian crisis of 1885–7, the German united left (Social Democrats, left-wing liberals, Catholic Centre Party) tried to push old Bismarck over the brink into war against Russia, hopefully in alliance with Britain. In 1887 they were in sight, after all, of their ideal constellation of 1848 for their ideological Armageddon – war against Tsarist Russia.

Radical German democrats in 1848 actually did get their war, against middle-sized Denmark, and for this they bought up their first Imperial fleet (*Reichsflotte*), the abortive model for the Kaiser's battle fleet: both German Left and Right emerged as the heirs of the confused revolution of 1848–9. Historical mechanisms first became visible in and around the Frankfurt Paulskirche to govern the 'course of German history', as it were, from the underground of the German Empire, whatever its ideological guise.

The Bismarck factor: *Realpolitik* = war

With historical hindsight, and insight from the vantage point of 1848–9, appealing to the mystique and *Reichsherrlichkeit* of the First Empire, we can better understand what happened after the founding of the modern Second German Empire – the First World War, the Weimar Republic, the Third Reich, the Second World War. Bismarck only put his personal imprint on a long-term process that was well under way at the very day of his birth, 1 April 1815. Probably he was just the one political factor in the ferment of German unification who saw and accepted most clearly the logic of historical mechanisms at work, and who was most able to translate them into concrete *Realpolitik* – through war.[5]

Riding the prevailing current towards national and economic unity, Bismarck's one grand speculation as the very basis of his *Realpolitik* succeeded triumphantly: in 1862 he promised to see through the controversial reform of the Prussian army (which threatened to crash on the rocks of the left-wing liberal majority in the Lower House of the Prussian parliament) without a civil war and the overthrow of monarchy, both of which King Wilhelm I feared might happen as they had happened in England in the seventeenth century, including the beheading of the king. The trick was done by going behind the back of the Prussian parliament and obtaining a secret loan from the German Rothschilds to finance army reform plus the two wars against Denmark (1864) and Austria (1866). During the battle of Königgrätz, Bismarck carried a purse with gold and silver pieces to the value of about 25,000 marks in today's (2000) currency, ready to abscond from the battle-field to Switzerland if the Prussian army were to lose and he were to be found out as a grandiose political hazardeur.[6] But the Prussians won, for objective reasons that worked in their favour. The momentum of victory in 1866 propelled Bismarck to victory over France in 1870 and to German unity in 1871.

The German gambling tradition

Although Bismarck's discreet financial transactions remained unknown for a long time, his daring bid for power established in Germany a tradition of reckless political gambling. It became self-destructive if it operated without a safety net and the gamble did not come off. After 1871, the general conditions of power politics changed dramatically with Bismarck's very success: while German unification appeared to be in line with the current *Zeitgeist* when the winds blew into the sails of the young *Reich*, the proud Imperial ship ran into rough waters as it embarked on a course of imperialist expansion and *Weltpolitik*.[7]

Bismarck, never too sure how long his own creation would last, had, during the crisis over Bulgaria in 1885–7, confided to his state papers one of his startling insights:[8] since the great antagonism in the world at the time was that between England and Russia, over the Straits and Central Asia, Germany would be safe as long as she did not poke her nose out too far from her continental home. The implication is clear: if Germany were to expose herself too much, she might divert the main lines of tension to herself. That is exactly what happened after Bismarck with the Kaiser's *Weltpolitik*, which led to colonies overseas and a powerful battle fleet strong enough to challenge England. German imperialism had existed, however, in accordance with the desires of German liberalism, since at least 1848.[9]

From then onwards, German policy-makers piled up one daring gamble after another:

1. While Germany's continental base was too narrow, though broadened by the dual alliance with Austria–Hungary in 1879, the Habsburg monarchy was an ally of doubtful value with all her national minority problems. Austria–Hungary might be rent from inside if it faced pressure from outside *in extremis* as well: the Great War of all Great Powers. That constellation had been seen by Austrian statesmen in 1853–4: Austria, still reeling from the revolution of 1848–9, when only Russian intervention against the national revolution of Hungary had saved her, abstained from active participation in the Crimean War. The reasoning of Austrian statesmen in 1853–4 was breathtakingly sober

and realistic: whatever its outcome, the cost of war would have been fatally high for Austria – it would have meant ruin by national and social revolution.[10] Meanwhile, the situation had gone from bad to worse, in particular with the rise of the South Slav movement with its missionary zeal of little Serbia to bring down, as the spearhead for Tsarist Russia, the Ottoman and Habsburg Empires.

2. In order to plunge into a course of imperialist *Weltpolitik*, Germany had to maintain a first-class army against France and Russia *and* build a strong battle fleet against England as well. Though any German battle fleet would hardly be able to match the British fleet in terms of quantity (number of capital ships and heavy guns), Tirpitz hoped to be able to outdo it in terms of quality – superior technology, training and tactics.

3. The strategic gamble also became a financial one by the way it was paid for – not with higher taxes, but with loans to be honoured after a victorious war by war indemnities from the vanquished.

4. The next gamble appeared sound enough – to go it alone without an alliance on the global level (with either England or Russia) because, according to the logic of pre-1914 power politics, alliance with one would have meant war against the other.

5. Another gamble was to take over the Ottoman Empire as a continental outlet for *Weltpolitik* by modernizing its infrastructures and army, with the Baghdad railway as its future backbone of economic development. Germany only dislodged France and England from their traditional role of protecting the Ottoman Empire against Russian pressure on Constantinople.

6. A grandiose strategic gamble was the Schlieffen Plan of 1905. It staked everything on a series of two successive *blitz* offensives, against France and Russia, all within five months. It operated against France with a dozen ghost army corps that did not exist, put all reserve corps into the front line, risked, by marching through Belgium, war with England, and pretended that Russia's weakness, after defeat against Japan in 1904–5 and the First Russian Revolution of 1905–6, would go on indefinitely.

7. When the general staff saw that Russia did recover, after all, they panicked and pressed for a 'preventive war' against Russia (and France) just before Sarajevo (28 June 1914), before Russia would fully recover her military strength (which was expected by 1917).

8. During the First World War, unrestricted U-boat warfare and blowing Tsarist Russia out of the war through Lenin and the Bolsheviks were two more gambles with far-reaching consequences: the first brought America into the war, the second, by virtue of its very short-lived success, prepared conditions that Germany had to cope with in

different ways – as the Weimar Republic, the Third Reich, and the postwar Germanies until unification in 1990.

9. Ludendorff's final offensives from March to July 1918 banked on success before the full impact of America's war effort would destroy all chances of victory in the west.

10. When the spring offensive failed and the collapse of Bulgaria, Turkey and Austria–Hungary opened the flanks of the Reich for Allied offensives through Tyrol and Bohemia, Ludendorff hoped to forestall a political collapse of the Reich from inside after military defeat outside. He sought an instant armistice and commandeered parliamentary government into existence to appease Woodrow Wilson and the war-weary masses of Germany.

11. When all these final gambles failed, Ludendorff brusquely changed his mind and pleaded for war *à outrance* to the last ditch and last man, but this only provoked his dismissal and revolution, when sailors of the high sea fleet sabotaged a last sally against the home fleet in a Wagnerian *Götterdämmerung* mood *à la* Ludendorff.

The Weimar Republic, 1918/19–1933: a systematic approach

This *détour de force* was necessary to explain adequately the wild fluctuations of German foreign policy after the First World War. Many apparently contradictory details, but also structural differences between the Weimar Republic and the Third Reich, fall into place against the background of inherited dilemmas, historical mechanisms from the rise of the German Question after the demise of the First Empire in 1806[11] and the Vienna Settlement of 1815, plus the tradition of gambling after Bismarck's coming to power in 1862, which turned self-defeating with the German move to *Weltpolitik* and the acquisition of a battle fleet from 1896–8. Only then can it be better appreciated what the foreign policy of the Weimar Republic, conditioned by domestic policies and its exigencies, had in common with that of the Third Reich and where there were genuine differences in substance and methods.

Germany and the Versailles settlement

The harsh conditions of the Armistice and Versailles shattered German illusions about a lenient 'Wilson Peace', sued by a Germany that had turned suddenly to parliamentary government. The hour of truth came out of the blue for a German public that had been systematically deluded into cock-sureness by unrealistic war bulletins. In the race between concluding an Armistice from above, before revolution overthrew the *Ancien Régime*, and revolutionary war-weariness in the face of certain military defeat from below, revolution in Berlin on 9 November won two days before the Armistice.[12] The main result was the extreme right-wing 'stab-in-the-back'-legend: the otherwise ever victorious German army had been struck down by a sinister left-wing motley of socialists, pacifists and Jews, robbing Germany of victory against a 'world of enemies' at the last minute. It turned out to be the *pons asinus* into the Third Reich, because a look at the map could have debunked it even at the time: Germany's strategic position after the Armistice with Austria–Hungary on 3 November was hopeless against a certain Allied final offensive by the spring of 1919, through Tyrol into Bavaria and through Bohemia into Saxony. It would have ended in a result comparable to that of spring 1945 – *debellatio*, total defeat for the Reich.

However grim Versailles was in detail, compared with the certainty of total defeat if Germany had held on in November 1918, and with that of 1945, when the potentialities of 1918/19 became realities, the position of the Reich was strong: though she had lost border regions with mostly unwilling national minorities and was weakened in economic terms, Germany remained a Great Power in Europe, like France after the defeat of Napoleon I in 1815. In particular, Germany was largely surrounded by weak successor states to the south and east. But in contrast to high-flung hopes for a 'Greater Germany', as articulated by German war aims, both official and unofficial,[13] if Germany had won the war, subjective national depression after defeat was sharpened by objective postwar hardships – revolution, bouts of civil war, economic dislocation and inflation.

Such hangovers from defeat were common enough after a great war. German inflation had been started by the method of financing armament before and during the war itself – with loans, instead of higher taxes, especially on war profits. In order to get rid of the burden of internal debts accumulated by war loans, the German *Reichsbank* indulged in a policy that actually cultivated inflation: it gave out credits to industrialists, who repaid them in nominally the same sum in marks, although the sum had fallen massively in value due to galloping inflation: 'Mark equals Mark' (*Mark gleich Mark*) was the cynical recipe of the President of the *Reichsbank*, von Havenstein, by getting rid of state debts at the expense of the general public. It was a continuation of pre-war and wartime gambling by different means in times of peace, again with disastrous results: the German middle class was ruined by *inflation*, its political backbone finally broken by a kind of repeat performance during the Great Depression of 1929 with gruesome *de*flation.

Germany and Soviet Russia – common hostility to Poland

In dealing with vanquished Germany, the Allies had to face a grave dilemma, bequeathed to them by the German Lenin–Bolshevik gamble during the war itself: Britain and America softpedalled French demands for even harsher conditions on the Reich for fear that conquered Germany might turn to Bolshevism. This would have made the ideal constellation hoped for by Lenin – Russian quantity and German quality (industrialization) concerted by his leadership – and would have paved the way for the traditional Russian 'drive to the West', now under the ideological auspices of communism: world revolution, born from the (First) World War.

The worst (or best) case scenario did not materialize: Germany did preserve her sovereignty, with Western encouragement, by putting down all internal attempts at communist revolution *à la russe*. But as a compromise, she remained ideologically neutral towards the West, containing communism by the French *cordon sanitaire* between Soviet Russia and Germany. Also, Rapallo (1922) re-opened the German line to (now Soviet) Russia, just to spite the Western Allies and to encircle Poland. According to Machiavelli's principle – the neighbour is the natural enemy; hence the neighbour to the neighbour is the natural ally – Germany and Russia, the two greatest of the vanquished, resumed traditional cooperation against Poland, their common neighbour (and enemy).

After 125 years of being partitioned, Poland had been resurrected in the power vacuum left by the simultaneous fall of all three partitioning powers, Russia, Austria–Hungary and Germany. Close cooperation against hated Poland was the logical upshot: during the World Economic Conference in Genoa in April 1922, which was meant to find a permanent settlement for reparations, Germany and Soviet Russia sent delegations, but were not admitted to the proceedings. As a surprise to everyone, the two outcasts of the international community struck a bargain in nearby Rapallo: they recognized each other, established diplomatic and consular relations, mutually renounced any financial claims (reparations from Germany, repayment of pre-war loans from Russia) and pledged economic cooperation. Another furtive result was military cooperation against Poland, unhappily wedged between Germany and Russia.

Rapallo became a nightmare for the West, because it gave back to Germany a first taste of freedom of action, to play off West and East to her own advantage. Secret military cooperation gave Germany the chance to build and test weapons, forbidden under the terms of the Versailles treaty, hidden in the vast expanses of Soviet Russia. In exchange, Soviet generals learned the higher arts of strategy from the (officially forbidden) German general staff, lessons which their successors successfully turned against their former masters in the Second World War, after the German invasion of the Soviet Union in June 1941.

'Revising' Versailles

From the remarks about Germany under the shadow of defeat and Versailles and her stance towards the East (Soviet Russia and Poland) there emerges the great common denominator of German foreign policy between the two world wars – revising Versailles. To a certain extent, revising a regime imposed by a victorious coalition is normal practice: France had done it after the War of the Spanish Succession (1713–14) and the Napoleonic Wars (1814–15), Russia after the Crimean War (1856), Soviet Russia after 1918–19, joined by Fascist Italy after 1922 and Japan, who both felt their war efforts had not been sufficiently rewarded by territorial gains. But revising the Versailles settlement was a euphemism for *destroying* it. 'Freedom' for another 'resurrection' (*Wiederaufstieg*) of the German Empire meant freedom of action to resume what had been denied to Imperial Germany by the Great War, establishing her hegemony over Europe as a basis for aspiring to the status of a full-blown world power in her own right.

Yet here is the rub, as has been rightly stressed by the most recent and detailed German treatment of the policy of the German Reich in its three different phases between 1871 and 1945. For all the impressive continuities of aims and partly even of personnel from the First World War to the Second, to do justice to the Weimar Republic, there is one great difference: the Weimar Republic did, overall, want to revise Versailles by peaceful means, using economic power and diplomatic pressure towards Germany's east, while to the west frontiers were formally recognized and guaranteed by the Locarno treaties in 1925.[14] But Hitler, from the outset, wanted to do it through war, and he aimed at more than just going back to the frontiers of 1914, which had been widely felt to be too narrow in the First World War.

In other words, Weimar revision was to be peaceful *and* limited in scope. Nothing more than regaining the territories in the east lost to Poland was the overall aim. Of course, we do not know what would have happened if the Weimar Republic had succeeded. Thus, it is useless to speculate whether it would have been satisfied with such gains, or whether it would have drifted into the same inexorable momentum of what the ancient Greeks called *pleionexia* – power calls for more power, as did Hitler after 1933. A less charitable interpretation of the link between the foreign policy of the Weimar Republic and the Third Reich could see the latter as the logical result of the frustration felt by the former over not achieving its ends (revision in the east) by incongruous means (peaceful revision), without being willing to give up the fatal juxtaposition of conflicting ends and means.

Furthermore, adamant Polish resistance to any territorial revision in favour of Germany would eventually confront Germany with the same dilemma that the Federal Republic had to face before and after unification in 1990 – the discrepancy between forward-looking aims that could only be achieved through war to change the frontiers of 1919 and 1945, but professing to do so only by peaceful means. The day would come when the incongruous combination of (offensive) aims and (defensive) methods would have to be resolved one way or the other: after the First World War Germany did it by going to war in 1939, after the Second by recognizing the frontiers of 1945, first de facto by the new German *Ostpolitik* of the Social Democrat–liberal coalition under Willy Brandt in 1970–2, which was ratified by international treaties, and then by the unification of Germany in 1990.

From Lesser to Greater Germany: the *Anschluß*

Yet however limited and peace-loving the Weimar Republic may have been in its territorial revisionism towards her east, in the end she came dangerously close to positions that would lead straight into the Third Reich. The central issue was the *Anschluß*, arising from the difference between *kleindeutsch* and *großdeutsch* – 'Lesser Germany' under Prussian leadership, 'Greater Germany' under Austrian hegemony, with or without her non-German territories. In the tradition of the Frankfurt Paulskirche of 1848–9, practically all Germans were *großdeutsch*-minded after the First World War. In that respect, there was no essential difference between Right and Left.

Since the dissolution of the Habsburg monarchy in 1918, however, *großdeutsch* had acquired a new meaning, subtle in content as apparently just a minor modification, but shattering in its consequences: with the demise of the Habsburg monarchy, *großdeutsch* no longer meant unification of Germany under Austrian leadership, at least collectively, although, with a remarkable twist of historical irony, the *Großdeutsch Reich* in 1938 was, in fact, headed by a *Führer* hailing from Austria who introduced a German adaptation of the Roman salute (*römischer Gruß*). At the turn of 1918–19, *großdeutsch* could only mean refuge to the Germans of Austria (and the fringe of Bohemia and Moravia) seeking *Anschluß* in the Lesser German Reich.

Despite the territorial losses imposed by Versailles, this would have amounted to a 'mini-Greater German solution',[15] the unification of 'Lesser Germany' only with the German territories of Austria, as preferred by patriots from 'Lesser Germany' in 1848 and briefly realized by Hitler in 1938 with the *Anschluß* proper of Austria plus the Sudetenland. The most reduced of all 'Greater German' solutions would have soothed the wounds of the German nation in 1918–19, but it was utterly unrealistic and promptly blocked by the Allies. From then on, the ban against the *Anschluß* rankled deep in the German mind and became another opening for the Austrian-born Hitler on his way to power in the Reich, first Lesser, then Greater German.

Foreign policy of the Weimar Republic: a chronological approach, 1918–1933

Following these structural observations, the sequence and consequences of the Republic's foreign policy after the November 1918 revolution can be explained within the historical context and continuities from Second to Third Reich. But first, the Weimar Republic had to consolidate and clear the debris of world war, defeat and revolution inside *and* outside its borders. Only then could it pursue more ambitious aims. Links between foreign and domestic policy are particularly close during the Weimar Republic: success in foreign policy was eagerly sought to stabilize the unpopular Republic. Deadlock in foreign policy often provoked serious political and government crises which were overcome only through the creation of a new coalition government. The critical issue of Weimar foreign policy remained Versailles.

The burden of Versailles

In November 1918 the provisional government, the Council of People's Commissioners (*Rat der Volksbeauftragten*), quickly broke off diplomatic relations with Soviet Russia when it found out that the Russian communists were trying to do to the German revolutionary government what the Kaiser's government had done so disastrously successfully with the Russian provisional republican government – to overthrow it by supplying arms, money and advice to German communists.

While putting down communist uprisings that imitated the Russian model of revolution, the most pressing business for the young Republic in postwar revolutionary turmoil was to get the best terms possible from the victorious Allies. Berlin could not do much directly, because Germany was not admitted to the peace congress. The peace terms caught Germany utterly unprepared, and it was only under Allied threats to renew war, and after severe crisis, that a new government and the National Assembly accepted the peace treaty, but under protest and with reservations. In the heated atmosphere, no rational debate about causes and effects of German policies in the past took place. That became possible only after the even harsher lessons of defeat in the Second World War and with the growing distance in time and mental detachment in the democratic Federal Republic.

Particularly sore points, apart from territorial losses and the ban on the *Anschluß*, were the 'war guilt clause' (article 231 of the Versailles treaty) and the reduction of the *Reichswehr* to just 100,000 men. Both had a disruptive impact on domestic developments: many of the soldiers and officers dismissed joined the half-regular 'Free Corps' for suppressing internal, communist-inspired uprisings and Soviet republics in Munich and Bremen. They also acted against Poles in Upper Silesia and against Bolsheviks in the Baltics, where they wanted to regain new *Lebensraum* as colonizing farmers. The Free Corps thus became the great reservoir for Hitler's SA and his hand-picked elite unit, the SS. Official and unofficial struggle against the 'war guilt lie' (*Kriegsschuldlüge*), as it was polemically called, always served as a spearhead for 'revising' Versailles, by 'proving' German innocence in starting the First World War.[16]

Reparations and inflation

Reparations, in both kind and money, were a constant heavy burden. The Weimar Republic, of course, tried to get Allied claims reduced and was, by and large, successful.[17] But at every stage of negotiations, Allied demands and initial German refusal provoked a severe government crisis in Germany. In the first years, usually a new government, after the resignation of its predecessor, had to shoulder the load, under Allied threats.

The peace treaty had not set any limit on reparations, because war damages were literally immense. When the Allied Reparations Commission did settle on a fixed limit in January 1921 (269,000 million goldmarks), Berlin refused. Three cities in western Germany were occupied as a reprisal (Düsseldorf, Duisburg and Ruhrort). The London Ultimatum of 5 May 1921 reduced the bill to 132,000 million goldmarks spread over 37 years, including a 25 per cent levy on German export proceeds. Germany gave in, under the threat of the Allies occupying the whole Ruhr area and renewing the blockade.

The heavy financial load of reparations contributed to the rise in German inflation. But by and large, German hyperinflation was home-made.

Politically, Germany was thrown into utter confusion by hyperinflation until late 1923, torn by a first period of polarization between extreme Left and Right: the communists staged regional and local uprisings in order to over-throw the weak Weimar Republic, while the young National Socialist Party under Hitler had its first upsurge in Bavaria, until it collapsed, after Hitler's Beer Hall Putsch on 8–9 November 1923 in Munich had failed. With the introduction of the new *Rentenmark* in November 1923 and the Dawes Plan in 1924, the German economy recovered and the Weimar Republic con-solidated, pushing back the extremist parties in the second general election of December 1924.

Stresemann and interim consolidation, 1923–1929

In the period of extreme internal polarization, Germany was paralysed in its foreign policy. From the turmoil Gustav Stresemann, with his right-wing liberal Deutsche Volkspartei (DVP), emerged as a leading political figure, first as chancellor of a 100-day 'grand coalition', which broke the internal deadlock and paved the way to financial, economic and political con-solidation. As chancellor of a grand coalition from the SPD to the DVP, Stresemann called off the costly passive resistance campaign against France over the Ruhr, ended inflation by a currency reform, dissolved the SPD–KPD governments of Saxony and Thuringia through the *Reichswehr* and weathered the crisis provoked by Hitler's abortive 'March to Berlin'. The end of paralysing political polarization made the currency reform effective. Stresemann dominated German foreign policy until his death at the end of 1929, just before the Wall Street Crash led to the great slump. As foreign minister in successive governments he gave German foreign policy consist-ency and continuity. He steered a course of reconciliation at least with the West, sanctioned by the Locarno Treaties of 1925.

In its turn, the new *Reichsmark* made the Dawes Plan possible in April 1924, which gave a sound financial basis to the Stresemann policies: German reparations were further reduced and Germany received 800 million in American credits to enable her to meet her reparations commitments by restarting industrial productivity. France agreed to withdraw her troops from the Ruhr area by July 1925. The Locarno Treaties cut German losses in the west by mending fences with France and Belgium, guaranteeing the frontiers of Versailles with Germany's two western neighbours. Germany adhered to the League of Nations in 1926, even as a Great Power with a permanent seat on the Council of the League.

But Germany expressly reserved the right to revise her eastern frontiers with Poland and Czechoslovakia. Stresemann also wanted to hold open the option of regaining German territories in the east because, as an outflow of even moderate revisionism, Germany denied similiar guarantees to Poland and Czechoslovakia. The rejection of an 'Eastern Locarno' became an ominous signpost to a more sinister future.

A third consequence emerged as a compromise between Germany joining the Western Powers wholesale and Soviet efforts to keep Germany from going west, i.e. to Locarno: the Soviet Foreign Minister Tschitscherin even tried to lure Stresemann into an outright alliance in order to reduce Poland to her 'ethnic borders', in other words to shear Poland of her eastern and western belts with heavy non-Polish minorities – Germans to the west, Lithuanians, White Russins, Ukrainians to the east. Stresemann flatly refused. But after Locarno, the Berlin Treaty with the Soviet Union of 1926 struck a precarious balance of German relations with the West and (communist) East, while ignoring Poland: Germany assured her neutrality, if the Soviet Union got involved in war with third powers, without being clearly the aggressor. What it meant was the Soviet fear that Germany might join another war of intervention, under the auspices of the League of Nations. The Western Powers gave Germany a free hand to assuage Soviet suspicions.

Locarno in 1925 and the Berlin treaty in 1926 together reflected the difficult situation of the Reich between the West and the Soviet Union. But the hostility of Poland's two great neighbours towards the hated 'seasonal state' persisted, as did secret military cooperation against Poland. In 1926 Stresemann even began a customs war in order to force Poland to cede territories in her west to Germany. In spite of economic dislocation, Poland held on and the German customs war failed to achieve its aim.

Further economic consolidation was to be achieved by the Young Plan of 1929. It replaced the Dawes Plan by further reducing German reparations and spreading them to annual payments until 1988. It also provided for yet another international loan, to enable German payments, and for the evacuation of the Rhineland by French troops in 1930, five years before the date set by the Versailles Treaty. Finally, international controls on German railways and the *Reichsbank* were lifted.

However beneficial the Young Plan may have been in economic terms, its best intentions were defeated by the great slump later in 1929. Perhaps even more ominously, it once more polarized Germany politically, even at the (apparent) high point of economic consolidation. Both the communists and the extreme Right, conservative German nationalists and Hitler's Nazi Party, opened a concerted campaign of bitter hostility, denouncing the Young Plan and the Weimar Republic. Internal polarization even inaugurated the agony of the Weimar Republic, while radicalizing its course of foreign policy, just before the great slump. In particular, right-wing agitation turned out to be the beginning of internal escalation, which swept Hitler into power only four years later. Although the extreme Right failed in its campaign for a referendum to raise enough votes against the Young Plan, it did provide a first public stage for Hitler and his party and made him respectable to wider circles within the German middle classes.

Post-Stresemann foreign policy: from slump to Hitler, 1929–1933

The decisive breakthrough for Hitler came with the great slump in October 1929. It almost coincided with Stresemann's death. Under the pressure of the slump and of Hitler's meteoric rise, the foreign policy of his successors became largely an instrument for scoring some 'success' abroad in order to survive politically at home. The net result was also a rapid drift to the right in foreign policy. Key issues remained: reparations as an inexorable *continuum*, *Anschluß*, disarmament. All of them were linked to each other in one way or another.

The last grand coalition, this time under an SPD chancellor, Hermann Müller, survived the slump by only five months. The authoritarian governments of Brüning (March 1930–May 1932) tackled all three subjects at about the same time, but with only limited success. At the height (or depth) of the slump in 1931, Brüning did achieve a moratorium for German reparation payments, through the mediation of the USA. But the Hoover Moratorium was cancelled out by the disastrous effects of home-made deflation and growing unemployment.

In 1931, the German plan for a customs union with Austria, which suffered even more from the slump, was to relieve the economic burdens of both by providing a larger common market and to bind the wounds of German national pride. As was to be expected, the *Zollunion* immediately raised in France the spectre of *Anschluß*, which, indeed, it was to prepare in economic terms. The customs union project, therefore, promptly provoked the French veto, in accordance with the Versailles Treaty. Instead of strengthening the Brüning government by a success in the touchy field of foreign policy, its failure only weakened the outgoing Weimar Republic and increased German resentment against Versailles and the West.

Ambitious sights were set far beyond little Austria: Hungary, Czechoslovakia, Yugoslavia and Romania might be attracted into the economic orbit of the Reich, reaching out even to the Baltic countries.[18] A German-dominated economic bloc under the cloak of *Mitteleuropa* could throw its weight against then isolated Poland and force her to yield to German revisionist pressures on her western frontiers. After that, the weight of a 'mid-European' economic union under German leadership could do the same against France, all with the aim of renewing, somehow or other, German *Weltpolitik* on a global scale. This, at least, was the concept of the secretary of state in the German *Auswärtiges Amt*, von Bülow, as officially outlined to the German ambassador in Paris in January 1931. Von Bülow was also the most energetic (hidden) protagonist of the German struggle against the 'war guilt lie'.[19]

The change after Stresemann became manifest when his successor as German foreign minister, Julius Curtius, also coming from Stresemann's right-wing liberal DVP, rejected out of hand Briand's plan for a European union, closely linked to the League of Nations.[20] True, Briand's plan would have established French hegemony on the continent by also freezing the territorial status quo in the east. That became the main reason for Germany's killing the whole plan without any further discussion.

The momentum rejecting Briand's European project carried the Weimar Republic even further to the right. Not satisfied with blocking any return to French hegemony on the continent, the Brüning government aimed at putting German hegemony in its place, however camouflaged by economic means. Brüning himself turned more and more anti-French, compensating for the new turn by cultivating relations with England, America and the Soviet Union. Internally, the *Reichswehr* pressed for German unilateral rearmament, to the point of breaking with Brüning and contributing massively to his downfall in the spring of 1932.

Rapid deterioration of the world economic crisis in 1931 also made reparations more urgent than ever before. Politically, the rise of Hitler's Nazi Party and the growing communist agitation conjured up the danger of political collapse, both of the Brüning authoritarian government and of Weimar itself. Brüning used his (realistic) worst case scenario of breakdown of the political centre and of some kind of Bolshevik–Nazi chaos in Germany to blackmail America into the Hoover Moratorium in 1931. By suspending the payment of international financial commitments, including war debts, it also suspended German reparations for a year. But Brüning aimed at getting rid of reparations altogether thereafter.

Meanwhile, the German Foreign Office speculated on profiting from Japan's aggression in the Far East against Manchuria in late 1931, which would weaken the League of Nations. It was almost a return to the continuities of Wilhelmenian gambling, banking again on war elsewhere (in the Far East) and, this time, speculating *à la baisse*, on economic collapse at home in order to justify new armaments.[21] The great slump thus encouraged German leaders to return to a policy of extreme national egotism, seeking German hegemony once again at any cost and not shirking conflict with her neighbours. They themselves raised the chronic problem of any German national state – 'its compatibility with Europe'.[22] In other words, a united

Germany would be too big and powerful for Europe and any European balance of power if Germany refused to let herself be integrated in the service of Europe.

Within such long-term structural perspectives, Weimar foreign policy in its last year appears just as an exercise in playing into the hands of Hitler, the more so since continuities of leading personnel from the Weimar Republic (and, indeed, from Imperial Germany) to the Third Reich is impressive and depressing enough. In any case, reparations, disarmament and unilateral rearmament were consciously joined to one explosive package deal: 'equality in security' (*Gleichheit der Sicherheit*) became the slick slogan to veil Germany's intention to let general disarmament crash on the rocks of German ambition and French suspicion, and then rearm unilaterally.

When Germany tried to get rid of reparations once and for all, she had a better case: the instalments of the Young Plan had banked on continuous economic growth. After only a few months, the great slump smashed all illusions, and in 1931 the Beneduce Report concluded from the catastrophic shrinking of the world economy that international liabilities had to be adapted to the new situation. The upshot was an International Conference on Reparations at Lausanne in mid-1932, where Germany theoretically achieved the end of reparations. The success came too late for Brüning: he fell under the growing pressure from the extreme Right before the conference even met.

In February 1932, an International Disarmament Conference was to bring an equivalent step forward for the official German line, but Brüning could only call for German 'equality in security', without any substantial effect. Under Brüning's successor, von Papen, Germany withdrew unilaterally from the disarmament conference on 23 July 1932, because French fears of German unilateral rearmament were too strong for her to agree to general disarmament. Although England, France and Italy conceded German equality later that year during the Lausanne Disarmament Conference on 11 December 1932, the emphasis, under German insistence, had fatally shifted – from *dis*armament to general, though internationally controlled, *re*armament. Another obstacle to the Second World War had been removed, with Hitler waiting in the wings, yet already throwing a long shadow on the foreign policy of the dying Weimar Republic.

The last chancellor of the Weimar Republic, General von Schleicher, was in office too briefly, from December 1932 to January 1933. Just as his audacious plans to find a new political basis without civil war at home quickly evaporated, so his idea of courting the Soviet Union to better balance correct relations with the West also came to nothing. But in changed conditions: Schleicher's flirtation with the communist East turned out to be another link in the German tradition of playing off East and West, exploiting Germany's position between the democratic West and the communist East.

151

The Third Reich, 1933–1945:
a systematic approach

Hitler's coming to power in early 1933 makes any analysis and assessment of German foreign policy under his direction much simpler: compared with the sometimes intriguing complexities of Weimar foreign policy, Hitler's aim was straightforward – war. One may even question the use of the phrase 'foreign policy', if Hitler's overriding aim was another world war.

Hitler's 'will' to the Second World War:
break and continuities

Much unnecessary confusion exists about Hitler's and Nazi Germany's drive for war due to muddled thinking. When one is talking about 'war guilt' in relation to any war, one has to make careful distinctions on two levels, which, in historical reality, interact with each other in a dialectical way. On the one hand between various stages of war, in the case of the two world wars between local, continental and world war;[23] on the other hand the *will* to start consciously the one or the other stage and merely *causing* higher stages of war. In other words, one has also to distinguish intent and effect.[24] Thus, Germany in 1914 willed local war, because she thought that Austria–Hungary might swiftly dispatch little intransigent Serbia. Berlin accepted the risk of a continental war against Russia and France because she thought she would win such a still limited war, even against her biggest continental neighbours. Only war with Britain was unwelcome, because Germany stood no chance of winning a real world war. It is useless to claim (or disclaim) that one or the other side *'willed'* war, in abstract and empty generalities. Instead it becomes necessary for any sober analysis to distinguish between intention and causing war on the one hand, and stages of war (local, continental, world) on the other.

Thus, Germany had the greatest share of responsibility for bringing about the First World War, while other powers had their own share, for example Serbia, who wanted to bring down Austria–Hungary, one way or the other, in order to erect her Greater Serbian Yugoslav Empire on the ruins of the Habsburg monarchy, as she had grown by ruining the Ottoman Empire through the two Balkan wars of 1912–13.

By the same token, it is mere moralizing, without any value for historical scholarship, to blame Hitler for *'willing'* the Second World War. No one in his senses *'willed'* a second world war, especially after the experience of the First World War. And even Hitler was not so foolish as to consciously launch a second world war, because he could not win it, just as no one can win a war against the rest of the world. Rather Hitler had 'learned' his lesson from the German failure in the First World War by following a diplomatic line that tried to evade the escalation into another regular world war by keeping the level of war commitment for Germany as low as possible.

Hitler and Göring had speculated that the West would continue its appeasement indefinitely. They preferred to isolate future victims and bring them down through threats of war, only to resort to war if necessary, and to keep war localized as far as possible. The master formula was, as Nazi propaganda in the first two years of the Second World War gloated, that Hitler, in his great wisdom, had avoided the dreaded war on two fronts – until 22 June 1941.

Hitler's magic wand worked well enough in the beginning, as long as victims of his aggression were small, weak, easy to isolate and lay within the pale of seemingly justified German revisionism. Then he could skilfully exploit the guilt complex of liberal minds in the Anglo-Saxon world, who felt that Germany had been unjustly treated in 1919 and therefore had a point in revising the Versailles Settlement. But the more 'successful' Hitler was in his early years, including the *Anschluß* of Austria and of the Sudeten Germans in Czechoslovakia, the sooner he reached the boundaries of what had become Western appeasement. Once Nazi Germany overstepped the invisible line between appeasement and resistance, she also breached the border between war and peace when risking a next step towards Greater German aggrandisement. Prague and Poland in 1939 were the two critical steps that made war inevitable – the Second World War, because war on a lower level was no longer to be localized.

That is why Hitler and his closest associates were aghast at the British declaration of war on 3 September 1939 and horrified by the prospect of another world war, but by then it was too late, and they were careful to hide their realistic fears of losing the war from the Germans and the world at large. The collapse of Hitler's policy of localized blackmail and aggrandisement heralded certain defeat. Yet Hitler used and risked war as an instrument for achieving his ends – German hegemony over Europe, one way or another.

At every step, Hitler tried to limit and minimize risks, to keep war, ideally for him and his Third Reich, on a level well below a general conflagration, by isolating his next victim. When he did follow in the footsteps of the Kaiser, the Führer doomed his Third Reich. Therefore, one must always be careful to distinguish between Hitler's *will* to war on levels below that of a second world war, and his overwhelming responsibility for unleashing it, much against his tactical and opportunistic grains. This fine difference does not make Hitler and his disastrous policy any better. But it is closer to historical realities and could help to defeat any paläo- or neo-Nazi apologetic excuses, half-lies and lies.

Given Hitler's general will for war, all his otherwise confusing tactical tricks and opportunistic changes make sense. The apparent paradox of conflicting images for assessing the general character of German foreign policy from 1933 onwards also dissolves and gives way to a sinister consistency. On the one hand, Hitler's foreign policy is described as a 'revolution' (by Hildebrand); on the other, it was just another step in a flight of German continuities. In fact, it was both at the same time – both 'revolution', in the sense of a brusque break with the 'feeble' Weimar past, *and* continuity, all in a complex dialectical relationship between various factors of German foreign policy, each of which have to be analysed in the light of their own intrinsic contexts. It all depends on the point of view from which one looks at the one or the other aspect of German foreign policy after 1933.

The state of Europe in 1933

A historical *tour d'horizon* in 1933, taking future developments into consideration, becomes necessary to better understand why Nazi Germany could emerge with such relative ease and breathtaking speed as the *großdeutsche* superpower on the European continent within just a few years.

Hitler could reap many fruits from the Weimar Republic, particularly as Germany's position even after Versailles had been much more favourable in terms of traditional power politics. Leaving aside the well-known complaints of Germany against the Versailles regime, Germany was, by 1933, stronger than ever, despite the economic havoc caused by the ravages of hyperinflation in 1922–3 and the great slump of 1929. With the dissolution of Austria–Hungary and Tsarist Russia, followed by the retirement of a territorially reduced and ideologically isolated Soviet Union, Germany was surrounded by weak smaller states and one middling power (Poland), except in the west, where France was still trying to re-establish *her* hegemony over the continent. The Anglo-Saxon powers had withdrawn from the continent more (USA) or less (Britain), the latter in renewing her long-standing historical rivalries with France.

Thus, Europe was again in a situation like the one that had existed after the Crimean War (1853–6), when Russia and Britain had largely withdrawn from the continent for reasons at home (reforms) and abroad (imperial expansion) and left France in awkward isolation, confronted alone with the terrible German Question. Now France was again all but isolated, facing the German giant. After 1856, Germany had become the Second Reich in 1871; in 1933, after the interregnum of the Weimar Republic, the

Third Reich started off as *kleindeutsch*, but grew within five years to become *großdeutsch*.

It was cold comfort for France to have picked up, from the debris of both Tsarist Russia and Habsburg Austria–Hungary, a motley of post-imperial successor states, as a meagre compensation for the Russian alliance lost through the October Revolution 1917 (with discreet German help). Structural reasons both internal (heterogeneous 'national' states, which tried to homogenize their sundry peoples by a centralist and assimilationist state *à la française*) and external (rivalries with neighbouring 'national' successor states) kept the new eastern European successor states too weak to fulfil three functions at a time – balancing, for France, German power, in place of Russia; keeping Germany and the Soviet Union apart; acting as a *cordon sanitaire* to contain communism. Instead, with the growing power of both Nazi Germany and Soviet Russia, the new states were crushed by and between the two giants, once they had recovered from their momentary paralysis after defeat and revolution. By doing so, the two totalitarian powers absorbed the buffer states between them as their satellite or client states, first Nazi Germany, then, after the Second World War as the upshot of Nazi Germany's 'foreign policy', the Soviet Union.

Only Yugoslavia resisted and had to be conquered by one of the German *Blitzkrieg* campaigns early on in the Second World War. She liberated herself largely on her own from German occupation in 1944–5, was never an outright satellite state of the Soviet Union, and was the first to break away from the Soviet Empire in 1948. But at the end of the Cold War she broke up in a welter of blood, murder, massacres and ethnic cleansing, while the other post-communist successor states are turning, more or less successfully, to the West, largely intact as national states (with the exception of Czechoslovakia).

Even the Western powers did not act in unison. Both England and France were largely paralysed by internal problems in societies that continued to suffer from shell shock, each with traumatic symbolic names of their own – Verdun for the French, Passchendaele for the British. They were war-weary, abhorred the idea of another great war, let themselves drift into the rot of wishful thinking, and thus rallied only when it was too late to save peace by more appeasement. Britain was plagued with a guilty conscience at having treated Germany too roughly in Versailles; France was about equally split between a Right that preferred Hitler to a Jewish socialist prime minister (Léon Blum) in a Popular Front government, and a Left whose extreme left wing, the strong Communist Party, followed Stalin in all his tactical twists to the point of refusing to join a national front against Hitler's Germany after the German–Soviet Pact against Poland of 23 August 1939 that opened the Second World War.

In any case, on the basis of the foreign policy of the Weimar Republic, Hitler carried on and reaped much of its 'achievements' by outdoing it, changing its quality of *limited and peaceful* revisionism into overthrowing Versailles, eventually through war. In its final year, the dying Weimar Republic had bequeathed to Hitler both the drastic revision of the burden of reparations and, at least theoretically, equality of Germany in the realm of (re)armament, symbolized by Lausanne and Geneva (1932). But what rankled most in the German mind was that no territorial revision, including the *Anschluß*, was even in sight. It was here that Hitler scored his most dazzling and daring early 'successes'. They were, however, of the stuff of which the famous Delphic oracle was made, which apparently promised King Kroisos of Lydia before his war against Kyros that by crossing the Halys he would destroy 'a great empire'. In fact, Hitler's Pyrrhic victories, to change the classical image, were self-destructive for the (Third) German Empire.

The Third Reich: a chronological approach, 1933–1945

Having cleared up the muddle about Hitler willing or not willing a whole second world war, it becomes easier to retrace the breathtaking course of his foreign policy. Although he was 44 when he became chancellor in 1933, he was always the young man in a hurry.

The general aim – super-empire and World Power

The Führer's overall aim was to raise Germany to the status of a World Power, just as the Kaiser had done: 'Germany will either become a World Power or it will not be', as Hitler himself wrote in *Mein Kampf* as early as 1925.[25] Hitler's Third Reich, therefore, amounted to Germany's second 'bid for world power' (Fritz Fischer) within one generation. Summing up continuities from the Second to the Third Reich, however modified by the Weimar Republic, Hitler even revived the Wilhelmenian tradition of daring gambles with a vengeance. His Third Reich was a collective mega-gamble, and its foreign policy plus military strategic planning for and during the Second World War contained a series of gambles that came off at first but later failed miserably and led to utter defeat. Also in that respect, Hitler with his foreign policy was the perfect embodiment of continuity from Second to Third Reich.

Himmler's and Hitler's *Großgermanisches Reich Deutscher Nation* (Greater Teutonic Empire of the German Nation) was a preposterously inflated racist modernization of the Old 'Holy Roman Empire of the German Nation', the First German Empire. As a maxi-Greater German Empire on the continent of Europe, it was to absorb all or most of its smaller neighbours and the minor powers, and to crush both the middling powers (Poland) and the great ones (France, Soviet Russia). The real enemy was communism, organized on a state level in the Soviet Union. For reasons of ideology and power politics, conquest of the USSR became the final or crowning object of Hitler's dazzling gamble. It apparently had two 'advantages' to offer – more *Lebensraum* for (allegedly) crammed-in Germans to 'colonize' the 'Slav East' on an imperial scale, and the chance to cash in on widespread aversion to the rigours of Stalin's (equally, but differently) totalitarian regime.

Yet, since the resurrection of Poland after the First World War, Germany had no common frontier with the Soviet Union. Therefore, at least with historical hindsight, Hitler's foreign policy after 1933 emerges as an attempt to clear the decks for the final showdown against the 'Jewish–Bolshevik world conspiracy', the world enemy no. 1 of the Nazi *Weltanschauung*. For this Hitler had to 'improve' Germany's strategic position, first to the east in 'peace' (Poland 1934), then to the west (Saarland 1935, Rhineland 1936), then east again (Austria, Sudetenland 1938, Prague 1939), then through war (Poland 1939, the west 1940, the south-east 1941), in order to be able to invade the Soviet Union. But he hoped to keep Britain out by some global arrangement – graciously 'guaranteeing' her Empire and Commonwealth.

If this was not, perhaps, Hitler's conscious intention from the start, at least that was the overwhelming effect of German 'foreign policy' until the German attack on the Soviet Union on 22 June 1941. Within that concept, Hitler's tactical opportunism knew no bounds. That objective historical effect is enough to serve as a guiding-line through the maze of Hitler's tactical zigzagging.

Preparing the ground for future expansion, 1933–1935

When Hitler came to power in Germany, his position in Europe was both relatively strong and weak. Despite the great slump, Germany had re-covered during the Weimar Republic to an astonishing degree and had already started on her strategy of using her still enormous economic power to dislodge France from south-east Europe, or *Mitteleuropa*. One pillar of the Versailles system would be eroded, the French *cordon sanitaire* and Litte Entente involving Czechoslovakia, Rumania and Yugoslavia. On the other hand, the Third Reich met with widespread suspicion. Poland's President Pilsudski even considered, for a while in 1933, a preventive war against Germany, in order to nip German aggression in the bud before it could flower and bear poisonous fruit. But since France rejected any such idea, nothing came of it. And Pilsudski, in his last year, even made a brusque turnabout and struck a spectacular deal with Hitler in January 1934.

A few days after becoming chancellor, Hitler told his *Reichswehr* generals in secret what he thought of the future. He was still uncertain, but what he actually said was clear enough, borne out as it was by events: 'Perhaps gaining new export chances by force (*Erkämpfung*), perhaps – and probably better – conquest of new *Lebensraum* and its reckless (*rücksichtslos*) Germanisation.'[26] But until the new *Wehrmacht* was built up, there were 'dangerous times ahead': in other words (relative) military weakness would require some diplomatic restraint abroad for a while.

Thus, Hitler indulged profusely in 'peace' overtures in order to buy time for consolidating his regime inside and rearming outside. The establishment of the one-party system was astonishingly quick, suspending the Weimar Constitution and superimposing on its political structures those of his one-party state with dictatorial power. The phase of internal consolidation was 'crowned' in a set-up that was, theoretically, still republican. After the death of President Hindenburg on 2 August 1934, Hitler also declared himself *Reichspräsident*, without any election to legitimize what was, in fact, a *coup d'état*, and he made all the military forces, *Reichswehr* and *Kriegsmarine*, swear an oath of *personal* loyalty to him.

Hitler's 'foreign policy' was dictated by the universal logic of power politics, geography and territorial conditions laid down at Versailles. First internal political unity, then rearming without arousing hostile suspicions abroad, then expanding in a piecemeal fashion, following the path of least resistance, i.e. against weakest and smallest objects first, keeping up appearances of moral respectability as long as was necessary and possible.

Even during internal consolidation until 1934 and in the following year, Hitler was able, by sheer 'luck' and blatant opportunism, to score his first successes in foreign policy, covered by the formalities of international law. Two were situated in a sphere of transition, where domestic and foreign factors overlapped. The Concordat with the Vatican on the national level of the Reich (*Reichskonkordat*, in contrast to former treaties on the level of the *Länder*) had been holding fire during the Weimar Republic. Hitler concluded it within a few months, on 20 July 1933, reaping political benefits on two fronts. Internally, it turned out for him as a god-sent, elegant way to neutralize the catholic Centre Party and to drive it into disbanding on its own, as other non-Marxist political parties had been doing under government duress. Externally, the new Third Reich achieved a measure of international respectability bestowed from the highest places.

Another step was Hitler's decision to leave the League of Nations in November 1933, using the alleged denial of 'equality' in disarmament/ rearmament as an excuse. Hitler even had the effrontery to get his move endorsed by the first of his plebiscites on foreign policy, which he won hands down.

In a similarly 'elegant' fashion to the Catholic Centre Party inside, Hitler in January 1934 neutralized Poland, his one middle-sized neighbour, outside, from whom he had even feared (realistically, as it turned out) a preventive coup in his first days as chancellor, while Germany was still weak. Hitler, as an Austrian, had never been anti-Polish as such, unlike the general mood in the Reich, especially so in the *Auswärtiges Amt* (the German Foreign Office). It was against hostile anti-Polish resentments and prejudices that he had to see through a sudden volte-face – a treaty of non-aggression and friendship with Poland – because for him it brought only tactical advantages against the grain of moods that had prevailed in Germany for almost a century. Hitler tore the strongest factor, Poland, from the French system of finding compensation for the former alliance with Russia against Germany. In a period of cultural exchange between the two countries, Poland came closest to the status of a near ally for Germany, earmarked by Hitler as a pliant client state in a crusade against Bolshevism and the Soviet Union. When Poland baulked in 1938 and the Greater German Reich seemed powerful enough, Hitler reverted to the traditional German anti-Polish stance in 1939.

The next easy success fell into Hitler's lap in German territory a year later. The Versailles Treaty had provided for a plebiscite by mid-January 1935 for the Saarland to decide its own final status – return to the Reich *sans phrase* or have a separate identity, as France wished. With the backing of the Reich, most political parties in the Saarland opted almost hysterically for a return to the Reich, confirmed by a popular vote of about 90 per cent. Territorial gain, small in quantity (size, population) but big in quality (heavy industry), brought an immeasurable gain in prestige to the Führer.

Two months later Hitler followed up his advantage, served to him on a silver platter provided by international law, with another move that was technically an internal affair but violated international law, the Versailles Treaty. On 16 March 1935 Hitler proclaimed general conscription, sovereignty for Germany to decide for herself in matters concerning her military forces (*Wehrhoheit*), and open rearmament. The semantic difference between the *Reichswehr* (the professional army of 100,000 men of the Weimar Republic, laid down by Versailles) and the *Wehrmacht* of the Third Reich symbolized the new German drive for more military power – in principle unfettered rearmament, including heavy weapons (heavy artillery, tanks), air power and capital ships beyond a 10,000 ton limit. The *Wehrmacht*, of course, was forged as a weapon for war, more offensive than defensive. The threatening effect on German foreign policy was obvious, not only because Hitler, for the first time, had openly and consciously violated international law.

Despite the obvious implications, the European powers acquiesced, because, for structural internal reasons and rival external interests, they were incapable of reacting adequately to the imminent threat to peace. The Stresa Front in April 1935 declared the intention of England, France and (Fascist) Italy to react with military measures if Germany were to proceed to the next logical step, remilitarization of the Rhineland on the west bank of the Rhine. But this show of verbal strength was neutralized by Hitler's next move, the Anglo-German Naval Agreement, which was signed only three months later. The bilateral treaty on 18 June 1936 (Waterloo Day) sanctioned Germany's naval rearmament beyond the limits imposed by Versailles and inaugurated outright appeasement – the conscious effort by the Western powers, led by Britain, to avoid another Great War by giving way to Hitler in order not to anger and 'provoke' him into open aggression.[27]

Fascist Italy as a new friend, 1935–1936

Stresa was the last time that Fascist Italy under Mussolini sided with Britain and France in a feeble effort to contain the rising Third Reich through a show of solidarity. Hitler fervently admired Il Duce as his shining model and predecessor in establishing an extreme right-wing totalitarian regime, whereas Mussolini, in secret, heartily despised the uncouth plagiarizer from the barbarian north. Of course, Hitler tried to win Mussolini as a future ally. A first visible symptom was Hitler's state visit to Venice, accompanied by a trainload of Nazi functionaries, in June 1934. The attempted *rapprochement* was quickly blocked by two events: first, the miscarried Austrian adventure of 25 July 1934, when Mussolini upheld his protégé, the clerico-fascist authoritarian regime in Austria; second, the murder of Chancellor Dollfuß by Austrian SA troopers. Mussolini even mounted his military 'guard on the Brenner' to uphold Austria against Nazi Germany.

One year later, soon after Stresa, Mussolini ended his jumping up and down while sitting on the European fence by starting his own war of aggression against Ethiopia in October 1935. Sanctions of the League of Nations against Fascist Italy, largely ineffective as such, only drove Mussolini into the open arms of the Third Reich. Both dictators were only too pleased to leave their respective diplomatic isolation. With the attack on Ethiopia, Mussolini had to rely henceforth on Hitler as his only ally, and for the supply of strategic raw materials. From then on began the dramatic *renversement des alliances* between the two dictators – Mussolini, once the senior partner, quickly became the junior partner in a 'brutal friendship'[28] as war approached, and he ended up as Hitler's virtual vassal or even hostage. But Nazi Germany, just like the Kaiser's Germany before 1914, had picked up an ally of doubtful military value, if only because Italy was exposed, with her long coastline, to naval pressure in the Mediterranean. Structurally, and even more telling, the Italians were loath to fight Western democracies to whom they felt ideologically and politically closer than to the Teutonic copy of classical Fascism.

/

More freedom of action, 1936

Hitler used the momentum of his newly won freedom of action by tearing up more bonds of international law: on 7 March 1936, Germany unilaterally denounced the Locarno Treaties and ordered the occupation of the left bank of the Rhine, demilitarized by the Versailles Treaty. This time, the risk was bigger than that of the previous year, when he had started open rearmament. By repudiating the recognition of Germany's western frontiers and occupying forward positions for future aggression, Hitler announced to the world at large his basic contempt for international law and, at least obliquely, hinted at what did actually follow only four years later – aggression against the West.

In fact, Hitler's risks turned out to be smaller than he had thought when taking the plunge in another round of (apparently sound) gambling: France, torn between Left and Right and caught during the polarizing election campaign that was to bring the Popular Front government and Léon Blum to power, was utterly paralysed internally to act with vigour and one voice externally. And Britain was at the height of its course of appeasement. Thus, the Western powers once more kept quiet.

Only four months later, in July 1936, the outbreak of the Spanish Civil War brought the two right-wing totalitarian systems even closer together in support for Franco and his putschist government, not only morally, by diplomatic recognition, but also by sending crucial equipment and even 'volunteers', in full-scale military units. For Germany, the *Legion Condor* tested new weapons in a limited war and the tactical cooperation of ground and air forces, especially tanks and fighting bombers. A macabre climax was the bombing of the Basque city of Guernica in 1937 by the fledgling *Luftwaffe*, heralding saturation bombing to terrorize civilian populations in the Second World War. On the other hand, the spectacular Olympic Games in August 1936, awarded to Berlin before the Nazis had come to power in 1933, provided Hitler with a heaven-sent opportunity to elaborate on the theme of his 'peaceloving' intentions. Even Jewish athletes were admitted into the German Olympic team, just to fool the public abroad and to counteract the ill-will produced by the anti-Semitic Nuremberg Laws of 1935.

Only two months later, three important events became further stages on the way to the Second World War, fusing both internal and external factors. In October 1936 Hitler appointed Göring his number 2 in the Nazi hierarchy as *Beauftragter zur Durchführung des Vierjahresplanes* (Commissioner for Executing the Four Year Plan), taking a leaf from Soviet Stalinism. Yet the German Four Year Plan did not introduce 'socialism' along international (communist) lines, but only the German national socialist version of coordinating and pushing economic preparations for future war efforts well within market ('capitalist') structures. Still, the Nazi policy of 'autarky' (that is, economic self-sufficiency) and stockpiling or securing access to strategic war materials was geared to the hasty expansion of the *Wehrmacht* and the navy to prepare Nazi Germany for a great war by 1943.

Second, a kind of ideological alliance with Italy, advertised by Mussolini as the 'Berlin–Rome Axis', was concluded in October 1936.[29] It welded the hard core of one side of the war alliances for the Second World War, namely Germany and Italy, and was 'reinforced' in May 1939 by a formal military alliance, the 'Pact of Steel'. Still, the name 'axis powers' stuck as the label for the counter-alliance to the 'United Nations', as the Allied powers of the Second World War were officially called.

Third, the 'Axis' in Europe was extended into the Far East by the even more ideological Anticomintern Pact with Japan in November 1936. Though it fitted beautifully into the Machiavellian neighbour-to-neighbour = enemy pattern, the Anticomintern Pact was geographically rather eccentric and, literally, too far-fetched for any effective coordination of war efforts and strategies. But in Europe, the Anticomintern Pact became a symbol for the 'Axis', which was joined by minor powers in south-east Europe, but not by Franco's Spain, as Hitler hoped in 1940.

Treacherous lull: Hossbach Protocol, 1937

While in 1937 the Spanish Civil War, the prelude to the Second World War in Europe, raged on, and the Second World War, in fact, had already started with the Second Japanese–Chinese War, all appeared quiet on the German front(s). Outwardly, the lull that followed the Berlin Olympic Games, though punctuated by the Four Year Plan, the Berlin–Rome Axis and the Anti-comintern Pact, spilled over into 1937. But towards the end of the 'quiet' year, in deepest confidence, behind closed doors, Hitler confided to his top military leaders his future plans: on 5 November 1937, more than four years after his first disclosure to top generals of the *Reichswehr*, Hitler was more precise about coming historical realities.

According to the only source, notes taken by Hitler's aide, known as the Hossbach Protocol,[30] Hitler wanted to 'safeguard' and 'preserve' the quantity and demographic growth of the German people. The necessary space (*Raum*) was not to be found overseas but in Europe, for agrarian settlements and sources of raw materials. For the 'solution of the German question' only the 'way of violence' was possible, which could never be without risks. For him it was only a matter of 'when' and 'how'. The best time would be 1943–5, when a high peak of German armament would be reached (this indeed happened in 1944 in the final phase of the Second World War!). Thereafter, things could only get worse for Germany. Action might become necessary at an earlier date if France became so paralysed internally and externally that she was incapable of acting against Germany. In such a case, he had earmarked the next two stages of German expansion, Austria and Czechoslovakia. Hitler even coolly gave a yardstick for measuring Germany's quantitive and qualitative increase of power – one division for every million additional Germans.

The Greater German Reich: *Anschluß* of Austria and Sudetenland, 1938

Sooner than he had thought possible in his boldest daydreams, Hitler could tick off the last two items on his internal agenda the following year – Austria and Czechoslovakia. Most Austrians and many Germans in Czechoslovakia had never accepted the Allied veto against their desire to join the Reich in 1918–19. If socialists had hoped to strengthen the Weimar Republic with their votes by removing an irritant to the collective German mind, the traditional Greater Germans in Austria were outright chauvinists of pan-German vintage, of the same flesh and spirit as Hitler himself. The abortive customs union of 1931 and Hitler's meteoric rise within the Reich fired popular imagination to make the NSDAP the strongest party in Austria.

In 1938 Hitler skilfully manipulated and exploited the slogan of 'national self-determination for the Germans', blissfully overlooking objective reasons as to why it could not work for all Germans – the Reich would then be too strong for Europe. Catholic Conservatives, backed by Mussolini's Fascism, tried to stem in vain the pro-Nazi tide with authoritarian structures, both against the Left (socialists) and extreme Right (NSDAP). In a combination of genuine popular enthusiasm for the Third Reich and the bullying of Dollfuß's successor Schuschnigg, Hitler installed a Nazi government in Vienna, marched into Austria with his brand new *Wehrmacht* on 13 March 1938 and annexed Austria, rudely shattering any illusions that Austria could keep internal autonomy within the Third Reich.

Austria's *Anschluß* had stirring repercussions throughout Europe. Here was another violation of international law in the form of the Versailles Treaty. Hitler's Germany was henceforth the Greater German Empire (*Großdeutsches Reich*), formally on the narrowest geographical basis (lesser Germany plus German Austria proper). Nonetheless, Bohemia and Moravia, the heart of the Czechoslovak Republic, were almost encircled by German territories, but for a narrow bottleneck between Upper Silesia and Lower Austria: the door was open to the Balkans, where weak successor states began to follow the lead from the new most powerful pole in the European system.

For purely geographical reasons, Czechoslovakia ranked next on Hitler's agenda after the Anschluß. It was the ideal victim, with 3 million Germans living mostly in the heavily industrialized and fortified border regions of Bohemia and Moravia. In a process comparable to that in Austria, their overwhelming majority had turned Nazi, while German socialists remained loyal to the Czechoslovak Republic. In concerted action Hitler whipped up the Sudeten Germans, as they were called by Nazi propaganda, through Konrad Henlein, leader of the Sudetendeutsche Partei, into disrupting the Czechoslovak Republic by raising their demands successively in such a way that, once they were fulfilled, they were stepped up once more. Under German threats of war, appeasement reached its peak when Britain and France forced Czechoslovakia to accede to her own dismemberment in Munich in autumn 1938, by annexation of the 'Sudeten German' border regions and the secession of Slovakia as a German client state.

Hitler's daring coup provoked both the first planning of military resistance against him inside Germany, which collapsed when he emerged triumphantly from his gamble, and widespread gloom among the German population at the prospect of another Great War. Yet the general outward impression prevailed – the Greater German Empire had become even greater and more powerful. Rump Czechoslovakia was almost strangled by surrounding German territories, clearly earmarked as the next victim, although Hitler protested to the contrary. The Sudetenland was allegedly his last territorial demand. A last resort for German political exile within the reach of the growing Reich was doomed. Finally, the first chapter of the German–Czech catastrophe in old Bohemia was brutally opened by the Germans in the autumn of 1938, provoking the grim Czech reaction of 1945 – mutual ethnic cleansing, first by Germans of Czechs, then by Czechs of Germans.

Expansion beyond Germany's ethnic borders in the east: Prague, Memelland, Poland, 1939

Hitler's next logical step in March 1939 was to occupy Prague and rump Czechoslovakia, converting it into a German Protectorate (*Reichsprotektorat Böhmen und Mähren*), with a very restricted internal autonomy for practical purposes of a kind of colonial indirect rule. He crossed the line between territorial aggrandisement on ethnically German grounds and expansion into non-German lands, but also the line between preserving peace through appeasement and Western resistance to further aggression. England gave guarantees to two further prospective candidates for Hitler's next acts of aggression – Poland and Rumania.

Poland was the more likely victim, because she was, by the destruction of Czechoslovakia, already more than half-encircled by the Reich plus its Slovak client state to the south. In 1938 she had provoked the Führer's wrath by refusing to join the Reich in a proposed crusade against Bolshevism – under German leadership, of course. The Polish dilemma was insoluble. If they granted passage for German troops to attack the Soviet Union, the Poles had to face two alternatives, both equally hateful. If Germany won, Poland would be relegated to a German vassal state; if Germany lost, Poland would be crushed by Soviet Russian revenge. On the other hand, Poland could easily be isolated by a return to traditional cooperation between Russia and Germany (of whatever political and ideological set-up). Any eventual help from far away Western powers could at best be indirect, and would be doomed to be largely ineffective.

Hitler ruthlessly exploited Poland's precarious position, hemmed in between Germany and Russia. As an answer to the British guarantee for Poland he denounced, in a fit of partial honesty, both the German–Polish Non-Aggression Treaty of 1934 and the Anglo-German Naval Agreement of 1936, because he gave away at least obliquely that he was bent on war. In the growing tension it hardly mattered any more that Hitler bagged his last 'peaceful' territorial gain before outright war, the 'return' of the part-German Memelland on 22 March 1939 'to the Reich', under threat, as usual, of military action against little Lithuania.

After Prague (15 March 1939), German 'foreign policy', or what was left of it, was focused on the Soviet Union, which became the key for unlocking the Polish obstacle. Hitler was realistic enough to expect resistance from his next victim of military planning, 'Fall Weiß', ordered secretly on 3 April. As he said, in one of his characteristic top secret conferences with the heads of the *Wehrmacht*, on 23 May 1939, two months after occupying Prague, he saw that further 'successes' could no longer be obtained 'without blood-shed'.[31] In order to reduce the risks, Hitler sought again to isolate Poland as effectively as possible. The Soviet Union, the neighbour to the German neighbour Poland, was the natural and (almost) ideal partner to do the trick.

Despite their ideological enmity, both totalitarian systems maintained normal diplomatic relations after 1933. Anti-communism and persecution of the German Communists in Germany on the one hand, anti-Fascism on the other, which even made them clash indirectly on the battleground of the Spanish Civil War, were no serious obstacles to traditional power politics. But the profile of relations had remained low. After Nazi Germany had left the League of Nations in late 1933, the Soviet Union had entered it in 1934, propagating its celebrated policy of 'collective security' – against the rising Third Reich. Even before his decision to attack Poland, Stalin, on 10 March 1939, had thrown out bait to Hitler with his famous 'chestnuts' speech, warning unnamed countries not to pull out the chestnuts from the fire for the capitalist West. Hitler eagerly took the hint and discreetly intensified economic relations with the Soviet Union. As he stepped up his pressure on recalcitrant Poland and completed his military build-up for 'Fall Weiß', the two totalitarian regimes also 'improved' their diplomatic cooperation.

Meanwhile, Stalin double-crossed the West by also negotiating with England and France over a defensive treaty for Poland. Stalin demanded, at that point even with strategic logic on his side, free passage for Soviet troops to fight Germany. The Poles, however, refused steadfastly, because they knew from bitter experience that Russian troops, once they came, would stay on indefinitely. Since the West could not force Poland to give in, Stalin broke off negotiations and turned to Hitler who had been waiting in the wings. Within a few days Hitler and Stalin rushed through their Non-Aggression Pact on 23 August 1939 before a stunned world. Poland was all but encircled by her hostile great neighbours, with only one narrow outlet to neutral Rumania, through which the Polish government could slip into exile after the inevitable military defeat. Stalin had made himself the junior partner for Hitler attacking Poland and thus starting the Second World War.

In his final drive to finish off Poland, Hitler uncannily summed up the continuities in German foreign policy since the Reich's becoming a Great Power in 1871, especially since the Weimar Republic. The will to more power through more expansion ostensibly 'only' sought to revise Germany's eastern frontiers, which had been studiously left out of formal recognition even under Stresemann. The refusal of an eastern Locarno now escalated to solving the German (self-made) dilemma between expansive aims (return to the eastern frontiers of 1918) and professedly peaceful means by opting for war. Hitler's propaganda harped on well-known themes: the plight of German minorities; the extension of the right of national self-determination to Germans; Poland's inability to keep up civilized standards; the right of the Free State of Danzig, under a kind of attenuated Polish suzerainty and under an even more indirect overview of the League of Nations, to join the German Reich. Hitler's 'final' demand, a railway and autobahn through the 'Polish Corridor', linking insulated East Prussia directly with the Reich, seemed 'modest' enough. But it was the bait to make Poland a German vassal state.

Thus, Hitler and Stalin between them, each in his own way, ruthlessly exploited Poland's basic dilemma and ground her to death. Hitler's Germany, no doubt, was the leading and more active partner. But Stalin's Soviet Union was indispensable to the way the Second World War began.

The Second World War, 1939–1945

Once the dam had burst, German war policy shed all remaining marks of diplomacy or foreign policy by carving up Poland with the Soviet Union. Nazi Germany surpassed by far the frontiers of 1914, the objects of 'peaceful' revision of the Weimar Republic against Poland, and even surpassed secret and public German war aims in the First World War to annex a border strip along the frontiers of Imperial Germany and to Germanize the new territories.[32] The Nazi Third Reich in the Second World War was also a more extreme and brutal extension of the Imperial Second Reich in the First World War: annexation and ethnic cleansing (*völkische Flurbereinigung*) as envisaged in Imperial Germany were executed on an even larger scale during war and by violent methods – mass deportations and massacres. If the Second Empire had been uncertain what to do with the many Jews – whether to keep them, with their Yiddish language and admiration for German culture, as a Germanizing element (the 'liberal' view), or to kick them out (the anti-Semitic view) – the Third Reich was single-minded (with individual modifications or aberrations) in its determination and its method – massacres escalating to genocide.

The attacks on Denmark, Norway, Luxemburg, Belgium and Holland in early 1940 showed a complete disregard for international law. After the defeat of France, Alsace-Lorraine (and Luxemburg) were drawn into the orbit of the Third Reich in an ambiguous form – there was no annexation, but an expansion of the Nazi Party structures and the school education system (in German only). Even more serious was the extension of general conscription to Luxemburg and Alsace-Lorraine, because it made conscripted soldiers accomplices of German war crimes in the east. Provisionally partitioned France along the Loire was made a client state, in particular through the collaboration of Vichy. Italy joined the war in the hour of certain French defeat, but became more of a liability than an asset, for reasons explained above. Efforts to enlist Franco's Spain failed in autumn 1940.

Hitler had easier game in south-eastern Europe, where he had wanted to make the weak successor states into client or vassal states ever since the 1938 *Anschluß* of Austria and the Sudetenland. The chief instrument for winning 'allies' was adherence to the Anti-comintern Pact. When Yugoslavia rescinded her joining the Axis powers after a military coup and returned to her traditional pan-Slav and pro-Russian orientation, she prompted Hitler in April 1941 into attacking Yugoslavia and Greece, an act also necessary to rescue Mussolini whose army had got stuck embarrassingly against Greece. Yugoslavia was split up, Greater Croatia became a German client state on the Slovak model, while parts of Slovenia were annexed into the Reich as late as 1944. Nazi Germany was drawn into the Balkan maze, thrusting on Hitler the burden of having to act as a mediator in two Vienna mediations (*Schiedsspruch*), one between Hungary and Slovakia (1938), giving the southern parts of Slovakia and of the Carpatho-Ukraine to Hungary, the other between Hungary and Rumania (1940), dividing Transuylvania between the two and as usual, satisfying no one.

Even more difficult and ineffective were efforts to coordinate war strategies with far-off Japan. While Hitler did not inform Japan of the impending attack on the Soviet Union in 1941, Japan remained neutral, being already over-committed in her war against China. Stalin could throw his Siberian divisions to the west to stall Hitler's offensive before Moscow. After Pearl Harbor in December 1941, Hitler was rash enough to launch his only formal declaration of war – against the USA, ending the twilight war on the Atlantic.

With total world war finally global, nothing was left of German foreign policy, but for feeble efforts in the bloody *Götterdämmerung* of the Third Reich to find some loophole of separate peace with the West against the Soviets, in order to save the skin of the highest-ranking Nazi leaders. Only after the war furies of the *furor teutonious* were finally spent by the *debellatio* on 8–9 May 1945, which had briefly appeared for a moment in November 1918 as a hint to future possibilities, could a new start be made from scratch, on the ruins of the Reich, in a Germany provisionally divided in the Cold War of 1945–90.[33]

Notes

1. For the most recent and most comprehensive *German* treatment of the whole period see the magisterial study by Klaus Hilderbrand, *Das vergangene Reich: Deutsche Außenpolitik von Bismarck bis Hitler, 1871–1945* (Stuttgart, 1995). See also Peter Krüger, *Die Außenpolitik der Weimarer Republik* (Darmstadt, 1993); Bern-Jürgen Wendt, *Großdeutschland: Außenpolitik und Kriegsvorbereitung des Hitler-Regimes* (Munich, 1993).

2. For a more detailed sketch see Imanuel Geiss, *The Question of German Unification, 1806–1990* (London, 1996).

3. Günter Wollstein, *Das 'Großdeutschland' der Paulskirche: Nationale Ziele in der bürgerlichen Revolution, 1848–9* (Düsseldorf, 1977).

4. Shlomo Na'man, *Lasalle* (Hanover, 1970), p. 242.

5. For an overview see Otto Pflanze, *Bismarck and the Development of Germany*, 3 vols (Princeton, NJ, 1991).

6. Fritz Stern, *Gold and Iron: Bismarck and the Building of the German Empire* (New York, 1977), p. 88.

7. Imanuel Geiss, *German Foreign Policy, 1871–1914* (London, 1976).

8. Unfortunately buried in the archives of the Auswärtiges Amt. I ran into the document but, stupidly enough, tired by the strains of archival work, did not copy the text, which, alas, can now only be recalled from memory.

9. Hans Fenske, 'Ungeduldige Zuschauer: Die Deutschen und die Expansion, 1815–1880', in Wolfgang Reinhard, ed., *Imperialistische Kontinuität und nationale Ungeduld im 19. Jahrhundert* (Frankfurt/Main, 1991).

10. Winfried Baumgart, *Der Friede von Paris 1856: Studien zum Verhältnis von Kriegführung, Politik und Friedensbewahrung* (Munich and Vienna, 1972), pp. 72–7. See also Paul W. Schroeder, *Austria, Great Britain and the Crimean War* (New York, 1972).

11. Geiss, *Question of German Unification.*

12. For a more detailed analysis, in a wider context of both modern German and universal history, see I. Geiss, 'Germany and the Armistice: Consequences and Coincidences', *The Poppy and the Owl* 25 (1999).

13. Fritz Fischer, *Germany's Aims in the First World War* (London, 1967).

14. Hilderbrand, *Das vergangene Reich*, pp. 454–64.

15. Geiss, *Question of German Unification*, pp. 57ff. Two more possible solutions, first realized by Hitler in 1938 and varying greatly in geographic scope, also existed: the 'maxi-Greater German solution', comprising 'Lesser Germany' plus all of the Austrian monarchy, as demanded in 1848–9 by Austrian 'Greater Germans'; the 'super-Greater German solution', adding vast territories (with essentially minuscule German minorities) in the East, as envisaged in Himmler's 'Greater Germanic Empire of the German Nation' (*Großgermanisches Reich Deutscher Nation*).

16. I. Geiss, 'Die manipulierte Kriegsschuldfrage: Deutsche Reichspolitik in der Julikrise 1914 und deutsche Kriegsziele im Spiegel des Schuldreferats des Auswärtigen Amtes, 1919–31', *Militärgeschichtliche Mitteilungen* 2 (1983), pp. 31–60. See also Ulrich Heinemann, *Die verdrängte Niederlage: Politische Öffentlichkeit und Kriegsschuldfrage in der Weimarer Zeit* (Göttingen, 1983).

17. Peter Krüger, *Deutschland und die Reparationen, 1918–19: Die Genesis des Reparations-problems in Deutschland* (Stuttgart, 1973).

18. Hilderbrand, *Das vergangene Reich*, pp. 519–48.

19. See Krüger, *Reparationen*, p. 16.

20. Antoine Fleury, ed., *Le Plan Briand d'Union fédérale européene* (Bern, 1998).

21. Hilderbrand, *Das vergangene Reich*, p. 544.

22. Ibid.

23. For an analytical sketch of the situation at the end of the First World War see I. Geiss, 'Armistice in Eastern Europe and the Fatal Sequels: Successor States and Wars, 1919–23', in Hugh Cecil and Peter Liddle, eds, *At the Eleventh Hour: Reflections, Hopes and Anxieties at the Closing of the Great War* (Barnsley, 1998), pp. 237–54.

24. I. Geiss, *July 1914: Selected Documents* (London, 1967), pp. 362–7.

25. Quoted in Hilderbrand, *Das vergangene Reich*, p. 570: 'Deutschland wird entweder Weltmacht oder überhaupt nicht sein'.

26. Hans-Adolf Jacobsen, *1939–1945: Der Zweite Weltkrieg in Chronik und Dokumenten* (Darmstadt, 1959).

27. Martin Gilbert, *The Roots of Appeasement*

28. Frederick W. Deakin, *The Brutal Friendship* (London 1962). See also Jens Petersen, *Hitler–Mussolini: Die Entstehung der Achse Berlin–Rom, 1933–36* (Tübingen, 1973).

29. Elizabeth Wiskemann, *The Rome–Berlin Axis: A Study of Relations between Hitler and Mussolini* (London, 1966).

30. Jacobsen, *1939–1945*, pp. 83–90.

31. Ibid., p. 93.

32. I. Geiss, *Der polnische Grenzstreifen 1914–1918: Ein Beitrag zur deutschen Kriegszielpolitik im ersten Weltkrieg* (Hamburg and Lübeck, 1960).

33. I. Geiss, 'The Federal Republic of Germany in International Politics Before and After Unification', in Klaus Larres and Panikos Panayi, eds, *The Federal Republic of Germany since 1949: Politics, Society and Economy Before and After Unification* (London, 1996), pp. 137–65.

PART THREE

Economics, Society, Politics and Diplomacy, 1919–1945: Key Themes

CHAPTER SIX

Big business and the continuities of German history, 1900–1945

J. ADAM TOOZE

Around the turn of the twentieth century the German economy came to be seen in a new way. The early phase of industrialization pioneered by Great Britain was revealed as no more than the prelude to an even more dramatic bout of economic development. From the early 1870s the European economies had been locked in a prolonged phase of painful price reductions and structural adjustment, popularly known as 'the great depression'. For many observers, including the elderly Marx and Engels, this had heralded the imminent collapse of capitalism.[1] However, in the mid-1890s the depression gave way to a phase of spectacular economic growth driven forward by technical innovation and unprecedented agglomerations of capital. The chief beneficiaries were the big names of German industry, firms such as Krupp, Thyssen and the Gelsenkirchener Bergwerke in heavy industry, the three dominant chemical corporations BASF, Bayer and Hoechst, or the electrical engineering giants Siemens and AEG, sponsored by the great banks of Berlin. But the broad mass of the population also appeared to be benefiting from the country's increasing prosperity.[2] The nation's centre of gravity in both political and cultural terms was shifting decisively towards the cities. After the gloom of the great depression there now seemed no end to the possibilities for economic advancement. In the next century Germany would stand alongside the United States and Britain as a true pioneer of modernity.

These extraordinary developments provoked both enthusiasm and anxiety and they were accompanied by a restless search for self-understanding. The great ideological traditions inherited from the eighteenth and nineteenth centuries – liberalism, conservatism and Marxism – were coming to seem increasingly anachronistic. Liberals struggled to make sense of an economy dominated by giant corporations and a society increasingly centred in the cities.[3] Early twentieth-century capitalism was far from the liberal utopia foreseen by the prophets of the eighteenth century, of a self-reliant citizenry founded on a free market economy. And yet the new world undoubtedly owed its existence to the process of economic development, which liberals had championed as progress. Conservatives could take pleasure in the discomfort of their traditional opponents, but their own recipes for turning back the clock were no less unrealistic.[4] The inherited foundations of the social and moral order appeared in irreversible decline. Germany's agrarian roots were unearthed as the course of economic development bound inexorably into a complex web of foreign trade. By comparison with liberalism and conservatism, the writings of Marx and Engels did provide intellectual tools with which to grasp capitalist development. But Marxism was not untouched by the passage of time. The *Communist Manifesto*, by far the most widely read text of social democracy, was beginning to show its age.[5] Composed on the occasion of the great liberal revolution of 1848, the *Manifesto* had little to say about many prominent features of the early twentieth century. Massive state intervention in infrastructure and welfare combined with global imperialist competition had not been on the agenda in the mid-nineteenth century. The general crisis of capitalism predicted in the mid-nineteenth century had not yet arrived. Nor was German society polarizing in the simple fashion Marx and Engels had foreseen.[6] There were few signs of proletarian immizeration. On the contrary, capitalism was giving rise to new strata with a considerable stake in the system – privileged manual workers and a large army of white-collar staff.

Of course, Germany was not an exception. All the developed societies of Europe were undergoing broadly similar processes of social and economic development. Across the continent, nineteenth-century ideologies were cast into doubt. However, Germany was in every respect an advanced case. Its industrial and financial development was the most rapid. Its corporations were the most gigantic. Its socialist party, the key indicator of political transformation, was the largest in the world. In the writings of economists and social theorists Germany was rapidly replacing Britain as a symbol of Europe's economic and social future. The significance attributed to the rise of capitalist big business varied from author to author. However, that it would be one of the chief forces shaping the economic and social future was beyond doubt.

Gustav Schmoller, the doyen of contemporary German economics, sought to calm conservative nerves by arguing that the rise of capitalist businesses with their elaborate office hierarchies would provide a new source of social stability.[7] The army of white-collar workers would provide a powerful counterweight to the blue-collar battalions of social democracy. The sociologist Max Weber was more grandiose and less optimistic in outlook. For him the interlocking bureaucracies of private business and the state represented the central rationalizing dynamic of the modern world, an ambiguous process enhancing power and knowledge but simultaneously threatening to confine the creative individual within an iron cage. The fashionable economist Werner Sombart offered an analysis of 'high capitalism', in which giant agglomerations of productive and financial capital were at the heart of the national economy.[8] From the radical left Lenin, Liebknecht and Luxemburg sought to puncture the veneer of apparent stability, pinpointing what they believed to be the self-destructive dynamics of monopoly capitalism, the interlocking of finance capitalism and the imperialist state.[9] Outside observers were equally impressed by Germany's corporate might. Writing in 1915, the American institutional economist Thorstein Veblen identified what he believed to be a peculiarly German form of economic organization, which efficiently harnessed modern industrial technology to the aims of the state.[10] At a lower level of intellectual sophistication, German business itself began to become conscious of its own history.[11] Corporate archives began to be collected from the turn of the century and friendly academics were commissioned to write the first business histories.

By the outbreak of the First World War Germany's giant industrial and financial corporations had thus come to be assigned a central role in the nation's narrative. There was little doubt that they would play a powerful role in shaping the country's economic, social and political future. And since the middle of the twentieth century there has been no lack of German historians willing to confirm this prediction. The giant corporations of industry and finance are far more conspicuous in the historiography of Germany than in the literature of its western European neighbours.[12] Only in the United States has the new structure of corporate capitalism occupied a similarly prominent position in historical writing.[13] The economic and technical development of German big business, its influence on German society and politics and its contribution to defining Germany's relations with the wider world, form a strong strand of continuity through the turbulent history of the first half of this century. In unpicking this skein this essay will move back and forth between two levels of analysis. It will sketch some of the principal findings of the literature, whilst at the same time seeking to explore the continuities in the way in which this particular aspect of modern German history has been understood and written about.

German business and the postwar historians

In the postwar period both the official Marxist history of East Germany and critical historians in the West turned to the intellectual legacy of the early twentieth century to construct interpretations of recent German history. East German authors had little choice in their selection of texts.[14] Lenin's interpretations of imperialism and the Dimitrov formula on Fascism made mandatory appearances in the footnotes. It was axiomatic that the development of the means of production, 'personified' by Germany's giant corporations, was the determining force in the evolution of capitalist society. In the West the selection of intellectual reference points was freer, though far from unconstrained.[15] Until the late 1960s the Federal Republic was deeply hostile to Marxism of any stripe. But Western historians such as Fritz Fischer and Hans-Ulrich Wehler had no difficulty in finding acceptable points of reference in the earlier theoretical debates. To construct their vision of Germany's special path, they drew on theories of imperialism, Weber's vision of bureaucracy, the American sociology of modernization which was itself heavily indebted to the classics of German sociology, and Hilferding's model of organized capitalism. This common intellectual heritage reinforced the common conviction that the aggressive, anti-democratic attitudes of Germany's capitalists formed a powerful and pernicious continuity in the country's history. Reactionary business elites were one of the most powerful forces militating against the success of democracy in modern Germany.

In the East a Leninist interpretation of the First World War was de rigueur. In the West, it took Fritz Fischer's sensational intervention to force the historical profession to confront the possibility that the First World War was more than an accidental derailment of international relations, or a 'natural' product of superpower rivalry. Fischer claimed to have proof that the conflict was, in fact, an imperialist war of aggression launched by the Wilhelmine regime in collusion with German business interests. The conspiratorial memorandum of September 1914 in which German big business plotted the postwar Empire revealed the true face of German capitalism. Terrified by the vulnerability of their overseas export markets, they sought to create a European Empire of their own. The draconian treaty of Brest Litovsk, imposed on Russia's Bolshevik regime in March 1918, turned this fantasy into reality. Meanwhile at home, 'social imperialism' served as a useful device with which to marginalize the left and to protect German capitalism from the demands of the organized working class.

For orthodox Marxists Germany's defeat changed nothing in the basic constellation. The influence of big business was challenged during the revolution, but order was soon restored by the craven Social Democrats and their proto-Fascist allies, the Freikorps paramilitaries. For this service, big business showed little gratitude. It was never reconciled to a Republic that granted new rights to the workers and extended welfare provision at the expense of the taxpayer. The great depression and the surge in popular support for the Communist Party triggered a new phase of violent reaction.

Following the example of their counterparts in Italy, German business found a willing tool in Hitler's Nazi Party. Big business 'paid for Hitler', fuelling the party's overwhelming flood of propaganda, and finally in early 1933 hoisted Hitler into power with the help of its agrarian and military friends. Nazism could thus be interpreted as a particularly brutal instance of a generic response to capitalist crisis, Fascism.

The interpretation of Hitler's rise to power offered by many Western historians differed little in detail. Crucially, they too were convinced of the importance of big business in undermining the Weimar Republic and setting the stage of Hitler's takeover. Where they differed from their Eastern counterparts was in the interpretation they gave to this collusion. Haunted by the guilty burden of the Holocaust, Western historians were insistent that the racist crimes of the Nazi regime required a special explanation.[16] This in turn had to be rooted in the unique character of German historical development. The complicity of German business with Nazism was not merely the normal response of capitalists to economic and political crisis. It reflected a deeper failure of German social and political development, the failure of the German bourgeoisie to assume its proper role as an agent of liberalism. In wider political terms this failure had its roots as far back as the defeat of the liberal revolution of 1848. The state-centred, militarist traditions of Prussia remained unbroken. The middle class failed to emancipate itself. For social historian Jürgen Kocka this deep cultural legacy could be seen even in the corporate hierarchies of modern German business. He claimed to detect the influence of military models even in the business organizations of modern German industry.[17] In political terms the crucial turning point came in the 1870s. In the wake of the first 'great depression' early in the decade, German liberalism suffered a second, decisive setback. Exploiting this loss of confidence, Bismarck lured the industrialists of the Ruhr into abandoning their support for free trade in favour of a nationalist alliance with the protectionist agrarian elites of East Prussia.[18] It was this same alliance of 'iron and rye' that asserted itself in the inter-war period to destroy the Weimar Republic.

German big business was thus corrupted in its infancy. It was not capitalism *per se* that was the problem, but the specific cultural and political tendencies of German business. It was in the heavy industry of the western Ruhr region that these were most pronounced: authoritarian and nationalist in its politics, paternalist and repressive in its policies towards its workforce and protectionist when it came to trade policy.[19] Of course, not all of German industry followed the lead of the reactionary Ruhr. The traders of Hamburg were more liberal in all but their attitudes to their workforce.[20] Electrical engineering giants such as Siemens and AEG did not dream of forsaking the world market, nor did the booming German chemicals industry.[21] Their corporate social policies were less authoritarian than those of the Ruhr. The liberal internationalism of Germany's more modern industries became a cliché in its own right. However, as Kocka found at Siemens, even the more 'modern' firms participated in the deliberate effort to marginalize the socialist left by fostering invidious divisions between blue-collar and white-collar employees.[22] The salaried bastion of social order became a seething hotbed of petty bourgeois resentment and fascism. And in any case, at the moment of crisis in the early 1930s, with the world economy in ruins, it was the reactionary, nationalist sector of German business that was able to reassert itself and to promote Nazism as a national solution to Germany's economic problems.

Though the Nazi regime proclaimed the end of liberal capitalism and a fundamental break with the past, this was easily dismissed as ideological window-dressing. To historians in both the East and the West, it was far more convincing to see a continuity of capitalist influence at work behind the scenes. The destruction of the KPD, the SPD and the independent labour movement in the first half of 1933 was undeniably in the interests of German business. Meanwhile, the public works programme put the economy back to work, and the armaments boom, engineered in direct collaboration with leading industrial corporations, guaranteed profits.[23] In 1936, with the announcement of Goering's Four Year Plan, German monopoly capitalism tightened its grip. If heavy industry was the bogeyman of Wilhelmine and Weimar Germany, the giant chemicals combine IG Farben played that role in the Third Reich. Originally assigned to the liberal, internationalist faction of German capital, IG Farben executives joined forces with the Nazis to outdo its capitalist rivals and to find substitutes for the foreign markets it had lost during the depression.[24] IG Farben occupied key positions in Goering's organization and the Plan not surprisingly provided a generous flow of state subsidies and guaranteed sales for Farben's latest generation of products, synthetic rubber, fuel and textiles. These were the vital ingredients that would make the Nazi economy ready for war. In turn, conquest would secure a protected economic *Grossraum* (economic space) for Farben to dominate. The corporation was thus viewed as a powerful force pushing the regime towards war, a crime for which it was put on trial by the Allies after the Second World War. Other investigations by the US authorities appeared to reveal a dense network of contacts interweaving Germany's major banks, its major industrial corporations and the Nazi regime.[25] For postwar historians this provided rich pickings. What was to be regretted was that the Allies did not follow the political logic of their own investigations. Instead, under the cloak of anti-communism Germany's business elite was allowed to effect a wholesale restoration. It was not until the 1960s that the reactionary continuity in German business was finally broken as a new generation of foreign-trained managers finally accommodated itself to European integration and the progressive liberalization of world markets.[26]

In the postwar decades, this line of historical argument was most unwelcome to German firms, struggling to draw a veil over the past and to concentrate on the business of the *Wirtschaftswunder*. The documents sequestrated by the Allied prosecutors were irrevocably in the public domain and provided ample ammunition for the critics. However, left-wing historians of business were never safe from lawsuits and injunctions, or from the hired guns of German business history.[27] In the postwar period scholars friendly to business produced a third, more optimistic version of the continuity thesis. They too could draw on a tradition of history writing that stretched back to the turn of the century. In the context of West Germany's economic miracle, they reconstructed a narrative linking the celebrations of the Wilhelmine period to the triumphs of the postwar era. German business embodied all the positive continuities in German history, an unpolitical tradition of technological and commercial endeavour, which brought prosperity to Germany and the benefits of German genius to mankind. This industrial tradition dated back to the nineteenth century and flourished until 1914. Thereafter, its peaceful development had been cruelly disrupted. Far from being under business control, the irrationality of politics had imposed itself on Germany's unpolitical capitalists.[28] Political extremes of left and right had created a deeply inhospitable environment. Since 1945 this ideological struggle had been successfully tamed. The curse of nationalism was lifting from Western Europe and communism was safely contained. Germany could now return to its true destiny as a peaceable economic superpower.[29]

This was an appealing version of events with at least some purchase on reality. It linked the positive achievements of the Wilhelmine era to the equally impressive reconstruction of West Germany. And it certainly served its purpose in commemorative Festschriften and official histories. However, it had one fatal flaw. Advocates of German business in the postwar decades proved incapable of dealing honestly with the Nazi past. One strategy was simply to gloss over the worst years with omissions and evasions. However, this left a gap in the narrative. A more convincing approach was to present German business as among the victims of the 1930s and 1940s. Deprived of commercial liberty, subject to the arbitrary decisions of bureaucrats and the whims of the Gestapo, businessmen like the rest of the German population had suffered unwillingly in silence. With their workforce they had shared the horrors of Allied bombing, the privations of foreign occupation, reparations and communist expropriation. Like millions of others, German businessmen had struggled to assert their innocence in the face of Allied *Siegerjustiz* (victor's justice). The final argumentative tactic was counter-attack. The claims of left-wing and liberal historians were rubbished. They were ideo-logues, not 'scientists', harbouring preconceived ideas about the relationship between business and Nazism. Business had given no substantial support to Hitler before 1933. The complicity of German industry in rearmament was brushed over. Even the Allied judges at Nuremberg had not convicted the executives of Krupp and IG Farben. This combination of evasion, self-pity and counter-attack was typical of German *Vergangenheitspolitik* (the politics of dealing with the past) in the immediate postwar decades.[30] It neutralized the accusations of academics and journalists and protected a guilty genera-tion of managers from serious repercussions. In this sense it was highly effect-ive. However, it was not successful in laying the past to rest. Indeed, it was the transparent evasions of German business that conferred credibility on the conspiratorial version of events offered by Fritz Fischer, the Bielefeld school and East German historians. German business clearly had something to hide.

Re-envisioning continuity

Three versions of continuity thus competed in the literature of the first three postwar decades: the enduring continuity of finance capitalism, which through ruthless manipulation of the political system secured its dominance across the ruptures of the twentieth century; the continuity of the authoritar-ian German *Sonderweg* (special path), which was not finally broken until the 1960s with the complete integration of the Federal Republic into the liberal, capitalist West; and the continuity of German enterprise, in which narrative the inter-war period appeared as a time of trial from which German busi-ness had emerged triumphant. Versions of these stories of continuity can still be found in the most recent literature. But since the 1980s the history of German business has also begun to be retold, by recombining the older narratives in a variety of new ways.

One common feature of the more recent literature is its understanding of the period 1914–45 as a distinctive epoch of catastrophe. 'World War I drove Germany mad.'[31] The war was a cataclysm, interrupting what had previously been Germany's 'normal' social and political development. It was the exertions of total war, the humiliating defeat and its traumatic aftermath that set Germany on its disastrous special path. The hyperinflation of 1914–23 and the confiscatory terms of the stabilization in 1924 destabilized what had previously been a confident bourgeois society.[32] German politics took a disastrous turn towards nationalism and anti-Semitism. And this political narrative is matched by the new literature in economic history.

Following in the steps of Knut Borchardt, the German economy in the inter-war period is now commonly described as passing through a pro-longed phase of low growth.[33] The details of Borchardt's interpretation are, of course, hotly contested. High wages, excessive taxes and social con-tributions, inflated government borrowing, unhelpful *Reichsbank* policy, depressed business expectations, technological uncertainty have all been cited as possible causes of inter-war stagnation. But, whatever the explanation, the broad chronological framework sketched by Borchardt has found wide acceptance.[34] The epoch of 1914–45 constitutes a disastrous unity distinct from the years both before 1914 and after 1945.

In business history, as well, the inter-war period has come to be seen as a period in its own right. The First World War and its aftermath posed fundamental challenges that shaped the strategies of German business well into the 1940s. At home, proprietors accustomed to the unproblematic assertion of their rights as 'Herr im Haus' were forced to operate in a far less deferential climate. The established class hierarchy was challenged both by the mobilization of the labour movement between 1914 and 1923 and more ambiguously in the 1930s by the popular mobilization unleashed by the Nazi Party. Abroad, German business suffered a very serious loss of markets to both domestic suppliers of substitute goods and to new trading powers such as Japan. The First World War marked a moment of transition in the global order of economic power. In 1900 the three-way industrial competition between Germany, Britain and the United States hung in the balance. In the first three decades of the twentieth century it was resolved decisively in favour of America. In virtually every area of commerce and industry the United States had by the 1920s established a dominant posi-tion. German businesses were faced with a series of fundamental technical and economic questions which came inevitably to be framed in relation to the US model. Should German corporations seek to compete head to head, or should they sidestep US competition? Should they imitate or adapt US techniques to European conditions? Did they have sufficient resources to sustain a role for themselves as pioneers in their own right?

Detailed investigation along these lines has yielded a far more complex picture of corporate strategy in the inter-war period, as a function of com-petitive environment, technology, labour relations and corporate organiza-tion. And this has reinforced a second broad tendency in the recent literature to reconsider the relationship between politics and business. The narratives of the postwar decades offered a stark choice between conspiratorial deter-minism and apolitical apologia. In light of recent research these stories have come to appear reductive in their treatment of both business strategy and the political process. Most recent studies start from the assumption of the autonomy of both the political and the economic sphere.[35] This does not mean that the two are unrelated, but that the nature of their interactions cannot be reduced to a crude scheme. The dynamics of their relationship need to be studied in minute detail and without the assumption that the pattern of influence runs one way, from a crudely defined 'business interest' to the determination of politics, or the reverse. What general picture emerges from this rewriting of Germany's political economy? Above all, it has revealed the period 1914–45 to be one of extraordinary, open-ended struggle over the boundaries between economics and politics. This certainly cannot be reduced to a simple matter of finance capital imposing its will on the political system. Nor is it well described in liberal terms, as a free market increasingly constrained by 'state control'.[36] It was a period of truly protean struggle in which both the identity of the state and the future of the capitalist system were at stake. It is the radical open-endedness of this struggle that constitutes the unity of the period.

The grand narrative of this period of history remains to be written. However, key moments are now well covered in the literature. The battle for power in inter-war Germany was unleashed by the collapse of state authority during the First World War. Faced with the demands of total war, the unprepared Wilhelmine civil service was elbowed aside by the military and their allies in German industry.[37] The hopeless inefficiency of the bureaucrats and the ruthless profiteering of business led to a catastrophic loss of legitimacy.[38] The idea of the German state, one of the founding myths of the German nation, evaporated.[39] Amidst the wreckage of the Wilhelmine Empire, German business struggled to assert its priorities against both the labour movement and the embattled political authorities.[40] Between 1918 and 1924 big business leaders repeatedly challenged the authority of the fledgling Republic over taxation, labour regulations, price controls, trade policy, reparations and even the general direction of foreign policy. By 1923 big business and their allies in the Reichstag were in a position to dictate the terms of Germany's domestic economic stabilization. In these years it is indeed meaningful to speak of a political system forced into a position of subservience to German capital.

By contrast, the second half of the 1920s was a period of uneasy stability. Liberal businessmen learned to live with the Republic they had so profoundly shaped, whilst the hardliners of the Ruhr grew increasingly restless at the necessary compromises of parliamentary politics.[41] In 1928 a bitter strike erupted in the iron and steel industry. And after 1929 the fragile balance was finally upset by the onset of worldwide depression. There is much still to be said about the shifting balance of power during the early 1930s between the state, the major political parties and various factions of capital. But it is certainly no longer plausible to view Hitler's movement as a puppet of big business.[42] His installation as chancellor followed from the bankruptcy of all the more conservative alternatives. This reflects the impasse within Germany's divided polity, but also the impotence of business interests. Even the strongest German corporations struggled in the depression. Unlike in the early 1920s they were unable to decouple themselves from the fate of the nation. The once great banks were hardest hit, surviving only with the assistance of the Reich.[43] Though the enemies of business in the labour movement were also weakened, German capital was in no position to dictate the course of political events. Hitler's surging mass movement was viewed with trepidation by the vast majority of businessmen. Nazism was a genuinely popular political force, with an ambivalent attitude towards capitalism. Insofar as Hitler was beholden to the old elites, it was to the *Reichswehr*, not to big business.[44] Comparing 1931–4 to the earlier phase of acute political crisis, 1918–24, reveals the loss of political influence suffered by German big business. By the end of the depression industrialists and bankers were no longer in a position to dictate the terms within which politics operated.

This is not to say that businessmen had much to complain about in the early years of the Nazi regime. The dangerous radicals in the SA were brutally silenced. Under Hjalmar Schacht, the Reich's Ministry of Economic Affairs stabilized a system of friendly cooperation with the most influential segments of German business.[45] But business was an opportunistic beneficiary rather than a decisive actor determining the course of events. This became clear after 1937 when the acceleration of rearmament began seriously to impinge on the equilibrium of the German economy.[46] Rearmament was stepped up in the face of business opposition. Raw materials and labour were rationed and the German economy was increasingly detached from the international division of labour. Far from indicating the reassertion of control by monopoly capital, Goering's Four Year Plan testified to the radical independence of the Nazi regime, what Tim Mason referred to as the 'autonomy of the political'.[47] The mighty interests of the Ruhr were forced into humiliated submission over Goering's plans for the development of German iron ore.[48] Far from dominating the Four Year Plan, the corporate hierarchy of IG Farben was itself subverted from within.[49] But it was not the Reich's economic administration that benefited from the political defeat of German business. The German economy was brought under 'state control' in name only. After Schacht's resignation from the Ministry for Economic Affairs in the autumn of 1937, the national economic administration itself was subject to thorough ideological 'coordination'. Henceforth, it was the party that issued orders, both to the German state and to German business.

The phase between 1937 and 1941, in which the Nazi leadership was able to subordinate both the powerful business lobby and the German state elite, was the climax of the inter-war crisis. In the early 1920s politics had been reduced to subservience by economic interests. Now the order was reversed. Having silenced the 'old elites', the Nazi regime seemed to have found a way to liberate ideological politics from all restraint. Hitler successfully defied conventional strategic calculation in launching the war and conquering western Europe by the summer of 1940. The radicalization of racial policy at home and on the Eastern Front tore up the rule book of the *Rechtsstaat* (law-bound state). Meanwhile, the successful wars of conquest promised to liberate Germany from the most basic economic constraints.[50] All Europe was sucked into a vicious spiral of conquest, exploitation and racial violence. German corporations certainly profited from the phase of conquest between 1939 and 1942. But it is illusory to imagine that they were in the driving seat. Within Germany there were no longer to be any forces capable of containing the drive of Nazi ideology. 'Monopoly capitalism' certainly did not have that power. The decisive check came from the outside. In the winter of 1941–2, in front of Moscow, the irrationality of Nazi ideology found its limit. 'Reality' reimposed itself in the form of the Red Army.

The frustration of Nazi plans in the Soviet Union forced a final phase of domestic reorganization and a new relationship between business and the regime. The established structures of the German state, at least in the area of economic administration, were by this time beyond repair. The civil service state was reduced to a shell. And Hitler even managed to convince himself that he could do without the army top brass. But the regime was now forced to rely more heavily on the technical and material resources of German business. The failure of the *Blitzkrieg* campaign in Russia restored the bargaining power of Germany's business lobby. The Second World War was, after all, no different from the First. It required a total industrial mobilization. Unlike in the First World War, leadership of the industrial war economy remained with a group of politicians, Nazi technocrats such as Fritz Todt, Albert Speer and Hans Kehrl. But as in the First World War, their organization of the war effort depended on the cooperation of Germany's leading industrial corporations.[51] German business returned to the centre of power. By 1942–3, however, this was power in a restricted sense. Nazi Germany was no longer the master of its own fate. The military initiative had passed to the Allies. Germany could do little more than respond to their overwhelming force. Defeat was merely a matter of time. And German business, for all its new-found influence, could do little more than struggle to preserve its facilities intact and plan secretly for a future after the war.

In this sketch narrative of the inter-war crisis, the theme of continuity is not the dominance of big business, but the fragile authority of the German state.[52] With the crisis of the First World War the German nation state forfeited its unquestioned right to act as the representative and directing institution of the German nation. It was in the context of this crisis that German business could emerge as such a powerful political actor in its own right. In the early 1920s men such as Hugo Stinnes sought to assert the absolute priority of the 'nation of producers', organized inwardly through giant corporations and represented outwardly by the might of German exports. With the stabilization of the Republic this quasi-syndicalist vision faded from view and business leaders moved increasingly into the background, remaining influential but no longer seeking to dictate to the politicians. The chief beneficiaries of the second crisis of the German state unleashed by the great depression were not big business, but the ideologues of the Nazi Party. The state both as a representative institution and as the real centre of power was now challenged more radically than ever. In its place the Nazis envisioned a militant race-nation united in personal loyalty to a single individual, the Führer. Business interests were certainly not averse to such visions of national unity. However, their own role in the Nazi scheme was strictly functional and subordinate. It was only with the frustration of Nazi plans in the Soviet Union that business groups were able to regain a strategic role.

Betriebsgemeinschaft: the community of labour

This recasting of the grand narrative restores autonomy to both the political and the economic. And in so doing it has opened the space for revisionist studies of two key areas of business strategy, both of which featured prominently in older narratives of continuity. The first of these is labour relations. In both the Marxist and the Bielefeld accounts of modern German history, the defence of proprietorial privilege was a key theme. Hostility towards the labour movement was central to the authoritarian politics of German capital. Fear of revolution led business to abandon the Wilhelmine Empire. Resentment against the gains made by labour motivated opposition to the Weimar Republic. And it was the fierce anti-Marxism of the National Socialists that supposedly made them an acceptable tool of capital. Recent literature has not overturned this consensus. What it has done is to explore in detail the strategies employed by German business to exclude trade unions and manage their workforce. In so doing, historians have moved from a largely 'negative' view of corporate power, the ability of capital to repress labour, to an exploration of the 'positive' strategies through which German firms sought to create a new kind of *Betriebsgemeinschaft*, or works community. Whereas the older literature stressed the continuity of reactionary strategies in industrial relations, recent writing has focused on the development of modern personnel and welfare policies as a strand of continuity between the Weimar Republic and the Third Reich.

Managerial concern to rationalize the labour process can be traced back to the 1920s. And the recent literature highlights a complex of factors that were at work.[53] In part the rationalization movement was a response to the new assertiveness of labour in the aftermath of the revolution. Management needed to re-establish control and cut costs. The movement was also a response to American models of Fordist production, struggling to adopt the methods of mass production to Germany's more restricted circumstances. But above all, the recent literature has reminded us that managing the labour process was of strategic importance, because so much of German industry remained highly labour-intensive. Despite the development of large-scale capitalist production in the late nineteenth century, highly capital-intensive sectors such as iron and steel and chemicals were far from typical. Most of German industry, particularly in manufacturing sectors such as motor vehicles or engineering, continued to rely heavily on artisanal skilled labour. Labour was the key factor of production and its efficient management was therefore central to restoring the competitiveness of German firms. On the whole, this did not involve the wholesale adoption of so-called Fordist strategies. The firms that adopted assembly line manufacture, employing specialized machine tools and semi-skilled labour, were the rare exception. Far more common were compromise strategies that involved the streamlining of existing production facilities, whilst retaining the flexibility of general purpose machinery. Productivity was further enhanced through the introduction of payment schemes such as group piece rates that abolished the incentive to go slow. And German industry continued to invest heavily in training.[54] To tie down the precious resource of skilled labour, larger firms also spent money on extensive programmes of corporate welfare.[55]

The ideal that motivated corporate social programmes was the *Betriebsgemeinschaft*. This was imagined as a harmonious social unit that extended from the work bench to the community beyond. It united workers, managers and owners in the common pursuit of efficient, high-quality production, and in the pride and honour that came with commercial and technical success. Often the scope of this imagined community was parochial, a small town or village, but it was nevertheless emphatically German, with the ideal of *Deutsche Wertarbeit* (German quality work) at its heart.[56] Relations between owners and workers were portrayed in the soft tones of paternalism. For all members of the *Betrieb* there was more at stake than mere material benefit. Efficiency was not merely the requirement of profit, it was a standard to which all should aspire and from which all would benefit.

186

Leistung (high performance) was an end in itself, though fairness demanded that performance should be duly rewarded. As it was envisioned in the 1920s, the *Betriebsgemeinschaft* was an ideal counterposed to the realities of contemporary Germany. It represented unity against the bitter conflicts of class war. It represented firm leadership and united purpose against the factious politics of the Republic. And the concept was all too easily translated into the language of the Third Reich. The terms of this translation are one of the core themes in the recent literature.[57]

The central issue is the relationship between corporate welfare and personnel strategies and the vision of labour relations developed by the Nazi regime, as represented by the Deutsche Arbeitsfront (DAF, German Labour Front).[58] Numerous case studies agree in stressing the ability of large corporations to resist unwanted intrusions by the Front. Elements of the DAF's agenda that were compatible with corporate strategies were readily taken up. Improvements to factory facilities and workwear to match the aesthetic and hygienic ideals of *Schönheit der Arbeit* (Beauty of Labour) were happily adopted. DAF thinking on remuneration, introducing finely calibrated pay scales to reflect the different content of different jobs, also meshed with corporate personnel strategies. The new pay scales for the German metalworking industry introduced in the early 1940s were a durable legacy of this uneasy collaboration.[59] They abolished traditional skill demarcations and specified rewards according to a 'scientific' assessment of job content. The DAF also introduced a new and systematic approach to industrial training. Here, however, the limits of collaboration between business and the Front were clearly visible. Managers baulked at the DAF's claims to define the curriculum of industrial training. Skilled labour continued to be regarded primarily as a corporate resource, not as a national asset. And the DAF's attempts to provide a genuine substitute for Germany's trade unions were resisted at every turn. In 1934, German heavy industry intervened massively to influence the drafting of the new labour law.[60] The so-called *Treuhänder der Arbeit* (Trustees of Labour) were restricted to providing legal aid and other forms of individual welfare. German big businesses were no more willing to allow labour relations to be controlled by the DAF than they were to tolerate an independent trade union.

The story is thus one of continuity. Corporate strategies directed towards the creation of an autarchic *Betriebsgemeinschaft* remained the determinant force in German industrial relations across the divide of 1933. Against this backdrop, the introduction of foreign workers and slave labour on a large scale after 1941 did represent a fundamental discontinuity.[61] And the recent literature is unanimous in its rejection of earlier apologetic accounts and unsparing in its judgements of German management. There can be no doubt that management from the shopfloor to the boardroom actively participated in the forced labour programme. This involved direct collaboration with the SS in the organization of slave labour columns, the management of barrack camps and the disciplining of foreign workers. However, as has recently been argued in the case of Daimler-Benz, even this can be seen as part of a cynical effort to preserve continuity.[62] The brutal exploitation of foreign workers was not viewed as a long-term strategy. Their abundant supply and ruthless exploitation allowed military production to be increased in the short run without an over-commitment of capital or any permanent reorganization of the labour process. In the long run firms such as Daimler-Benz fully intended to return to their familiar methods of production employing a highly skilled German workforce. The expenditure of slave labour was designed to ensure that the transition was as smooth as possible.

Corporate diplomacy

The second major response to the challenges facing corporate Germany in the inter-war period was a determined drive to re-establish Germany's position in the world economy. The earlier literature stressed the long-standing plans for eastward expansion.[63] Having defeated Russia by 1917 the German conquerors planned an extensive economic empire in eastern and south-eastern Europe. Even after the frustration of these plans, big business in the 1920s continued to sponsor organizations such as the Mitteleuropäischer Wirtschaftstag, dedicated to promoting the idea of an economic *Grossraum* (large economic space) in the east. And after 1933 the drive to the east became a central theme in Nazi trade policy. Through a series of bilateral agreements, it has been claimed, the Third Reich established an informal economic empire in eastern and south-eastern Europe. After 1939 this informal system of dependency and exploitation was converted into a brutal regime of military occupation. Whilst agreeing that there are clear continuities in the international strategies of German big business in the first half of the twentieth century, recent histories have shifted the focus firmly from east to west.[64] The central aim of German big business in the aftermath of the disastrous First World War was to recover their share of the richest markets in the world, all of which lay in western Europe or across the Atlantic. This in turn would consolidate a position from which German firms might resist the competition of their dominant rivals in the United States. In this global competition, the raw materials and impoverished markets of eastern Europe were a sideshow.

The international strategies of Germany's largest exporters in the 1920s certainly represent a form of economic revisionism. They meshed well with the efforts of Germany's foreign minister in the 1920s, Stresemann, to rebuild Germany's diplomatic position through the strength of its international trade. Competition with the US required size and this in turn could only be achieved in stable markets. The strategy of Germany's steel producers, chemicals firms, and electrical engineering corporations therefore revolved around consolidating first the German and then the European markets.[65] In chemicals the merger of IG Farben was completed in 1925. In steel the formation of the giant Vereinigte Stahlwerke in 1926 marked a major step towards 'rationalization' of the industry. In electrical engineering a duopoly, AEG and Siemens, had existed since the 1890s. These national champions then reached out to form international cartels. The international steel agreement of 1926 began the process. The carving up of the world market for dyestuffs began a year later. Agreement on the division of the nitrogen market was reached in 1929. By the late 1930s most major international markets were the subject of one or other cartel arrangement and in Europe it was German corporations that took the lead.[66]

The incompatibility between this complex strategy of corporate diplomacy and the militant racism of the Nazi regime is obvious. It is true that the international cartels of the 1920s and early 1930s tended already to assign to Germany a dominant share of Scandinavian, eastern and southeastern European markets. However, these were minor bargaining chips in the struggle for access to the major markets of western Europe and overseas. Not surprisingly, trade policy became, by the late 1930s, an area of major conflict between corporate Germany and the Nazi regime. There was a fundamental clash of priorities. After 1936 heavy industry wished to take advantage of the brief revival in world trade to boost exports and shift production accordingly. At the same time, however, the regime was seeking to accelerate its drive towards rearmament and autarchy. The clash resulted in a humiliating defeat for the Ruhr. The histories of firms such as Siemens tell of a similar struggle to avoid over-commitment to the rearmaments programme.[67] However lucrative the profits from German rearmament, in the long term German producers simply could not afford to abandon their share of the international civilian market. For manufacturers of innocent consumer goods such as musical instruments the challenge posed by the Nazi regime was even more fundamental. They could not count on vast government orders at home. And foreign sales were badly hit by deteriorating international economic relations and boycotts in protest at the regime's anti-Semitism. Meanwhile, the complicated marketing arrangements characteristic of Germany's most successful exporters entangled them in a war of attrition with Schacht's trade bureaucracy.

The successful military assaults on Poland, Scandinavia and western Europe in 1939–40 were certainly not the product of capitalist imperialism.

As late as 1939, British and German industrialists were engaged in high-level corporate diplomacy and the iron and steel cartel continued to function smoothly.[68] There was little enthusiasm for war when it came and Germany's lightning victories of 1940 were an astonishing surprise to both sides. In their aftermath corporate Germany struggled to take advantage. However, private firms on the whole proceeded with caution.[69] Many of the best facilities had been damaged in the early months of the occupation. Furthermore, the long-term risks of over-capacity and the uncertain pattern of future trade arrangements were disincentives to unfettered expansionism. The Reichsverband der Deutschen Industrie (Reich's Association of German Industry) envisioned a form of customs union, creating an economic zone in Europe free from the obstructions of national regulations, open to organization through private cartel arrangements. The political dominance of Nazi Germany would be paralleled by the economic superiority of German producers. However, the basic aims were still those of the 1920s, to secure in Europe a base for successful competition with the United States.

It was not western Europe but the Soviet Union that was to feel the full weight of German imperialism. The unprecedented military successes of Hitler's armies in western Europe by the summer of 1940 triggered a wave of aggressive euphoria among the elites of the Third Reich. The attack on the Soviet Union in June 1941 was preceded by extensive planning for a savage new racial order, and German businessmen played their part in these breathtaking deliberations.[70] Their enthusiasm for Imperial conquest, however, was largely to be disappointed. The chaotic activities of the German occupation authorities, the irrationality of racial policy and the sheer destructiveness of the war in the east were not good for business. It was, as always, in the west that the really rich pickings were to be had. To supply the war in the east, Albert Speer initiated a division of labour within Germany's western European empire that anticipated the trade patterns of the 1950s and 1960s. The heavy industrial capacity of Belgium and northern France was integrated into the core of the war economy.[71] Firms such as Phillips in the Netherlands or Renault in France became major sub-contractors to the Nazi war effort. It is the imperative for western integration, not eastern European conquest, that has proved to be the really powerful continuity in the history of German business.

What links industrial relations and corporate diplomacy, and how do these issues relate to the broader themes addressed in this article? Clearly, both rationalization and the strategy of national and international cartelization were responses to the economic disaster of the First World War and the overwhelming threat of American competition. These were defensive business strategies, cutting costs, controlling the workforce and restricting competition. But the twin visions of a harmonious *Betriebsgemeinschaft* and a world economy regulated by corporate diplomacy can also be interpreted in political terms. They can both be seen as responses to the crisis of the German state. In the vacuum created by the collapse of the Wilhelmine Empire, the capitalist corporation emerged as an alternative model of political and economic order.[72] The *Betriebsgemeinschaft* offered an attractive alternative to the disunity of the political sphere, a harmonious community of producers and their families, united around the firm as a unit of both production and reproduction. In the moments of most acute crisis in the worst years of the First and Second World Wars, this vision took on a concrete reality. The workplace became a precious site of normality, a source of everyday necessities, of food and clothing, but also a place of coercive order. The corporate diplomacy of the inter-war years can also be interpreted in these terms. This was not the imperialist fusion of business and state power anticipated by Lenin, far from it. Certainly from the German point of view the international cartels of the inter-war period are far more plausibly interpreted as an attempt to stabilize the international economic order in the vacuum left by the failure of conventional diplomacy. Hence the enthusiasm for an economic *Grossraum*, an economic space in which German corporations could realize their visions of self-government on a larger, continental plan.

Conclusion

Over the last two decades there has thus been a profound change in the way in which historians view the role of business in modern German history. However, for all their revisionism recent accounts have remained indebted to the classic interpretations of the turn of the century in one fundamental respect: their continued emphasis on the 'commanding heights' of German capitalism. Our in-depth knowledge of modern German business history continues to be restricted to the experience of no more than a dozen giant firms. The same names – Deutsche Bank, Dresdner Bank, Siemens and AEG, IG Farben, Vereinigte Stahlwerke, Krupp, GHH, Daimler-Benz – recur again and again in the literature.[73] Of course, there are practical reasons for this. It is the large firms that have left the most substantial archives. But this selection of firms is also dictated by the more or less explicit conception that size matters, often accompanied by the claim that it is in the largest firms that we can best study the most advanced and the most modern practices at work. In many ways this is of course right and reasonable. However, from this innocent truism it is only a short step back to the excited contemporary comment of the early twentieth century.

Through our focus on 'the biggest and the best', we continue, almost a century later, to participate in the initial, awed response to the 'birth of organized capitalism'.

This is certainly a sublime spectacle. However, it is becoming increasingly clear that our abiding fascination with the world of the giant corporations has had a distorting effect on our broader understanding of the political economy of modern Germany.[74] The continuity in our conceptual tools has obscured other more fundamental structures. We have tended to forget that until well into the second half of the century, the largest firms embraced only a limited segment of the German economy. The corporate giants certainly contributed disproportionately to national output. But in the inter-war period their share of the total was well below half. Only in a few sectors of the industrial economy, such as steel, chemicals and electrical engineering, did the giants truly rule. Even in mechanical engineering, a 'modern industry' by any account, production continued to be distributed across a mass of small and medium-sized workshops. Most theorists of the turn of the century assumed that this complex reality would soon be simplified through the acceleration of industrialization, urbanization, the extinction of smaller producers and their absorption by the larger firms. In fact, it was not until the economic miracle of the 1950s and 1960s that agrarian and small-town Europe was visited by wrenching social and economic change. It is arguably one of the most characteristic features of the inter-war period that this predicted development failed to occur.[75] It must therefore be a priority of future research to explore more fully the survival of this world of small and medium-sized producers, its relationship to the realm of big business and to the sphere of politics.[76] Such research will give us a much fuller understanding of the political economy of inter-war Germany. We may also gain the necessary intellectual distance from which to historicize the theoretical legacy of the turn of the century, which for so long has shaped our understanding of Germany's past.

Notes

1. For the developing view from the left, see R. Walther, '. . . *aber nach der Sündflut kommen wir und nur wir.' 'Zusammenbruchstheorie', Marxismus und politisches Defizit in der SPD, 1890–1914* (Frankfurt, 1981); F. R. Hansen, *The Breakdown of Capitalism: A History of the Idea in Western Marxism, 1883–1983* (London, 1985), pp. 32–67.

2. For an influential contemporary analysis see K. Helfferich, *Deutschlands Volkswohlstand, 1888–1913*, 3rd edn (Berlin, 1914).

3. See for example J.J. Sheehan, *The Career of Lujo Brentano: A Study of Liberalism and Social Reform in Imperial Germany* (Chicago, 1966).

4. K.D. Barkin, *The Controversy over German Industrialization, 1890–1902* (Chicago, 1970).

5. L. Kolakowski, *The Main Currents of Marxism*, vol. 2 (Oxford, 1978).

6. See Bernstein's classic revisionist critique, first published in 1898: E. Bernstein, *Evolutionary Socialism* (New York, 1961). For the ensuing debate see H. Tudor and J.M. Tudor, *Marxism and Social Democracy: The Revisionist Debate, 1896–1898* (Cambridge, 1988).

7. G. Schmoller, 'Was verstehen wir unter dem Mittelstand?', *Verhandlungen des 8. evangelischen Kongresses* (Göttingen, 1897).

8. W. Sombart, *Die deutsche Volkswirtschaft im neunzehnten Jahrhundert* (Berlin, 1912).

9. Most famously V.I. Lenin, *Imperialism the Highest Stage of Capitalism* (Moscow, 1982).

10. T. Veblen, *Imperial Germany and the Industrial Revolution* (London, 1915).

11. For the history of business history see F. Redlich, 'Unternehmungs- und Unternehmergeschichte', *Handwörterbuch der Sozialwissenschaften*, vol. 10 (Stuttgart, 1959), and H. Jaeger, 'Unternehmensgeschichte in Deutschland seit 1945. Schwerpunkte – Tendenzen – Ergebnisse', *Geschichte und Gesellschaft* 18 (1992), pp. 107–32.

12. In the British historiography organized business interests are accorded a far less significant role. See, for example, their cursory treatment in the survey by P. Clarke, *Hope and Glory, 1900–1990* (London, 1996).

13. For a representative overview see E.W. Hawley, 'The Discovery and Study of "Corporate Liberalism"', *Business History Review* 52 (1978), pp. 309–30.

14. A. Dorpalen, *German History in Marxist Perspective: The East German Approach* (Detroit, 1985).

15. G. Iggers, 'Introduction', in G. Iggers, ed., *The Social History of Politics: Critical Perspectives in West German Historical Writing since 1945* (Leamington Spa, 1985), pp. 1–48.

16. J. Kocka, 'German History before Hitler: The Debate about the German Sonderweg', *Journal of Contemporary History* 23 (1988), pp. 3–16.

17. J. Kocka, 'Family and Bureaucracy in German Industrial Management, 1850–1914', *Business History Review* 45 (1971), pp. 133–56.

18. H.U. Wehler, *The German Empire, 1871–1918* (Leamington Spa, 1985), and D. Stegmann, *Die Erben Bismarcks. Parteien und Verbände in der Spätphase des Wilhelminischen Deutschlands. Sammlungspolitik, 1897–1918* (Cologne, 1970).

19. G. Feldman, *Iron and Steel in the German Inflation, 1916–1923* (Princeton, NJ, 1977).

20. N. Ferguson, *Paper and Iron: Hamburg Business and German Politics in the Era of Inflation, 1897–1927* (Cambridge, 1995).

21. G. Plumpe, *Die I.G. Farbenindustrie AG: Wirtschaft, Technik und Politik, 1904–1945* (Berlin, 1988).

22. J. Kocka, *Unternehmensverwaltung und Angestelltenschaft* (Stuttgart, 1968), and *idem, White-Collar Workers in America, 1890–1940* (Beverly Hills, 1980).

23. H.-E. Volkmann, 'Die NS-Wirtschaft in Vorbereitung des Krieges', in W. Deist, M. Messerschmidt, H.-E. Volkmann and W. Wette, *Ursachen und Voraussetzungen des Zweiten Weltkrieges* (Stuttgart, 1979), pp. 211–435. On the surging profits of German business under Nazism see M. Spoerer, *Von Scheingewinnen zum Rüstungsboom* (Stuttgart, 1996).

24. D. Petzina, *Autarkiepolitik im Dritten Reich. Der nationalsozialistische Vierjahresplan* (Stuttgart, 1968).

25. See the reports of the Office of Military Government, US (OMGUS), into IG Farben, Deutsche Bank and Dresdner Bank, republished in the 1980s.

26. V. Berghahn, *Unternehmer und Politik in der Bundesrepublik* (Frankfurt, 1985).

27. In the 1970s both Siemens and Deutsche Bank used legal action to suppress damaging accounts of their history. The offending sections were blanked out in F.C. Delius, *Unsere Siemens-Welt. Eine Festschrift zum 125. jährigen Bestehen des Hauses S.* (Berlin, 1975), and G.W.F. Hallgarten and J. Radkau, *Deutsche Industrie und Politik von Bismarck bis in die Gegenwart*, 2nd edn (Frankfurt, 1986).

28. The final volume of the official history of Siemens is entitled *Die Dämonie des Staates*, which translates roughly as 'The demon state'. See G. Siemens, *Geschichte des Hauses Siemens*, vol. 3 (Munich, 1951).

29. For the official version see L. Erhard, *Germany's Comeback in the World Economy* (London, 1953).

30. See R.G. Moeller, 'War Stories: The Search for a Useable Past in the Federal Republic of Germany', *American Historical Review* 101 (1996), pp. 1008–48.

31. J. Steinberg, *All or Nothing: The Axis and the Holocaust* (London, 1990), p. 236.

32. This is the theme of Ferguson, *Paper and Iron*.

33. K. Borchardt, *Wachstum, Krisen, Handlungsspielräume der Wirtschaftspolitik* (Göttingen, 1982).

34. For the outline of an alternative narrative see C. Buchheim, 'Zur Natur des Wirtschaftsaufschwungs in der NS-Zeit', in C. Buchheim *et al.*, eds, *Zerrissene Zwischenkriegszeit: Wirtschaftshistorische Beiträge* (Baden-Baden, 1994).

35. Most radically, Plumpe in his study of IG Farben has espoused the closed-systems theory of Niklas Luhmann: see Plumpe, *Die I.G. Farbenindustrie*, pp. 34–9. But the basic idea is common to most recent work: see for example

L. Herbst, 'Der Krieg und die Unternehmensstrategie deutscher Industrie-Konzerne in der Zwischenkriegszeit', in M. Broszat and K. Schwabe, eds, *Die deutschen Eliten und der Weg in den Zweiten Weltkrieg* (Munich, 1989), pp. 72–134, and N. Gregor, *Daimler-Benz in the Third Reich* (New Haven, CN, 1998).

36. As attempted by R. Overy, 'State and Industry in Germany in the Twentieth Century', *German History* 12 (1994), pp. 93–118.

37. The best account is still G. Feldman, *Army, Industry and Labour in Germany, 1914–1918* (Princeton, NJ, 1966).

38. See J. Kocka, *Facing Total War: German Society, 1914–1918* (Leamington Spa, 1984).

39. J. Caplan, *Government Without Administration: State and Civil Society in Weimar and Nazi Germany* (Oxford, 1988).

40. See the magisterial account by G. Feldman, *The Great Disorder: Politics, Economics, and Society in the German Inflation, 1914–1924* (Oxford, 1996).

41. B. Weisbrod, *Schwerindustrie in der Weimarer Republic. Interessenpolitik zwischen Stabilisierung und Krise* (Wuppertal, 1978).

42. This was established beyond reasonable doubt by H.A. Turner, *German Big Business and the Rise of Hitler* (Oxford, 1985).

43. See L. Gall *et al.*, *The Deutsche Bank, 1870–1995* (London, 1995), pp. 130–356, and C. Kopper, *Zwischen Marktwirtschaft und Dirigismus. Bankenpolitik im 'Dritten Reich', 1933–1939* (Bonn, 1995).

44. I. Kershaw, *Hitler, 1889–1936: Hubris* (London, 1998), p. 425.

45. Hjalmar Schacht had been the business choice for president of the *Reichsbank* in 1924. After resigning over the Young Plan he drifted into the orbit of the Nazi Party, but was never a card-carrying member. On the Ministry under Schacht see W. Boelcke, *Die Deutsche Wirtschaft, 1930–1945. Interna des Reichswirtschaftsministeriums* (Düsseldorf, 1983).

46. See M. Geyer, 'Rüstungsbeschleunigung und Inflation', *Militärgeschichtliche Mitteilungen* 30 (1981), pp. 121–86; M. Geyer, 'Zum Einfluss der National-sozialistischen Rüstungspolitik auf das Ruhrgebiet', *Rheinische Vierteljahresblätter* 45 (1981), pp. 201–64.

47. T.W. Mason, 'The Primacy of Politics – Politics and Economics in National Socialist Germany', in H.A. Turner, ed., *Nazism and the Third Reich* (New York, 1972), pp. 175–200. This is a somewhat misleading phrase in that the 'primacy of politics' seems to imply an autonomy from the economic. As Mason himself insisted, this did not mean an ability magically to overcome real material constraints. The limitations of Germany's resources soon caught up with the Third Reich. The primacy of the political actually consisted in the temporary silencing of business interests and all those who articulated economic

constraints within the political system. This did not, of course, eliminate the problem of scarcity. It simply allowed the Nazi leadership to ignore temporarily the constraints and to impose its own interpretation on the difficulties that arose once the economy did hit the buffers.

48. G. Mollin, *Montankonzerne und 'Drittes Reich': Der Gegensatz zwischen Monopolindustrie und Befehlswirtschaft in der deutschen Rüstung und Expansion, 1936–1944* (Göttingen, 1988); R.J. Overy, 'Heavy Industry in the Third Reich: the Reichswerke Crisis', in R.J. Overy, *War and Economy in the Third Reich* (Oxford, 1994), pp. 93–118.

49. P. Hayes, *Industry and Ideology: IG Farben in the Nazi Era* (Cambridge, 1987).

50. M. Geyer, 'The Nazi State Reconsidered', in R. Bessel, ed., *Life in the Third Reich* (Oxford, 1986), pp. 57–68.

51. The literature, East and West, remains remarkably unanimous on this point: see D. Eichholtz, *Geschichte der deutschen Kriegswirtschaft*, vol. 2, 1941–1943 (Berlin, 1985); L. Herbst, *Der Totale Krieg und die Ordnung der Wirtschaft. Die Kriegswirtschaft im Spannungsfeld von Politik, Ideologie und Propaganda, 1939–1945* (Stuttgart, 1982); G. Janssen, *Das Ministerium Speer. Deutschlands Rüstung im Krieg* (Frankfurt, 1968).

52. M. Geyer, 'The State in National Socialist Germany', in C. Bright and S. Harding, eds, *State-making and Social Movements: Essays in History and Theory* (Ann Arbor, MI, 1984), pp. 193–232.

53. T. von Freyberg, *Industrielle Rationalisierung in der Weimarer Republik. Untersucht an Beispielen aus dem Maschinenbau und der Elektroindustrie* (Frankfurt, 1989).

54. J. Gillingham, 'The Deproletarianization of German Society: Vocational Training in the Third Reich', *Journal of Social History* 19 (1986), pp. 423–32.

55. For a comparison of social policies at a number of major corporations see W. Zollitsch, *Arbeiter zwischen Weltwirtschaftskrise und Nationalsozialismus. Ein Beitrag zur Sozialgeschichte der Jahre 1928 bis 1936* (Göttingen, 1990), pp. 108–78.

56. A. Lüdtke, 'The "Honour of Labour", Industrial Workers and the Power of Symbols under National Socialism', in D.F Crew, ed., *Nazism and German Society, 1933–1945* (London, 1994), pp. 67–109.

57. For a comprehensive survey see M. Frese, 'Sozial- und Arbeitspolitik im "Dritten Reich": Ein Literaturbericht', *Neue Politische Literatur* 38 (1993), pp. 403–46.

58. M. Frese, *Betriebspolitik im 'Dritten Reich': Deutsche Arbeitsfront, Unternehmer und Staatsbürokratie in der westdeutschen Großindustrie, 1933–1939* (Paderborn, 1991), pp. 10–26.

59. R. Hachtmann, *Industriearbeit im 'Dritten Reich'* (Göttingen, 1989), pp. 204–23.

60. Frese, *Betriebspolitik*, pp. 93–113.

61. The German economy had made use of foreign labour since the late nineteenth century. However, the scale of the Nazi foreign labour programme was novel, as was the employment of foreign workers not only in agriculture and mining, but throughout German industry: see U. Herbert, *A History of Foreign Labour in Germany, 1880–1980: Seasonal Workers/Forced Laborers/Guest Workers* (Ann Arbor, MI, 1990).

62. Gregor, *Daimler-Benz.*

63. For a neo-traditionalist account see Volker R. Berghahn, 'German Big Business and the Quest for a European Economic Empire in the Twentieth Century', in V.R. Berghahn, ed., *Quest for Economic Empire: European Strategies of German Big Business in the Twentieth Century* (Providence, RI, 1996), pp. 1–33.

64. L. Herbst, 'Der Krieg und die Unternehmensstrategie deutscher Industrie-Konzerne in der Zwischenkriegszeit', in M. Broszat and K. Schwabe, eds, *Die deutschen Eliten und der Weg in den Zweiten Weltkrieg* (Munich, 1989), pp. 72–134.

65. H.G. Schröter, 'Europe in the Strategies of Germany's Electrical Engineering and Chemical Trusts, 1919–1939', in Berghahn, ed., *Quest for Economic Empire*, pp. 35–54.

66. For an overview see H. Schröter, 'Cartelization and Decartelization in Europe, 1870–1995: Rise and Decline of an Economic Institution', *Journal of European Economic History* 25 (1996), pp. 129–53.

67. W. Feldenkirchen, *Siemens, 1918–1945* (Munich, 1995), pp. 120–34.

68. J. Gillingham, *Coal, Steel and the Rebirth of Europe, 1945–1955: The Germans and French from Ruhr Conflict to Economic Community* (Cambridge, 1991), pp. 1–44.

69. The initiative was taken by the so-called *Parteiwirtschaft* (party-controlled businesses as opposed to private or state-controlled firms) led by the Reichswerke Hermann Goering, the steel conglomerate that emerged from the crisis of 1937. See R.J. Overy, 'German Multi-Nationals and the Nazi State in Occupied Europe', in Overy, *War and Economy in the Third Reich*, pp. 315–42.

70. R.-D. Müller, 'Von der Wirtschaftsallianz zum kolonialen Ausbeutungskrieg', in H. Boog *et al.*, *Der Angriff auf die Sowjetunion* (Frankfurt, 1991), pp. 177–84.

71. J. Gillingham, *Belgian Business in the Nazi New Order* (Ghent, 1977), and *idem*, *Industry and Politics in the Third Reich: Ruhr Coal, Hitler, and Europe* (New York, 1985).

72. Extending somewhat the argument first made by C.S. Maier, 'Society as Factory', in C.S. Maier, *In Search of Stability: Explorations in Historical Political Economy* (Cambridge, 1987), pp. 19–69.

73. And this restricted sample is unrepresentative even of the largest firms in German industry. A list of the top 200 industrial firms in Germany in 1913 starts with Krupp, with a capital of almost 600 million marks, but it ends with

the Schlossbrauerei Schöneberg, a large Berlin brewery with a capital of only 12.6 million.

74. G. Herrigel, *Industrial Constructions: The Sources of German Industrial Power* (Cambridge, 1996).

75. B. Lutz, *Der kurze Traum immerwährender Prosperität* (Frankfurt, 1984).

76. For an exemplary history of a medium-sized manufacturing firm see H. Berghoff, *Zwischen Kleinstadt und Weltmarkt: Hohner und die Harmonika, 1857–1961* (Paderborn, 1997).

CHAPTER SEVEN

Women and the family

LISA PINE

This chapter analyses the impact of state policy upon women and the family in Weimar Germany and the Third Reich, focusing on the themes of eugenics, marriage, divorce, birth control, abortion and family welfare. By placing the subject within its historical context, this essay examines the strands of continuity and change that were evident between the two periods. The First World War had brought about a large upheaval in family life and had created a substantial change to traditional attitudes and values. One reason for this was that conscription had created a social vacuum, in the sense that countless families now lacked the patriarchal authority upon which the functioning of family life had previously depended.[1] Conscription also meant a decrease in family income. The immediate aftermath of the war brought problems too, inflation and unemployment among them. At the family level, there were problems of grief for family members who had died in battle, but also the burden of many men who returned home crippled or psychologically disturbed. The mid-1920s, however, became years of relative stability for the German family, as most people sought an ordered home and a sense of peace and security.[2] The family was a place of refuge.

The postwar period witnessed some significant changes in German society. In the new Weimar Constitution of 1919, women achieved suffrage. New educational initiatives on sexual hygiene and birth control were introduced by organizations such as the Association for Sexual Hygiene and Life Reform and the National Union for Birth Control and Hygiene, set up in 1923 and 1928 respectively.[3] There was a movement towards a more rational approach to sex, with an emphasis upon sexual health and hygiene, such as contraception advice and information about venereal disease. Yet, simultaneously, there was a call for traditional values and protection of the genetic stock of the nation. The Weimar Republic was characterized by an ambivalence towards liberalization and the dropping of old taboos. There were some moves towards modernization, but the impact of these modernizing forces generated a conservative backlash.[4] Sexual promiscuity, rising divorce and abortion rates, and higher numbers of married women at work were considered to be signs of the demise and decline of the family. Crude birth rates declined faster in the 1920s than at any other point in German history.[5] The decline in the birth rate was seen by conservative forces not as a 'rationalization of sex life' but as a 'national catastrophe'.[6] Predictions about the 'death of the nation' and the depletion of the race were clearly extant in Weimar society and were not new under National Socialism.

The impact and achievements of the women's movement diminished considerably during the course of the Weimar period. Once the right to vote had been achieved in 1919, together with a constitutional promise of equality, progress dwindled and the organized women's movement itself was crippled.[7] In addition, despite the rhetoric of emancipation in the Weimar Republic, patriarchal ideology and attitudes remained dominant in political, social and economic life.[8] In these respects, National Socialist ideology towards women and the family was not new and a foundation for Nazi policies already existed.

The position of the family waned with the effects of the economic crisis engendered by the Wall Street Crash in 1929. This time it was largely a financial burden that families faced. The economic crisis eroded the material basis of middle-class family life, as savings were lost, and of working-class family life, as mass unemployment meant that workers lost their jobs and incomes. This placed a considerable strain on the mother to search for cheap provisions, mend clothes and maintain the cohesion of the family. Young, unemployed family members sometimes left home, wandering across Germany, and even beyond the borders, to relieve the strain on the family of 'unnecessary eaters'.[9] The economic climate of the early 1930s created many social rifts, for example between the employed and the unemployed and between generations. Inter-generational conflict sharpened considerably as parents lost their status and prestige through unemployment and impoverishment, and many were no longer in a position to provide their children with protection and security. Such tensions were advantageous to the Nazi Party, which capitalized upon the 'crisis of the family'. Loss of savings and financial security, as well as utter desperation, and the host of other problems associated with the depression, attracted many women to vote for the Nazi Party – which promised employment and recovery of the economy – in the hope that they would be able to feed their families again. In addition, the ideological image of women promoted by the Nazis found ready acceptance among many women as well as men during the last years of the Weimar Republic.[10]

When Hitler came to power in January 1933, the National Socialist government had to formulate policies not only to ameliorate the plight of the German economy, but also to redress the 'crisis of the family' and the decline in the nation's birth rate. Capitalizing upon the conservative backlash against the loosening of patriarchy and the changes in sexuality and family life during the Weimar era, the new regime claimed that its policies would restore traditional models of the family. Organicist theories of the state, which had evolved over the previous two decades, became part of the policy-making process. The state was conceptualized as an organism, in which the family represented a crucial elemental cell.[11] 'The family is the primordial cell of the *Volk*, that is why the National Socialist state places it at the centre of its policy.'[12] These were the words of Wilhelm Frick, Reich Minister of the Interior, in a broadcast to the nation on 13 May 1934. They sum up the image that the National Socialist government wanted to portray publicly, that is, of a very firm and solid commitment to family life.

The National Socialists attributed the dwindling birth rate to the spiritual and ideological setbacks that had affected German society in the years preceding the *Machtergreifung*. The senseless, extravagant enjoyment of the individual during the Weimar Republic had taken precedence over collective moral obligations. Hence, 'duty' towards the community through kinship and family, marriage and childbirth, had been lost in a flurry towards 'internationalism', 'pacifism' and 'racial mixing'. The National Socialists claimed that the Weimar governments had encouraged egocentricity and independence, with taxation laws that showed a hostility to marital and familial life. Bachelorhood and childless marriages had been completely acceptable in Weimar society. The average family had had two children, while large families had been seen as abnormal, and as inimical to the good of society. Large families, often living in poverty and hunger, had been the subjects of scorn and derision in Weimar society, which failed to recognize, according to the National Socialists, that it was these very families that were fulfilling their biological obligations to the continued existence of the nation. From 1933 onwards, these Weimar attitudes were completely reversed. As one eugenicist put it: 'The worth of a nation is shown in the preparedness of its women to become valuable mothers . . . Germany must once again become a fertile land of mothers and children . . . the existence or non-existence of our people is decided solely by the mother.'[13] While men fought on the battlefield, women also had a battle to fight – to produce a new generation of Germans.[14] Parents of large families were to be proud of their 'swarm of children'.[15] Now there was a stigma attached to being unmarried or childless, with peer pressure among colleagues to marry and have children becoming increasingly apparent.[16]

The family had a key social function in Nazi society because it had a specific duty to fulfil. It was seen as the 'germ cell' of the nation and as the source of '*völkisch* renewal', through reproduction. As such, it became the most important eugenic tool. Racial hygiene played a significant part in Nazi policies pertaining to the family. Indeed, it became a cornerstone of state policy under National Socialism, with the introduction of legislation designed to improve not only the quantity but also the quality of the German population. Before examining eugenics under National Socialism, an overview of the origins and development of racial hygiene in Germany in the years prior to the Nazi era is helpful in order to establish continuities and discontinuities.

Eugenics

The eugenics movement in late nineteenth- and early twentieth-century Germany was a heterogeneous one.[17] Although its members were largely from the educated middle class, there were two key distinctions within the movement. First, there was that of political orientation, for eugenics was not solely a right-wing phenomenon. It spanned the entire political spectrum in the years preceding the Nazi *Machtergreifung*. Alfred Grotjahn, for example, was a prominent socialist eugenicist, and the *Deutscher Bund für Volksaufartung und Erbkunde*, formed in 1926 in Berlin and chaired by Carl von Behr-Pinnow, was a centre-left eugenics society. Secondly, not all eugenicists readily accepted ideologies of Nordic or 'Aryan' supremacy. Many central figures in the racial hygiene movement, such as Alfred Ploetz, Max von Gruber, Ernst Rüdin and Fritz Lenz, did indeed embrace these ideologies, advocating the use of racial hygiene to promote the Nordic race. Ploetz and Lenz founded a secret 'Nordic ring' within the eugenics movement in 1911 for this purpose.[18] But there were also a number of influential eugenicists, including Wilhelm Schallmayer, Hermann Muckermann and Alfred Grotjahn, who rejected Nordic supremacy. This conflict manifested itself in the two main centres of the *Deutsche Gesellschaft für Rassenhygiene*. The Berlin institute was rather moderate, rejecting any unscientific notions of 'Aryan' supremacy, while the Munich institute was pro-Nordicist and much more right-wing.

Apart from these two important distinctions, the common aims of the eugenics movement were to promote and increase the nation's 'fit' elements, and to 'eliminate' the 'unfit' – that is, the anti-social and the 'asocial'. This reflected the middle-class prejudices of the racial hygienists, and like other eugenics movements both in the United States and elsewhere in

Europe, racial hygiene in Germany before 1933 was more concerned with class than race. Advocates of racial hygiene believed that rational management of the German population, by controlling the reproductive capacities of various groups within it, would lead to the attainment of a healthier and more productive nation. The social, political and economic problems that beset Germany during the Weimar Republic required quite radical solutions, and it was during this time that eugenics – as a means of boosting the level of productivity and 'fitness' within the German population – flourished.[19] Two new research centres were set up – the German Research Institute for Psychiatry, founded in 1918, in Munich (renamed the Kaiser Wilhelm Institute for Psychiatry in 1924), and the Kaiser Wilhelm Institute for Anthropology, Human Heredity and Eugenics, founded in 1927, in Berlin. In addition, the *Deutscher Bund für Volksaufartung und Erbkunde* and the *Deutsche Gesellschaft für Rassenhygiene* merged in 1931 into a larger, more popular and more influential organization, the *Deutsche Gesellschaft für Rassenhygiene* (*Eugenik*). Political and ideological differences were put aside, so that its members could try to achieve their common goal of using eugenics as a scientific solution to social and welfare problems.

During the Weimar era, racial hygiene aimed to arrest the decline of the German *Volk* and state. Class prejudices continued to play a key role in racial hygiene. The 'inferiority' of specific social groups was considered to be a reflection of their innate characteristics. High fertility among the socially unstable sectors of the population was seen as a serious threat to the future well-being of the nation.[20] Influential figures such as Lenz aimed to preserve their class from biological extinction. Hence the term 'fit' was applied almost exclusively to the educated and 'socially valuable' elements in society. Essentially, 'performance' and 'success in social life' were the yardsticks by which the 'worth of individuals and families' was measured.[21] Indeed, by 1931 the dire economic situation meant that rationalization and the efficient use of resources became key preoccupations. Muckermann's view that it was necessary to 'reduce the number of hereditarily ill individuals . . . by means of eugenics' became quite widely accepted in influential circles beyond the medical profession.[22] In 1932, a sterilization bill was drafted by the Prussian Health Council, allowing for the voluntary sterilization of certain types of hereditarily ill individuals. The proposals were welcomed by a number of medical organizations, but as a result of the prevailing political problems, the bill was not passed during the Weimar Republic. However, that a sterilization bill was introduced at all demonstrates the achievements of the eugenics movement and the sizeable increase of its influence by 1933.[23] The developments in racial hygiene during the Weimar period also show that Nazi eugenic policy did not emerge as a novelty, but followed on from existing trends.

Under National Socialism, however, the course and scope of racial hygiene changed dramatically. No longer just the concern of a fairly narrow elite of intellectuals and medically trained professionals, racial hygiene became a central part of state policy, in accordance with the National Socialist *Weltanschauung* and Hitler's pathological obsession with the preservation of the 'Aryan' race. The *Deutsche Gesellschaft für Rassenhygiene (Eugenik)* lost its independence and became a government organ within the domain of the Ministry of the Interior. The Berlin, non-racist eugenicists quickly lost their influence as the Nazi government imposed its brand of racial hygiene upon the movement. Figures such as Muckermann and Ostermann were removed from their offices and forced into early retirement, while many others left the society of their own volition and Jewish members were expelled from the society by 1934.[24] An overtly racist line was taken by Germany's leading eugenicists – especially Lenz, Ploetz and Rüdin – whose earlier unattained desires for 'nordification' now became a firm priority on the government's agenda.

On 14 July 1933, the Law for the Prevention of Hereditarily Diseased Offspring was passed. It went much further than the proposal of 1932, by calling for the compulsory sterilization of individuals suffering from certain 'hereditary diseases'.[25] These were: 'congenital feeble-mindedness', 'schizophrenia', 'manic depression', 'Huntingdon's chorea', 'hereditary blindness', 'hereditary deafness' and 'serious physical deformities'. In addition, chronic alcoholics could be compulsorily sterilized. The law was officially declared to embody the 'primacy of the state over the sphere of life, marriage and family'.[26] Between January 1934, when the decree came into effect, and the outbreak of war in September 1939, approximately 320,000 people (0.5 per cent of the German population) were sterilized under the terms of this law.[27] The quantitatively and strategically most important group sterilized were the 'feeble-minded'. This category made up some two-thirds of those sterilized, and almost two-thirds of these were women.[28] Many of these people were of German ethnicity, but from the poorest sectors of society, while others were from ethnic minority groups or were the inmates of asylums and psychiatric institutions.[29]

Under National Socialism, eugenicists were expected to aid the regime in carrying out its objective of improving the German race, by 'eliminating' the 'hereditarily ill' as well as the 'socially unfit'. The implementation of eugenic policies demonstrated a very close alliance between science and the state.[30] Racial hygienists played a significant part in the realization of Nazi policy by teaching eugenics to state-employed and SS doctors, providing expert testimony in the sterilization cases brought before the hereditary health courts, composing racial genealogies and at least half-heartedly accepting both the regime's 'euthanasia' programme and the 'Final Solution'.

In order to maintain their own positions and obtain finance for their institutes and research, leading eugenicists joined the Nazi Party and accommodated themselves to the racial policy of the Nazi government. Even when government policy became much more extreme than they themselves might have thought necessary, the eugenicists continued their work, despite the atrocities carried out by the Nazi government in the name of science. Ultimately, the logic of eugenics was translated by the Nazi regime into a practice for its own ends, far more sinister than those anticipated by the welfare-orientated eugenicists of the Weimar era.

Marriage, divorce, birth control and abortion

The National Socialists' objectives of an increased birth rate, racial homogeneity and a regimented social life invaded the private domain of the family quite profoundly. In 1934–5, the Nazi regime began to reorganize and expand the public health system, making it a modern tool for enforcing Nazi population and racial policy.[31] These policies had a considerable impact upon laws relating to marriage, divorce, birth control and abortion, and significant changes from the Weimar era can be traced in this respect.

In *Mein Kampf*, Hitler spoke of the necessity to raise the status of marriage and to 'give it the consecration of an institution which is called upon to produce images of the Lord'.[32] In addition, he stressed the need for early marriage as the prerequisite for 'healthy and resistant offspring'. He claimed that 'marriage cannot be an end in itself, but must serve the one higher goal, the increase and preservation of the species and the race'.[33] Indeed, this became one of the central themes of both Nazi propaganda and policy directives concerning the family. Yet, as leader of a nation upon which such codes of behaviour were unremittingly urged, Hitler did not set the example himself. Publicly, he claimed that he remained single because he was devoted to the community of his nation. Privately, he said: 'It's lucky I'm not married. For me, marriage would have been a disaster.'[34] He claimed: 'I am a completely non-family man with no sense of the clan spirit.'[35]

Despite Hitler's failure to set an example in this respect, marriage was of great significance to the National Socialists. Hitler believed that 'where marriage itself is concerned, it is, of course, essential that both parties should be absolutely healthy and racially beyond reproach'.[36] In this respect, marriage had a large part to play in the 'racial preservation' of the nation. 'In the blood alone resides the strength as well as the weakness of man . . . People who renounce their racial purity renounce with it the unity of their soul in all its expressions.'[37] The prohibition of marriages between 'racially pure', 'healthy' Germans and the 'unfit' or 'racially inferior' was a method of preventing this kind of 'renunciation'. It took the form of new Nazi legislation in 1935. The Law for the Protection of German Blood and Honour – one of the Nuremberg Laws, 15 September 1935 – prohibited marriages and sexual relationships between Jews and 'Aryans'.[38] On 18 October 1935, the Law for the Protection of the Hereditary Health of the German People or Marriage Health Law was issued, which effectively excluded the 'inferior' and 'alien' from the *Volksgemeinschaft*.[39] This law required all prospective spouses to produce a 'certificate of fitness to marry', issued by the local health authorities. Such certificates were denied to those with serious infectious or 'hereditary' diseases. These measures demonstrate that, to the National Socialists, marriage was not a free community of two people, but purely an institution for procreation.[40] The biologization and medicalization of marriage led to an unprecedented restriction of individual liberties.

The case of Else K. provides a typical example of the marriage health law and sterilization policies of the Nazi regime.[41] Else K. had to undergo a medical examination in order to ascertain her 'fitness to marry'. She failed her 'intelligence test'. In addition, information came to light about her deceased brother, who had been in an asylum for 'schizophrenia'. As a result of these two factors, she was sterilized in 1935. Furthermore, she was denied the right to marry the man of her choice, as he was 'hereditarily fit'. A marriage between a sterilized 'hereditarily ill' person and a 'hereditarily healthy' person went against the interests of the *Volksgemeinschaft*, as the marriage would be childless and 'valuable' offspring would be lost.

On the positive side, incentives to promote early marriages between healthy, 'Aryan' partners included the marriage loan scheme, which was contained in the Law for the Reduction of Unemployment, 1 June 1933.[42] According to this law, an interest-free loan of up to RM 1000 could be made to a German couple in the form of vouchers for the purchase of furniture and household equipment. The granting of a loan was conditional upon the woman giving up paid employment. The two main reasons for this were to encourage women back into the home and to create job opportunities for men. In addition, it was hoped that the scheme would lower the male marriage age and decrease men's need for prostitution.[43] The loans were to be repaid at the rate of 1 per cent per month. A supplementary decree of 20 June 1933 stated that the sum to be repaid would be cut by one-quarter for each child born to the couple, so that, in effect, on the birth of the fourth child the repayment was waived altogether.[44] This measure was aimed at encouraging newly-weds to start having children as quickly as possible.

Another salient feature of the decree was that it made the granting of a loan conditional upon the political attitude and way of life of the couple.

Hence, if one or both of the partners had any affiliations to the KPD or its associated organizations, the loan was denied to them. Conversely, in the case of members of the SS, SA, NSF and other Nazi organizations, political reliability was assumed and the loan was granted. Marriage loans were denied to persons who were or had been 'asocial', for example tramps, prostitutes, alcoholics and those considered to be 'workshy'.[45] Marriage loans could also be refused if either prospective spouse was suffering from a 'hereditary mental or physical disease'. A second supplementary decree of 26 July 1933 required all applicants for a marriage loan to undergo a medical examination.[46] Hence, suitability for marriage had to be proved. Loans were most commonly denied to prospective marriage partners on grounds of psychiatric disorders and infertility.

Between August 1933 and January 1937 some 700,000 marriages, one-third of all those contracted within that period, were assisted by marriage loans. In 1937, the revocation of the prohibition of women's paid employment as a prerequisite of the loans resulted in a sharp increase in applications. In 1939, 42 per cent of all marriages were loan-assisted.[47] However, the loans did not have the desired effect of boosting the nation's birth rate. The long-term trend towards one- and two-child families was not altered appreciably by this measure, as the loans were inadequate to cover the costs of a larger family.[48] Couples granted marriage loans on average had only one child.[49]

In 1938, a reform of the marriage law was introduced, incorporating a new divorce law that facilitated divorce.[50] Under paragraph 53 of this decree, 'premature infertility' became a ground for divorce, as did either partner's 'refusal to procreate', in both cases because the primary purpose of marriage, the preservation and increase of the race, could not be fulfilled. Paragraph 55 allowed for a divorce if the couple had lived apart for three years or more and the marriage had 'irretrievably' broken down. After the enactment of this law, by 1941 21,293 men and 6,648 women had filed for divorce on the grounds of the 'irretrievable breakdown' of their marriage. In the same period, 'premature infertility' accounted for 383 divorces and 'refusal to procreate' for 1,771 divorces.[51]

The facilitation of divorce, however, did not stem from liberalistic ideals or from any attempt on the part of the regime to ameliorate the position of private individuals. Instead, it was for the benefit of the *Volk*. The objective was to dissolve marriages that were of no value to the *Volksgemeinschaft*. The logic behind this law was that once a divorce had been granted, the two partners involved might remarry and provide the *Volk* with children. Judges could reduce or entirely waive a husband's obligation to make alimony payments to his former wife if he had subsequently remarried and started a new family.[52] This provision led to 'frequent disgruntlement', according to

SD reports, as women felt that the divorce law, leaving them inadequately protected, contradicted the regime's promotion of large families. Contradictory as it may have seemed, the 1938 divorce law was another method by which the National Socialist regime sought to fulfil its population policy objectives.

The pronatalist imperatives of the Nazi regime could not be met with the prevailing climate in German society of relatively easy access to birth control advice and contraceptives, and with the effects of the relaxation of the abortion laws during the Weimar era.[53] The birth control centres, marriage and sexual counselling centres set up during the Weimar Republic were either closed down by the new Nazi government or absorbed into the public health offices.[54] This suited the political aims as well as the pronatalist ambitions of the Nazi regime, as many of these centres were run by the KPD. Hence, the regime was able to use the Law for the Protection of the People and State of 28 February 1933 to ban birth control organizations on the grounds that they were 'Marxist'.[55] However, the practice of birth control in Germany could not be easily eradicated by the regime. Nazi laws and propaganda merely meant that such practices were reduced and continued underground, rather than eliminated altogether. The real crackdown occurred in January 1941, when Himmler's Police Ordinance categorically banned the production and distribution of contraceptives, but even this did not ensure total success for the regime in this respect.

Abortion legislation in Germany had been incorporated into the Penal Code on 1 January 1872, in the form of paragraphs 218–220.[56] Paragraph 218 stated that a pregnant woman who purposely caused herself to abort was subject to imprisonment for up to five years, unless there were mitigating circumstances, in which case the sentence was reduced to a minimum of six months. The same punishment was applicable to any person who helped in the procurement of an abortion. According to the provisions of paragraph 219, any person who administered an abortion for profit could be imprisoned for up to ten years. Paragraph 220 called for the imprisonment of any person who purposely caused a pregnant woman to abort without her knowledge or consent for at least two years, or, if the woman died as a result of this action, for a minimum of ten years.

Social agitation for a liberalization of these abortion laws had been initiated before 1900, but without success. During the Weimar era, KPD and SPD representatives had introduced demands into the Reichstag for the legalization of abortion. Despite the opposition of the Catholic Centre Party and a number of nationalist groups, in May 1926 a Reichstag majority voted for the consolidation of paragraphs 218–220 of the Penal Code into a single paragraph, paragraph 218. The severity of the sentences was reduced. Detention for a period of between one day and five years was prescribed for a woman who induced her own abortion or allowed it to be carried out by a practitioner. The same punishment applied to the practitioner. If an abortion was carried out for profit or without the consent of the woman, a prison sentence of between one and fifteen years was meted out to the practitioner.

On 26 May 1933, the National Socialist government tightened up the abortion laws again. Paragraphs 219 and 220 were reintroduced.[57] Paragraph 219 stated that any person who advertised, exhibited or recommended articles or procedures for abortion could be fined or imprisoned for up to two years. Paragraph 220 prescribed the same punishment for any person publicly offering his or her services, or those of a third party to carry out an abortion. Abortion on eugenic grounds, however, was permissible, and in some cases, even mandatory.[58]

Illegal abortionists were increasingly punished by imprisonment, rather than by fines. In 1936, Himmler created the Reich Central Office for the Combating of Homosexuality and Abortion, headed by Josef Meisinger, to deal with matters of 'public morality'.[59] Abortion and homosexuality were conceptually linked, as both implied individual choice. In 1937, the anti-abortion campaign led by the Gestapo intensified, with nine times as many abortionists facing legal charges as in the previous year.[60] During the war, measures against abortion became increasingly stringent. It was made almost impossible to have an application for a legal abortion approved, which led to an increase in the number of illegal abortions. On 9 March 1943, a new sub-paragraph was added to paragraph 218, which stated that the death penalty could be imposed upon any person who continually impaired 'the vitality of the German *Volk*' by carrying out abortions.[61]

Family welfare

During the Weimar era, many advances had been made in public health and welfare, including improvements in infant care and welfare for mothers.[62] Although the National Socialists built upon these welfare measures, family welfare in the National Socialist state was aimed primarily at serving the nation, rather than at helping families in need *per se*. Erich Hilgenfeldt, the leader of the *NS-Volkswohlfahrt* (NSV) organization, claimed, 'we want to be fanatical servers of the health of the German *Volk*'. On 28 February 1934, a special agency of the NSV – the *Hilfswerk 'Mutter und Kind'* – was set up to facilitate Nazi population policy. The sphere of work of the *Hilfswerk 'Mutter und Kind'* was split into a number of main functions, including welfare and recuperation for mothers, welfare for small children, and the establishment of help and advice centres.[63]

Welfare for mothers who had recently given birth but did not have sickness insurance had existed since the end of the First World War.[64] However, it was only under the Nazi regime that this whole sphere of welfare became a central element of state policy. Welfare for mothers meant, above all, help in the home. Mothers in financial need were given assistance, although this did not usually entail direct financial aid.[65] Instead, it meant material assistance, such as the provision of beds, linen and children's clothes or food allowances. *Kinderreich* mothers, pregnant mothers or those who had recently given birth were assigned assistance in their household chores by home helps. There were also house visits from welfare workers and/or nurses to help pregnant women avoid miscarriages, illness or premature births, by advising and examining them. Their role was to educate and care for expectant mothers, to prevent problems connected with breast-feeding, to give practical advice on childcare and to observe the general behaviour of the family.[66] Whereas during the Weimar era, welfare was for all, welfare visits to 'hereditarily ill' or 'abnormal' children under National Socialism were restricted 'to a minimum'.[67]

Welfare for mothers also took the form of various recuperation measures. Some moves towards such measures had already been initiated during the Weimar era.[68] However, convalescence for mothers prior to 1933 was not so ideologically motivated nor so fundamental to state family policy as that of the National Socialist period. Recuperation homes were situated in tranquil surroundings, such as in the mountains or by the sea, or at natural springs and spas. The average stay was for 26 days.[69] The practice of ascertaining the 'hereditary-biological' value of each woman was a dominant feature of this whole area of work, and the 'hereditarily inferior' were not considered for recuperation benefits. The recuperation homes had a strong educational aspect to them, not least because of the strong focus upon community life within them. The course of daily activities was quite politicised, so that along with convalescence, in the form of rest, good, wholesome food and exercise, mothers coming to these homes received a large dose of National Socialist ideology. For example, the definition of the special role of women in the National Socialist *Volksgemeinschaft* was the subject of considerable attention in these homes. The aim of the mothers' rest care was 'to toughen up German women for their tasks in the house and family'. The staff of the recuperation homes observed the mothers carefully and made reports about their behaviour and attitudes. The work of the recuperation homes was not purely for the benefit of the individual mothers who visited them, but, more importantly, for the good of the entire *Volk,* for mothers returned home with renewed strength and spirit to undertake their familial duties, which benefited their children as well as themselves.[70] According to official NSV statistics, 40,340 women were sent to recuperation homes in 1934. This number rose to 77,723 in 1938.[71]

With regard to health policy, special attention was devoted to the prevention of infant mortality by means of wider education of the public in childcare. The infant mortality rate of 7.7 per cent in 1933 was reduced to 6.58 per cent by 1936.[72] Prevention of childhood disease was also a central aim of NSV work – 'what is prevented in childhood is prevented for life'.[73] It was considered dangerous for the future of the nation for infants and small children to be negatively affected by factors such as lack of care and bad nutrition, hence the promotion of their health was a key function of the *Hilfswerk 'Mutter und Kind'*. Advice and consultation centres were essential in contributing both to the population policy objectives of the regime and to a heightened awareness of issues such as prevention of illness, the importance of breast-feeding and correct nutrition.[74] General health education was also served by a pamphlet entitled 'The Adviser for Mothers', of which almost 1.2 million copies were distributed in 1937.[75]

Childcare was an important aspect of welfare work. Children under six were sent to day nurseries or kindergartens, where they could be looked after properly, especially if their mothers had jobs outside the home. The 'Guidelines for Day Nurseries' in 1936 set out the following among its tasks: to sponsor the physical, mental and spiritual development of the children, to educate them in National Socialism and service to the *Volksgemeinschaft*, and to instil in them a sense of care for the German nation. Hence, the nurseries clearly had the function of socializing small children in the spirit of National Socialism. NSV kindergartens were considered to be 'essential bases . . . for the education of young German people'.[76] According to official NSV statistics, the number of day nurseries rose from approximately 1,000 in 1935 to 15,000 in 1941. In addition to ordinary nurseries, 'harvest kindergartens' were set up in rural areas. These freed agricultural women from their familial responsibilities during the day, allowing them to carry out their harvesting. 'Harvest kindergartens' were first set up in the summer of 1934, to take in healthy, unsupervised children from the age of two upwards. The number of 'harvest kindergartens' increased from 600 in 1934 to 8,700 in 1941 and to 11,000 in 1943.[77] They promoted the physical, mental and spiritual development of the children and educated them in the ideas of National Socialism.[78]

A network of help centres was set up throughout Germany to offer advice to mothers who sought it. These centres were an important focus of *Hilfswerk 'Mutter und Kind'* work. By 1935, 25,552 such centres had been set up.[79] They offered advice about all aspects of household management, nutritional questions, health, care of babies and education of children, as well as all types of family problems. In 1937, 3,274,049 people visited these centres, as compared to 2,824,932 the previous year. The most important function of the centres was educational. Their staff were in direct contact with the population and as such were able to spread National Socialist ideology quite easily.[80] There were 28,936 such centres in 1941, of which 8,136 incorporated professional medical advice.[81] However, not least because of problems connected with the war, the need for more centres was urgently felt in 1943.[82] The NSV aimed to expand the scope of the centres, so that each would have a catchment area of between 3,000 and 8,000 inhabitants. Medical advice was made available every eight days in the big cities, every four weeks in small towns and large villages, and every six to eight weeks in small, rural communities.

Although nascent welfare measures already existed in the Weimar Republic, the ideological conception of the NSV under National Socialism meant a change from traditional welfare care to one which was primarily understood in population policy terms.[83] In this sense, the NSV provided 'preventive welfare', promoting 'racially pure' and 'fit' Germans and discriminating against the 'inferior', regardless of the level of their need or suffering.

Conclusion

In conclusion, there were many links and continuities between policies directed at women and the family during the Weimar Republic and the Third Reich. The starkest contrast, however, was that in order to regenerate the 'body of the nation', Nazi policy increased state intervention into the private sphere, on racial and biological grounds. Under National Socialism, family rights were suppressed as the regime aimed to control, define and categorize both sexuality and the family. This was a clear contrast to the liberal conception of the family as the last place of refuge for the individual against the encroachment of state intervention.[84] Despite its allegations about the negative implications of the Weimar period for the family and its claims to re-establish the true meaning of the family after the 'liberal capitalists' and 'Marxists' had destroyed its 'moral foundations', the Nazi regime, in reality, itself undermined the German family in an unprecedented way. It did so by subjecting the family to encroachment and mechanisms of control, by reducing its socialization function, by attempting to remove its ability to give emotional shelter and provide for its members, and by subjecting it to the racial thinking that was so central to Nazi ideology. The Third Reich imposed an unprecedented supervision and control of births, marriages and sexuality. The Nazis' investment into marriages and families was also much greater than that of Weimar governments. Yet the legacy of the National Socialist era for the German family was the ultimate destruction of the private sphere, in physical and practical terms, as well as morally and spiritually. At first, the Nazis delivered on their promise of recovery of the economy and employment, and the promotion of the family, but in the end they did not. Their claims to restore traditional family values and the family *per se* were not upheld and remained just rhetoric. Ultimately, both Nazi policy and the impact of the Second World War left the family in total disarray.[85] The legacy of the war and of the Nazi regime meant that it was only in the 1950s that everyday family life began to regain any true sense of unity and concord.[86] In 1953, the German Federal Republic set up a Ministry for Family Concerns. This was a reflection of the status regained by the family as a source of renewal and stability. By the early 1950s, the family had regenerated, stabilized and strengthened itself. Once again it became a source of emotional support to its members, something it had not been permitted to be under the Nazi dictatorship.

Notes

1. R. Sieder, *Sozialgeschichte der Familie* (Frankfurt am Main, 1987), p. 212.

2. Ibid., p. 213.

3. U. Frevert, *Women in German History: From Bourgeois Emancipation to Sexual Liberation* (Oxford, 1989), p. 189.

4. D. Peukert, *The Weimar Republic: The Crisis of Classical Modernity* (London, 1991), p. 104.

5. I. Weber-Kellermann, 'The German Family between Private Life and Politics', in A. Prost and G. Vincent, eds, *A History of Private Life. V: The Riddle of Identity in Modern Times* (London, 1991), p. 515.

6. Frevert, *Women in German History*, p. 188.

7. R. Bridenthal and C. Koonz, 'Beyond *Kinder, Küche, Kirche*: Weimar Women in Politics and Work', in R. Bridenthal, A. Grossman and M. Kaplan, eds, *When Biology Became Destiny: Women in Weimar and Nazi Germany* (New York, 1984), pp. 33–65.

8. Ibid., p. 35. See also Peukert, *The Weimar Republic*, p. 99.

9. Sieder, *Sozialgeschichte der Familie*, p. 225.

10. Peukert, *The Weimar Republic*, p. 101.

11. On the origins and development of this ideology, see P. Weindling, 'The Medical Profession, Social Hygiene and the Birth Rate in Germany, 1914–18', in R. Wall and J. Winter, eds, *The Upheaval of War: Family, Work and Welfare in Europe, 1914–1918* (Cambridge, 1988), p. 428.

12. W. Frick, *Wir bauen das Dritte Reich* (Berlin, 1934), p. 54.

13. A. Mayer, *Deutsche Mutter und deutscher Aufstieg* (Munich, 1938), p. 38.

14. R. Wiggershaus, *Frauen unterm Nationalsozialismus* (Wuppertal, 1984), p. 21.

15. Frick, *Wir bauen das Dritte Reich*, p. 54.

16. R. Proctor, *Racial Hygiene: Medicine under the Nazis* (London, 1988), p. 121.

17. On the origins and early development of German eugenics, see P. Weingart, J. Kroll and K. Bayertz, *Rasse, Blut und Gene. Geschichte der Eugenik und Rassenhygiene in Deutschland* (Frankfurt am Main, 1992), pp. 36–42. See also J. Noakes, 'Nazism and Eugenics: The Background to the Nazi Sterilisation Law of 14 July 1933', in R. Bullen *et al.*, eds, *Ideas into Politics* (London, 1984), pp. 75–84.

18. S. Weiss, 'The Race Hygiene Movement in Germany, 1904–1945', in M. Adams, ed., *The Wellborn Science: Eugenics in Germany, France, Brazil, and Russia* (Oxford, 1990), p. 34.

19. On population policy and racial hygiene debates in the Weimar Republic, see J. Flemming, K. Saul and P. Witt, eds, *Familienleben im Schatten der Krise. Dokumente und Analysen zur Sozialgeschichte der Weimarer Republik* (Düsseldorf, 1988), pp. 28–35.

20. M. Teitelbaum and J. Winter, *The Fear of Population Decline* (Orlando, 1985), p. 50.

21. E. Baur, E. Fischer and F. Lenz, *Grundriss der menschlichen Erblichkeitslehre und Rassenhygiene* (Munich, 1923), vol. 2, p. 192.

22. H. Muckermann, 'Illustrationen zu der Frage: Wohlfahrtspflege und Eugenik', *Eugenik* 2 (1931), pp. 41–2.

23. On the campaign for sterilization during the Weimar era, see P. Weindling, *Health, Race and German Politics between National Unification and Nazism, 1870–1945* (Cambridge, 1989), pp. 450–7.

24. Weiss, 'The Race Hygiene Movement', pp. 41–2.

25. 'Gesetz zur Verhütung erbkranken Nachwuchses vom 14. Juli 1933', *Reichsgesetzblatt 1933*, 1, pp. 529–30. See also Weingart, Kroll and Bayertz, *Rasse, Blut und Gene*, pp. 464–80.

26. A. Gütt, E. Rüdin and F. Ruttke, *Gesetz zur Verhütung erbkranken Nachwuchses vom 14. Juli 1933* (Munich, 1934), p. 5. On this law and its effects on marital life, see also J. Schottky, *Ehe und Krankheit* (Vienna, 1940), pp. 27–36.

27. G. Bock, 'Racism and Sexism in Nazi Germany', in Bridenthal, Grossman and Kaplan, eds, *When Biology Became Destiny*, p. 279.

28. G. Bock, 'Antinatalism, Maternity and Paternity in National Socialist Racism', in G. Bock and P. Thane, eds, *Maternity and Gender Policies: Women and the Rise*

of the European Welfare States, 1880s–1950s (London and New York, 1994), p. 236.

29. Bock, 'Racism and Sexism in Nazi Germany', in Bridenthal, Grossman and Kaplan, eds, *When Biology Became Destiny*, pp. 281–2.

30. G. Czarnowski, *Das kontrollierte Paar. Ehe- und Sexualpolitik im Nationalsozialismus* (Weinheim, 1991), p. 231.

31. G. Czarnowski, '"The Value of Marriage for the *Volksgemeinschaft*": Policies towards Women and Marriage under National Socialism', in R. Bessel, ed., *Fascist Italy and Nazi Germany: Comparisons and Contrasts* (Cambridge, 1996), p. 98.

32. A. Hitler, *Mein Kampf*, trans. R. Mannheim, with an introduction by D.C. Watt (London, 1992), p. 366.

33. Ibid., p. 229.

34. *Hitler's Table Talk, 1941–1944: His Private Conversations*, introduced by H. Trevor-Roper (London, 1953), p. 245.

35. Ibid., p. 650.

36. Ibid., p. 440.

37. Hitler, *Mein Kampf*, p. 307.

38. 'Gesetz zum Schutze des deutschen Blutes und der deutschen Ehre vom 15. September 1935', *Reichsgesetzblatt 1935*, 1, pp. 1146–7.

39. 'Gesetz zum Schutze der Erbgesundheit des deutschen Volkes vom 18. Oktober 1935', *Reichsgesetzblatt 1935*, 1, p. 1246.

40. See H. Kessler, *'Die deutsche Frau'. Nationalsozialistische Frauenpropaganda im 'Völkischer Beobachter'* (Cologne, 1981), pp. 13, 51.

41. On what follows, see A. Nitschke, *Gesundheit im Dienst der Rasse. Zur Geschichte des öffentlichen Gesundheitsdienstes Bremens im Dritten Reich am Beispiel des Bezirksgesundheitsamtes Bremen-Nord* (Bremen, 1993), pp. 8–11.

42. 'Gesetz zur Verminderung der Arbeitslosigkeit vom 1. Juni 1933', *Reichsgesetzblatt 1933*, 1, pp. 323–4.

43. Bock, 'Antinatalism, Maternity and Paternity', in Bock and Thane, eds, *Maternity and Gender Policies*, p. 242.

44. 'Erste Durchführungsverordnung über die Gewährung von Ehestandsdarlehen vom 20. Juni 1933', *Reichsgesetzblatt 1933*, 1, pp. 377–8.

45. J. Noakes and G. Pridham, eds, *Nazism, 1919–1945: A Documentary Reader*, Vol. 2, *State, Economy & Society, 1933–1939* (Exeter, 1984), pp. 455–6.

46. 'Zweite Durchführungsverordnung über die Gewährung von Ehestandsdarlehen vom 26. Juli 1933', *Reichsgesetzblatt 1933*, 1, p. 515.

47. Noakes and Pridham, eds, *Nazism*, p. 451.

48. See M. Burleigh and W. Wippermann, *The Racial State: Germany, 1933–1945* (Cambridge, 1991), pp. 251–2. See also H. Focke and U. Reimer, *Alltag unterm Hakenkreuz* (Hamburg, 1979), pp. 122–3; K. Jurczyk, *Frauenarbeit und Frauenrolle. Zum Zusammenhang von Familienpolitik und Frauenerwerbstätigkeit in Deutschland von 1918–1945* (Frankfurt am Main, 1977), p. 67.

49. J. Stephenson, *Women in Nazi Society* (London, 1975), p. 47.

50. 'Gesetz zur Vereinheitlichung des Rechts der Eheschließung und der Ehescheidung im Lande Österreich und im übrigen Reichsgebiet vom 6. Juli 1938', *Reichsgesetzblatt 1938*, 1, pp. 807ff. On this law, see Noakes and Pridham, eds, *Nazism*, pp. 468–9. See also Stephenson, *Women in Nazi Society*, pp. 42–4.

51. Czarnowski, ' "The Value of Marriage for the *Volksgemeinschaft*" ', in Bessel, ed., *Fascist Italy and Nazi Germany*, pp. 107–8.

52. Ibid., p. 109.

53. On contraception during the Weimar era, see C. Usborne, *The Politics of the Body in Weimar Germany: Women's Reproductive Rights and Duties* (London, 1992), pp. 119–33. See also A. Grossmann, *Reforming Sex: The German Movement for Birth Control and Abortion Rights, 1920 to 1950* (Oxford, 1995).

54. Czarnowski, ' "The Value of Marriage for the *Volksgemeinschaft*" ', in Bessel, ed., *Fascist Italy and Nazi Germany*, p. 99.

55. Stephenson, *Women in Nazi Society*, p. 61.

56. On what follows, see H. David, J. Fleischhacker and C. Höhn, 'Abortion and Eugenics in Nazi Germany', *Population and Development Review* 14 (1988), pp. 83–4.

57. On what follows, see 'Gesetz zur Änderung strafrechtlicher Vorschriften vom 26. Mai 1933', *Reichsgesetzblatt 1933*, 1, pp. 295–6.

58. Proctor, *Racial Hygiene*, pp. 122–3.

59. Burleigh and Wippermann, *The Racial State*, p. 191.

60. David, Fleischhacker and Höhn, 'Abortion and Eugenics in Nazi Germany', p. 94.

61. See Stephenson, *Women in Nazi Society*, p. 69, and *Reichsgesetzblatt 1943*, 1, pp. 140–1.

62. Peukert, *The Weimar Republic*, p. 139.

63. On this, see L. Pine, *Nazi Family Policy, 1933–1945* (Oxford, 1997), pp. 23–38.

64. C. Sachße and F. Tennstedt, *Geschichte der Armenfürsorge in Deutschland. Band 2. Fürsorge und Wohlfahrtspflege, 1871–1929* (Stuttgart, 1988), p. 147; *idem, Der Wohlfahrtsstaat im Nationalsozialismus. Geschichte der Armenfürsorge in Deutschland. Band 3* (Stuttgart, 1992), p. 129.

65. H. Vorländer, *Die NSV. Darstellung und Dokumentation einer nationalsozialistischen Organisation* (Boppard, 1988), p. 67.

66. Bundesarchiv (hereafter BA) NS 37/1010, 'Arbeitsanweisung für die offene Fürsorge für werdende Mütter, Wöchnerinnen, Säuglinge und Kleinkinder', 20 Jan. 1943, pp. 6–7.

67. Ibid., p. 7.

68. See E. Goldacker, *Die deutsche Mutterschaftsfürsorge der Gegenwart* (Leipzig, 1932), p. 71.

69. BA R 89/5242, 'Hilfswerk Mutter und Kind', p. 11.

70. 'Mutter hat Ferien', *Neues Volk*, July 1939, p. 20.

71. See E. Hansen, *Wohlfahrtspolitik im NS-Staat* (Augsburg, 1991), p. 159, for a table showing the growth and development of Hilfswerk 'Mutter und Kind' activities between 1935 and 1942.

72. O. Walter, 'Die NS-Volkswohlfahrt im Dienste der Mutterschaftsfürsorge', *Der Öffentliche Gesundheitsdienst, Teil A*, 20 June 1937, p. 282.

73. H. Rees-Fac, 'Unser Werk für Mutter und Kind', *NS-Frauenwarte*, May 1939, p. 729.

74. On this, see Dr Hoffmann, 'Über Mütterberatungsstunden für Säuglinge und Kleinkinder als wertvollste staatliche Fürsorgeeinrichtung', *Der Öffentliche Gesundheitsdienst, Teil B*, 20 July 1937, pp. 335–9.

75. Institut für Zeitgeschichte Db 36.21, 'Hilfswerk Mutter und Kind', p. 12.

76. BA R 89/5242, 'Hilfswerk Mutter und Kind', p. 14.

77. Vorländer, *Die NSV*, p. 70.

78. BA NSD 30/25, 'Richtlinien für Erntekindergärten im Rahmen des Hilfswerkes "Mutter und Kind"', p. 3.

79. D. Kramer, 'Das Fürsorgesystem im Dritten Reich', in R. Baron and R. Landwehr, eds, *Geschichte der Sozialarbeit* (Weinheim and Basel, 1983), p. 192.

80. BA NSD 57/8–8, 'Im Hilfswerk Mutter und Kind. Arbeit in den Hilfstellen', p. 27.

81. Vorländer, *Die NSV*, p. 266.

82. On what follows, see BA NS 37/1010, 'Arbeitsanweisung', p. 3.

83. H. Vorländer, 'NS-Volkswohlfahrt und Winterhilfswerk des deutschen Volkes', *Vierteljahrshefte für Zeitgeschichte* 34 (1986), p. 359.

84. J. Donzelot, *The Policing of Families* (London, 1980), p. 5.

85. On this, see Pine, *Nazi Family Policy*, pp. 184–7.

86. Frevert, *Women in German History*, p. 265.

CHAPTER EIGHT

Continuities and discontinuities in race: Jews, Gypsies and Slavs under the Weimar Republic and the Third Reich[1]

PANIKOS PANAYI

Introduction

Any discussion about the uniqueness of Nazi Germany would have to focus, above all else, upon racial policy. From the outset of his political career Adolf Hitler, the true Nazi ideologue, wore his anti-Semitism, racism and pan-German nationalism very much on his sleeve. If he ever seized power, he would clearly pursue policies which put such ideas into practice. While he may not have represented the first German politician to hold such views, he became the first one to gain national political control. The period 1933–7 meant the exclusion of minorities through largely legalistic methods, but, from 1938 to 1945, especially during the war, the Nazis acted as they wished.

Nazi ideology revolved around the concept of a superior German Aryan race under threat from other inferior groups both inside and outside German borders. These essentially fell into three categories in the form of Jews, gypsies and Slavs, the last of which consisted of a series of national groupings, both before and after 1939. These three groups became the central racial victims of Nazi ideology. By 1919 all constituted minorities within the German nation state, founded in 1871, although both Jews and gypsies had existed as minorities for centuries before that time.

The Jews represent the oldest ethnic grouping within Germany, existing as a people centuries before the Germans and for over 1,500 years before German unification in 1871, a fact that played a role in the rise of modern German anti-Semitism. However, the modern manifestation of this ideology has roots which are thousands of years old. Wherever Jews had settled historically, hostility had followed them: Germany was no exception. The major manifestations during the medieval period included the slaughter of Jews in towns on the Rhine and Moselle in 1096, in connection with the First Crusade, and the massacres of Jews in 350 towns in 1349, when suspicion circulated that the Jews had caused the spread of the plague. Even when such violence did not occur, Jews had no doubt of their exclusion from Christian society because of numerous restrictions on their activities.[2]

The eighteenth-century Enlightenment meant an improvement in the position of Jews within Germany, and under the Constitution of the German state established in 1871 they became fully emancipated. Nevertheless, while official anti-Semitism may have declined, popular manifestations thrived between 1871 and 1918, witnessed by the rise of anti-Semitic parties, so that German Jewry continued to endure the hostility that had characterized its entire history within Germany. Despite this, German Jewry at the end of the First World War represented a vital and generally wealthy community, enjoying more freedom than at any other time in its history. In 1925 the Jewish population of Germany totalled 564,400, less than 1 per cent of the population.[3]

While gypsies may not have lived in German areas of Europe for quite as long as Jews, their histories of persecution tie these two quintessential outgroups together. Gypsies were first recorded in Germany in Hildesheim in 1407,[4] arriving there after a process of migration originating in northern India about 1,000 years previously and which had resulted in the settlement of gypsies throughout eastern Europe by this time. While they initially faced a mixture of hostility and curiosity from the settled populations, their history from the sixteenth to the eighteenth centuries involved constant persecution. Like the Jews they faced a stream of legislation from rulers of German states of all sizes. The eighteenth century was 'an extremely terrible period of suffering' for the German gypsies, as they 'were hunted, tortured, enslaved and murdered'.[5] The Enlightenment meant attempted forced assimilation rather than emancipation for this uneducated, poor and itinerant group.

While overt hostility may have lessened during the nineteenth century, witnessed most clearly by the fact that some gypsies obtained citizenship for the first time under the *Kaiserreich*, the new German state made attempts to control the movement and way of life of the gypsies. In Bavaria, for instance, the police kept track of the activities of gypsies passing through their area of jurisdiction, while Prussia issued a directive in 1906 for the control of gypsies. By 1926 only about 26,000 gypsies lived in Germany, a dramatic increase from the 2,000 who lived in the country around 1900, largely due to immigration from the Balkans,[6] despite official efforts to keep them out.

The Slavic minorities living in Germany by 1919 divide into several related groups, present in the country because of migration before or after 1871. The largest minority consisted of Poles, with a common origin, but dividing into several groups. While the border between Germany and the Slavic states had changed regularly, it stabilized as a result of eighteenth-century partitions of Poland, which brought about 3 million Polish speakers into Prussian domains, although this number fell by half in 1815.[7] The late nineteenth century witnessed the rise of both Polish and German national-ism in the Prussian areas with Polish populations. The creation of Poland at the end of the First World War reduced the Polish minority in Prussia, although just under 200,000 people who claimed Polish as their native language still lived within German borders in 1925, together with around 400,000 who used both German and Polish.[8] The Polish minority in the Weimar Republic included migrants who had moved to the industrializing Ruhr, from Prussian Poland, after the 1850s and whose numbers may have totalled half a million by the outbreak of the First World War. The size of the figure depends upon whether it includes Masurians, a group who spoke a Polish dialect but practised Protestantism, and who, decisively, did not back Polish nationalism. They may have numbered 150,000 in the Ruhr before 1914.[9] The Kashubians, living in Prussian Poland, viewed them-selves as a separate group because of their distinct language and may have numbered only 2,387 in 1910, which fell further by the start of the Weimar Republic.[10] The Sorbs represented a final Slavic group quite distinct from the Poles. Situated on the border with Czechoslovakia, and using their own language, Wendish, they had experienced a national awakening during the nineteenth century. The 1925 census revealed that 70,908 people used Wendish as their mother tongue.[11] As well as the Slavs, indigenous within the German borders, the *Kaiserreich* had also begun to import foreign workers during the late nineteenth century as domestic labour supplies dried up, a process which involved force during the First World War and set the precedent for the massive Nazi exploitation of foreign labour. While most of the migrants working in Germany on seasonal contracts before 1918 consisted predominantly of Russians and Poles (from the parts of historical Poland under Russian and Austro-Hungarian control), substantial numbers also came from the west, especially Italy, the Netherlands, Belgium and Switzerland. The foreign workers found employment in both industry, especially in the Ruhr, and agriculture, particularly in Prussia, with numbers fluctuating around 1 million for much of the period 1900–18.[12]

The different types of minorities living within Germany at the end of the First World War very much realized their status. Many endured inferior social and economic conditions to ethnic Germans, especially gypsies, Poles, foreign workers, and Jewish immigrants who had recently arrived from Russia. All of these groups had their own languages. These minorities, together with indigenous Jews, also received attention from the pan-German nationalists, who wanted to see German expansion in the east, and racists and anti-Semites, who very much represented a central strand of the political life of the *Kaiserreich*.

The Weimar Republic

The Weimar Republic appears to represent a period of contradiction in German history in which differing forces vied with one another for superiority, and in which the Nazi Party eventually seized power. This also reflects the position of minorities. While they may have experienced some short-term improvements in their position, by the dying years of the Weimar Republic, even before the Nazis seized power, it would be difficult to see an improvement in the position of any ethnic minority group in Germany.

Part of the explanation for this lies in the fact that every section of German society, whether minority or majority, experienced the negative consequences of the economic catastrophe that was Weimar. However, ethnic groups also became ever more visible and victimized in the increasingly racialized political agenda which the Nazis set as they rose to power. Nevertheless, the Nazis were certainly not the only extreme right-wing party in Weimar. One of the most important of the early Weimar groups was the Deutschvölkisher Schutz- und Trutz-Bund, which evolved out of the pre-war Pan German League in 1919 and represented a link to the Nazis, ceasing to exist by 1923. Other smaller local groupings, such as the Bavarian People's Party, also existed during the Weimar period, while student societies represented hotbeds of anti-Semitism and nationalism. Furthermore, the mainstream right-wing parties, in the form of the German People's Party and the German National People's Party, also banged the nationalist drum.

'Antisemitism was endemic to Weimar Germany',[13] with numerous manifestations which affected the lives of the Jewish community in the country. However, the Jews remained an ethnic minority characterized by privilege rather than disadvantage, which, of course, fuelled the resentment against them. Nearly 75 per cent of Jews 'made their living from trade, commerce, banking, and the professions, especially medicine and law' at a time when only 25 per cent of the gentile population worked in such occupations.[14] Nevertheless, like everybody else, Jews suffered under the impact of Weimar inflation and depression which meant, for instance, a decline in their incomes, a reduction in the number of Jewish firms, and unemployment rates on a similar level to gentiles'.[15] Jews played a particularly significant role in the rich cultural life of the Weimar Republic, another cause of Nazi anti-Semitism. Many Jews made their living as theatre directors, actors, film producers, critics, artists, composers and authors. One need only mention names such as Fritz Lang, Max Reinhardt, Arnold Zweig and Otto Klemperer.[16] The centrality of Jews to Weimar culture is explained both by their generally superior economic position and by their concentration in urban areas. In 1925 nearly 70 per cent of German Jews lived in the largest cities, compared with 25 per cent of gentiles, with 31 per cent of all Jews residing in Berlin.[17]

The centrality of Jews to German cultural life points to the extent of acculturation and assimilation that had taken place as part of the emancipation process which had begun during the eighteenth-century Enlightenment. Other indications of these processes include a decline in religious practice so that, during the late 1920s, only 41 per cent of Jews in Frankfurt attended services even on the holiest days.[18] An extreme manifestation of assimilation consisted of the development of a literary Jewish self-hatred from the end of the nineteenth century.[19] Nevertheless, this form of complete assimilation was not the norm, with most Jews retaining their religious identity while at the same time taking pride in their German nationality. The participation of Jews in the German army during the First World War provides the best indication of this, as 17.5 per cent of the Jewish population fought in the conflict.[20] Part of the acculturation process had involved moving out of the ghettos characteristic of medieval Jewish settlement patterns throughout Europe. In accordance with their economic position, over two-thirds of Jews 'lived in sophisticated, upper middle class districts of the largest cities' during the Weimar Republic.[21]

Nevertheless, Jews also made efforts to perpetuate their ethnicity, most clearly indicated by the existence of Jewish organizations. The largest of these was the Central Verein Deustcher Staatsbürger Jüdischen Glaubens, established in 1893 to defend Jews against the slurs of anti-Semites. Several Zionist groups also existed, holding particular attraction for those Jews who had migrated to Germany from Russia before the First World War. In addition, there were organizations which reflected the different religious divisions among German Jews.[22] Like the German population as a whole, Jews organized themselves according to any number of issues which held particular groups together. The organizations that existed during the Weimar Republic included, for instance, the Kentrallverband Jüdischer Studenten and the Preußische Landesverband Jüdischer Gemeinde.[23] A Jewish women's grouping, the Jüdischer Frauenbund, had come into existence in 1904 and survived into the Nazi period.[24]

The evolution of Jewish ethnicity from the late nineteenth century mirrored developments in German society, but the fact that separate Jewish organizations did develop points to the existence of the endemic anti-Semitism that characterized the new German state that came into existence in 1871 and which certainly did not disappear with the foundation of the new Republic in 1919. The hatred of Jews manifested itself in all manner of ways. The rise of the Nazis did as much to galvanize anti-Semitism as to create it. At the start of the Weimar Republic there existed 400 *völkish* organizations together with 700 anti-Semitic journals.[25] Against this background Jews faced constant discrimination and violence, which helps to explain their residence patterns. One of the nastiest manifestations consisted of the defiling of Jewish cemeteries, which occurred regularly throughout the Weimar period. Eleven such incidents occurred in 1926, for instance. One of these, in Breslau, resulted in the knocking over of ten headstones on the night of 14–15 December. As the Nazis increased their appeal, an increasing number of synagogues were damaged, totalling 18 in 1930.[26] By this time attacks upon Jews had become a regular occurrence, especially in connection with Nazi demonstrations. Jews also faced economic boycott, becoming increasingly victimized in the dire economic climate of the dying years of the Weimar Republic.[27] Throughout the 1920s all manner of organizations had tried to exclude Jews. In 1926, for instance, the Munich Section of Alpinists passed a motion introducing a *numerus clausus* 'limiting the acceptance of new Jewish members'.[28]

The Weimar Republic clearly represented a period in which the position of German Jews became increasingly difficult as anti-Semitism reached new peaks, although it clearly existed as a potent force before the rise of the Nazis. Nevertheless, Jewish life in Germany, in which anti-Semitism had historically played a central role, remained 'normal', affected as much by economic crisis as racism after 1929.

The Weimar governments did not pass anti-Semitic measures, as the Nazis would. But legislation did come into operation with the aim of controlling the gypsies, representing an intensification of the official concern with this minority which had existed before the First World War. The gypsies continued to differ from the Jews because of their distance from mainstream society, epitomized in their desire to continue their itinerant lifestyle, the main concern of the legislation passed against them during the Weimar Republic. Gypsies technically had the same rights as the rest of the population, but their lack of education limited their ability to exercise them.

Traditional negative views about the gypsies continued to circulate. At the end of the First World War their detractors claimed that they had done well out of the conflict as currency and horse dealers. More generally, stereotypes circulated about them as aimless wanderers who were dirty and lazy and made a living from begging and stealing. Such ideas fed into official policy, initiated on a local level, through police forces, which often had special units to deal with the 'gypsy plague'. Many senior policemen perpetuated the stereotypical views about gypsies. The main concern of the measures introduced during the Weimar Republic consisted of either settling or expelling gypsies from areas over which local governments had control.

As early as 1918 the Interior Ministry of Württemberg passed a measure to prevent gypsies from camping near the settled population and, with the aim of settling gypsies, set up a gypsy settlement in 1925. In 1926 there followed the Bavarian Law for the Combating of Gypsies, Travellers and the Workshy, which implemented severe restrictions upon itinerant populations. In the following year the Prussian Ministry of the Interior decided to fingerprint all gypsies within its territory, while the Interior Ministry of Hessen also introduced its own Law to Combat the Gypsies in 1929, with the aim of registering and keeping track of those within this state. By the end of the Weimar period German gypsies could camp only in police-controlled locations for specific periods of time. The settled population generally supported such measures. In Frankfurt, for instance, local residents with gypsy neighbours complained to the city authorities about their effect upon the surroundings.[29]

Although the Weimar state certainly made life more difficult for gypsies, the measures introduced remain typical of those passed by other twentieth-century liberal democratic states. While the new measures may have eased the task of the Nazis in passing further anti-gypsy legislation, they took hostility towards this minority to new levels, which had been absent from Europe for centuries.

The main pressure upon the settled Slavic minorities in the Weimar Republic consisted of an assimilatory one, again characteristic of a liberal democratic state. Like the Jewish minority, the Polish one managed to survive as an ethnic group, although this remained more the case for those living in parts of eastern Germany which did not become incorporated in the newly created Polish state at the end of the First World War. In fact Poles in Upper Silesia actually staged three unsuccessful uprisings between 1919 and 1921 which German troops suppressed.[30] After this time the Union of Poles in Germany, which also represented those living in the Ruhr, came into existence. This acted as an umbrella organization for smaller Polish groups in the country. The continued existence of Polish schools in both the Ruhr and Prussia played a role in the perpetuation of Polish ethnicity, although under 6,000 children may have received instruction in Polish schools in Germany in 1930.[31] Two more negative factors working against the continued survival of the Polish minority in the Ruhr consisted of emigration and the existence of prejudice. Between 1918 and 1933 one-third of the population of the Ruhr town of Bottrop moved either to the new Polish state, to other parts of Germany or to France.[32] Polonophobia existed throughout German society during the Weimar period, continuing nineteenth-century traditions. It affected all sections of the political spectrum from the extreme right-wing groupings to Otto Braun, Social Democratic Minister President of Prussia, who could speak of the existence of an east–west cultural division. Hostility towards Poles also existed in the German press, with much attention focusing upon Polish schools. Such views filtered through to children and even teachers and helped to intensify the classic assimilatory act of name changing.[33]

The Union of Poles actually worked together with the Sorbs and smaller minorities to establish the Union of National Minorities in Germany in 1924.[34] The position of the Sorbs resembled that of the other Slavic Weimar minorities in the sense that national consciousness survived but declined in a not too favourable climate. Between 1910 and 1933 the number of people who used Sorbish declined by half.[35]

The economic crisis of the Weimar years meant that the numbers of foreign workers entering the country declined, making this period fairly exceptional in terms of the history of labour importation in modern German history. However, while numbers may have decreased, foreign workers did not disappear altogether from the Weimar Republic, although their numbers fluctuated according to the existing economic conditions. Nevertheless, whatever short-term economic determinants may have operated, further structural factors facilitated the importation of foreign labour. These included a continuing fall in the birth rate and the emigration of 603,000 Germans between 1919 and 1932. The importation became more formalized through the establishment of an Imperial Labour Office in 1922 which issued short-term work permits.

Immediately after the end of the First World War the vast majority of the 2 million foreign workers and prisoners of war who had laboured for the German war economy rushed home to Poland, France and Belgium. Despite the mass demobilization of German soldiers, there still remained labour shortages, especially in the eastern agricultural areas, where many foreigners had worked during the war. Persuading Germans to work on Prussian land would have proved difficult and, at the same time, the junkers preferred to employ foreigners because they were cheaper, worked harder and complained less. Consequently, throughout the Weimar period, Prussian agriculture employed an annual average of over 100,000 Polish workers. Continuing the traditions set by the *Kaiserreich*, most foreign workers had short-term annual work permits. Some also laboured in industry and service employment, so that, in 1928, the peak Weimar year in which the economy used non-German workers, 90,999 out of 236,870 people employed worked in non-agricultural activity. The depression meant a decline in foreign worker recruitment, which fell to 10,866 in 1932.[36]

Peacetime Nazism

With the Nazi seizure of power, the position of resident minorities within German borders would seriously deteriorate. For the first time in the history of the modern German state, an overtly racist party gained power. This meant that the endemic and potent anti-Semitism and racism of the *Kaiserreich* and Weimar Republic now became official policy rather than circulating on the fringes. The first six peacetime years of the new regime essentially prepared the way for the hell created during the Second World War. Before 1939 the Nazis displayed some concern for the legitimacy of their actions but certainly did not shy away from using force. The position of minorities consequently deteriorated due to a combination of violent and legalistic changes, which aimed at creating a racial state.

Minorities would have had few doubts that the seizure of power by the Nazis would mean a deterioration in their position. Jews in particular had witnessed the brutalization of politics in the last years of Weimar as well as the increase in violence against them. Furthermore, Nazi ideology, as outlined in *Mein Kampf*, the credo of the new German chancellor, clearly pointed to the fact that a racial party had taken control of Germany. This blueprint for the state that would gradually emerge created the fiction of an Aryan race, epitomised by contemporary Germans, which must remain as pure as possible, as racial mixing led to decline. The main obstacle to German Aryan success consisted of the Jews, whom Hitler described using terms such as 'vermin' and 'parasites'.

During the peacetime Nazi period the new regime introduced a series of important racial laws which wiped away the progress made by indigenous German minorities, above all Jews, since the Enlightenment. In fact, the Nazis passed a total of 400 laws against the Jews alone during their twelve years of power.[37] On 7 April 1933, just a month after the Nazis had gained sole control, the Law for the Restoration of the Professional Civil Service dismissed non-Aryans, overwhelmingly Jews, from government, including academic, employment.[38] Perhaps the most important legislation for the formalization of the racial state consisted of the Nuremberg Laws passed at the end of 1935, which forbade Germans from marrying or having sexual relations with Jews, gypsies or Negroes, and also restricted citizenship to people of 'German blood'.[39] Such measures simply represented the legal basis for a regime which made race a central tenet of its social, economic and, in time, foreign policy.

Immediately upon seizing power the Nazis turned their violent attention to the Jews, so that Jewish life in Germany once again returned to the historical pattern of struggling for everyday survival against a practising

226

anti-Semitic state. In Worms, for instance, 'Jewish stores were tear-gassed' on 12 February, while on 9 March, 'several Jews were brutally beaten by contingents of the local SA'. Such incidents occurred in the town throughout March.[40] The early violence came to an end on boycott day, 1 April 1933. Although in most towns and cities members of the SA and Hitler Youth 'positioned themselves in front of Jewish businesses, carrying posters printed in advance', with the aim of attempting to stop customers from entering, physical attacks also occurred in, for instance, Berlin, Dortmund and Saxony.[41]

While violence may have declined until the *Kristallnacht* pogrom of November 1938, normality in peacetime Nazi Germany meant an experience of everyday discrimination and prejudice in which the state increasingly controlled the activities of Jews while propagating anti-Semitism in all manner of ways, whether through films, newspapers or academic research. A book from the Institute for the Study of the Jewish Question in 1937 tackled questions such as 'Jewish Criminality' and the 'Racial Degeneration of the Jews'.[42] Under such a pervasive anti-Semitism Jews faced constant verbal abuse from 'Aryans' whom they did not know and the ending of long-term friendships, while organizations of all types 'Nazified' themselves by excluding Jews as members.[43] Violence also remained an everyday occurrence, especially in smaller towns and villages, where Jews were particularly visible. On Palm Sunday of 1934, for instance, two Jews were killed during a riot in Gunzenhausen in Franconia.[44] The hostility also filtered through to children especially after schools became segregated in 1935 and 1936. Hannele Zürndorfer remembers children 'teasing and baiting me and pushing me about' while she was growing up in suburban Düsseldorf.[45]

The struggle for survival in peacetime Nazi Germany also meant trying to make ends meet in a situation in which Jews became deprofessionalized due to Nazi legislation. Some turned to itinerant selling, a traditional Jewish occupation, while others had to live off Jewish welfare organizations.[46] Nevertheless, until the *Kristallnacht* pogrom many Jewish shops continued as some Germans still functioned as rational beings when making purchasing decisions.[47]

A semblance of normality also existed in social and religious life. In fact, between 1933 and 1938 Jewish theatre, music, art, film and sport continued.[48] However, social and religious activity did not escape the attention of the state. In the small town of Minden the activities of the synagogue, the Jewish Cultural Association, the Imperial Association of Jewish Front Soldiers, the Zionist Work Association and the Jewish Sports Association Helmannia faced restriction from 1935 and closure in 1937.[49] Not surprisingly, in view of the level of persecution and the spiritual need it created, religious observance and synagogue attendance increased dramatically where possible.[50] Other Jews took more drastic measures including suicide. Although this phenomenon had been higher among Jews than gentiles even before the Nazi era, it 'took on the character of a mass phenomenon' after 1933.[51] Emigration represented another way out, although the Nazis attempted to make this difficult. Nevertheless, about 150,000 of the approximately 520,000 Jews living in Germany in 1933 had left by the beginning of 1938.[52] Some towns had witnessed an even more drastic decrease in their Jewish communities. The Jewish population of Worms, for instance, fell by 65 per cent from 1,104 people in 1933 to 400 by 1938,[53] while that of Munich declined from 9,005 to 6,392 in the same period.[54]

Any semblance of normality that may have remained in Jewish life between 1933 and 1937 had disappeared by the end of 1938, especially after *Kristallnacht*. Anti-Semitism gained a new lease of life following the *Anschluss* with Austria in March, which resulted in pogroms against the Jewish communities there. The Nazis publicized the assassination of an official at the German embassy in Paris on 7 November, leading to the nationwide explosion of anti-Semitic violence on the night of 9–10 November, which resulted in the destruction of 7,500 shops and more than 250 synagogues, as well as at least 236 deaths. In addition, 30,000 Jews faced arrest and incarceration in concentration camps, a clear indication of the unleashing of the Holocaust.[55] Although the surviving internees were released by the spring of 1939, as many as 2,500 may have died within the camps due to a typhus epidemic.[56]

In the ten months between *Kristallnacht* and the outbreak of the Second World War further measures meant that Jews had to pay for the damage caused by the Holocaust, while they faced a ban on attending public entertainment and control of their movement in the areas where they lived.[57] The final few months of peace therefore witnessed an increase in the emigration of Jews from the expanded Reich, which, by the outbreak of war, incorporated Austria and the whole of Czechoslovakia. Despite the obstacles put up by the Nazis and the reluctance of other states to accept Jews, about 115,000 left in the final ten months of peace.[58] Many of these were children leaving behind parents whom they would never see again. Hannele Zürndorfer recalled 'the last clinging embrace: my face against the familiar tweed of my father's coat and the comforting feel of my mother's fur collar'.[59] Peter Gay, on the other hand, was lucky enough to escape with his mother and father, who eventually made their way to the USA.[60]

Like the Jews, the gypsies also faced increasing persecution under the Nazis. They became victims of some of the same racial laws, but also had specific measures directed against them. Nazi ideology increasingly focused upon the gypsies as a 'non-Caucasian' ethnic minority linked 'to Afro-Germans by their darker skin pigmentation and classified like the Jews as aliens and criminals'. The press increasingly backed the elimination of the 'gypsy plague'.[61] Nazi ideology regarding the gypsies developed fully under Robert Ritter, who in 1936 established the Research Unit on Racial Hygiene and Population Biology, within the Imperial Health Office. This proceeded to carry out research on the origins of the gypsies with the aim of providing genealogical and biological data to demonstrate the hereditary nature of gypsy criminal and asocial behaviour, as Nazi ideology revolved around the core of the healthy, normal Aryan. The research involved registering the approximately 30,000 gypsies in Germany.[62]

Against this background the Nazis took new steps to deal with the 'gypsy plague', although the new measures very much fit into the tradition of previous gypsy persecution within Germany, which became increasingly organized under the Weimar Republic. In September 1933 the SA and SS arrested a small number of gypsies for begging and placed them in the camps in Buchenwald, Dachau and Sachsenhausen.[63] The first year of Nazi rule also saw the extension of the 1926 Bavarian legislation to cover the whole country, although several other regions introduced additional legislation. Furthermore, new measures allowed for the sterilization of gypsies.[64]

Persecution of the gypsies increased from 1936. In that year, in the lead-up to the Olympic Games, the police escorted all Berlin gypsies with their caravans and horses to a camp established in the suburb of Marzahn, where they would remain to carry out forced labour.[65] The gypsies of Frankfurt also experienced increasing control in 1936, which again meant the establishment of a camp in which to concentrate them.[66]

By the outbreak of the Second World War, the Nazis had prepared the way for the deportations and murders of gypsies that would take place during the conflict. The year 1938 saw an intensification of persecution for gypsies as well as Jews. The Imperial Police Office in Berlin took over the task of dealing with the gypsies on a nationwide basis.[67] In both 1938 and 1939 the number of gypsies in concentration camps, especially Buchenwald, Dachau and Sachsenhausen, increased.[68] Nevertheless, a degree of normality remained, so that 200 gypsies still lived in Munich at the outbreak of war, either within houses or caravans,[69] despite the history of Bavaria as the centre of gypsy persecution in Germany. But even for those gypsies who remained free before 1939 'life was haunted by the fear of persecution'.[70]

The position of the Slavic minorities in Germany also deteriorated under peacetime Nazism. The Polish population in the Ruhr, for example, faced increasing hostility and pressure to assimilate. In keeping with their heavy-handed tactics, the Nazis closed down Polish societies in the region and increasingly tightened controls over the use of the Polish language.[71] A similar situation developed in Lusatia. Although the Nazis initially treated the Sorbs with caution, especially in view of the fact that they had voted for them in significant numbers, their interests clashed with those of the more racially correct League of Germans of the East, leading to increasing persecution from 1937, including the abolition of the Sorbish organizations, most notably the Domowina, and a ban on the use of Wendish.[72]

In contrast to the situation after the outbreak of war, the Nazis put limited effort into the importation of foreign workers in peacetime, due largely to the desire to solve the German unemployment problem. Nevertheless, foreign workers never disappeared from Germany, despite the closing of the German border to Polish workers in 1932, and, as labour shortages began to develop from about 1936, the Nazi economy increasingly utilized foreigners. Thus, the 148,455 foreign workers in Germany in 1933 had increased to 229,374 in 1936 and 435,903 in the last year of peace, meaning that foreigners constituted 2.12 per cent of the German workforce in 1938–9, divided fairly equally between agriculture and industry. The countries of origin included Poland, whose migrants included a 66 per cent quota of women, Italy, Yugoslavia, Bulgaria and Hungary. Economic conditions in the land of origin encouraged people to move to Germany despite long working hours, which could stretch to twelve per day. As with all sections of the German population, the Nazi state made sure it controlled its imported workers, establishing a Reich Agency Labour Exchange and passing a Foreigner Police Ordinance in 1938.[73]

The ethnic hell of wartime Nazism

The peacetime racial measures of the Nazis simply prepared the way for the genocidal state that would surface following the outbreak of war, especially in the areas in eastern Europe over which the Nazis gained control. Hitler had outlined his attitude towards the east in *Mein Kampf*, which brought ideas which had circulated during the *Kaiserreich* to their logical conclusion. Hitler wanted to seize control of eastern Europe for the purpose of creating *Lebensraum* (living space) for Germans. By moving into this part of the continent, the Nazis could fulfil a further racial goal in the form of eliminating the Jews, as the vast majority of European Jews lived in the eastern half of the continent, especially Poland and the Soviet Union. Furthermore, the Nazis could also make use of what they viewed as racially inferior Slavs as manual labourers in the 'Thousand Year Reich'.

The Nazis therefore had clear racial aims in mind when they invaded an eastern European country, Poland, in 1939. This state, which had deep anti-Semitic traditions like other European states, became the scene of the Final Solution, finally decided upon at the Wannsee conference of January

1942, after which the death camps came into operation. Before then war-time Nazi anti-Semitism had gone through another stage, which essentially destroyed the Jewish communities of Germany and invaded eastern Europe. This involved the establishment of ghettoes, which had characterized medieval European Jewish settlement but had also begun to materialize during peacetime Nazism in Germany. Operating at the same time as the ghettoes were the mobile *Einsatzgruppen*, German and east European troops who shot local Jewish populations in the Soviet Union.

For German Jews the first years of the war meant the further elimination of any lingering traces of freedom that might have survived. In the first place, following the 1938 pogrom, new employment restrictions meant that most of those who had continued practising as doctors and lawyers during the early Nazi period could no longer do so, while the 'Aryanization' of German economic life meant that other Jews whose businesses had survived the pogrom now lost them, either through forced sale or, after the outbreak of war, through confiscation. In 1941 both male and female German Jews of all ages, most of them with middle-class backgrounds, became victims of conscripted labour programmes and found themselves working long hours in factories for meagre pay. In the first few years of the war, the Jews also endured restrictions on their movements, were forced to wear the yellow star and were moved to concentration camps within Germany. While some died within the German camps, others were forced to the Polish death camps.[74] About 28,000 Jews survived the Holocaust in Germany and Austria by going underground.[75] The number of Jews in Munich had declined to just 430 at the end of the war, a number which included those who had gone into hiding and those not considered 'full Jews'.[76] Smaller towns lost their Jewish communities altogether, in the case of Worms by the end of 1942.[77]

Similar patterns of persecution evolved throughout Nazi Europe. The German invasion of Poland led to direct control. This country contained 3 million Jews making up 10 per cent of the population[78] and provided the ground upon which the Final Solution was implemented. The invading Nazis came into contact with a much poorer Jewish community than that in Germany, concentrated in particular areas of some of the largest cities. Like their German brethren they faced a loss of civil rights, recruitment into labour battalions as well as constant violence. In 1940 the Nazis established ghettoes in cities with the largest Jewish populations including Warsaw and Lodz, which took in the surrounding Jewish populations.[79] Life in the ghetto meant humiliation, starvation and the prospect of death at any time. In the Warsaw ghetto on 17–18 April 1942 '52 Jews were shot down in the streets like dogs'.[80] By this time the Polish ghettoes had also begun to take in the deported Jewish populations of other invaded European states and cities. One SS officer drew attention to the 'catastrophic conditions' in the Lodz ghetto which 'was permanently overcrowded'.[81] In addition to forcing Jews into Polish cities the Nazis also quickly established concentration camps in Poland, which would eventually develop into the death camps that killed most European Jews. These consisted of: Auschwitz, Belzec, Chelmno, Majdanek, Sobibor and Treblinka. In statistical and non-personal terms anti-Semitism in Second World War Poland meant the virtual elimination of Jewish life, with one of the oldest and most developed Yiddish traditions in eastern Europe, from Polish soil, reducing the Jewish population to around 250,000 souls, a fall of 90 per cent.[82]

A few Polish Jews attempted to move eastward into the Soviet Union on the outbreak of war while others were temporarily saved by the fact that they fell into the eastern half of the country annexed by the Soviet Union, as agreed by the Nazi–Soviet Non-Aggression Pact of August 1939. However, with the Nazi advance into the Soviet Union after the launch of Operation Barbarossa at the end of 1941, the Nazis soon began to implement the racial order that they had already perfected in Poland during the preceding two years. Local anti-Semitism, which had manifested itself in violence in the Russian borderlands from the late nineteenth century until the end of the First World War, assisted Nazi policies. The Nazis were further helped by local anti-Soviet nationalist inhabitants in the Baltic States and the Ukraine who willingly participated in hunting down and killing Jews in the occupied lands. About 1 million Jews were murdered in the Soviet Union in this way during 1941 and 1942.[83] In one typical incident in the Rumbuli Forest just outside Riga on 30 November 1941 'a narrow cordon, which was formed by SS units, a contingent of the Special Task Unit Riga, and Latvian Units' shot Jews, who would then fall into prepared pits. The victims included 'over one thousand Jews from Berlin' who 'were pulled off a train, herded immediately up to the pits, and shot'.[84] As a result of the Rumbuli Forest massacres in November and December 1941, about 20,000 Riga Jews died, leaving about 7,000 survivors.[85] Overall more than 2 million Soviet Jews were murdered either by the actions of the *Einsatzgruppen*, or by deportation to the death camps. This meant that Jewish losses were about four times as heavy as those of the Soviet population as a whole.[86]

Large-scale murder of Jews also occurred elsewhere in eastern Europe. Hungary had a strong anti-Semitic tradition which resulted in the passage of discriminatory legislation throughout the inter-war years and acted as a background factor to the deportation of its Jews to Poland,[87] meaning that the Jewish population shrank from about 825,000 to 255,000.[88] In Czechoslovakia, annexed by Hitler just before the outbreak of war, about 240,000 Jews were killed, leaving just 22,000 in the Czech areas and

3,500 in Slovakia.[89] Romania lost about 300,000 of its 757,000 Jews.[90] In Greece, 'At the outbreak of War there were between 70,000 and 80,000 Jews . . . of whom over 50,000 lived in the city of Salonika. Fewer than 10,000 survived, and some of the oldest Jewish communities in Europe perished as a result.'[91] Bulgaria represented the classic exception to the rule in eastern Europe and the Balkans in the fact that it saved virtually all of its Jews because the government did not hand them over for deportation to the death camps.[92]

In western Europe the picture varied from one country to another for similar reasons to those in the eastern half of the continent. In Scandinavia much effort went into supporting and hiding Jews within Denmark with assistance from neutral Sweden.[93] Holland, however, witnessed the deportation of 110,000 of its Jews to the Nazi extermination camps in Poland, meaning that only about 30,000 Dutch Jews survived the Second World War.[94] France had one of the deepest anti-Semitic traditions in western Europe and passed its own racial laws under the Second World War Vichy regime – as well as setting up its own concentration camps. Nevertheless, about 70 per cent of the 350,000 Jews living in France in 1939 survived.[95] Italy, without much of an anti-Semitic tradition, had one of the most impressive survival rates, losing only 8,000 of its 57,000 Jews,[96] due to a popular refusal to surrender to the Nazi will, despite the alliance of Mussolini and Hitler.[97]

In all, Lucy Dawidowicz estimates that 5,933,900 out of 8,861,800 Jews in the countries occupied by the Nazis were murdered, meaning a death rate of 67 per cent.[98] The extent to which the Nazis fulfilled their aims in individual states depended on a series of factors including the nature and extent of German occupation in a particular state and the levels of anti-Semitism and sympathies of the local non-Jewish population. Areas annexed by the expanded Third Reich or contiguous with it, passing under direct Nazi rule, also tended to be those with the strongest anti-Semitic traditions and, consequently, those which lost the highest proportion of their Jews. Those under less direct control and with less developed traditions of anti-Semitism were those with the lowest death rates, notably Italy and Bulgaria. There remains no scientific equation that determined the rates of survival, so Greece, with less developed traditions of modern anti-Semitism, nevertheless suffered significant Jewish losses.

As well as containing the majority of Europe's Jews, eastern Europe also housed the bulk of the continent's gypsies, especially Bulgaria (80,000), Yugoslavia (100,000), Poland (50,000), Rumania (300,000), Slovakia (80,000), the Soviet Union (200,000) and Hungary (100,000), with a total European population of over 1 million.[99] While European gypsies endured similar racial persecution to the Jews, they had a higher survival rate.

Immediately after the outbreak of the war a decree prevented gypsies from travelling within German territory, and plans developed to deport German gypsies to Poland, which eventually began in April 1940, although only about 2,000 deportations occurred. As German troops marched into the Soviet Union at the end of 1941 the *Einsatzgruppen* began murdering gypsies there. By this time gypsies also faced deportation to concentration and forced labour camps established in eastern Europe, although most of those in Germany remained to face continually deteriorating conditions. The Nazis decided upon the final solution to the gypsy question in December 1942, which involved deportation to camps throughout Europe, including Auschwitz, BIIe, which accounted for the deaths of 20,078 people. The gypsies also continued as subjects of Nazi research. Much concern focused upon their racial origin, but they also became guinea pigs in concentration camp experiments, especially in attempts to find a vaccine for spotted fever.[100]

The Nazis had an impact upon the gypsy populations of Europe almost as dramatic as that on the Jews, resulting in as many as half a million deaths.[101] In Germany, as we might expect, gypsy life was virtually destroyed.[102] The few thousand who remained included people who survived the concentration camps and those who managed to evade arrest by the various Nazi policing authorities.[103] In the Soviet Union up to 35,000 gypsies were killed by the Nazis, including almost all of those in Latvia and Estonia, but, like the Jewish population of the Soviet Union, those who lived beyond the area of German occupation were protected by the Soviet authorities.[104] In Poland the gypsies initially found themselves concentrated in ghettos. In November 1941 they were gathered in the Lodz ghetto with a view to their extermination, subsequently being sent to the death camp at Chelmno.[105] However, even in the heartland of Nazi genocide as many as 20,000 gypsies may have survived either by hiding 'in the depths of the forests' or the 'mountain fastnesses', moving to the Soviet Union or cheating death in the camps.[106] Elsewhere in Europe between 36,000 and 39,000 gypsies were murdered in Rumania, while around 30,000 suffered a similar fate in Hungary.[107] The situation for gypsies in Yugoslavia varied according to the fate of the area in which they lived. The highest death rate occurred in the Nazi-supported Croatian state, where over 25,000 gypsies were killed, while 12,000 of the 60,000 Serbian gypsies suffered a similar fate. The safest were those living in Macedonia and Slovenia.[108] Despite the higher survival rates of gypsies compared with Jews, if the Nazis had won the Second World War, it seems likely that the gypsies would have faced extermination. They had no place in the new world order envisaged in *Mein Kampf*, the blueprint for Nazi policies during the Second World War.

The third racial group that became a victim of Hitler's push to the east, again as set out in his credo, consisted of Slavs. Those groups resident within the German boundaries of 1937 did not stand a chance of saving the overt signs of their ethnicity as the peacetime persecution moved into its wartime phase. Seven days after the outbreak of the Second World War all surviving Polish organizations in the Ruhr faced dissolution, and on 11 September 1939 the Nazis arrested 249 leading Polish functionaries from the Ruhr and threw them into concentration camps. Although most of these were released in the spring of 1940, at least 60 Ruhr Poles were shot, beheaded or died in concentration camps, although, as a group, these western Poles, away from the eastern front, came off relatively lightly.[109] In Lusatia Sorbian leaders faced incarceration and at least 23 Sorbian priests had to leave their parishes. At the same time, any overt signs of Sorbian ethnicity disappeared. Nevertheless, plans to resettle this ethnic group never became reality.[110]

The Slavic majorities in the territories that the Nazis invaded in eastern Europe became victims of a scorched earth policy. The Soviet Union, as the homeland of both the racially inferior Slavs and communism, suffered particularly badly, meaning the deaths of up to 20 million of its citizens and the destruction of around 1,700 towns and 70,000 villages. The invading Nazis commandeered agricultural produce, shot all communists, and brutally treated prisoners of war, meaning that about 3.3 million out of the 5.7 million seized between June 1941 and May 1944 actually died, mostly due to starvation, although the SS may have executed about half a million.[111] Although it contained just racial, and not ideological, enemies, Poland came off as badly as the USSR under Nazi rule. The Nazi occupation meant not only the murder of 3 million Jews, but also the deaths of a further 3 million gentiles, who, collectively, died as a result of combat, the camps, disease, and labour exploitation.[112]

While the rapacious and brutal policies of the Nazis in the lands which they occupied in the east may represent a new departure in German practices towards racial groups under their control, the exploitation of labour has links with the periods both before Weimar and after Nazism. Once again, ideology dictated the use of eastern European workers. With the move into eastern Europe outlined in *Mein Kampf*, the Germans would become the ruling race, meaning that they could exploit indigenous labour. In addition, much of the Nazi hierarchy refused to mobilize German women as workers, because such an action 'would inflict both physical and mental harm' upon them 'and damage their psychic and emotional life and possibly their potential as mothers',[113] the last demonstrating the role of women in Nazi ideology. Furthermore, the number of German men needed to fight wars on several fronts and police local populations and concentration camps made an increase in the number of foreign workers inevitable. In fact, the Nazis used labour power from territories which they had conquered in both the east and the west, although, as different racial groups, they received varying treatment, with more of those from the west moving to Germany voluntarily. This applied to Denmark, for instance, although the reason for taking up work in Germany lay in the dire economic consequences of the Nazi invasion, which meant a rise in unemployment.[114]

As a result of the labour shortages in the German wartime economy, it became fundamentally dependent upon civilian foreigners and prisoners of war. Total numbers increased from 301,000 in 1939 to 7,126,000 in 1944, or from 0.8 to 19.9 per cent of all workers employed in the German economy. While the majority consisted of Poles and Russians, the 1944 total included 253,648 Belgians, 1,254,749 French people, 584,337 Italians and 270,304 Dutch. The 1944 total counted 5,295,000 civilians and 1,831,000 prisoners of war.[115] While some of the former may have worked for the Nazis voluntarily, the vast majority did so through force, especially as the result of the introduction of compulsory labour laws in the countries occupied by the Nazis.[116] Fritz Sauckel, who became responsible for the recruitment of foreigners in March 1942, estimated two years later that out of the 5 million foreigners who had made their way to Germany, not even 200,000 had done so voluntarily.[117]

Agriculture, mining and industries connected with war production employed the largest numbers of foreign workers,[118] but some individuals found themselves employed in surprising occupations. A small number of Polish women worked as nursemaids for German families in Poland, representing a relatively comfortable existence[119] compared with the experience of numerous Nazi employees, both male and female. In many cases recruited foreigners would find themselves working in the inhuman conditions of camps. Ravensbrück contained women from both eastern and western Europe who made clothes under strict discipline in individual barracks that could contain up to 1,000 women each, with bunk beds stacked three high.[120] The recruitment process operated by Sauckel provided big and small German companies with the necessary labour power they required. The Ford factory in Cologne, for instance, started using predominantly Russians, both men and women, from 1942 and by 1944 they made up 50 per cent of employees in the plant.[121]

Clearly, foreign workers faced difficult working and living conditions, although the Nazis aimed primarily to exploit rather than, as in the case of Jews and gypsies, to exterminate them. They had to endure low food rations, a problem which increasingly affected the entire German population as the war progressed. The Nazis treated different groups of workers in different ways in terms of accommodation, living conditions, wages and diet, so that Germans came at the top, followed by people from western Europe, southern Europe, and, at the bottom, Poland and the Soviet Union.[122]

Interaction of foreigners, especially those from the east, with racially pure Germans caused concern among the Nazis. Poles had to wear a badge marked 'P' and lived in separate housing.[123] If they had sexual relationships with German women they could be hanged. Between 18 April 1941 and 7 January 1942 this fate befell nine men who were seen with German women in Alsace and Baden. The women had their hair shaved off in public in front of other young women under orders from the SS.[124]

For 'most of the eastern workers and some of the western workers, life in the Third Reich was one long, continual nightmare of hard work, insufficient food, inadequate quarters, personal discrimination, and cruelty'.[125] Not surprisingly, at the end of the war the vast majority of the foreign workers who found themselves in Germany streamed back home to areas devastated by Nazi policies.

Continuities and discontinuities

The racial order established by the Nazis would have to be regarded as unique in the history of both modern Germany and modern Europe. The uniqueness lies in the legalistic primacy of race in all aspects of life and death in areas controlled by the Nazis and the enthusiasm with which the German Nazis and their east European supporters carried out the policies. The banality of murder fits into the context of a war in which killing became the function of, not just the Nazi state, but the whole of 'civilized' Europe. In such circumstances the move from killing soldiers to exterminating civilians was not a great one, especially in a war in which, by 1945, all participating countries had dispensed with any concept of wartime ethics. The Nazis essentially began the descent into barbarism as early as their seizure of power in 1933 and the instant attacks upon Jews. As a revolutionary racist party they displayed no concern for the rule of domestic or international liberal democracy. The drive to war to redesign the racial and political map of Europe had always been Hitler's aim.

The political methods and goals of the Nazis may have been unique, but racial exclusion has deep roots in German and European history. Jewish settlement in pre-modern Europe essentially represented a struggle for survival with endemic prejudice, discrimination and violence. Similarly, the gypsies who reached Germany in the fifteenth century faced constant persecution wherever they went. The Enlightenment, which began the emancipation process of Jews, did not even touch the gypsies. Even the escape from the medieval shackles for Jews involved setbacks, notably the 1819 Hep-Hep Riots, which affected Jewish communities throughout

Germany.[126] Once the Jews gained equal rights in 1871, unofficial anti-Semitism rocketed. Under the *Kaiserreich* the gypsy and Polish minorities, as well as the imported east European workers, had no doubt about their position as outsiders.

This situation continued into the Weimar period, which, from the point of view of the position of minorities, had little positive to offer. For gypsies this period simply laid the groundwork for the Nazis, as Weimar legislation tightened already existing controls on them. For Jews anti-Semitism simply increased and combined with the consequences of the economic depression to leave many in an unenviable situation in 1933.

But the Nazis made racism and return to medieval exclusion official policy once they seized power, so that by the outbreak of the Second World War, Germany had basically abolished minority ethnicity through the implementation of increasingly brutal methods in which both the state and the populace played a role. The killing culture of the war meant that the murder of minorities became legitimate.

In the postwar period ethnicity has continued to play a large role in the existence of inequality. While Jews in Germany may have full civil rights, persecution of gypsies has continued. But the largest outgroup consists of foreign workers, mostly from southern Europe and Turkey, who are recruited using methods that originate in the late nineteenth century. With a nationality law dating from 1913, neither the migrants nor their descendants have citizenship and, consequently, full civil rights.

To suggest that this is a legacy of Nazism may be putting the case too strongly, but the second-class status of foreign workers in both political and social terms points to the fact that ethnic exclusion continues to play a role in Germany. Nevertheless, in this sense the Federal Republic does not differ from several other European states, most notably Switzerland, although no postwar state is free from racism. To speak of continuities, it may therefore be more useful to draw links between the postwar and pre-Nazi periods. Nazi racial policy separates the two in terms of the centrality of racial persecution and the brutality of this persecution. Nevertheless, modern Germany, like most nation states, has always been an ethnic democracy which practises exclusion according to origin. This makes Nazism unique, yet also rooted in modernity and German history.

Notes

1. I am very grateful to the Alexander von Humboldt Foundation for financing two visits to Germany, which allowed the research for this article.

2. See, for instance, Ruth Gay, *The Jews of Germany: A Historical Portrait* (London, 1992), pp. 9–28.

3. Avraham Barkai, 'Die Juden als sozio-ökonomische Minderheitsgruppe in der Weimarer Republik', in Walter Grab and Julius H. Schoeps, eds, *Juden in der Weimarer Republik* (Stuttgart, 1986), p. 330.

4. Rainer Heheman, '"Jederzeit gottlose böse Leute" – Sinti und Roma zwischen Duldung und Vernichtung', in Klaus J. Bade, ed., *Deutsche im Ausland – Fremde in Deutschland: Migration in Geschichte und Gegenwart* (Munich, 1992), p. 272.

5. These are the phrases of Joachim S. Hohmann, *Geschichte der Zigeunerverfolgung in Deutschland*, 2nd edn (Frankfurt, 1988), p. 27.

6. Ibid., p. 67.

7. Martin Broszat, *Zwei Hundert Jahre deutsche Polenpolitik*, 2nd edn (Frankfurt, 1972), pp. 68, 86.

8. Gerard Labuda, 'The Territorial, Ethnical and Demographic Aspects of Polish–German Relations in the Past (X–XX Centuries)', *Polish Western Affairs* 3 (1962), p. 250.

9. Christoph Kleßmann, 'Long-Distance Migration, Integration and Segregation of an Ethnic Minority in Industrial Germany: The Case of the "Ruhr-Poles"', in Klaus J. Bade, ed., *Population, Labour and Migration in 19th- and 20th-Century Germany* (Oxford, 1987), pp. 103–5.

10. Emil Kurónski, *Die Polen nach dem amtlichen Volkszählungen* (Berlin, 1938), p. 22.

11. Martin Kasper, 'Sorbische Sprache und Kultur unter dem Hakenkreuz', in Karin Bott-Bodenhausen, ed., *Unterdrückte Sprachen: Sprachverbote und der Recht auf Gebrauch der Minderheitensprachen* (Frankfurt, 1996), p. 106.

12. Ulrich Herbert, *A History of Foreign Labour in Germany, 1880–1980: Seasonal Workers/Forced Labourers/Guest Workers* (Ann Arbor, MI, 1990), pp. 21, 107–8.

13. Daniel Goldhagen, *Hitler's Willing Executioners: Ordinary Germans and the Holocaust* (New York, 1997), p. 83.

14. Donald L. Niewyk, *The Jews in Weimar Germany* (Baton Rouge, IN, 1980), p. 13.

15. Donald L. Niewyk, 'The Impact of Inflation and Depression on the German Jews', *Leo Baeck Institute Yearbook* 27 (1983), pp. 19–36.

16. Jost Hermannd, 'Juden in der Kultur der Weimarer Republik', in Grab and Schoeps, eds, *Juden in der Weimarer Republik*, pp. 9–37.

17. Ibid., p. 16.

18. Niewyk, *Jews in Weimar Germany*, p. 102.

19. See Walter Grab, *Der deutsche Weg der Juden-Emanzipation, 1789–1938* (Munich, 1991), pp. 152–80.

20. Rolf Vogel, *Ein Stuck von Uns: Deutsche Juden in Deutschen Armeen, 1873–1976* (Mainz, 1977), p. 139.

21. Niewyk, *Jews in Weimar Germany*, p. 85.

22. See *Das Deutsche Judentum: Seine Parteien und Organisationen* (Berlin, 1919).

23. Alphons Silbermann, 'Deutsche Juden oder jüdische Deutsche? Zur Identität der Juden in der Weimarer Republik', in Grab and Schoeps, eds, *Juden in der Weimarer Republik*, pp. 352–3.

24. Marion A. Kaplan, *The Jewish Feminist Movement in Germany: The Campaigns of the Jüdischer Frauenbund, 1904–1938* (Westport, CT, 1979).

25. Trude Maurer, 'Die Juden in der Weimarer Republik', in Dirk Blasius and Dan Diner, eds, *Zebrochene Geschichte: Leben und Selbstverständnis der Juden in Deutschland* (Frankfurt, 1991), p. 107.

26. Central Verein Deutscher Staatsbürger Jüdischen Glaubens, *Friedhofsschändungen in Deutschland, 1923–32* (Berlin, 1932).

27. Fritz Marburg, *Der Antisemitismus in der Deutschen Republik* (Vienna, 1931), pp. 52–6.

28. Werner J. Cahman, *German Jewry: Its History and Sociology* (New Brunswick, NJ, 1989), p. 115.

29. See: Eva von Hase-Malik and Doris Kreuzkamp, *Du Kriegst auch einen schönen Wohnwagen: Zwangslager für Sinti und Roma während des Nationalsozialismus in Frankfurt am Main* (Frankfurt, 1990), pp. 33–6; Michael Schenk, *Rassismus gegen Sinti und Roma: Zur Kontinuität der Zigeunerverfolgung innerhalb der deustchen Gesellschaft von der Weimarer Republik bis in die Gegenwart* (Frankfurt, 1994), pp. 351–6; Michael Burleigh and Wolfgang Wippermann, *The Racial State: Germany, 1933–1945* (Cambridge, 1991), pp. 114–17; Hohmann, *Geschichte der Zigeunerverfolgung*, pp. 73–7; Wolfgang Wippermann, *Geschichte der Sinti und Roma in Deutschland: Darstellung und Dokumente* (Berlin, 1993), p. 24; Karin Reemstma, *Sinti und Roma: Geschichte, Kultur, Gegenwart* (Munich, 1996), pp. 98–100; Michael Zimmerman, *Rassenutopie und Genozid: Die nationalsozialistische 'Lösung der Zigeunerfrage'* (Hamburg, 1996), pp. 66–71.

30. Wolfgang Wippermann, *Geschichte der Deutsch-Polnischen Beziehungen: Darstellung und Dokumente* (Berlin, 1992), p. 29.

31. Harald von Riekhoff, *German–Polish Relations, 1918–1933* (Baltimore, 1971), p. 199.

32. Richard Charles Murphy, 'Polish In-Migration in Bottrop, 1891–1933: An Ethnic Minority in a German Industrial City' (University of Iowa unpublished PhD thesis, 1977), pp. 279, 285, 286.

33. R. Oenning, *'Du da mitti polnischen Farben'* . . . : *Sozalisationserfahrungen von Polen im Ruhrgebiet, 1918–1939* (Münster, 1991), pp. 57, 60–100, 111, 114.

34. Wojciech Wrzensiński, 'The Union of Poles in Germany (1922–1939)', *Polish Western Affairs* 9 (1968), pp. 30–1.

35. Elke Gemkov, Marco Heinz and Stefan Neumann, 'Die Sorben in der Lausitz', in M. Heinz and S. Neumann, eds, *Ethnische Minderheiten in West Europa* (Bonn, 1996), pp. 113–14.

36. See, for instance: Joachim Tessarz, *Die Rolle der ausländischen landwirtschaftlichen Arbeiter in der Agrar- und Ostexpansionspolitik des deutschen Imperialismus in der Periode der Weimarer Republik (1919–1932)* (Halle, 1962); Johann Woydt, *Ausländische Arbeitskräfte in Deutschland: Vom Kaiserreich bis zur Bundesrepublik* (Heilbronn, 1987), p. 54; Herbert, *History of Foreign Labour*, pp. 121–7.

37. Nora Levin, *The Holocaust Years* (Malabar, FL, 1990), p. 16.

38. Wolfgang Wippermann, *Geschichte der deutschen Juden: Darstellung und Dokumente* (Berlin, 1994), p. 77.

39. Burleigh and Wipperman, *Racial State*, pp. 49–50.

40. Henry R. Huttenbach, *The Destruction of the Jewish Community of Worms, 1933–1945: A Study of the Holocaust Experience in Germany* (New York, 1981), p. 14.

41. Avraham Barkai, *From Boycott to Annihilation: The Economic Struggle of German Jews, 1933–1943* (London, 1989), pp. 17–25.

42. Institut zum Studium der Judenfrage, *Die Juden in Deutschland* (Munich, 1937).

43. Marion A. Kaplan, *Between Dignity and Despair: Jewish Life in Nazi Germany* (New York, 1998), pp. 40–6.

44. Steve M. Lowenstein, 'The Struggle for Survival of Rural Jews in Germany, 1933–1938: The Case of Bezirksamt Weissenberg, Mittelfranken', in Arnold Paucker, ed., *Die Juden im Nationalsozialistischen Deutschland* (Tübingen, 1986), p. 117.

45. Hannele Zürndorfer, *The Ninth of November* (London, 1983), p. 46.

46. Barkai, *From Boycott to Annihilation*, pp. 77–99.

47. Cahman, *German Jewry*, p. 126.

48. Volker Dahm, 'Kulturelles und geistiges Leben', in Wolfgang Benz, ed., *Die Juden in Deutschland, 1933–1945: Leben unter nationalsozialistischer Herrschaft*, 3rd edn (Munich, 1993), pp. 75–222.

49. Hans Nordsiek, *Juden in Minden: Dokumente und Bilder jüdischen Lebens von Mittelater bis zum 20. Jahrhundert* (Minden, 1988), p. 66.

50. Kaplan, *Between Dignity and Despair*, pp. 52–3.

51. Konrad Kwiet, 'The Ultimate Refuge: Suicide in the Jewish Community under the Nazis', *Leo Baeck Institute Yearbook* 29 (1984), pp. 135–48.

52. Michael Marrus, *Unwanted: European Refugees in the Twentieth Century* (New York, 1985), pp. 129–30.

53. Huttenbach, *Jewish Community of Worms*, p. 16.

54. Cahman, *German Jewry*, p. 83.

55. Anthony Read and David Fisher, *Kristallnacht: Unleashing the Holocaust* (London, 1991), pp. 73–4.

56. Ibid., pp. 134–5.

57. Wippermann, *Geschichte der deutschen Juden*, p. 84.

58. Konrad Kwiet, 'To Leave or not to Leave: The German Jews at the Crossroads', in Walter Pehle, ed., *November 1938: From Kristallnacht to Genocide* (Oxford, 1991), p. 146.

59. Zürndorfer, *Ninth of November*, p. 71.

60. Peter Gay, *My German Question: Growing up in Nazi Berlin* (London, 1998), pp. 138–54.

61. Sybil Milton, 'Antechamber to Birkenau: The *Zigeunerlager* After 1933', in H. Gubitz, H. Bästlein and J. Tuckel, eds, *Die Normalität des Verbrechers: Bilanz und Perspektiven der Forschung zu den nationalsozialistischen Gewaltverbrechen* (Berlin, 1994), p. 241.

62. Ibid., p. 244; Reemstma, *Sinti und Roma*, p. 103.

63. Schenk, *Rassismus gegen Sinti und Roma*, p. 114.

64. Milton, 'Antechamber to Birkenau', pp. 241–3.

65. Ibid., p. 245.

66. Hase-Mihalik and Kreuzkamp, *Du Kriegst auch einen schönen Wohnwagen*, pp. 40–1, 46.

67. Milton, 'Antechamber to Birkenau', p. 249.

68. Zimmermann, *Rassenutopie*, pp. 118–24.

69. Ludwig Eiber, Eva Strauß and Michael Krausnick, *'Ich wußte, es wird schlimm': Die Verfolgung der Sinti und Roma in München, 1933–1945* (Munich, 1993), p. 30.

70. Alfred Lessing, *Mein Leben in Versteck: Wie ein deutscher Sinti den Holocaust überlebte* (Düsseldorf, 1993), p. 30.

71. Oenning, *'Du da mitti polnischen Farben'*, p. 115; Christoph Kleßmann, *Polnische Bergarbeiter im Ruhrgebiet, 1870–1945* (Göttingen, 1978), pp. 177–83.

72. Burleigh and Wipperman, *Racial State*, pp. 133–5; Kasper, 'Sorbische Sprache', pp. 105–12.

73. Woydt, *Ausländische Abeitskräfte*, p. 54; Herbert, *History of Foreign Labour*, pp. 127–31; Lothar Elsner und Joachim Lehmann, *Ausländische Arbeiter unter*

dem deutschen Imperialismus, 1900 bis 1985 (Berlin, 1988), pp. 155–81; Karl Liedke, '. . . *aber politisch unerwünscht': Arbeitskräfte aus Osteuropa im Land Braunschweig, 1880 bis 1939* (Braunschweig, 1993), pp. 138–42.

74. Kaplan, *Between Dignity and Despair*, pp. 145–228; Konrad Kwiet, 'Nach dem Pogrom: Stufen der Ausgrenzung', in Benz, *Die Juden in Deutschland, 1933–1945*, pp. 545–613; Barkai, *From Boycott to Annihilation*, pp. 152–74.

75. Lucy Dawidowicz, *The War Against the Jews, 1933–45* (Harmondsworth, 1987), p. 448.

76. Constantin Goschler, 'The Attitude towards Jews in Bavaria After the Second World War', *Leo Baeck Institute Yearbook* 36 (1991), p. 445.

77. Huttenbach, *Jewish Community of Worms*, pp. 38–9.

78. Arno J. Meyer, *Why Did the Heavens Not Darken?: The Final Solution in History* (London, 1988), p. 69.

79. Ibid., pp. 186–92.

80. Abraham Lewin, *A Cup of Tears: A Diary of the Warsaw Ghetto* (Oxford, 1988), p. 70.

81. Hans Mommsen, *From Weimar to Auschwitz: Essays in German History* (Cambridge, 1991), p. 246.

82. L. Dobroszycki, 'Restoring Jewish Life in Post-War Poland', *Soviet Jewish Affairs* 3 (1973), p. 59.

83. Philippe Burrin, *Hitler and the Jews: The Genesis of the Holocaust* (London, 1994), p. 93.

84. Gerald Fleming, *Hitler and the Final Solution* (Oxford, 1986), pp. 78–80.

85. Mayer, *Why?*, p. 275.

86. Alec Nove and J.A. Newth, 'The Jewish Population: Demographic Trends and Occupational Patterns', in Lionel J. Kochan, ed., *The Jews in the Soviet Union Since 1917*, 3rd edn (Oxford, 1978), p. 149.

87. Randolph L. Braham, *The Politics of Genocide: The Holocaust in Hungary*, vol. 1 (New York, 1981).

88. Martin L. Kovacs, 'National Minorities in Hungary, 1919–1980', in Stephan M. Horak, ed., *Eastern European National Minorities, 1919–1980* (Littleton, CO, 1985), pp. 167–8.

89. H. Renner, 'The National Minorities in Czechoslovakia After the Second World War', *Plural Societies* 7 (1976), p. 30.

90. Dawidowicz, *The War Against the Jews*, pp. 458–61.

91. Mark Mazower, *Inside Hitler's Greece: The Experience of Occupation, 1941–44* (London, 1993), p. 256.

92. Estha Benbassa and Aron Rodrigue, *The Jews of the Balkans* (Oxford, 1995), pp. 173–9.

93. Myrna Goodman, 'Foundations of Resistance in German-Occupied Denmark', in Ruby Rohrlich, ed., *Resisting the Holocaust* (Oxford, 1998), pp. 213–37.

94. Richard A. Stein, 'Antisemitism in the Netherlands – Past and Present', *Patterns of Prejudice* 19 (1985), p. 19.

95. Robert S. Wistrich, *Anti-Semitism: The Longest Hatred* (London, 1992), pp. 132–4.

96. Dawidowicz, *The War Against the Jews*, pp. 441–3.

97. See Jonathan Steinberg, *All or Nothing: The Axis and the Holocaust, 1941–43* (London, 1990).

98. Dawidowicz, *The War Against the Jews*, p. 480.

99. These approximate figures are given by Ulrich König, *Sinti und Roma unter dem Nationalsozialismus* (Bochum, 1989), pp. 44–5.

100. See, for instance, ibid., pp. 80–9; Burleigh and Wipperman, *Racial State*, pp. 120–7; Bernhard Steck, 'Die nationalsozialistische Methoden zur "Lösung" des Zigeunerproblems', *Tribüne* 20 (1981), pp. 53–78; George von Soest, *Zigeuner zwischen Verfolgung und Integration: Geschichte, Lebensbedingungen und Eingliederungsversuche* (Weinheim, 1979), pp. 41–6.

101. Hohmann, *Geschichte der Zigeunerverfolgung*, pp. 177–8.

102. König, *Sinti und Roma*, p. 44.

103. Michael Zimmermann, '"Jetzt" und "Damals" als imaginäre Einheit: Erfahrungen in einem lebensgeschichtlichen Projekt über die national-sozialistische Verfolgung von Sinti und Roma', *BIOS* 4 (1991), pp. 228–31.

104. David M. Crowe, *A History of the Gypsies in Eastern Europe and Russia* (London, 1995), p. 186.

105. Isabel Fonseca, *Bury Me Standing: The Gypsies and their Journey* (London, 1995), pp. 265–71.

106. I. Ficowski, *The Gypsies in Poland* (Warsaw, 1989), p. 49.

107. See the relevant contributions on Hungary and Romania in David M. Crowe and I. Kolsti, eds, *The Gypsies of Eastern Europe* (Armonk, NY, 1991).

108. Crowe, *History of the Gypsies*, pp. 220–1.

109. Kleßmann, *Polnische Bergarbeiter*, pp. 183–6.

110. Kasper, 'Sorbische Sprache', pp. 112–14; Burleigh and Wippermann, *Racial State*, pp. 134–5.

111. Jürgen Förster, 'The German Army and the Ideological War Against the Soviet Union', in Gerhard Hirschfeld, ed., *The Policies of Genocide: Jews and Soviet Prisoners of War in Nazi Germany* (London, 1986), pp. 15–29; Mayer, *Why?*, pp. 159–275, 313–47; Georgily A. Kumanev, 'The German Occupation Regime in Occupied Territory in the USSR (1941–1944)', in Michael Berenbaum, ed., *A Mosaic of Victims: Non-Jews Persecuted and Murdered by the Nazis* (New York, 1990), pp. 128–41.

112. Wolfgang Jacobmeyer, 'Die deutsch-polnischen Beziehungen in der Neuzeit als Konfliktgeschichte', in D. Storch, ed, *Polen und Deutchland: Nachbarn in Europa* (Hanover, 1996), p. 28.

113. Gordon A. Craig, *Germany, 1866–1945* (Oxford, 1981), p. 735.

114. Thenkel Straede, 'Dänische Fremdarbeiter in Deutschland während des zweiten Weltkrieges', *Zeitgeschichte* 13 (1985–6), pp. 400–4.

115. Herbert, *History of Foreign Labour*, pp. 154, 156.

116. Edward L. Homze, *Foreign Labour in Nazi Germany* (Princeton, NJ, 1967), p. 200.

117. Jochen August, 'Die Entwicklung des Arbeitsmarkts in Deutschland in den 30er Jahren und der Masseneinsatz ausländischer Arbeitskräfte während des Zweiten Weltkrieges', *Archiv für Sozialgeschichte* 24 (1984), p. 305.

118. Herbert, *History of Foreign Labour*, p. 155.

119. Annekatrein Mendel, *Zwangsarbeit im Kinderzimmer: 'Ostarbeiterinnen' in deutschen Familien von 1939 bis 1945* (Frankfurt, 1994).

120. Helga Kohne, 'Der Weg in die Hölle von Ravensbrück', in Helga Kohne and Christoph Lane, eds, *Mariopol–Herford und Zurück: Zwangsarbeit und ihre Bewältigung nach 1945* (Bielefeld, 1995), pp. 202–3.

121. *Zwangsarbeit bei Ford: Dokumentation der 'Projektgruppe Messelager' im Verein EL-DE-Haus e.V. Köln* (Cologne, 1996), p. 24.

122. Herbert, *History of Foreign Labour*, pp. 162–3.

123. Ibid., p. 135.

124. Eva Seeber, *Zwangsarbeiter in der Faschistischen Kriegwirtschaft* (Berlin, 1964), p. 178.

125. Homze, *Foreign Labour*, p. 297.

126. Jacob Katz, *Die Hep-Hep Verfolgungen des Jahres 1819* (Berlin, 1994).

CHAPTER NINE

The extreme right

LEE McGOWAN

Any attempt to provide an account of the fortunes of the extreme right in the period from 1919 to 1945 is an exhausting task. The force of right-wing extremism in modern German history reached its apex within the time frame covered by this book. Indeed, the period from 1919 to 1945 spans the life and times of the National Socialist Party of Germany (NSDAP), the most potent and extreme right political movement in modern German – and European – history. Its impact on the world has long surpassed the twelve-year rule of dictatorship and terror that engulfed one of Europe's most cultured nations and hurled it towards war, defeat and dismemberment.

The NSDAP was only one of the multitude of extreme right *völkisch* parties that emerged at the very outset of Weimar Germany. The attraction and growth of such extremism owed much to the changed political circumstances after 1919, the disbelief in the realities of a 'lost war', feelings of national humiliation after the Versailles peace settlement and the search for national rejuvenation. The NSDAP rapidly emerged as the pre-eminent force on the extreme right of the political spectrum. Interest in the Nazi Party fails to diminish with time. This period continues to repel and fascinate. Books, articles and films strive to satisfy popular demand. All seek to analyse every conceivable aspect of this regime. They cover its origins and historical development, its leadership and its *Führer*, Adolf Hitler, its policy objectives (both in the fields of domestic and foreign policy), its war aims, its efforts to eradicate European Jewry and its impact on the German population at the national, regional and increasingly the local levels. All offer varying insights and (some highly sensationalist) interpretations of this period.

Accounts of the NSDAP are often divided into two distinct periods: first, in its guise as a protest and minor political party (with peaks and troughs) under the Weimar period, and second, in its role as the government of the

Third Reich from January 1933 until Germany's unconditional surrender to the Allied powers in May 1945. As such these can be presented as distinct periods of German history and government. Readers need to apply caution because just as the myth of 1945 as year zero (*Stunde Null*) has become increasingly discredited, so the same applies to both 1919 and 1933. There are common threads of ideological continuity and personality that traverse both periods. Neither phase should be studied nor can be fully comprehended in isolation.

This chapter aims to highlight the degrees of continuity and commonality that shaped the force of right-wing extremism in Germany between 1919 and 1945. It focuses particular attention on the leading party to emerge after 1918, the German National Socialist Workers' Party. It plots the elements of continuity that link the National Socialists to their challengers on the right of the political spectrum and argues that there was nothing particularly unique about the National Socialist movement or its ideology. Indeed, its programme was merely an amalgam of attitudes that had long found favour among all sections of the conservative and extreme right. The key to understanding the continuity versus discontinuity debate rests ulti-mately with the Nazi movement's ability after 1933 to transform much of its ideological agenda into government policy. On the one hand the new regime demonstrated degrees of continuity with its emphasis, for example, on expansion, but on the other it revealed new and extreme approaches to policy processes and implementation, not least in its approach to providing its solution to the Jewish question.

The political backdrop: the Weimar Republic

The Weimar Republic was conceived at a time of national crisis. Weimar is often portrayed as a lost cause. With hindsight it is clear that the new democratic order was beset with economic and social difficulties stemming from the war and the sudden and bloodless collapse of the 'old imperial order'. Ultimately its failure rested with its inability to establish itself in the hearts and minds of the German electorate. True, there were externalities, such as Germany's diplomatic isolation, her harsh reparations schedule and the world recession over which successive German governments had no control. Internally, however, there were also formidable obstacles, not least in the form of the former ruling elites of the old right. They remained resolutely opposed to Weimar's democratic credentials and cherished the hope of a return to authoritarian government, while the middle classes, the erstwhile supporters of the new order, were to become alienated by the two economic slumps of this period. Moreover (and this point requires particular emphasis), the allegiance of many within the army, the civil service, the universities, the business world and the legal profession was not fastened to this democratic republic. Put simply, although not many were actively to resist or thwart the Republic's aims, significantly few were ready to support it with much enthusiasm.

This new democratic regime represented a decisive break in the continuity of German government. Its birth marked the sequestration of the traditional power and patronage of the old right (comprising the conservative, aristocratic and large landowning circles) and placed them at the mercy of the forces that Bismarck had labelled the enemies of the state. In short, the installation of democracy transformed the earlier patterns and distribution of power in favour of the Catholics (Centre Party), the Socialists (the SPD) and the German Democratic Party (DDP), the heirs of the old progressive tradition.

In the autumn of 1918 in the wake of the naval mutinies, the collapse of the monarchies and the upsurge in radical left activity, the forces on the conservative right were pushed onto the defensive and adopted a relatively low profile in an effort to salvage their survival and possessions. Once, however, the fear of the extreme left had receded they immediately began a period of open hostility to the Republic. In the changed political circumstances after 1919 the former rulers of the old and conservative right were given and indeed used every opportunity to search repeatedly for scapegoats, which they found in the form of democracy, the SPD, the Communists and the Weimar Republic.

Politically, the interests of the conservative nationalists after the First World War were, to a large extent, catered for forcefully in the Reichstag by the *Deutschnationale Volkspartei* (the German National People's Party or DNVP), which had arisen from the ashes of the old Conservative Party. Its base was those vocal right-wing forces that had proliferated throughout the Imperial period, namely, junkers, free Conservatives, anti-Semites, Christian socialists, pan Germans and elements of the minority *völkisch* movement. Essentially, the neo-conservative DNVP programme was constructed around an ardent opposition to the Weimar system, the rejection of democracy, the renunciation of the Versailles Treaty, the assertion of distinct nationalist objectives, the dissemination of the *Dolchstoßlegende* (stab-in-the-back legend) and strong anti-Bolshevik sentiments. It is important to draw attention to the opposition from the conservative right to the new regime, for it helped, albeit unintentionally, in turn to legitimize the antipathies to and the charges of the newly emerging forces of the extreme right against the democratic system.

The label of right-wing extremism is applied to the numerous *völkisch* organizations that emerged after 1918. Although the term 'extremism' was

248

rarely evoked in the inter-war period, it is applied in contemporary terminology to those movements and parties that express anti-pluralist, anti-parliamentarian, authoritarian, racist and anti-communist views in addition to espousing nationalist, military and ethno-centric ambitions.[1] According to the *Bundesamt für Verfassungsschutz* (German Federal Office for the Protection of the Constitution), right-wing extremists can be classified as those

> Striving for a totalitarian or at least an authoritarian state. They reject
> the representative parliamentary democracy. Their motivating forces are
> a nationalism that severely restricts individual civil liberties and is directed
> against international understanding, as well as racism.[2]

This description lends itself very well to the *völkisch* parties, who all placed emphasis on 'extreme nationalism, racial anti-semitism, and mystical notions of a uniquely German social order, with roots in the Teutonic past, resting on order, harmony, and hierarchy'.[3]

In retrospect, it can be seen that the events and after-effects of the First World War came to radicalize the right in Germany. The Weimar period heralded the decline and gradual usurpation of the old conservative styled and led DNVP by a younger and more militant breed who cared little for a return to the old pre-1914 political order, but rather were intent on creating something totally new. Whereas before 1914 *völkisch* nationalism had been of strictly limited appeal to groups such as the Pan German League (*Alldeutscher Verband*) and the Eastern Marches Association (*Ostmarkenverein*), it was to flourish under Weimar.

By 1919 there were some 73 such groups in Germany. Most were small, local and rather insignificant. There were, it must be noted, some notable exceptions such as the Thule Society and the German People's Protection and Defiance League (*Deutschvölkischer Schutz- und Trutz-Bund*).[4] Both these groups sought to disseminate anti-Semitic propaganda and to foster alliances and mergers with other *völkisch* groups. In terms of membership, the ranks of the extreme right were often swollen by students, young demobilized officers who were not prepared or could not easily adapt to a postwar world, and large elements of the lower middle classes. The latter feared both the economic and political insecurity as well as the trenchant and ongoing activities of the extreme left.

In terms of commonality, the conservative forces and the small *völkisch* groups of the radical right shared common tenets of belief: they were highly nationalistic, displayed strong anti-Semitic and anti-Marxist tendencies, and were collectively united by their desire to destroy the democratic Republic and restore German pride. The manner in which the message was conveyed to their targeted audiences was remarkably different. Whereas the forces of the conservative right tried to base their arguments on a philosophical level and through the deployment of refined theories (Wilhelm Stapel or Moeller van den Bruck), the proponents of the *völkisch* right opted for a more direct approach. They focused on simple slogans, made use of friend/foe dichotomies, and stirred up anger and resentment among their target audiences, usually in beer cellars. Their message was essentially a rather crude and bastardized amalgamation of ideas and issues that had been in circulation for some time. In other words, from an ideological standpoint the extreme right had little to offer. What distinguished them was their propensity for agitation, their ability to incite their audiences and on occasion to inaugurate the use of violence, and none more so than the *Nationalsozialistische Deutsche Arbeiterpartei*, or the NSDAP, which was to emerge as the most infamous variant of German right-wing extremism.

The German National Socialist Workers Party

At the start of the 1920s the NSDAP was merely one of numerous *völkisch*-orientated parties thriving on feelings of injustice, hatred and economic hardship. Its origins lie with the Deutsche Arbeiterpartei (DAP), or the German Workers' Party. This faction, established by Anton Drexler in Munich in 1919 on an initiative of the Thule Society, sought to convert the working classes to a nationalist and anti-Semitic agenda. Reconstituted as the *Nationalsozialistische Deutsche Arbeiterpartei* in 1920, this party was eventually to destroy the Weimar system and propel Germany into war. Few, however, from the perspective of the early 1920s, could have predicted this outcome or the impact and enduring significance this party would have on the three succeeding generations of Germans born after 1945.

In all probability the NSDAP would have been (as was the fate of many of its rivals) either consumed by larger and more active radical right forces or simply dissolved – without, that is, the personality and oratorical skills of one individual, Adolf Hitler. Much has been written about the leader of the National Socialist movement who emerged from obscurity to become the leading politician of the Weimar period and the Führer of the German people.[5] Although time and space prevent any lengthy discussion of Hitler here, care is taken to inform readers of the most salient points in his political development from agitator to dictator.

Without the First World War and its aftermath, Hitler would almost certainly have remained an obscure and unfulfilled watercolour painter in Munich. The war transformed his existence. It brought him comradeship, a sense of purpose, a career (initially in the army), and led him to discover (while employed by the army as an informer, or *V-Männer*, to inculcate nationalist and anti-Bolshevik sentiments among the troops) his powers as a speaker and his ability to compel his audience. He came, listened and joined the DAP in 1919. Possessing political genius and belief in himself and his abilities, Hitler, almost single-handedly, through his speeches, his style of rhetoric and the popularity of his slogans, enabled his fledgling party to distinguish itself from all its rivals. Hitler was undoubtedly the NSDAP's major asset and the most outstanding of all his contemporaries on the extreme right-wing scene. He used his knowledge of this fact to good effect (often through tantrums and on occasions through resignations to demonstrate his opposition to any proposed mergers with other similar-minded parties) to capture the leadership of the NSDAP in 1921. Once installed, he skilfully presented the party as a new and vibrant force that could steer Germany on a new and better course to prosperity and success. The NSDAP grew rapidly from filling the beer cellars of Bavaria in the early 1920s into a national phenomenon by the end of the decade.

Ultimately, although something called National Socialism could have emerged without Hitler, the particular course that it and history took would in all probability have been rather different. The movement's fate was bound entirely to Hitler. It was principally his visions and aspirations that shaped the party's programme in power. His outlook on the world (*Weltanschauung*) and the ideological platform of the Nazi Party are essentially contained in his book *Mein Kampf* ('My Struggle') and to a lesser extent in the NSDAP's 25-point programme of 1920.[6] It is misleading to regard National Socialism as a distinctive doctrine. It was neither unique nor innovative in the German political landscape of the 1920s and the 1930s. On the contrary, the ideological components of Nazism comprised a hotch-potch of ideas and sentiments that by and large encapsulated the familiar slogans of both the conservative and the extreme variants of right-wing politics. This 'unalterable' party manifesto, which was proclaimed in a Munich beer cellar (*Hofbräuhaus*) on 24 February 1920, sought to be innovative by presenting a distinctive slant to the NSDAP's aims and objectives that would enable it to distance itself from its rivals. The programme constituted a mixture of nationalist and anti-capitalist aspirations. The nationalist side contained the familiar analogous and customary slogans and aspirations of the extreme right (i.e. they included demands for a Greater Germany, self-determination for the German people, land and colonies, discrimination against Jews, the prevention of any further immigration, the expulsion of all those non-Germans who had entered the Reich since 1914, and the notion of common good before individual good). In contrast, the socialist side attested to some degree of originality at least from the right of the political spectrum. This placed emphasis on such precepts as the nationalization of all publicly owned companies, the abolition of all monies earned during the war, profit-sharing by large companies, the breaking of 'interest slavery', and substantive property and land reform. In the early 1920s NSDAP agitation and propaganda centred on three predominant issues: anti-Semitism, overt nationalism and anti-capitalism. The first two became clarion cries of the Nazi Party until the very end of its regime. In contrast, the strong anti-capitalist language was deemed counter-productive in the medium to longer term and was gradually discarded, its supporters silenced and, once in power, abandoned.

Political violence and the extreme right

Political violence materialized as a hallmark of the political extremes during the Weimar period and peaked both at the outset and in the final years of this regime. Elements of right-wing orchestrated violence surfaced almost immediately through, for example, the activities of the *Freikorps*, a paramilitary-style organization that comprised ex-army, and especially young, officers, former soldiers and university students. The members of the *Freikorps* rapidly immersed themselves in continual skirmishes in 1918–19 not only with the *Räte* (the Bolshevik-style governments in major German cities) but also in the defence of Germans and German territory against the Poles and the German Communist Party's (KPD) *Rote Frontkämpferbund* in Silesia and West Prussia.[7]

The inherent dangers from the right were most visibly displayed in the abortive putsch led by Friedrich Kapp to overthrow the Reich government in March 1920, the assassination of the Foreign Minister, Walther Rathenau, by the right-wing terrorist Organisational Consul in June 1922 and the unsuccessful Hitler putsch in Munich of November 1923. Although the Reich government had been able to move swiftly to disband large sections of the *Freikorps* in accordance with the Versailles Treaty, it remained essentially powerless to counter the opposition posed by right-wing parties and the activities of right-wing terrorist organizations (and their counterparts on the left). This ineffectiveness came to damage public confidence in law and order and in the final phase of the Republic, which accounted for over 80 per cent of the violence, only served to polarize the political atmosphere.

National Socialist violence may be accurately divided into two periods. The first covers the period 1919–34. It was generally orchestrated by the *Sturmabteilung* (storm troopers, or the SA), which was 'born quite naturally with the first meeting-hall brawl . . . in 1920'.[8] The extreme right's general propensity to participate in, pursue and orchestrate widespread violence as a means of political discourse clearly demarcated them from the conservative right. From Hitler's perspective the masses could not be swayed to the

NSDAP's cause through an ideology, but only through action and protest.[9] The role of violence in the National Socialist struggle was not designed as a means to bring about revolution directly, but to generate propaganda, to mobilize the masses, to capture the streets from the KPD, and ultimately to enable the NSDAP to emerge as a credible political force that could topple the Republic. The SA-inspired violence and confrontation was a means to this end:

> What we needed then and need now, was and is not a one hundred or two wrong headed conspirators, but a one hundred thousand and a further one hundred thousand fanatical fighters to establish our vision of the world. This work must be done, not in secret conventicles, but by powerful massed strokes; the road cannot be cleared for the movement by dagger or poison or pistol, but by conquering the man in the street. We have to destroy Marxism, so that future control of the streets may be in the hands of National Socialism now, just as it will be in the future.[10]

In the closing years of Weimar the SA became synonymous with the politics of protest and violence. By 1932 it had attracted over 2 million members. The raw recruits to the SA were particularly the young, especially those aged under 35, who were moved not so much by the ideology as by the feelings of camaraderie, a commitment to a new beginning and a greater sense of their own personal security. Significantly, SA activities and violence were never envisaged as a frontal attack on the state and its representatives, against whose forces the SA would have stood little chance. Instead they concentrated their activities on two groups: first, the communists and socialists, and second, the Jews and other minorities.

The relevant feature of this physical violence and intimidation lay in its spontaneity and its sporadic nature. Brawls and street battles became the calling card of the SA and by 1933 very few urban areas had escaped their violence. This was ongoing and was accompanied by a rise in the number of Nazi 'martyrs': this climbed from 5 in 1928 to 15 in 1930 and to 70 in the first half of 1932.[11] The worst excesses took place in the run-up to the Reichstag elections of July 1932, which witnessed 461 political riots in Prussia and led to 24 fatalities and hundreds of injuries.[12]

The failure of his 1923 putsch in Munich convinced Hitler of the need to pursue a legal path to power. To this end he conceived the idea of using propaganda as a means to lambast the Republic and the Marxists, to foster resentment especially among the middle classes and to promote extremely vague notions of future action. In retrospect, that this formula worked is illustrated by the party's surprise electoral breakthrough in 1930 and in its spectacular results in June 1932 (see Table 9.1). At this point Hitler was the leader of the largest political party in the Reichstag. Under these

Table 9.1 The rise of the radical right: a comparison between the anti-Weimar parties in the Reichstag, 1928–1933 (number of seats)

	1928 (May)	1930 (Sept)	1932 (July)	1932 (Nov)	1933 (Mar)
KPD	54	77	89	100	81
	(10.6%)	(13.1%)	(14.3%)	(16.9%)	(12.3%)
NSDAP	12	107	230	196	288
	(2.6%)	(18.3%)	(37.3%)	(33.1%)	(43.9%)
Total	66	184	319	296	369

Table 9.2 The decline of the pro-Weimar parties in the Reichstag, 1928–1933 (number of seats)

	1928 (May)	1930 (Sept)	1932 (July)	1932 (Nov)	1933 (Mar)
SPD	153	143	133	121	120
	(29.8%)	(24.5%)	(21.6%)	(20.4%)	(18.3%)
DDP	25	20	4	2	5
		(3.5%)	(1%)	(1%)	
DVP	45	30	7	11	2
		(4.7%)	(1.2%)	(1.8%)	
DNVP	73	41	37	52	52
	(14.2%)	(7%)	(5.9%)	(8.3%)	(8%)
Centre Party	62	68	70	73	73
	(15.2%)	(14.8%)	(15.6%)	(15%)	(13.9%)
Total	358	302	251	259	252

Adapted from: Detlev J.K. Peukert, *The Weimar Republic* (1993), and Thomas Childers, 'The Limits of National Socialist Mobilisation: the Elections of 6 November 1932 and the Fragmentation of the Nazi Constituency', in *idem*, ed., *The Formation of the Nazi Constituency, 1919–1933* (1986), p. 233.

circumstances it was inevitable that the conservative right would push for much closer contacts and cooperation with the National Socialists and propel Hitler into the chancellery as head of a coalition (and supposedly conservative-dominated) government in January 1933. Ultimately, the SA's prominence was correctly discerned by Hitler as a potential threat to his own authority and position and also represented a serious thorn in his side insofar as its aspirations promised to sour his relations with the *Reichswehr*. Consequently, to ensure his control and to appease the army, the SA's leadership was eliminated in June 1934 and responsibility for state security was passed to the fledgling SS. This marked the onset of the second phase of Nazi violence and terror, 1934–45.

The central question at the heart of this chapter is the degree to which continuity or discontinuity marks the National Socialist movement in both opposition and government and in relation to other political forces on the right and previous political regimes. The next two sections explore the themes of continuity in relation to both ideology and policy initiatives in government.

Distilling continuity and discontinuity: the case of Nazi ideology

Any attempt to provide a coherent account and definition of Nazi ideology proves rather more difficult than might have been expected. Despite the vast material that continues to accumulate on Nazism, any notions of unanimity need to be discarded. Differing political orientations and social perceptions provide considerably divergent and conflicting theses. Kershaw aptly delineates the complexities when he remarks that:

> Studies of Nazi ideology have been regarded by some as genuinely revolutionary in content, and branded by others as quintessentially counter-revolutionary. Leading historians have seen Nazism as dynamic nihilism devoid of ideological commitment, and Hitler as an opportunist without principle or ideology seeking power for power's sake, while others have distinguished Nazism from Italian and other forms of fascism on the grounds of its theoretical basis in a doctrine of race and have interpreted Hitler as a politician driven by a remarkably consistent and coherent, if hateful and repulsive ideology.[13]

National Socialism was a variant of Fascism, and, as with all fascist movements, the ideology was rather thin. A strict ideological platform never fully materialized. The policies and meanings of a future National Socialist government were never really spelt out in any substance. The starting point for any consideration of a National Socialist ideology must be the aspirations and objectives of its Führer, as laid down in *Mein Kampf*.[14] In ideological terms Nazism reflected the familiar concepts and prejudices of the extreme and conservative right: anti-parliamentarianism, anti-Marxism, nationalism, the promotion of the *Volksgemeinschaft* and, increasingly, racism. All were bound together by the primacy of the German state. Taken together, these features can hardly be classified as either exclusive or original in nature.

If the dissemination of such ideas and slogans suggests consistency and continuity on the part of the right, the attempts by the Nazis to realize them once in power clearly exposes a unique determination and new approach to policy implementation. Herein lie the elements of discontinuity that have come to distinguish the Nazi government from previous regimes and to characterize its leaders and the movement as fanatical. Few could have predicted the series of events that would take place between 1933 and 1945. Arguably, many of the directions and personal opinions in *Mein Kampf* that appear so conspicuous when viewed from a post-1945 perspective remained largely misunderstood or were perceived as mere propaganda and fantasy by a maverick adventurer in the 1920s. Yet behind all the confusion, frustrations and hatreds of its author lay the core of a political conviction that was largely translated into policy after 1933.[15]

The notion that ideology was simply a means to woo the masses is enticing, not least because the National Socialist leadership was prepared to sacrifice policy and make adjustments to suit prevailing political needs. In other words, no aspects of the 'doctrine' could be considered as taboo. Official documentation and statements from the Nazi Party were often riddled with contradictions and ambiguities. The Nazi doctrine proved highly susceptible to being reshaped and redefined according to the party's needs. Hitler's emphasis, for example, on the right to German self-determination was utterly abandoned with regard to the South Tyrol question in favour of closer collaboration with Mussolini. Likewise the socialist and anti-capitalist agenda of the NSDAP's 1920 party programme was simply discarded by Hitler, in face of ardent opposition from the left of the party, for essentially two reasons: first, to make the party more marketable to the middle-class electorate, and second, to avoid alienating either the army or the conservative right.[16] It was already clear by this stage that the NSDAP could not expect to make any serious inroads into what essentially represented the communist constituency.

In pure policy terms what distinguished the NSDAP from all its rivals was its ability to present itself successfully to the electorate as a new and vibrant force and to take traditional concepts and values to new lengths and extremes. The Nazi movement did not hanker after some former glorious period such as Imperial Rome or Napoleonic France, but instead promised a new dawn for a 1,000-year Reich. This manifested itself in its promotion of the struggle and the role of leadership. For large sections of the electorate the attraction of the Nazis lay not with their ideology (or arguably the lack of it) but with the style and presentation of their message. National Socialist ideology was constructed upon ardent opposition to democratic, liberal and humanist values.

Distilling continuity and discontinuity: the extreme right ascendant, 1933–1945

Explanations for the sudden breakthrough and rapid advance of the NSDAP in the early 1930s centre on the party's use of propaganda, its promotion of violence, the capabilities of its *Führer* and the onset of economic recession (1929–32) which completely destabilized the Weimar Republic. However, the NSDAP's arrival in power was also dependent on the fateful decision taken by the old right, led by Franz von Papen, to appoint Hitler as chancellor. Although in retrospect this decision was obviously a serious miscalculation, it needs to be set against the backdrop of the deepening recession, the growing cohorts of unemployed, the persistent communist and fascist violence, the indecisive elections and the endless cabinet crises that marked Germany from 1929–32. The conservative right viewed Hitler's chancellorship as nothing more than a transition to their restoration of authoritarian rule. In the short term, it also enabled them to pit the NSDAP against the Communists. Subsequent events were to reveal just how much they had underestimated Hitler's abilities and actual ambitions.[17]

Within two months and with only two cabinet colleagues initially (though one did control internal affairs) Hitler had in effect consolidated his hold on power to the detriment of the conservative forces. Yet to what extent did the National Socialist experiment mark a new chapter in German politics? Did it in reality pursue a new agenda or was it merely a continuation of traditional German policy orientations? This chapter now turns to address these issues. For purposes of clarity, and given the limited space available, this section divides the period of Nazi rule into three separate sections: domestic policy, foreign policy, and Germany at war. Each aims to provide a brief summary and to trace the themes of continuity and discontinuity.

Domestic policy

From Hitler's perspective the immediate question after January 1933 centred on how to maintain power. The means to this end were achieved by setting fire to the Reichstag on 27 February 1933 and skilfully placing the blame on the Communists. This staged episode enabled Hitler to persuade

President Hindenburg of the need for the imposition of martial law under article 48 of the Weimar Constitution. It is somewhat ironic that Hitler was able to dismantle democracy and consolidate National Socialist rule through the use of the Weimar Constitution. Thousands of Nazi-decreed laws were based on this emergency legislation, which remained in place until the collapse of the Third Reich. Simultaneously, the Nazis set out to eliminate or deter all other forms of political opposition. The persecutions began. Members of the KPD, for example, were either arrested, fled or went underground, and by the time of the Enabling Act (*Ermächtigungsgesetz*) of 23 March only the SPD were in a position to oppose (vainly) a law which gave Hitler very wide-ranging legislative functions. In the next few months all other political parties were dissolved and the NSDAP became the party of the state. The rapid Nazi takeover of the entire state apparatus was, it should be emphasized, greatly assisted by the failure of all the opposition groups to form an effective resistance strategy.

The consequences of Nazi control were substantial and displayed clear examples of discontinuity with the two previous political regimes. The federal structure of Germany, as established under Bismarck, was simply terminated in March 1933. At the local level democracy was simply obliterated and by the end of 1934 all the new provinces were placed under the control of governors (*Gauleiter*) who were all personally selected by Hitler. By the middle of 1933 serious discussions had ceased to occur within the cabinet. Consequently such meetings essentially became superfluous and none were convened after 1938. Overall policy priorities and objectives were simply dictated by Hitler. In practice, many cabinet functions were delegated to some 42 special agencies, but once again all fell directly under Hitler's jurisdiction. How such policies were to be operationalized was an issue that Hitler left to the discretion of those to whom he had assigned the responsibilities.

The NSDAP's significance as a party quickly subsided once power had been attained. The new weapon in German life became state-sponsored, through various security organizations from the SA initially to the SS, the SD and the Gestapo. Concentration camps were erected (Dachau in 1933 became the forerunner of the more infamous death camps at Auschwitz and Treblinka) to house political opponents, asocials (such as homosexuals), religious minority groups such as Jehovah's Witnesses, criminals and others who dared to insult the Nazi leadership, denigrate the swastika or spread lies about the regime's atrocities.[18]

President Hindenburg's death in 1934 enabled Hitler to consolidate his power further when, in direct violation of the Weimar Constitution, which forbade the chancellor from tampering with the presidency, he assumed the role of president. Nevertheless, this occurred without incident and seemed to prove rather unproblematic if the overwhelming majorities for Hitler in a series of plebiscites in 1933–5 are considered.[19] The Nazi government, however, remained in a somewhat precarious position in the early years. Resistance was still possible from two sources: the army and big business. The army was a state within a state and a bastion of the old conservative aristocracy. Support from the army, or at the very least its apathy, was essential in Hitler's plans to restructure the state and ultimately pursue an expansionist foreign policy agenda. To appease the army, Hitler had been only too willing to sacrifice Ernst Röhm, one of his earliest comrades, and the SA leadership during the Night of the Long Knives on 30 June 1934. More, however, was necessary if the Nazis were to soften this potential source of friction.

Some leading conservatives were suspicious and did attempt to engage the army's opposition to Hitler as early as 1934, but the military elite was not interested in staging a *Staatsstreich* (coup). Many felt obliged by their oath to Hitler, while most refrained from any form of resistance to the very end. In reality, the army was neither supportive of the Third Reich nor did it oppose it. It tolerated events and monitored Hitler's moves. Indeed, there were certainly themes of commonality between National Socialism and the army, including a common hatred of the Versailles Treaty and support for the rearming of Germany. This relationship was further consolidated by common agreement on the coveting of expansion eastward into Poland and, possibly, the Soviet Union. However, the army elite did not envisage and were resistant to the idea of a major war in the immediate future. Where open opposition did arise to Nazi expansionist policy within the army, as occurred with General Blomberg and War Minister Fritsch over Hitler's designs on Czechoslovakia in 1938, they were swiftly replaced with more subservient individuals (in this case Generals Jodl and Keitel). Secretly, opposition was mounting, but Hitler's growing popularity and a reluctance on behalf of other powers to support the putschists prevented any forcible attempt to remove him.[20]

With the army essentially under control Hitler was able to pursue his principal ideological objectives: expansion abroad, economic stability and full employment at home and the creation of a racially pure Germany at home. The most pressing concern in the early years was the urgency of restoring economic prosperity to Germany. Although the Nazis had arrived in power without any grand economic blueprint, they secured in Hjalmar Schacht an excellent and highly capable individual who as President of the *Reichsbank* and later head of the Economics Ministry transformed Germany's economic fortunes and doubled national income between 1933 and 1937. This period saw unemployment slashed from 6 million to 1 million. This German 'miracle' was essentially attained through the introduction of mass public works schemes. Many were forms of low-paid employment, but they proved a sufficient and successful means to reduce the number of unemployed, boost government credit and of course advance the rearmament drive. Schacht was not a Nazi and would almost certainly have been an instrumental figure in any conservative government. In other words, there was nothing particularly novel about the Nazis' economic boom.

The links between business and the Nazis have been a recurrent and controversial theme of the literature. On the one hand there is the view, proffered relentlessly by GDR historians, that Nazi policy was dictated by monopoly capitalism and the interests of big business.[21] This is a gross misreading of events. The business community certainly became intertwined with Nazism, but largely for its own interests. It accepted economic planning and willingly agreed to the cartelization of many sectors of German industry, a process that had been occurring in any case since the 1890s, to assist production and profits. Balance sheets were to show an impressive fourfold rise in profits between 1929 and 1939. The more rearmament was pushed the more raw materials were needed which made expansion more urgent, thus intensifying the need for weapons. Ultimately many leading industrialists, including Krupps and Flick, were to participate in the plunder, exploitation and destruction and ultimately in the mass murder programmes. In short, Hitler was anything but an instrument of the capitalists. These 'co-operating experts and economists were instruments and objects, not originators of this policy'.[22]

In the domestic policy arena, once all political opposition had been effectively silenced and control had been firmly established, the National Socialist regime turned its attention to transforming core elements of its earlier agitation into policy. Notions of creating a new racially pure Germany led to a spate of anti-Jewish laws, efforts to reshape and re-educate Germans into the creeds of eugenics and race theory and the initiation (albeit short-lived) of a euthanasia programme to target the physically impaired and disabled.

Anti-Semitism was the most pronounced of these policies. Under the Nazi government the pursuit of anti-Semitism revealed elements of both continuity and discontinuity. Their adoption of an anti-Semitic agenda was hardly surprising and scarcely unique. It had for centuries been a fact and way of life in all European societies and cultures. Persecution in a variety of forms (exclusion from certain trades, expulsion, murder) was for the most part based largely on religious, economic and social grounds. It was far from being simply a German issue: anti-Semitism at the end of the nineteenth century was particularly pronounced in both France and Austro-Hungary, while Russia was the land of persecution. Before 1914 'anti-Semitism was very much comparable to a stubborn low-grade infection that did not seriously impair the health of the social body but defied all attempts to cure it'.[23] Indeed, many Jews in Germany (in spite of certain career avenues still being closed off) deemed their future prospects to be reasonably healthy.

Although they would have been aware of some of the more extreme racist literature circulating particularly in the 1890s, it was evident that the small and one-issue anti-Semitic parties of the Imperial period were in decline.[24] Nevertheless, the seeds of anti-Semitic prejudice in all its religious, cultural, political and increasingly racial variants had been sown. Its true malignance materialized in the aftermath of the First World War and this 'disease' spread virulently throughout the body politic. One of the strongest elements within *völkisch* nationalism was its adoption of the social Darwinian values of 'survival of the fittest' and its consequent emphasis on race and its propagation and dissemination, through popular tracts by Fritsch and Chamberlain, of racial anti-Semitism. This represented a new and highly significant variant of the age-old anti-Semitic tradition in Europe. Now conversion to Christianity was no longer an exit route from persecution. From here nothing less than the eradication of Jewry from German soil was deemed sufficient to cleanse Germany.

The NSDAP did not invent anti-Semitism, it merely repackaged it. It was the National Socialist emphasis on race doctrine that clearly demarcated Nazism from other forms of European Fascism and broke all continuity with previous German government philosophies.[25] The endorsement of racial theory enabled the classification of different races and the identification of primary and secondary branches. The most gifted was the 'Aryan': although the term has Indo-European origins, it came to be associated with the Germans. Nazi propaganda proclaimed the superiority of the German race and its right to rule while, in contrast, it condemned 'inferior' peoples to a state of enslavement and drudgery or even extermination. The supposed credibility of this new science was immediately evident with the establishing of chairs in race theory in universities across Germany after 1933.

The acceptance and pursuit of racial theory complemented the promotion of an excessive nationalism within a *Volksgemeinschaft* (national community). On the one hand this led logically to the identification of outsiders and those excluded from this national community; on the other, racial theory enabled the Nazis to promote a new strain of anti-Semitism that superseded earlier prejudices against well poisoners, butchers of babies and sexual deviants. During the Nazi years contempt for outsiders fell mostly on the Jews and to a lesser extent on the gypsies and the Poles. The Jews were not only classified as an inferior race, but as the counter-race (*Gegenrasse*) that was intent on destroying and corrupting all the positive values and achievements of the 'Aryan civilization'. Hitler's extreme anti-Semitic convictions and vilification of the Jewish community are clearly on display in *Mein Kampf*.[26]

Nazi propaganda came to identify the Jews as plotters of a world conspiracy. They were held responsible for Germany's defeat in 1918 and for the Bolshevik menace that confronted Europe and were accused of planning to destroy the creativity and strength of the Aryan race through the process of deeper integration and essentially through mixed marriages. Hitler held such 'mixing of the races' to be contrary to the rules of nature and held firmly to the belief that pure blood lines should be maintained. This simple mythology was helped by several generations of 'patriotic professors' and 'pseudoprophets', and ultimately, all this hatred and venom led directly to the concentration camps. Nevertheless, despite Hitler's strong anti-Semitic feelings and those expressed in party documentation in the early 1920s, anti-Semitism played no more than a secondary role in the transformation from *völkisch* sect to mass party. This is not to deny the significance of the party's anti-Semitic credentials, or its common feature among all radical right parties, but to recognize the leadership's view that it was an insufficient means to bolster support among the wider electorate. In contrast, the adoption and pursuit of a zealous anti-Marxist rhetoric proved a much more useful weapon in terms of both recruitment and impressive electoral returns.

The Nazis differed from the anti-Semitic writers at the turn of the century insofar as they possessed both the will and the conviction to amplify the theories of racial anti-Semitism to their most extreme variant under the Final Solution (*Endlösung*) programme. The beginnings of the persecution of German Jews under Nazi Germany commenced in the days after Hitler had assumed power. It initially assumed the form of intimidation and physical assault, window-smashing and the plundering of Jewish-owned department stores, and even the first boycott of Jewish goods in April 1933. Again, there was nothing particularly unique about such cruelty and beatings. They represented continuity with events throughout the second Christian millennium across Europe. What ultimately came to distinguish the National Socialists' approach to the Jewish question was a compulsion not only to exclude the Jewish community from all aspects of daily society, but ultimately to attempt to eradicate German and European Jewry.

The road to this end commenced in a series of anti-Jewish laws where the non-Aryans were deprived of their citizenship and rights under German law. The Press Law of 1934, for example, excluded Jews from the arts and the theatre and revoked the law of naturalization (on all Jews who had been awarded German citizenship since 1914). The now infamous Nuremberg Laws of 1935 effectively reduced the Jews to second-class citizens, forbade their marriage with non-Jews and even prohibited sexual relations with non-Jews. Jewish possessions and property were confiscated (in 1937) and increasingly they were dismissed from their positions of employment within initially the public sector and then the private sector. The *Kristallnacht* (Night of the Broken Glass) in November 1938 bore witness to one of the most notorious and horrific episodes in the history of anti-Semitism when 7,000 Jewish businesses and synagogues were set alight. Thousands were beaten and intimidated. Essentially, from the mid-1930s onwards the people of the Jewish faith were systematically purged from all levels of the state bureaucracy: from the judiciary, from the professions, from the universities, and from access to higher education. While many Jews fled abroad, many more opted to remain in Germany. Few at this stage could have predicted the next phase and the radicalization of Nazi anti-Jewish policy. This, under cover of war, brought the mass deportations to the concentration camps in eastern Europe, and the decision taken at Wannsee in January 1942 to eradicate European Jewry.[27]

Foreign policy

Assessments of Nazi foreign policy are open to two focal interpretations. The first centres on the degree to which the process was carefully planned and executed. In contrast, the second portrays Hitler as a mere opportunist and 'coffee-house dreamer' seizing the chances as they emerged and the head of a regime which stumbled from one crisis to another.[28] Are we to depict Hitler and his regime simply as unprincipled opportunists or as radical visionaries following a coherent programme? If the latter, does this programme reveal degrees of continuity with traditional German foreign policy objectives or does Nazism represent something radically different and innovative? Certainly most historians writing in the 1950s and early 1960s spurned any notion of Hitler operating to a set agenda. Instead they preferred to portray him as an unscrupulous individual bereft of any talent.[29] On the contrary, it has been argued that it is only 'hindsight that gives some air of consistency'.[30] Others have deemed Hitler a stooge of other vested interests, namely the military and big business, and classified his foreign policy as only a continuation of the social imperialist drive that had been apparent in the Imperial period. Only in more recent decades have judgements come to counter such initial conclusions and to argue that Hitler's foreign policies (and their centrepiece of territorial expansion) were consistent and reflected his fanatical *Weltanschauung*.

As to the questions of whether Nazi foreign policy reflected German preoccupations on the foreign stage after 1919 and whether it truly represented revolutionary change, the answers to both must be in the affirmative. The Nazis in common with previous Weimar governments demanded a revision of the Versailles settlement and the restoration of Germany's

1914 borders.[31] This was their common starting point with the conservative right. However, in power the Nazi regime was to prove far more radical, expansionist and aggressive than any of their immediate predecessors and arguably more territorially ambitious than any conservative-led government would have been in the 1930s.

Hitler was a genius, albeit an evil genius, intent on establishing in the first instance German mastery in Europe and in the longer term, and after his death, global supremacy after a war with the United States.[32] He envisaged a simple step-by-step plan (*Stufenplan*) to world domination. If successful, it would have proven immensely costly in terms of lives, financial resources and economic prosperity.[33] It is the intentionist debate that has gained the upper hand in recent decades. Certainly, it is impossible to talk of any particular timetable or timescale, but the aims were unambiguous. In reality, the difficulty for the Nazi leadership lay in predicting the responses of other states to Germany's intentions. This was the gamble inherent within Hitler's plans. In stark contrast to his almost total disinterest in domestic affairs, Hitler was the architect of Nazi foreign policy. It was his particular fiefdom where he set the tone and style and overrode the views of his own foreign ministers, Konstantin Freiherr von Neurath (1933–8) and Joachim von Ribbentrop (1938–45).

However, the appointment of the conservative von Neurath as foreign minister initially concealed the significant and imminent changes in German approaches to foreign policy. Von Neurath's personality, politics and disposition suggested continuity and revisions to Versailles by peaceful means, whereas in reality the Nazi regime came to embody the pursuit of more aggressive and racist intentions. Overturning the Versailles settlement was only the first stage of an expansive foreign policy whose main objective was the destruction of the Soviet Union.

Lebensraum (living space in the east) represented the cornerstone of Nazi foreign policy. Its realization, however, necessitated the conquest of Russia and the enslavement of the Slavs. From Hitler's perspective a war between Germany and the Soviet Union was not only an inevitability, but a necessity to allow for much-needed German expansion. This theme marked a considerable continuity in German ambitions. Already during the 1880s Germany had initiated her campaign for a 'place in the sun' and a drive for overseas colonies. While this mirrored the activities of her continental rivals, it concealed the fact that Germany's real expansive goals lay not in Africa, but in eastern Europe, and more specifically in Russia. The Treaty of Brest-Litovsk of 1918 between Russia and the Central Powers (which ended Russian participation in the war) clearly revealed German ambitions.[34]

Any successful campaign against Stalin's state was to be followed by plans to Germanize the western territories of the Soviet Union with mass

German migration programmes. This would not only enable German colonization of eastern Europe, ensure the defeat of Bolshevism and solve the Jewish question, but also position a new, greater and racially pure Germany as a world power and prepare her for a subsequent confrontation with the United States. The sheer arrogance of this *Pax Germanica*, a plan for total world domination, was enough to signal its own failure. Policy can be divided into three distinct periods.

The period 1933–6 witnessed the first cautionary steps of Nazi foreign policy. This was directed to end Germany's isolation and to search for allies (in Great Britain, Italy, France, the Soviet Union, Poland). It was also used to attempt to profit from the disruption of the international system caused by events such as the Spanish Civil War, the Italian invasion of Abyssinia, Japan's invasion of Korea and China, and British/Soviet tensions over India in the early 1930s. Significantly, one of Germany's first moves centred on her decision to leave the League of Nations in 1933. This move was obligatory for any German government intent on rearming. German remilitarization duly followed to increase the size of the army from 100,000 men. This move was clearly in violation of Germany's treaty commitments, but was simply ignored by both the UK and France.

The second phase (1936–9) brought major successes for Nazi Germany, and each success fortified Hitler's position at home. They began tentatively with the remilitarization of the Rhineland in 1936. France and Great Britain watched these events but failed to react to yet another breach of the Versailles Treaty. This passivity, which was wedded to a British and French appeasement policy, only inspired Hitler towards a more radical agenda. His aspirations and expansionist ambitions were clearly revealed at a secret conference of top military and Foreign Office officials in the autumn of 1937. In a sensational four-hour monologue the Führer reiterated his views on the need for German territorial expansion.[35] Austria and Czechoslovakia were identified as the first targets of Nazi expansion.[36] Both countries were duly annexed.

The failure by both France and Great Britain ardently to oppose Nazi aggression only encouraged Hitler to further adventures. The Nazi–Soviet Pact of August 1939 took all Europe by surprise. No-one had expected an agreement between two such implacable foes. On the one hand this pact was designed to dissuade both London and Paris from any interference in Hitler's next plans, as his attention turned towards the free city of Danzig and another (the fourth) German–Russian initiative to erase Poland from the European map. It also enabled Germany to reduce the possibility of facing a war on two fronts, for should war be declared by both France and Great Britain on Germany, Hitler was determined to knock them out of the war before turning his attentions to the Russian steppes. By September 1939 both London and Paris were determined to resist any further German aggression and territorial expansion, even if it meant war. The German invasion of Poland therefore heralded the outbreak of the Second World War.

To conclude this section, it is almost certain that even without Hitler German foreign policy would have been expansionary, insofar as it would have sought to restore Germany's dominant position in central Europe and her 1914 borders, and to seek further expansion eastwards as at Brest-Litovsk in 1917. Whether this would have culminated in a general European and world war must remain an issue of conjecture.

Germany at war, 1939–1945

Debate may continue to rage over the degree of German culpability and responsibility for the outbreak of the First World War, but in 1939 Nazi Germany was unquestionably the aggressor. The decision to strike militarily was a gamble. Germany was simply not totally prepared, either militarily or economically, for a full-scale war.[37] Hitler's decision to launch war reflected a need to maintain the energy and momentum of the Nazi crusade, a belief in the rejuvenating force of conflict and the capabilities of the German people, and utter confidence in the superiority of the German war machine. The decision was also facilitated by the fear that Germany's own position and strength would deteriorate once her rivals, and particularly the Soviet Union, had completed their rearmament policies:

> No treaty and no agreement can ensure lasting neutrality on the part of Soviet Russia . . . The best security against Russian attack is to make a clear display of superior German strength and a quick demonstration of our power.[38]

However, although the Soviet Union was the main target of Nazi aggression, it was first of all necessary to crush the West to avoid a war on two fronts:

> Everything that I undertake is directed against Russia. If those in the West are too stupid and too blind to understand this, then I shall be forced to come to an understanding with the Russians to beat the West, and then, after its defeat, turn with all my concerted force against the Soviet Union.[39]

In retrospect, it is obvious that the war led directly to Nazi Germany's downfall, but this gamble very nearly paid off. A series of lightning attacks in late spring 1940 defeated the western European democracies (with the exception of Britain).[40] Although the UK's survival was greatly assisted by the Battle of Britain (September 1940), much to Hitler's anger and frustration, the Führer felt compelled to maintain the initiative and to pursue his expansionary aims eastwards. Indeed, it was assumed that once the Soviet Union had capitulated, British compliance and acceptance of German supremacy in Europe would ensue. It was against this backdrop, with Nazi Germany at the height of its powers, that plans for the invasion of Russia were drawn up in 1941.

The Barbarossa campaign, as it was called, began gloriously in July 1941. The *Wehrmacht*, supported by the *Luftwaffe*, made rapid advances across the Soviet Union. However, the successes were to prove shortlived and the failure to capture Moscow in the autumn of 1941 and to force Leningrad's submission heralded the first major setbacks in Germany's wars. The Russian campaign, which had been scheduled to last for six weeks, simply overstretched Germany's resources and logistics, and her difficulties were compounded by the severe Russian winter. Despite promising victories in Russia and North Africa at the start of 1942 which led German troops into Egypt and the Caucasus, the tide was turning against Germany. The entry of the United States into the war in December 1941 tipped the balance heavily against Germany. Germany's surrender at both Stalingrad in February 1943 and North Africa in May 1943 together with the Allied landings in Italy in the summer of 1943 marked the beginnings of the end for the Third Reich.

Hitler and most of the Nazi leadership simply failed to come to terms with the changed circumstances. The war continued. The Allies successfully drove the Germans out of southern Italy in 1943 and France in 1944 whilst they intensified their campaigns to bomb Germany into submission. Hitler's frenetic and rabid ramblings grew more intense as his plans began to dissolve around him, particularly after the assassination attempt in July 1944.[41] The failure of this ensured the continuation of the war for another year. Hitler conjured up all sorts of deals to the very end. He conceived of alliances with Britain and the USA against the common Soviet menace or even toyed with a rapprochement with Russia against the West. In reality, Hitler's room for manoeuvre was non-existent. Although both Britain and the United States demanded Germany's unconditional surrender, he still hoped that the Reich could be saved even as Berlin was disintegrating around him in April 1945. Finally Hitler, who was determined not to suffer the same fate as Mussolini, committed suicide on 30 April 1945.[42] Leadership of the Reich passed to Admiral Dönitz who on 9 May declared Germany's unconditional surrender. Hitler's war was over.

Conclusions

The extreme right in Germany between 1919 and 1945 has become synonymous with National Socialism, but what are we to make of this movement? Was it unique, and did the Third Reich mark a distinctive break in German history? Certainly in the 1920s Nazism displayed striking similarities with other right-wing extremist forces. It was far from novel and was largely dismissed. Much of its platform and agenda reflected the popular slogans and sentiment of its times. In its role as a protest and opposition party the trends of continuity with the right in general are clearly discernible. The decisive moment in the NSDAP's history and development, however, is its arrival in power.

Once installed, this new regime set about attempting to realize its radical agenda. It is from this point that it is possible to identify breaks in continuity with previous German governments as Hitler's regime became the most extreme, the most anti-Semitic, the most anti-communist and the most anti-democratic force to attain political power that modern German history has yet known. There are, however, also salient consistencies, most particularly in the field of foreign policy. Nazism's legacy is far-reaching. Indeed, as Hitler's self-imposed isolation in power and his megalomania grew, so the outcome of his particular brand of conviction politics ironically attained everything that he had so vehemently opposed during his political struggle. Hitler's war concluded with the division of Germany, the implementation of democracy in West Germany, the advance of communism into central and eastern Europe and the creation of the state of Israel in 1948.

The military defeat of Nazi Germany in May 1945 ended this most distinctive and destructive period of German right-wing extremism. Although the NSDAP was immediately prohibited, and despite the Allied programmes of denazification and re-education that took place in the late 1940s, vestiges of Nazism have continued to persist on the very fringes of the German political system. On three occasions the extreme right has momentarily prospered on the political landscape. Hitler's successors, whether they have consisted of the *Sozialistische Reichspartei* (1949–52), the *Nationaldemokratische Partei Deutschlands* (1966–9) or the *Republikaner* (1989–92), have excited much media speculation, but all three right-wing extremist political parties have failed to gain any lasting footholds in the German political system. The emergence of the much smaller and militant neo-Nazi groups in the later 1980s and throughout the 1990s only reinforced the images of persecution and the dangers that have come to characterize Nazism and compelled the Federal Republic of Germany to address and confront Germany's past.

Notes

1. SINUS, '5 Millionen Deutsche sagen, '*Wir wollen wieder einen Führer haben*' (Reinbek bei Hamburg, 1981); K. Faller and H. Siebold, *Neo-Faschismus* (Frankfurt am Main, 1986).

2. H. Knutter, *Hat der Rechtsextremismus in der Bundesrepublik eine Chance?* (Bonn, 1988), p. 36.

3. I. Kershaw, *The Nazi Dictatorship: Problems and Perspectives of Interpretation* (London, 1989), p. 135.

4. The league, sponsored by the Pan German League, was never envisaged as a political party. Despite a rapid growth which boosted its membership to some 200,000 by the early 1920s, many of its members were to drift to more politically conscious and active forces and mainly to the fledgling Nazi Party.

5. Hitler's formative years and his political awakenings have been skilfully charted and interpreted by A. Bullock, *Hitler: A Study in Tyranny* (London, 1962); J. Fest, *Hitler: Eine Bibliographie* (Frankfurt am Main, 1962); and I. Kershaw, *Hitler: Hubris, 1889–1936* (London, 1998).

6. This was written while Hitler was serving the rather lenient nine-month prison sentence for his involvement in the attempted putsch to topple the Bavarian government in Munich in November 1923. Had this proved successful, Hitler had planned to stage a march on Berlin.

7. At its height in 1919 the *Freikorps* boasted some 200,000 members. Its activities took place against the persistence of strong nationalist sympathies that stemmed back to the outbreak of the Great War and centred on the appeals of a *Volksgemeinschaft*. It was a powerful force in conservative circles and was to be complemented on the extreme right after 1919 by the emergence of numerous small right-wing extremist parties.

8. P. Merkl, 'Approaches to Political Violence: The Stormtroopers 1925–33', in W.J. Mommsen and G. Hirschfeld, eds, *Social Protest, Violence and Terror in Nineteenth and Twentieth Century Europe* (Basingstoke, 1982), p. 370.

9. Hitler's lack of interest in the use of ideas as a means of attracting support and his belief in the use of propaganda were already evident in *Mein Kampf* (Paternoster Library, London, 1938), esp. ch. 6.

10. Hitler, *Mein Kampf*, pp. 216–17.

11. R. Bessel, 'Violence and Propaganda: The Role of the Stormtroopers in the Rise of National Socialism', in T. Childers, ed., *The Formation of the Nazi Constituency, 1919–33* (London, 1986), p. 133.

12. J. Noakes, 'The Origins, Structure and Functions of Nazi Terror', in N. O'Sullivan, ed., *Terrorism, Ideology and Revolution* (Brighton, 1986), p. 76.

13. I. Kershaw, 'Ideology, Propaganda and the Rise of the Nazi Party', in P. Stachura, ed., *The Nazi Machtergreifung* (London, 1983), p. 162.

14. *Mein Kampf* has become a standard text into the mindset of Adolf Hitler in spite of his style and the lack of any clear evidence of any process of rational thought. On an initial examination the book is difficult to read, being written in a very verbose and dry style. It is badly structured and contains some very dubious sections, most notably that on syphilis. The turgid style explains why the book was exclusively ridiculed and why its author attained the guise of an adventurer. Hitler himself was far from a coherent thinker and his views were shaped and formed and confirmed by his own experiences, prejudices and lifestyle.

15. It is in the pages of *Mein Kampf* that Hitler pours substantive scorn on the Jews and shows his enthusiasm for the concepts of Social Darwinism. He urges the necessity of prohibiting interracial marriages, illustrates his contempt for bourgeois society and the concepts of democracy, utterly rejects the Versailles peace settlement and purports his views on how to restore German supremacy in Europe and acquire new territory.

16. For the left wing of the NSDAP this new direction constituted a betrayal of policy, and it continued to campaign on a much more socialist-inspired platform. The Strasser brothers were instrumental in this reworking of Nazi ideology and were strongly motivated by the SPD and attracted substantial support in the NSDAP's northern associations. This group stuck very closely to the genuine aims of the 25-point programme by placing particular emphasis on the need for nationalization and the introduction of curbs on private ownership. It sought the elusive third way between capitalism and socialism.

17. Detlev J.K. Peukert, *Die Weimarer Republik* (Frankfurt am Main, 1987).

18. K.D. Bracher, *The German Dictatorship: The Origins, Structure and Organisation of National Socialism* (London, 1982), pp. 435–50.

19. In August 1934, 38 million Germans (90 per cent of registered voters) approved Hitler's own elevation to the party–state position of Führer and Reich Chancellor with full emergency powers. Only just over 4 million opposed him.

20. A summary is provided by Bracher, *German Dictatorship*, pp. 483–94.

21. This is the idea that Hitler was simply following the orders of the landowning and industrial classes who had allowed him to become chancellor in the first place to break the power of the working class. In the GDR anti-Facism was effectively enshrined as an indispensable pillar of the state's ideology and legitimacy. It was used as a tool to attack the forces of capitalism and imperialism epitomised by the West German state. The Marxist–Leninist interpretation is a real travesty given what we know; see, however, D. Eichholtz, *Geschichte*

der deutschen Kriegswirtschaft, 1939–1945 (East Berlin, 1969), and D. Eichholz and K. Gossweiler, eds, *Faschismusforschung. Positionen, Probleme, Politik* (East Berlin, 1980). Too much has been made of contacts between leading Nazis and industrialists: it is simply the case that industry seeks to secure access to government whatever its hue. Seeking to exert pressure is one thing, influencing policy direction is another.

22. Bracher, *German Dictatorship*, pp. 416–17.

23. G. Craig, *The Germans* (London, 1984), p. 140.

24. Of the more influential texts see Houston Stewart Chamberlain's *Grundlagen des 19. Jahrhunderts* ('Foundations of the Nineteenth Century') (Munich, 1899); Theodor Fritsch's *Handbuch der Judenfrage* ('Handbook of the Jewish Question') (Hamburg, 1887); and Wilhelm Marr, *Der Sieg des Judentums über das Germanentum* ('The Victory of Jewry over Germanness'), 10th edn (Berlin, 1879), as well as a range of popular literature of the time.

25. K. Hildebrand, *The Third Reich* (London, 1984).

26. See Hitler, *Mein Kampf* (London, 1996), pp. 272–99.

27. H. Krausnick and M. Broszat, *Anatomy of the SS State* (London, 1982).

28. A.J.P. Taylor, *Origins of the Second World War* (London, 1961).

29. See Bullock, *Hitler*, for example.

30. Hans Mommsen, 'National Socialism: Continuity and Change', in W. Laqueur, ed., *Fascism: A Reader's Guide* (Harmondsworth, 1979), p. 177.

31. Under the terms of the Versailles Treaty, Germany was, for example, deprived of her colonies, lost territory to Belgium, France, Denmark and Poland, was forced to accept responsibility for the war and was faced with a huge reparations bill. This was a highly emotive issue and the treaty was denounced by the right as nothing less than a *Diktat*. Contrary to right-wing propaganda in the 1920s, had the German government opted not to sign the treaty then it is certain that the Allies would have invaded to dismember Germany and extract reparations directly.

32. These ideas, which are now commonly held by historians, were first given expression in A. Hillgruber, *Hitlers Strategie: Kriegsführung und Politik, 1940–1941* (Frankfurt-am-Main, 1965). The global theme has been developed most notably by K. Hildebrand.

33. Hillgruber, *Hitlers Strategie*, and Klaus Hildebrand, *The Foreign Policy of the Third Reich* (London, 1973).

34. Under the terms of this treaty the Soviet Union surrendered the Ukraine, the Baltic coast, the Caucasus, White Russia, Poland and Finland to Germany. The right's foreign policy ambitions not only sought the return of the territories lost under the Versailles settlement, but coveted the expanse won at Brest-Litovsk.

35. The summary of this speech was minuted by Colonel Hossbach at the meeting but fell into American hands in 1945. It was used at Nuremberg to provide clear proof of Germany's actions but its authenticity has often been questioned. In reality, there remains little doubt that it is a genuine account of what was said. See H.W. Koch, 'Hitler and the Origins of the Second World War: Second Thoughts on the Status of Some of the Documents', in E.M. Robertson, ed., *The Origins of the Second World War: Historical Interpretations* (London, 1982), pp. 158–88.

36. Fest, *Hitler*, pp. 539–43.

37. Millward and Carroll both rightly argue that the German economy was not geared up to total war until 1942: Alan Millward, *The German Economy at War* (London, 1965), and Bernice Carroll, *Design for Total War: Arms and Economics in the Third Reich* (The Hague, 1968).

38. Hildebrand, *The Third Reich*, p. 51.

39. This much used quote was spoken by Hitler to the Swiss Commissioner to the League of Nations in 1939. It must be regarded as a warning to the Western powers not to obstruct Germany's intentions. In practice it did not produce the desired responses from either London or Paris. See Carl J. Burckhardt, *Meine Danziger Mission, 1937–1939* (Munich, 1962), p. 272.

40. Norway and Denmark had been invaded earlier to prevent the supply of necessary raw materials from Sweden through Norwegian waters.

41. Various plots were planned but the most notorious of these, and the one that was almost successful, was that of 20 July 1944 in East Prussia. The Generals' Plot, led by Stauffenberg, was one of numerous opposition groups to the Nazi government. It was a clear indication that the war was seen as lost.

42. The noble solution. Hitler's body was burnt and buried in the gardens of the Chancellery. His remains were quickly exhumed by the Russians and spirited away for proper identification and, more importantly, to prevent the grave becoming a future shrine to National Socialism. The early confusion as to whether Hitler had indeed committed suicide or been able to flee, and the intrigues of the Russians and life in the bunker during the closing months, have been portrayed in Hugh Trevor-Roper's now classic account, *The Last Days of Hitler*, 4th edn (London, 1971).

CHAPTER TEN

The SPD

STEFAN BERGER

On 23 March 1933 the Reichstag voted on Hitler's Enabling Law.[1] When Otto Wels, chairman of the Social Democratic Party (SPD), stood up and walked to the lectern, he knew that his speech would not prevent the adoption of the law, for the Catholic Centre Party, for so long the democratic ally of Social Democracy in the Weimar Republic, had struck a deal with the devil: they would vote for the law in return for promises by the Nazis that they would respect and tolerate organized Catholicism. As the Communist members of parliament were already in concentration camps or in hiding, Social Democracy was the only political force left in the Reichstag which defied the Nazis' demand for total power in the state:

> Ladies and Gentlemen! The foreign policy demands made by the Herr
> Reichskanzler for the full equality of Germany are supported by us
> Social Democrats, all the more so as we have always made similar
> demands . . . There has never been any basic principle which hindered our
> party from representing the just demands of the German nation vis-à-vis
> other nations or peoples of the world . . . An unjust peace has never been
> able to lay the foundations for stable foreign and domestic policies. It does
> not sustain a true people's community (*Volksgemeinschaft*) which needs, above
> all, equal rights at home and abroad. A government may protect itself
> against the worst lies, it may use all necessary force to prevent violence, but
> it has to do so on every occasion and without taking sides. And it has to
> do so without treating defeated opponents as if they were outlaws. You
> can rob us of our freedom and you can even kill us, but you cannot take
> away our honour. Following the recent wave of persecution that Social
> Democrats have suffered, no one can reasonably demand or expect that
> the party votes in favour of this Enabling Law. The elections of 5 March
> have brought a majority to the governing parties and have thus opened up

the opportunity to govern strictly according to the letter and meaning of the constitution . . . Never before, since the German parliament came into existence, have elected representatives of the people been so massively excluded from exercising any control over public affairs as now and as will come to be the case still more thanks to the new Enabling Law. . . . The gentlemen of the National Socialist Party call the movement they have unleashed a national revolution – not a national socialist one. The link between their revolution and socialism has so far been reduced to the attempt to destroy the Social Democratic movement which, for more than two generations, has been and will continue to be central to the socialist project . . . We Social Democrats have carried the burdens of responsibility during the most difficult of times, and we have been pelted with stones as a result. Yet our achievements in the reconstruction of the state and economy, and in the liberation of the occupied territories, will stand before history. We have created equal rights for everyone and a socially just industrial law. We have helped to make a Germany where the highest offices of the state are open not only to dukes and barons but to men from the working class . . . In vain, the attempt to roll back the wheel of history! We Social Democrats know that power cannot be defeated by making simple appeals to adhere to the rule of law. We recognize the power-political facts of your current rule. But the people's consciousness of their rights is a political power too, and we will not cease to appeal to that consciousness. The Weimar constitution is not a socialist one. But we stand firm by the principles of the rule of law, and the equal and social rights enshrined in it. In this historic hour we Social Democrats solemnly profess our belief in the principles of humanity and justice, freedom and socialism. No Enabling Law gives you the right to obliterate ideas which are eternal and indestructible . . . The Anti-Socialist Law had not managed to destroy Social Democracy. German Social Democracy will also emerge from this new persecution as a stronger and healthier party. We send out our greetings to the persecuted and the tormented. We salute our friends in the Reich. Their steadfastness and loyalty deserve admiration. Their courage and their unbroken optimism guarantee a brighter future.[2]

This extract from Wels's speech highlights in exemplary fashion a number of issues which were of central importance for the character of the SPD between 1919 and 1945 and which will be discussed below.[3] First, the reference to the Anti-Socialist Law underlines the extent to which the party was rooted in the Imperial German past. Secondly, the insistence on the Social Democrats' willingness to defend the republican state and play by its rules indicates the importance of the revolution of 1918–19 as a reference point for the SPD's self-understanding in the Weimar Republic. Thirdly, in the light of the party's repression and persecution under National Social-ism, its strategy of containing the National Socialist threat to the republic had clearly failed. Wels's appeal to the Nazi-led government to adhere to the legal framework provided by the Weimar Constitution reflected the deep-seated belief of Social Democrats in the rule of law, which partly explains the SPD leadership's refusal to prepare for illegality at an earlier date. Wels's speech also reveals the party's commitment to a vague notion of German national interest. This commitment to the nation was to spark off heated controversies at several important junctures in the SPD's history, and it was always difficult for the party to delineate its 'good' patriotism from the integral 'bad' nationalism of the political right.[4] Fourthly, the 1930s and 1940s was a time of major rethinking of the Social Democratic ethos. The party's gradualism, reformism and social republicanism were questioned by many Social Democrats, and instead Social Democracy underwent a 'renaissance of radicalism'[5] which was spurred on by the rank and file as well as by diverse left-wing splinter groups. The history of the SPD in Weimar and Nazi Germany cannot be adequately understood without appreciating its awkward positioning between its transformatory ambitions and its gradualist policies. If the early 1930s witnessed a radicalization of Social Democracy, the failure to achieve some form of united front policy in the 1930s and the general disillusionment on the left about Stalinism was enough to stabilize Social Democratic reformism. Finally, a brief look at the failures of the SPD post-1945 will reveal their rootedness in both the continuities and discontinuities that characterized the party between 1919 and 1945.

The Weimar SPD and the burden of its history

When the Weimar Constitution was formally adopted on 11 August 1919, the SPD could look back on ten months as a party of government and on 40 years of persecution and discrimination. Hence, it is hardly surprising that the character of the Weimar SPD was determined largely by the legacy of the party's history in Imperial Germany. Worried by the Social Democrats' success at the polls and in search of an internal enemy against which to unite the liberal–conservative political forces, Bismarck outlawed the Social Democratic Party between 1878 and 1890, when the Anti-Socialist Law was allowed to lapse. Under this law, individual Social Democrats were allowed to stand for elections to legislative assemblies, including the Reichstag, but the party's associations were forcibly dissolved, its newspapers repressed and many of its activists forced into exile or imprisoned. In the 1890s, Social Democrats were still widely dubbed 'enemies of the Reich' (*Reichsfeinde*) and 'vagrants without a fatherland' (*vaterlandslose Gesellen*), and there were several successive attempts to renew anti-socialist legislative measures throughout the decade. Yet, despite such repression and accompanying attempts to wean industrial workers away from Social Democracy by introducing basic social reform in the 1880s, the SPD continued to grow. Under the Anti-Socialist Law the party was able to increase its share of the vote from 7.5 per cent in 1878 to 19.7 per cent in 1890, and it was to become the largest party in the Reichstag in 1912 with 34.8 per cent of the vote and 110 of 397 overall seats. On the eve of the First World War, the SPD had over 1 million individual members. It was the largest and most successful socialist party in the world and was closely allied to the fast-growing trade union and cooperative movements, members of which numbered in the millions.

Nevertheless, the SPD did not mobilize more than 50 per cent of the working-class vote in elections, and it only brought a distinct minority of workers into its organizational orbit. In fact, the 'typical' Social Democrat was a specific kind of worker: male, skilled, employed, urban, young, Protestant and 'respectable', often the archetypal printer, building or metal worker. Social Democracy in Imperial Germany formed a separate social milieu that had little contact with other social milieux, e.g. the Catholic one or the Protestant middle-class milieu. The division of Imperial German society into different vertical pillars continued in the Weimar Republic and formed a major obstacle to the cooperation of political parties in coalition governments. As every political party was firmly tied to representing the interests of a specific social milieu, their willingness and ability to compromise were bound to have tight limits, especially given the fact that none of the political parties had any experience of parliamentary government.

Within the Social Democratic milieu the experience of repression and isolation in Imperial Germany left a three-fold legacy. First, the SPD was to concentrate on building up its own organizational empire, complete with a wide range of ancillary organizations which catered for every thinkable aspect of workers' lives 'from the cradle to the grave'. Social Democracy created localized 'communities of solidarity' which enveloped members' lives and isolated them from other social and political groups.[6] Secondly, the SPD adopted an explicitly Marxist programme in 1891. The Erfurt programme offered a vision of the future in which the ever more intense class struggles between the bourgeoisie and the working class would lead to revolution and social transformation. Thirdly, Social Democrats were afraid of renewed repression that would endanger the fruits of their organizational patriotism. Consequently, they emphasized their legalistic outlook and rejected any direct revolutionary action. The party became characterized by what Dieter Groh has called 'revolutionary attentism', that is, the adherence to a revolutionary rhetoric that was coupled with practical powerlessness and inactivity.[7]

Revolutionary attentism and political isolation, however, did not adequately reflect the position of Social Democracy in Imperial Germany. Social Democrats also engaged in a gradualist reformist practice which aimed at democratizing the political system and improving the living standards of the working class. Especially in the south-western states of the German Reich, the SPD became increasingly integrated and accepted into the existing system of political parties. The reformist drive of the party in Imperial Germany should not be underestimated.[8] The SPD in Imperial Germany stood somewhere in between integration and isolation and, by 1914, it was badly divided into a revolutionary left wing (headed by Rosa Luxemburg and Karl Liebknecht, among others), a revisionist right wing (often connected with Eduard Bernstein, Eduard David and Ignaz Auer) and a Marxist centre (including Karl Kautsky and August Bebel). However, the SPD was also badly divided between those who wanted the SPD to play a more active role in politics and those who seemed content to sit back and wait for the collapse of capitalism. The former included representatives from the left and the right (characteristically, both Luxemburg and Ludwig Frank were in favour of using the general strike as a political weapon, albeit for very different purposes!), while the latter could be found largely among the Marxist centre and the officials heading the huge Social Democratic organizational apparatus. At the outbreak of the First World War, these political and ideological divisions came to the fore and, together with the conflict surrounding the continued support of the German war effort, resulted in the split of the party in 1917, when the Independent Social Democratic Party (USPD) constituted itself as a separate party, forcing local SPD associations to choose between the Majority Social Democrats (MSPD) and the USPD.[9] The ideological divisions in the party between those championing gradualist reformism and those advocating the revolutionary transformation of the existing political and economic system, together with the legacy of the party's prolonged repression and (self-)isolation in a specific Social Democratic milieu, weighed heavily on the Weimar SPD. However, the outsider of Imperial German politics was suddenly and unexpectedly catapulted into power by the revolution of 1918.

The legacy of the 1918 revolution for the self-understanding of the Weimar SPD

The democratic revolution of 1918 was not of Social Democratic making, but the MSPD and USPD leaderships decided to lead the revolution.[10] While initially there had been high hopes for a united response to the revolutionary upheaval, the differences between diverse factions of the labour movement were exacerbated by events and proved insurmountable. The wartime split of the labour movement was deepened and became one of the central features of its history after 1919.[11] The USPD had 750,000 members by the end of 1919, and in the June 1920 general election it received 17.9 per cent of the vote (in comparison with the MSPD's 21.7 per cent). Although it had become the party of hope for many workers in the revolution, it was too heterogeneous a party to survive for long.[12] In 1920, its left wing seceded from the party to join the small Communist Party (KPD), which transformed the KPD (founded on 1 January 1919) into a mass party. The bulk of the party's right wing reunited with the MSPD in 1922. Subsequently, Social Democrats and Communists presented industrial workers with a stark choice. The KPD championed the building of a Soviet Germany along the lines of Lenin's Soviet Union. It derided the Weimar Republic as a bourgeois and capitalist state in which no true emancipation was possible for the working class. Its insurrectionary tactics during the first years of the Weimar Republic gave way to a more legalistic outlook later on, but its principled hostility to the Republic was never in doubt. By contrast, the SPD did more than any other party to establish and, subsequently, to defend the Republic against its many enemies.[13] It recognized that it was not yet the perfect socialist state of the future, but it was at least a step in the right direction. The SPD aimed at building a social republic which would lead to a gradual transformation of capitalism and the emergence of a socialist state. Rudolf Hilferding's theory of 'organized capitalism' provided the theoretical framework for the SPD's adherence to reformist gradualism. It described the state as a neutral instrument of change in the hands of whoever commanded political power. Furthermore, Hilferding argued, the capitalist economy was moving towards socialism by its own logic. Competitive capitalism was being steadily replaced by organized capitalism and planned production. Such developments, according to Hilferding, would necessarily pave the way towards the socialization of the means of production in a socialist economy of the future.

The SPD, however, could only hope to achieve political power if it was to convert other social groups to its cause. Despite strenuous efforts, party membership could not be significantly extended beyond the 1 million mark, which was crossed just before 1914. Electorally, support for the Social Democrats peaked in 1919, when MSPD and USPD together received 45.5 per cent of the vote. After 1922 the SPD's performance varied between 29.8 per cent in 1928 and 20.4 per cent in November 1932. The main reason for the stagnation of the SPD's growth was the fact that the growth of the industrial blue-collar working class, which had traditionally formed the bulk of the SPD's support, slowed down in the 1920s. The fastest growing sector of the population was now comprised of white-collar workers (*Angestellten*). Hence, many in the SPD wanted to build bridges to the members of this new middle class as well as to agricultural workers and sections of the old middle class. A minority within the Weimar SPD aimed at transforming the party into a 'people's party' or 'catch-all party' which would draw support from diverse sections of the population.[14] Such attempts could draw on a strong tradition (in particular in south-western Germany) of presenting the SPD as a people's party rather than a class party.[15] In the early years of the Republic, it had some success in recruiting agricultural workers and white-collar workers, but decades of prejudice and mistrust could not be overcome in a matter of a few years. Nationalist conservatives remained far better at organizing these groups than Social Democrats.

Furthermore, the SPD tried hard to build coalitions with the bourgeois centre parties, in particular with the German Democratic Party (DDP) and the Catholic Centre Party. Yet there were firm limits to such a remodelling of the SPD's ethos in the Weimar Republic. Heinrich August Winkler has argued that the party's left wing and its continued championing of Marxism had much to answer for in the failure of the SPD to break through to be a genuine people's party in the Weimar Republic.[16] And indeed, especially after 1922, the reunified SPD emphasized the transformatory aims of Social Democracy more so than the MSPD between 1917 and 1922. The famous chant of the Young Socialists, that 'Democracy is not much, Socialism is the Aim', indicated a certain ambivalence of sections of the SPD towards the Weimar Republic. It also revealed the subterranean continuity of the transformatory ambitions of sections of Social Democrats. At no time in the Weimar Republic did the SPD become a mere reformist party along the lines of post-Second World War west European social democracies.

The continued ambivalence between the SPD's willingness to work within the existing political and economic system and its determination to over-come and transform it was not, however, primarily the result of Marxist ideology and the continued (self-)isolation of Social Democratic commun-ities of solidarity, which, incidentally, found their widest-ever expansion in the middle years of the Weimar Republic.[17] Rather, the professed Marxism of many Social Democrats was the direct outcome of their experiences with other political and social forces within the Republic. However much the SPD had tried to build bridges to the bourgeois centre parties, time and again the latter had put impossible demands on the SPD. In both 1923 and 1930 coalition governments failed, not so much because of the SPD's reluct-ance to compromise but because of the bourgeois parties' insistence on demands which were simply unacceptable to an SPD which constantly had to look over its shoulder to a KPD keen to capitalize on anything that could be interpreted as a betrayal of working-class interests.

The material and psychological reality of class society in the 1920s did not allow for any genuine transformation of the SPD into a catch-all party. Class was not only an ideology in Weimar, it was a fundamental every-day experience. On the shop floor workers were confronted with despotic foremen and the dangers of hard industrial labour which could easily lead to accidents and the loss of life or limb. In the neighbourhoods, Social Democratic workers suffered from unemployment and struggled to make ends meet to pay for rent, food and clothes, while their children received minimal schooling. The neighbourhood and class-specific youth cliques were much more important for the socialization of working-class youth than the state schools. Workers were subjected to high levels of violence by police and right-wing paramilitaries. Strikes and demonstrations were part and parcel of the daily struggle for emancipation. A 'popular Marxism' (*Volksmarxismus*) had penetrated the Social Democratic milieu and was meaningful to many rank-and-file members, as it corresponded with their everyday experience of exploitation and social injustice. It was this sense of class injustice that could bind Social Democratic and Communist workers' milieux together in the neighbourhoods and at the workplace, but prevented any bridge-building to other social classes.[18] The revolution of 1918 had badly divided the proletarian milieu of Imperial Germany. However, the supporters of the SPD and the KPD arguably perceived more commonalities between themselves than between workers and the middle-class supporters of the bourgeois centre parties. This made the position of the SPD in the Weimar Republic a difficult one. On the one hand, it had to form coalitions with those bourgeois parties if it wanted governmental power; on the other, it had to be wary not to lose the support of its traditional clientele to the KPD, all the more so as the continued separation of German society into separate milieux made it impossible for the SPD to gain support from other sections of the population.

The SPD's fight against National Socialism

When the Nazis came to power in 1933 it seemed to confirm the SPD's continued isolation. The bourgeois parties had either become so insignificant as to be meaningless (DDP and DVP), or they were willing to reach a compromise with National Socialism (Centre Party) in the hope of organizational survival. On 30 January 1933, the SPD's strategy for avoiding a National Socialist government lay in tatters. After 1930 so-called presidential cabinets ruled Germany without a parliamentary majority. The Weimar Constitution allowed for such measures in times of crisis, but they were to become a permanent feature between 1930 and 1933. The SPD opposed most of the deflationary measures of the first presidential cabinet under Chancellor Heinrich Brüning. It voted against Brüning and new elections were called in September 1930. The SPD lost over 5 per cent of the vote and the Nazis gained over 15 per cent, making them the second strongest party in the Reichstag – just behind the SPD. Subsequently, the SPD found itself in a dilemma. Every time it voted against Brüning, his legislation would be defeated and the president would use his powers to dissolve parliament and call new elections. The only beneficiaries would be the Nazis. Consequently, the SPD decided to 'tolerate' Brüning, both to keep the Nazis out of office in the short term and in the hope that, once the economic crisis was overcome, the threat posed by the Nazis to Weimar democracy would dissolve into thin air.

The success of 'toleration' was limited. While the presidential cabinets did keep the Nazis at bay for a while, the SPD looked increasingly immobile. Social Democratic officials in the neighbourhoods and ADGB officials in the factories found it difficult to explain to the rank and file why the party accepted legislation which one-sidedly burdened workers. Although there were some in the SPD, like Carlo Mierendorff, who argued that the SPD needed to activate its extra-parliamentary mass movement to combat Nazism outside parliament, the majority of Social Democrats found reassurance in the party's determinist view of history. Had the intellectual leaders of the party from Bebel to Kautsky and Hilferding not taught them over and over again that, at the end of the day, victory would necessarily have to belong to socialism? If that was the case, the best policies with which to weather the storm of the great depression were surely those that would allow them to sit out the crisis.

The SPD leadership's endorsement of 'toleration' also revealed the effects of the professionalization, rationalization and bureaucratization of policy-making on the parliamentary party and the party at large. Many Social Democrats·were all too accustomed to look at politics through the lenses of professional politicians engaged in a rational political discourse conducted through highly bureaucratized institutional channels. They therefore failed to recognize that the radical threat of Nazism made a more activist political ethos of the SPD all the more necessary. Furthermore, tactical considerations helped to confirm the SPD in its view that there was no realistic alternative to 'tolerating' Brüning. He was, after all, a leading Centre Party politician. The coalition of the SPD and the Centre Party ensured the stability of the government of Prussia – the last democratic bulwark of the Republic. Prussia had been known as 'Red Prussia' in the Weimar Republic. It was a bastion of Social Democratic strength and, ever since 1920, the SPD had formed stable coalition governments there with the Centre Party. From 1920 to 1932 the prominent SPD politician Otto Braun acted as minister president of Prussia.[19] So, as leading SPD politicians argued in private, nothing should be done to strain further the ties between the two major republican parties. Brüning's various attempts to build Centre Party–Nazi coalitions in the *Länder* only underscored the difficult position of the SPD, which saw itself increasingly isolated and abandoned even by its former republican allies.

In July 1932 Brüning's successor, Franz von Papen, toppled the Prussian government and replaced it with a Reich Commissar who was directly responsible to Papen. The SPD leadership was shocked and challenged the legality of Papen's action in court, but in the same month, barely eleven days after the so-called Prussia Coup (*Preußenschlag*), the SPD received a second major blow: the NSDAP became the strongest party in the Reichstag. It more than doubled its vote and commanded over 37.4 per cent of the total votes cast. The SPD lost a further 3 per cent and came a poor second with 21.6 per cent. While the Social Democratic milieu remained relatively intact and proved fairly resistant to overtures made by the Nazi Party, the latter could make massive inroads into the non-politicized sections of the working class and rely on the solid support of lower middle-class and middle-class voters. The question became more and more urgent: how could the Nazis be stopped? As early as 1930 leading Social Democrats such as Rudolf Hilferding took the threat posed by Nazism very seriously and spent much time analysing the rise of the NSDAP.[20] They focused on developing strategies which would prevent the National Socialists from gaining power and destroying the Republic. Social Democrats in the *Reichsbanner* and in the youth groups especially urged the party to adopt a more energetic and combative response to the National Socialist threat. They were discontented with the policy of 'toleration' and instead urged the adoption of more innovative forms of propaganda, the formulation of more positive policy goals and the espousal of a more militant extra-parliamentary stance against Nazism. At the same time, however, several leading Social Democrats (including Carl Severing, Otto Braun and Ernst Heilmann) toyed with the idea of letting the Nazis into government, arguing that, within a bourgeois coalition capable of restraining the Nazis' anti-system tendencies, governmental responsibility would soon show up their promises as mere propaganda. A minority, among them Siegfried Aufhäuser, even considered tactical alliances with sections of the NSDAP (such as the Strasser wing and National Socialist trade unions) on the basis of an alleged minimum consensus about purportedly shared socialist values.

The SPD's adherence to long-term historical optimism, tactical considerations and ingrained passivity ensured that the party remained true to its strict legalistic outlook (which it had developed in Imperial Germany) and refused to step outside the law in defence of the Republic. Caught between the concepts of a class party and a catch-all party, between the transformation of existing society and working within its limits, between internationalism and nationalism, between the ethos of an extra-parliamentary movement and the self-understanding of a parliamentary party, and both isolated from and tied to bourgeois society, the SPD ended up paralysed in the crucial years between 1930 and 1933. Its response to the Prussia Coup of 1932 was characteristic of its general inertia. Social Democratic organizations, ADGB members and the republican paramilitary formation, now gathered in the Iron Front, had waited for the moment when they could respond to the apparent attempts of the ultra-conservative entourage of President Hindenburg to do away with key components of Weimar democracy. On the day of the Prussia Coup, many organized workers in the factories and the working-class neighbourhoods waited for the signal from their leaders for a general strike and, possibly, armed resistance. But the signal never came.

The SPD and ADGB leadership were afraid of a bloody civil war, and they were painfully aware that, in the midst of a devastating economic crisis, with 40 per cent of unionized workers unemployed in the summer of 1932, the prospects of success for a general strike were not good. Furthermore, wherever the labour movement had challenged state power in inter-war Europe, it was the state that had emerged victorious in open confrontation, thereby demonstrating the limits of working-class power. Nevertheless, would it not have been better for the German labour movement to have risked open confrontation in July 1932 rather than to have passively accepted its total destruction at the hands of the Nazis in the spring of 1933? In July 1932 many workers had been ready. As one report of the Reich Interior Ministry concludes:

> Wherever close examination is possible, one constantly comes to the same conclusion: Communists, members of the Fighting League against Fascism, members of the *Reichsbanner* and other Social Democrats have set up a system of couriers who sound the alarm whenever National Socialists enter their territory and who mobilize 'self-defence formations' . . . Despite the mutual enmity of both Marxist parties, a united front is de facto established in the bloody battles against National Socialists . . . Meetings are held in which the methods of cooperation between the working-class parties are discussed. Anti-Fascist unity committees and self-defence units are founded . . . [21]

Barely nine months later, many Social Democratic rank-and-filers were too disillusioned and demoralized to be mobilized again. Would it not have been preferable to risk a fight rather than go down without a whimper, as was to happen after January 1933? Such judgements are, of course, always easier with hindsight. After all, in the summer of 1932, the Social Democrats who had to take the decisions did not yet know that Hitler would come to power in January 1933. However, they could be fairly certain that a confrontation with the Papen government would not result in victory but in a massive loss of life. Who, therefore, can blame the Social Democratic officials who shied away from a bloody civil war?

The failure of gradualism? Reconsidering Social Democracy after 1933

The legalistic outlook of the SPD leadership also prevented any early preparation of the party for the conditions of illegality that it was to encounter after 22 June 1933, when the National Socialists officially banned the SPD. In fact, as late as 5 April, Erich Schmidt, the leader of the Berlin Socialist Youth organization, was kicked out of the party for organizing illegal underground networks of five-person cells. There were desperate overtures to the National Socialist government. Wels and Friedrich Stampfer attempted to strike a deal with Hermann Göring in March. In return for their going abroad to dissuade the foreign press from reporting negatively on the 'new Germany', the Hitler government would consider lifting the ban imposed on all SPD print media. On 17 May 1933 the parliamentary party of the SPD agreed to a foreign-policy declaration of the Nazis which called for equal treatment of Germany on the international scene. Leading Social Democrats wanted to demonstrate national sentiment and reliability. As in 1914, the German parliament stood united. For a moment it seemed as though the SPD would become part and parcel of the *Volksgemeinschaft*. Yet, even if they had wanted to (and a clear majority of Social Democrats did not), the National Socialists never had any intentions of letting them. The months between January and June 1933 saw some unpleasant rivalries between those sections of the SPD's leadership who had remained in Berlin and those who had already gone into exile in Prague. The party ban in June resolved the conflict in favour of the Prague group.

The Social Democratic Party in Exile (SOPADE), resident in Prague, now attempted to support Social Democratic resistance groups inside Germany. It set up so-called border secretariats which were to maintain contact with groups operating from within Germany. The information received by the executive via these border secretariats was published in the 'Reports on Germany' – an invaluable source of information for historians of everyday life under National Socialism. Furthermore, SOPADE published the *Sozialistische Aktion* which was distributed illegally inside Germany with an estimated readership of 200,000–300,000. Much of the executive's work focused on collecting and disseminating information. Many of the clandestine resistance cells in Germany were reluctant to make and maintain contact with the executive. The disappointment and disillusionment about the failure of their leaders' strategies for containing National Socialism ran too deep. The executive had attempted to take account of these feelings by introducing new and younger members to the innermost circle of Social Democratic power, people such as Erich Rinner, Erich Ollenhauer, Georg Dietrich, Franz Künstler, Carl Litke, Anna Nemitz, Wilhelm Sollmann and the left-wingers Karl Böchel, Siegfried Aufhäuser and Paul Hertz. However, Social Democratic exile politics and the active resistance of Social Democrats in Germany often were at odds, and it remains questionable whether the Social Democratic resistance fighters inside Germany accepted the authority of Social Democratic exile politicians outside Germany.

In the proletarian city quarters, the SA blocked off whole streets in February and March 1933. Their residents, including women and children, were beaten. Some were taken away for further beatings in the Nazi torture chambers that sprang up all over Germany. Many never returned, others did – often with broken bodies and spirits. In response to the Nazi terror, approximately 20,000 Social Democrats formed about 300 local resistance groups in SPD strongholds such as Berlin, Thuringia, Saxony, the Ruhr and the Rhine–Main–Neckar region. They engaged in acts of sabotage, the spraying of anti-Nazi slogans on walls and monuments, leafletting and the production and distribution of anti-Nazi literature. Furthermore, they supported the families of those who had fallen victim to National Socialist terror, arranged hiding places for comrades on the run and smuggled information out of the country. Those active in the Social Democratic resistance inside Germany included in particular members of the former Social Democratic paramilitary organization Iron Front as well as members of the Socialist Youth and of left-wing splinter groups such as the Socialist Workers' Party (SAP),[22] the International Socialist Fighting League (ISK)[23] and New Beginning (NB).[24] Working-class resistance to the Nazi regime was carried out from within the urban working-class milieux, in particular where a strong network of socialist, Communist or Catholic working-class associations had existed prior to 1933. The socialist bastion of Leipzig, for example, earned itself a reputation as 'Reich-No-City' (*Reichs-Nein-Stadt*). However, the Nazis found it easier to gain a foothold in places such as Berlin–Neukölln, where the milieu had been badly split between socialists and Communists.[25]

Many former Social Democrats who did not flee abroad or join the underground resistance withdrew from active politics. Some kept informal contacts with former party comrades and friends. Funerals of well-known Social Democrats could turn into demonstrations of Social Democratic solidarity, when thousands came out, defied the Nazi spies and paid their last respects to their erstwhile comrades. Even though many were afraid of losing their jobs – and maybe their lives – in what must have seemed an increasingly senseless struggle, few Social Democrats actively participated in Nazi organizations. Some registered their dissent through small gestures such as not raising the arm for the Nazi salute, not flying the Nazi flag, listening to foreign radio stations or even privately singing Social Demo-cratic songs and displaying socialist insignia. In some areas, oppositional micro-milieux could be sustained well into the 1930s. Socialist, communist and Catholic sports, singing and other ancillary organizations would some-times join the bourgeois associations en masse and effectively continue with their activities as before. Such actions can hardly be classified as active resistance (*Widerstand*), but they were recognizable as a form of withstanding (*Resistenz*).[26] Only a minority of Social Democrats went further. Julius Leber, SPD member of the Reichstag between 1924 and 1933 and the party's spokesperson on defence and military matters, for example, took part in the attempt on Hitler's life in July 1944. He was a personal friend of the coup leader, Colonel von Stauffenberg, and was designated interior minister in a post-Nazi government of the resistance. After the failure of the putsch, Leber, like hundreds of others, was put on show trial and executed.

By this time SOPADE was far removed from any direct involvement with active resistance inside Germany. The 1930s had been a time for rethinking Social Democratic ideology and strategy. Much acrimonious debate characterized the discussions. The left-wingers Aufhäuser and Böchel wanted a decisive break with the legacy of the SPD and even demanded the dissolution of the old party and the formation of a new working-class party uniting Communists and Social Democrats. The majority on the executive finally forced both of them out of the party in 1935. The old authoritarian-ism of Social Democracy prevailed and prevented the executive from deal-ing with debate and dissent in a more productive fashion. Instead, the SPD leadership continued to put unity above open discussion and showed itself willing to violate the rules of intra-party democracy if it meant uprooting oppositional tendencies within the party. Yet even the old warhorses of the SPD such as Wels and Stampfer had to confront the fact that much rank-and-file opinion was dissatisfied with the Social Democratic record and was rapidly radicalizing its own rhetoric.[27] Many rank-and-filers argued for a united front of all socialist and communist forces in the fight against the mutual enemy: German fascism. Among the ranks, pro-unity feelings were especially strong where Communists and Social Democrats had been mem-bers of the same networks of sociability, where local leaders of either party were respected across the spectrum of the left and where intermediary groups such as the SAP and ISK were present.

The executive's Prague Manifesto of January 1934 paid lip-service to such radical sentiments. The manifesto signalled a theoretical return to Marxism and a radicalization of party theory which was in line with the development of many European Social Democratic parties in the 1930s. Capitalist society, the SPD executive argued, faced its most severe crisis and the revolutionary situation had contributed to the rise of Nazism as the last defence of capitalism. The Social Democratic movement was portrayed as being committed to the overthrow of Nazism and ultimately also to the abolition of capitalism. The manifesto positioned the SPD as spearheading a mass movement which aimed at the defeat of Nazism. Such an assessment incorporated considerable criticism of the legalistic and reformist practice of the SPD during the Weimar Republic, but it was also a criticism without any practical consequences. No mass movement against Nazism appeared in Germany, and the Social Democratic leadership remained wary of the united front tactics championed by the Communist Party after 1935. There was only one top-level meeting of representatives of the SOPADE executive and the KPD central committee, which took place in Prague in November 1935. Nothing much emerged from it. Overall, the attentism of SOPADE continued, with most of its energies channelled into intra-party debates and plans for a post-Hitler Germany.

In 1938, when Hitler's expansionism turned to Czechoslovakia, SOPADE decided to move its headquarters to Paris. After Germany attacked Poland in 1939 it moved across the Channel to London. Social Democratic emigrants in Britain, the United States and other temporary home countries concentrated much of their efforts on relief and rescue operations. They also sought to represent the 'other Germany' vis-à-vis the Allied governments. Most were convinced that a National Socialist minority was repressing the majority of 'good' Germans, and they showed themselves incapable of understanding how deeply National Socialist ideology had penetrated wide sections of the German population. Those who, like Curt Geyer and Walter Loeb, openly raised the issue of German majority support for Hitler were driven out of the party. Geyer and Loeb were accused of fostering the anti-German sentiments prevalent in all Allied countries during the war.[28] By contrast, SOPADE saw itself as representing 'true' German interests and insisted that it should be entrusted with the rebuilding of the country after the defeat of Nazism. Its identification with the German nation and its attempted defence of German national interests produced conflict with Allied governments and fostered illusions about the role of Social Democracy in a post-Hitler Germany.

In April 1941, SOPADE united with a number of smaller socialist exile groups to form the Union of German Socialist Organizations in Great Britain.[29] The smaller socialist organizations such as ISK, NB and the SAP had been seeking such an alliance for some time, especially after they had been thoroughly disappointed by the Hitler–Stalin pact of 1939. The leaders of SOPADE in London, Hans Vogel and Erich Ollenhauer, were also more open to the idea than exiled Social Democrats elsewhere. Furthermore, the British Labour Party exerted pressure on the Social Democrats to form a united organization. Finally, it was important that the socialist trade union group in London, headed by Hans Gottfurcht, had already incorporated ISK, NB and SAP members into its organization in March 1940. In the war, the *Union of German Socialist Organisations* cooperated with the Allied secret services and aided the Allies in their propaganda. Furthermore, it engaged in broad discussions about the outlook of the future Germany which resulted in a harmonization of views among diverse groups of socialists and, at the same time, an increased dissociation from the Communists. The cooperation of all socialists within the Union paved the way for the re-emergence of a united Social Democratic movement after 1945. The Union published its 'Programmatic Guidelines' in 1945 which, in rather lofty and general terms, proclaimed its aim of transforming Germany into a radical democratic republic. A parliamentary system and a planned non-capitalist economy producing full employment and general prosperity – these were the key pillars on which Germany was to be rebuilt, if Social Democrats were to have their way.

The legacy of Weimar and Nazi Germany for the postwar development of Social Democracy

Social Democrats were going to be disappointed in both the postwar successor states of the German Reich. In the GDR the Social Democratic tradition became marginalized and finally subsumed under the Communist-dominated Socialist Unity Party (SED). At the end of the war, sentiments to the effect that the fateful division of the labour movement had to be overcome were widespread. Many argued, with the leader of the Thuringian SPD, Hermann Brill, that the SPD should not be rebuilt along the lines of the Weimar party but that the time had come for a united left-wing party. Yet, in the Soviet zone of occupation, the Communists, with the help of the Soviet Military Authority, ultimately enforced the merger against the will of substantial sections of the SPD. While many Social Democrats subsequently left the party and others were purged from it, substantial numbers remained in the SED where they bowed to the dictat of a dogmatic communism prescribed by Walter Ulbricht.

In the West, the party leadership under the staunch anti-Communist Kurt Schumacher and the traditionalist Ollenhauer attempted to rebuild the Weimar SPD – with some modifications. So, for example, the SPD became the main champion of Germany's national interests against the Western Allies. Schumacher's postwar nationalism, however, badly backfired as it alienated the party from the Allied occupiers while, at the same time, it failed to win much popular support from Germans. In the West, the party suffered from the fact that the old class milieu, which had sustained Social Democracy in Weimar Germany, had disappeared. Already the propagation of the National Socialist *Volksgemeinschaft* had dented the strict separation of social milieux, and, much more importantly, the war had eroded much of what was still left. In the 1950s, under the conditions of the Cold War and the Pax Americana in western Europe, and after repeated electoral failures, the SPD embarked on a course of shedding for good any transformatory aims and redefining itself – in line with other west European social democracies – as a party championing welfare capitalism and Keynesian economics.

The historiographies of the two Germanies adequately reflected this postwar development, with GDR historians writing the hagiography of the KPD while in the FRG historians of Social Democracy wrote the history from the vantage point of the 1959 Bad Godesberg party conference which symbolized the move of the party from a class party to a people's party. As Geoff Eley has rightly emphasized, both of these perspectives miss an important point about the history of the SPD, namely that the SPD was, over vast parts of its history, a party which represented to many of its followers an alternative to capitalism.[30] In other words, it had, at certain times and in certain places, a transformatory potential that was different from communism and was also far removed from the adherence to welfare-state capitalism that has come to characterize the party since Bad Godesberg. Without this element of a 'third way' socialism, the history of the SPD in Weimar and Nazi Germany cannot be adequately understood.

Notes

1. The Enabling Law rendered parliament powerless, gave legislative power to the government and therefore has rightly been described as the constitution of National Socialist Germany.

2. *Stenographische Berichte über die Verhandlungen des Deutschen Reichstages*, vol. 457 (1933), pp. 32–4, my translation. Used with permission of Bundesarchiv, Berlin.

3. For a more extensive discussion of the issues discussed below see Stefan Berger, *Social Democracy and the Working Class in Nineteenth and Twentieth Century Germany* (London, 2000).

4. On the SPD's unholy relationship with nationalism over the *longue durée* see Stefan Berger, 'Nationalism and the Left in Germany', *New Left Review* 206 (1994), pp. 55–70.

5. Erich Mathias, *Sozialdemokratie und Nation* (Stuttgart, 1952), p. 25.

6. For the notion of the SPD as a 'community of solidarity' (*Solidargemeinschaft*) see Peter Lösche and Franz Walter, *Die SPD. Klassenpartei – Volkspartei – Quotenpartei* (Darmstadt, 1992). For a comparative perspective on 'communities of solidarity' see Stefan Berger, *The British Labour Party and the German Social Democrats, 1900–1931* (Oxford, 1994), ch. four.

7. Dieter Groh, *Negative Integration und revolutionärer Attentismus: Die deutsche Sozialdemokratie am Vorabend des Ersten Weltkrieges* (Frankfurt-on-Main, 1973).

8. For more details see Gary P. Steenson, *'Not one Man – Not one Penny': German Social Democracy, 1863–1914* (Pittsburgh, PA, 1981), pp. 54–65. See also Ralf Roth, *'Bürger* and Workers: Liberalism and the Labor Movement in Germany, 1848 to 1914', in David E. Barclay and Eric D. Weitz, eds, *Between Reform and Revolution: German Socialism and Communism from 1840 to 1990* (Oxford, 1998), pp. 113–40.

9. Carl Schorske, *German Social Democracy, 1905–1917: The Development of the Great Schism* (Cambridge, MA, 1955) sees the wartime split of the SPD as rooted in incompatible ideological factionalism which had already characterized pre-war Social Democracy. In contrast to Schorske, Susanne Miller, *Burgfrieden und Klassenkampf* (Düsseldorf, 1974) has argued that wartime conditions were crucial for the split. For a more recent synthesis of this long-standing debate see Wolfgang Kruse, *Krieg und nationale Integration. Eine Neuinterpretation des sozialdemokratischen Burgfriedensschlusses 1914/15* (Essen, 1993).

10. On the revolution see F.L. Carsten, *Revolution in Central Europe, 1918–1919* (London, 1972). On labour unrest at the end of the First World War in a comparative perspective see Chris Wrigley, ed., *Challenges of Labour: Central and Western Europe, 1917–1920* (London, 1993).

11. This is rightly foregrounded by Klaus Schönhoven, *Reformismus und Radikalismus. Gespaltene Arbeiterbewegung im Weimarer Sozialstaat* (Munich, 1989).

12. The history of the USPD is the topic of Robert F. Wheeler, *The Independent Social Democratic Party and the Internationals: An Examination of Socialist Internationalism in Germany* (New York, 1970), and D.W. Morgan, *The Socialist Left and German Revolution: A History of the German Independent Socialist Democratic Party, 1917–1922* (London, 1975).

13. William H. Maehl, *The German Socialist Party: Champion of the First Republic, 1918–1933* (Philadelphia, 1986).

14. For the concept of a 'people's party' or 'catch-all party' see Otto Kirchheimer, 'Wandel des westeuropäischen Parteiensystems', *Politische Vierteljahresschrift* 6 (1965), pp. 20–41.

15. Jonathan Sperber, *The Kaiser's Voters: Electors and Elections in Imperial Germany* (Cambridge, MA, 1997), has presented highly interesting and innovative evidence for his thesis that the SPD in Wilhelmine Germany was not, in fact, a class party but a party based on cross-class alliances and appeals to 'the people' rather than to the working class. However, much of his qualitative evidence comes from south-western Germany, and the picture in Prussia surely was a different one.

16. Heinrich August Winkler, 'Klassenbewegung oder Volkspartei? Zur Programmdiskussion in der Weimarer Sozialdemokratie, 1920–1925', *Geschichte und Gesellschaft* 8 (1982), pp. 9–54. It is also one of the major themes in Winkler's three-volume history of the labour movement in the Weimar Republic entitled *Geschichte der Arbeiter und Arbeiterbewegung in der Weimarer Republik* (Bonn, 1984, 1985 and 1987).

17. For the extensive labour movement culture in Weimar Germany see Willi L. Guttsman, *Workers' Culture in Weimar Germany: Between Tradition and Commitment* (Oxford, 1990). For the lacunae separating this labour movement culture from both working-class and popular culture see Geoff Eley, 'Cultural Socialism, the Public Sphere, and the Mass Form: Popular Culture and the Democratic Project, 1900–1934', in Barclay and Weitz, eds, *Between Reform*, pp. 315–40.

18. Klaus Michael Mallmann, 'Milieu, Radikalismus und lokale Gesellschaft. Zur Sozialgeschichte des Kommunismus in der Weimarer Republik', *Geschichte und Gesellschaft* 21 (1995), pp. 5–31, has presented a convincing argument for analysing the SPD–KPD relationship in the Weimar Republic against the background of a common proletarian milieu. The 'complex web of possibilities for co-operation and separation' that existed depended on the exact nature of the relationship between the two parties in the localities.

19. Hagen Schulze, *Otto Braun oder Preußens demokratische Sendung: Eine Biographie* (Frankfurt-on-Main, 1977).

20. On the Social Democratic analysis of and response to National Socialism see in particular Michael Ruck, *Bollwerk gegen Hitler? Arbeiterschaft, Arbeiterbewegung und die Anfänge des Nationalsozialismus* (Cologne, 1988); Wolfram Pyta, *Gegen Hitler und für die Republik: Die Auseinandersetzung der deutschen Sozialdemokratie mit der NSDAP in der Weimarer Republik* (Düsseldorf, 1989); Donna Harsch, *German Social Democracy and the Rise of Nazism* (Chapel Hill, NC, 1993).

21. Cited in Joachim Petzold, 'SPD und KPD in der Endphase der Weimarer Republik' (my translation), in Heinrich August Winkler, ed., *Die deutsche Staatskrise 1930–1933. Handlungsspielräume und Alternativen* (Munich, 1991), p. 92.

22. The SAP had split from the SPD in 1931. Unsuccessful electorally, it included some of the most perceptive analysts of the rise of National Socialism. After

1933 the SAP was led by Jacob Walcher. It sought to unite the left in anti-Fascist action, and its members included prominent post-Second World War Social Democrats such as Willy Brandt.

23. The ISK was founded by the philosopher Leonard Nelson in 1926. His ethical socialism, including teetotalism, atheism, vegetarianism and adherence to an elitist, anti-democratic leadership ethos, dominated the organization. Following Nelson's death in 1927, Willi Eicher, who in the late 1950s was to draft the Bad Godesberg programme of the SPD, emerged as the strongman of the ISK. In the early 1930s it had a mere 200 members, yet it was to play an important role in underground activities as well as in exile politics, commanding both excellent relations with other socialist parties in Europe and (until well into the 1930s) a functioning network of anti-Fascists inside Germany.

24. NB was founded in 1933 and had approximately 500 members, many of whom were former Social Democratic officials such as Richard Löwenthal, Waldemar von Knoerringen and Erwin Schoettle. It established no formal organizational structures and acted more as a discussion forum about what direction German socialism should take after its defeat by Nazism.

25. On the diverse reactions to National Socialism in the diverse working-class milieux see Detlef Schmiechen-Ackermann, *Nationalsozialismus und Arbeitermilieus: der nationalsozialistische Angriff auf die proletarischen Wohnquartiere und die Reaktion in den sozialistischen Vereinen* (Bonn, 1998).

26. Such a useful distinction was introduced by Martin Broszat, 'Zur Sozialgeschichte des deutschen Widerstandes', *Vierteljahreshefte für Zeitgeschichte* 34 (1986), pp. 293–309.

27. Gerd-Rainer Horn, 'Radicalism and Moderation within German Social Democracy in Underground and Exile, 1933–1936', *German History* 15 (1997), pp. 200–20. For a superb comparative perspective on diverse Social Democratic parties' reaction to Fascism in western Europe see *idem, European Socialists Respond to Fascism: Ideology, Activism and Contingency in the 1930s* (Oxford, 1996).

28. In Britain, for example, Lord Vansittart, a senior civil servant, had popularized the idea that Germans were an aggressive race *per se*. Such inverse racism became known as Vansittartism and had widespread repercussions in wartime Britain. See Isabel Tombs, 'The Victory of Socialist "Vansittartism": Labour and the German Question, 1941–5', *Twentieth Century British History* 7 (1996), pp. 287–309.

29. Ludwig Eiber, *Die Sozialdemokratie in der Emigration. Die 'Union deutscher sozialistischer Organisationen in Großbritannien' 1941–1946 und ihre Mitglieder. Protokolle, Erklärungen, Materialien* (Bonn, 1998).

30. Geoff Eley, 'Reviewing the Socialist Tradition', in Christiane Lemke and Gary Marks, eds, *The Crisis of Socialism in Europe* (Durham, NC, 1992), pp. 21–60.

CHAPTER ELEVEN

'Preaching the gospel of reasonableness': Anglo-German relations, 1919–1939

G.T. WADDINGTON

In the shadow of Versailles, 1919–1923

For all the contradictions and inconsistencies that were enshrined in the Treaty of Versailles, nothing augured less brightly for the prospects of a smooth transition from conflict to cooperation during the early 1920s than the fact that the two powers upon whom the burden of enforcing the peace settlement ultimately came to rest, France and Great Britain, had sharply contrasting visions of Germany's future role in European affairs. Driven by what they perceived as their own unique experience of the 'German problem', the French had initially desired a settlement that would permanently reduce Germany to such a state of weakness and subservience that she would never again be in a position to threaten the security of France. Indeed, the basic French aim at the peace conference, from which Clemenceau and his associates were only moved under protest and with extreme difficulty over some of the more contentious issues, had been unequivocally formulated in a Quai d'Orsay memorandum drawn up shortly before the armistice. 'In order to assure Europe of lasting peace,' it argued tersely, 'Bismarck's work must be destroyed.'[1] The peace negotiations in Paris, however, soon demonstrated the fundamental incompatibility of this objective with British concerns for the restoration of a European balance of power, the establishment of a stable democratic Germany shielded from Bolshevik encroachments and the reconstruction of the European economy, to which a significant degree of German economic recovery was increasingly deemed essential.[2] This conflict of ideas, which soon developed into serious disagreements over basic principles of policy, was aptly summarized by Sir Maurice Hankey, secretary to the British delegation in Paris, only two months after the Treaty of Versailles came into force. Commenting on the incessant disputes with the French about the German settlement, he wrote: 'The fact is that they wanted a stiffer treaty and we wanted an easier one. Moreover, from the first we always intended to ease up on the execution of the treaty if the Germans played the game. With the French, the exact opposite is the case.'[3]

Dissension among the Allies had not passed unnoticed by the Germans during the peacemaking process and provided them with a solitary ray of hope in what otherwise seemed a dark and dangerous situation. For although successive German postwar administrations were plagued by internal unrest and economic chaos, each had as its foremost, and practically predetermined, goal in foreign affairs the dismantling of the peace settlement as rapidly and in as comprehensive a form as possible. To their own population the German leaders could claim that domestic strife, political instability and economic misery were the result of a criminal *Diktat*. At the same time, the new regime could seek to exploit the differences between the Allies and plead for some alleviation of the treaty lest a worse – possibly 'soviet' – fate befall the German nation. From the outset therefore the Germans drew a distinction between Britain and the United States, to whom they looked for some understanding of their situation, and France, from whom patently nothing of the sort was to be expected. Indeed, when formal diplomatic relations between Britain and the Weimar Republic were finally established in the summer of 1920, the new German ambassador, Friedrich Sthamer, received a set of guidelines from Berlin which reveal much about German tactics towards Britain in the immediate postwar period. Starting from the premise that Germany's position vis-à-vis France was that of a 'debtor' whose only option was to put up whatever defence she could against additional onerous demands from Paris, the foreign minister, Walter Simons, drew attention to the fact that Britain's interest in the German economy provided a 'welcome counterweight' to the French tendency to seek a further weakening, if not the total destruction, of the German state. Consequently, although care had to be taken to ensure that Germany did not become 'a British economic colony', cooperation with the British in the economic and, where possible, other spheres was certainly not to be discouraged. Moreover, Germany should be equally wary of giving any appearance of sympathy for the aims of Britain's enemies. Should there be any suspicion of such activity, warned Simons, Britain would forthwith abandon Germany to the tender mercies of the French.[4]

Anglo-French discord over Germany was no more intense or obvious in the early 1920s than in the case of reparations where, in British eyes, the

French seemed to be pursuing the contradictory policies of seeking to ruin Germany economically while simultaneously demanding full and immediate satisfaction of their financial and other demands. 'How was it possible', asks Frederick Northedge with some point, 'to have golden eggs and roast goose at the same time?'[5] To be sure, the British were determined to extract their own substantial quotas from Germany after the final reparations total had been fixed in 1921, but it seemed to them wholly illogical, not to say dangerous, to wreck the German economy in the process. Consequently, while the French held that the Germans were wilfully evading their treaty obligations, the British were more inclined to give a sympathetic hearing to the German claim that in present circumstances they simply could not meet the demands of the repayment schedule. The two major international conferences on economic problems held at Cannes in January 1922 and at Genoa three months later not only failed to produce any agreement, but, on the contrary, marked a further sharp deterioration in the general situation. During the Cannes conference the French premier, Aristide Briand, resigned as a result of accusations of subservience to Britain and was replaced by Raymond Poincaré whose 'obsession' with Germany, writes Sally Marks, was 'nearly total'.[6] Moreover, the only tangible result of the subsequent gathering at Genoa was the Russo-German Treaty of Rapallo which introduced a new element of uncertainty into an increasingly unstable environment. Anxious at this latest development and angered by French intransigence, Lloyd George personally told the German chancellor, Joseph Wirth, that any isolated action by France in pursuit of her own interests would mean 'the end of the alliance'.[7]

During 1922 the German economy had already begun the slide into chaos that was to result in the astronomical inflation and abominable privations of the following year. With America having evidently washed its hands of European affairs following the Senate's refusal to ratify the Treaty of Versailles, and in view of British efforts to provide them with a forum to state their case at Cannes and Genoa, it was perhaps understandable that by the autumn the Germans should have come to view the British as their 'first, and even only line of defence against French aggression'.[8] It was thus equally understandable that they followed with great interest and not a little anxiety the general election that followed the fall of Lloyd George in October 1922. The new conservative government, however, did not, and indeed could not, deviate from the policy pursued by its predecessor. The differences between Britain and France over Germany, and indeed other issues, were of such a fundamental nature and concerned such vital British interests that they could not be relegated to the cut and thrust of party politics. In a memorandum of 20 November 1922 the head of the British department at the Wilhelmstrasse, Carl von Schubert, predicted that the conservatives would, if anything, take a stronger line against France in accordance with the basic principles of British foreign policy which dictated that no European power should ever become so strong that it could pose a threat to the British Empire. The conservatives, in Schubert's opinion, were determined to make this the keystone of their policy.[9]

The fact that by early 1923 the *Entente Cordiale* was distinctly lacking in cordiality was demonstrated by an incident at the Gare du Nord following a further acrimonious round of Anglo-French discussions in January. Having taken leave of Poincaré, the prime minister, Bonar Law, slammed the carriage window shut and hissed: 'Now you can be damned!'[10] The Franco-Belgian occupation of the Ruhr which began only a few days later was thus hardly likely to ease the very considerable strains that continued to burden Anglo-French relations. Although there was never any serious risk of a complete breakdown between London and Paris, the Ruhr crisis not only united the German people behind their government's call for passive resistance, but also threw into sharp relief the divergence between the British and French attitudes towards German reintegration. Speaking at the Imperial Conference of October 1923, the British foreign secretary, Lord Curzon, who had already fired off a highly critical note to Paris in August, publicly attacked the Franco-Belgian action which, he claimed, was 'productive of no good result and was leading to disaster and ruin'.[11]

In the meantime, however, a decisive development had occurred in Germany with the appointment of Gustav Stresemann as chancellor and foreign minister. Although his term of office as chancellor lasted only until November, Stresemann bravely took the decision to call an end to passive resistance on 26 September. He thus played an important part in breaking the deadlock and preparing the ground not only for a revised, and for Germany more manageable, reparations settlement, the Dawes Plan, which came into force in August 1924, but also for the end of the Franco-Belgian occupation of the Ruhr which had had baleful repercussions for all concerned. Moreover, according to a German assessment of September 1923, Stresemann had succeeded in making a very positive impression on all shades of British opinion which was now almost universal in its condemnation of French policy. The chancellor, it was felt, had done all he could to accommodate France and had nothing left to offer. Stresemann had thus 'achieved a great political success', for there was 'almost no one in Britain who doubts his sincerity in desiring an understanding with France for which he is prepared to make the greatest sacrifices'.[12] It now remained to be seen whether Stresemann, who continued as foreign minister in the new cabinet, could capitalize on this apparently favourable situation.

Tea for three? The Locarno honeymoon, 1924–1929

Although controversy still exists over Stresemann's ultimate aims,[13] it is clear that from the outset he accorded a high priority to Britain's role as mediator in Franco-German disputes. Stresemann brought a new coherence and direction to German foreign policy which made possible the remarkable successes achieved between 1925 and 1930. And in each of those successes, the Treaty of Locarno, Germany's entry into the League of Nations, and ultimately, although he did not live to see it, the evacuation of the Rhineland, he sought and to some degree received the support and cooperation of the British government. Stresemann naturally harboured no illusions that Britain's attitude in these questions was determined by anything other than a sober evaluation of her European and imperial interests. But he fully appreciated that, however much British statesmen might claim to value the friendship of France and criticize Germany, the simple fact was that the most fundamental British concepts of European stabilization required an improvement in the German economic position and thus some modification of the oppressive policy pursued by France since the end of the war.

As Marshall Lee and Wolfgang Michalka have noted, Stresemann was one of a 'bare handful of Western politicians fully to comprehend the political and diplomatic changes wrought by the First World War, and one of an even more exclusive number who realized that the only victor of that conflict was the United States'.[14] Thus, while on the one hand he was concerned to develop economic and financial ties with America in an effort to curb French power, he was also fully alive to the contradictions within the entente that the Ruhr crisis had so clearly revealed. Unlike Hitler, who drew his own conclusions from the Ruhr crisis,[15] Stresemann was too much of a realist to entertain any ideas about a future Anglo-German alliance, but he was nonetheless convinced that Britain had an important role to play in his efforts to restore Germany to the ranks of the Great Powers. As he declared to a Berlin audience in December 1925, Britain's participation in the Locarno pact had once more cast her in the role of the 'arbitrator of Europe' whose interest by definition lay in the suppression of French hegemony. 'If I am told that I pursue a policy friendly to England,' he continued, 'I do not do so from any love of England, but because in this question German interests coincide with those of England, and because we must find someone who helps us to shake off the stranglehold upon our throat.'[16]

It might seem somewhat ironic that much of the progress that Stresemann made towards this end came during a period when the threads of British foreign policy were in the hands of Austen Chamberlain, who in February 1925 described himself to the British ambassador in Paris as 'the most pro-French member' of His Majesty's Government.[17] Chamberlain had taken office in November 1924 determined to provide France with a measure of security which, he hoped, would not only repair the damage inflicted on Anglo-French relations since 1919 but also pave the way for a 'general relaxation of European tension in which the causes of legitimate German grievance could safely be removed'.[18] When it became clear that the Geneva Protocol would be rejected by Britain and the Dominions, Chamberlain's instincts led him to favour the conclusion of a security agreement with France and Belgium which might in due course be extended to include Germany provided that in the interim she played the part of a good European and complied with the terms of the peace settlement. The idea of an alliance with France, however, met with strong and eventually decisive opposition from several of Chamberlain's cabinet colleagues who feared that, far from engendering a more reasonable attitude in Paris, it would simply serve to stiffen the French and encourage them to continue their provocative policy towards Germany. While these issues were being debated in London, Stresemann, prompted by the British ambassador in Berlin, Lord D'Abernon, came forward with his famous proposal for a regional security agreement centred on the Rhineland which twelve months later had evolved into the Treaty of Locarno.

Judging by some of the contemporary French criticism of British policy,[19] and given the general consensus that Germany was the chief beneficiary of Locarno, one is almost tempted to look for elements of an Anglo-German deal lurking behind the clauses of the new security arrangements. It is certainly undeniable that both Stresemann and Chamberlain had cause for considerable satisfaction with their achievements, more so than the French foreign minister, Briand, who had signally failed to interest his British and German counterparts in the security of eastern Europe, where France had contracted alliances with Czechoslovakia and, more importantly, with Poland, the *bête noire* of successive postwar German governments. Stresemann's immediate gains lay in averting an Anglo-French alliance and in securing the first of the three scheduled withdrawals of Allied troops from the Rhineland which, although due in any case in late 1925 under the terms of the 1919 settlement, had threatened to provoke a further serious crisis in view of Germany's failure to comply with the disarmament provisions of Versailles. In the longer term, however, Stresemann believed that Locarno offered Germany a great deal more. As he wrote in April 1925: 'Our policy regarding the security offer was undoubtedly correct; it secured the Rhineland against a French policy of persecution, split the Entente, and opened new prospects for the East.'[20]

That Stresemann hoped for British assistance in exploring these 'prospects' is clear from a letter written a year later to Friedrich Sthamer. The revision of the eastern frontier, he argued, was 'not only the most important task of our policy, but perhaps also of European diplomacy as a whole'. British cooperation towards a solution, which admittedly could only be sought through peaceful means, was, in Stresemann's opinion, an 'imperative prerequisite'.[21] Chamberlain was doubtless gratified to learn from Sthamer in March 1925 that Germany had no intention of resorting to arms in her numerous quarrels with Poland, and to see that assurance enshrined in the German–Polish arbitration treaty that was built into Locarno, but he was certainly not prepared to support Stresemann in any confrontation with Warsaw. One of the great attractions of Locarno had been that it had limited Britain's commitments to western Europe, where her vital interests were at stake, and contained no provisions involving Britain east of the Oder, where they decidedly were not. In Chamberlain's view the question of the German–Polish frontier paled into insignificance in comparison with the central issue of Franco-German reconciliation, and, in the hope that the passage of time itself would dampen passions and thus facilitate a solution, he was determined to have as little direct involvement with it as possible.[22] However, Chamberlain and Stresemann independently understood and welcomed the fact that Locarno had compromised the French alliance with Poland. For Britain this meant that some restriction had now been placed on France's freedom of manoeuvre which made her less likely in future to back Poland unreservedly against Germany and thus hamper the general process of appeasement. Stresemann, on the other hand, clearly stood to gain from any weakening of Franco-Polish relations. In this sense the repercussions of Locarno in eastern Europe were, as Chamberlain said at the time, 'all in the German interest and in ours'.[23]

The Locarno pact and the rather short-lived 'era' that it is commonly held to have inaugurated represented the high watermark of Anglo-German relations during the inter-war years. This is not to suggest, however, that the period 1925–9 witnessed the development of a rapprochement between Britain and Germany, or even that the cordial relations between Chamberlain and Stresemann contributed significantly to an Anglo-German détente. The atmosphere during some of the so-called 'Locarno tea parties' was certainly fraternal, but this could not disguise the fact that neither the treaty nor Germany's subsequent entry into the League had in themselves solved the basic problem of how French fears could be reconciled with German ambitions.[24] Chamberlain, who saw Locarno not as 'the end of the work of appeasement and reconciliation, but as its beginning',[25] continued to view Britain as the key to this dilemma, and much of his diplomacy in Europe after 1925 was geared towards the promotion of the Franco-German understanding that he had hoped would follow from Locarno. Indeed, Briand's failure to carry through the programme for re-conciliation discussed with Stresemann at Thoiry in September 1926, and the repercussions of that failure on Stresemann's position vis-à-vis his own domestic opponents, only served to underline the importance of Britain's continued commitment to a role in continental affairs. The British reaction to Thoiry is itself instructive in this respect. For although Chamberlain and his advisors approved of the meeting, some concern was expressed both at the time and later about the prospect of a direct Franco-German settlement that failed to take sufficient account of British interests. Having committed themselves to Europe through Locarno, the British were determined that their voice should and must be heard. Small wonder therefore that the foreign secretary should later warn of the dangers of 'a second Thoiry with its immense expectations and absolutely negative result'.[26] A telling indication of Chamberlain's perception of Britain's task, and of his own effectiveness in discharging it, came in March 1927 when the League Council debated the relatively minor issue of the Saar Railway Defence Force. Here his intervention as adjudicator between France and Germany had been crucial in securing a compromise acceptable to Briand and Stresemann who had found it impossible to reach agreement between themselves. It was dis-appointing, Chamberlain wrote to his sister, that the press did so little to highlight the 'decisive role' played by Britain, or even 'hint at the fact (which was obvious to every soul in the room) that if there was to be an agreed solution, it must be found by us; for we alone could speak with sufficient authority and were sufficiently possessed of the confidence of both parties'.[27]

Chamberlain thus hoped to continue in the role of 'honest broker' be-tween France and Germany which he had claimed for Britain as early as March 1925.[28] However, as Frank Magee has demonstrated, this policy was not dictated by any altruistic considerations but by a realistic assessment of British interests which demanded stability between the major continental powers as the essential prerequisite for continued pacification and prosper-ity.[29] As one Foreign Office official succinctly observed in April 1926, 'With-out our trade and our finance we sink to the level of a third-class Power. Locarno and the unemployed have an intimate connexion.'[30] Over the next three years, however, numerous factors conspired to make it extremely difficult for Chamberlain to capitalize on the promising start that had been made at Locarno. Foremost among these was the fact that Britain's role as a world power demanded much greater attention after 1926 than had hitherto been the case. Indeed, German affairs were discussed at cabinet level only once between December 1926 and September 1928.[31] Moreover, internal developments in both France and Germany did little to facilitate Chamberlain's task. For while Stresemann was forced to defend his policy against the nationalists who accused him of complying all too readily with the wishes of Britain and France and clamoured noisily for further treaty revision, Briand too had increasingly to shield himself against those who argued that far too much had already been conceded. While Chamberlain fully appreciated the magnitude of the domestic problems faced by Briand, he was perhaps rather less understanding of those confronting Stresemann, who once remarked with a mixture of humour and despair that he had friends in all German political parties, even his own.[32] Notwithstanding Stresemann's personal determination to wring further concessions from the western powers, his pressing need to appease domestic opinion sometimes infuriated Chamberlain, who was convinced that progress on outstanding issues had to be achieved 'step by step' if it were to have any prospect of lasting success.[33]

The implications of Britain's cool rationalization of her European interests through the Treaty of Locarno were not lost on the German ambassador in London. In a perceptive review of British policy submitted in early 1927 Sthamer argued that the Rhineland pact had erected an 'insurmountable political barrier to the German drive to the West' and had thus fulfilled one of Britain's foremost aims on the continent. Combined with the fact that Germany had already been severely weakened by the Treaty of Versailles, this aim now appeared to have been secured long into the future provided that Britain continued to harmonize her policy with that of France, the only other power which might threaten her in western Europe. In these circumstances it was clear that Germany could expect no support from Britain that might serve to weaken the entente, and it was this paramount consideration, Sthamer believed, that explained London's current 'perceptible lack of interest' in German issues. Moreover, recent experiences had demonstrated 'that Germany becomes a matter of indifference to Britain as soon as a particular goal involving Germany is achieved', and that Britain's interest in German affairs was only revived 'when Germany's co-operation is required to achieve specific British aims, following which it once more immediately expires'.[34]

Subsequent developments would bear out much of this analysis. On questions of major importance such as reparations, German disarmament and the evacuation of Allied troops from the Rhineland, Chamberlain was prepared to support Stresemann only insofar as was compatible with the maintenance of cordial relations with France, which, in the words of Walford Selby, Chamberlain's private secretary, remained 'the axiom of British foreign policy'.[35] In other areas where British and German interests simply happened to coincide, as in September 1927 when the Poles sought to bring before the League Assembly a proposal to extend the Locarno guarantees to eastern Europe, he was prepared to offer Germany his diplomatic backing, but once more only in concert with Briand.[36] Moreover, although Chamberlain professed to fear any further strengthening of the ties between Germany and Russia that went beyond the 1926 Treaty of Berlin, he also hoped to make use of Stresemann's special relationship with Moscow to promote European appeasement following the breach of Anglo-Soviet relations in mid-1927.[37] Chamberlain equally took no pains to spare German sensibilities in pursuit of British interests. That much was demonstrated in July 1928 by his announcement of the ill-conceived Anglo-French Compromise on Armaments which not only brought forth criticism of his 'francophile' foreign policy at home, but also provoked a wave of indignation in Germany and the United States.[38] Stresemann was thus far too optimistic in declaring to the representatives of the Dresden press in October 1925 that the 'time of alliances' was over, and by 1929 he had few fair words for either Chamberlain or Briand whose original intentions he feared he had misjudged.[39]

In his celebrated letter to the former crown prince of September 1925 Stresemann outlined the 'three great tasks' that would confront German foreign policy in the immediate future, namely a 'tolerable' solution of the reparations question, the protection of German minorities abroad and a revision of the territorial settlement in eastern Europe. The essential prerequisite for progress on the first of these objectives, he argued, was the complete evacuation of Allied troops from the Rhineland, and it was this issue that dominated his final years at the Wilhelmstrasse.[40] Stresemann was naturally determined to see the Rhineland question solved prior to and separate from that of reparations due to his well-founded fears that the French would seek to use the continued presence of their troops on German soil as security against a final reparations settlement. Moreover, in view of the return of Poincaré to the French premiership in July 1926, the obstructive attitude of the French military and Briand's failure to commend the Thoiry project to his colleagues, it was clear that Stresemann would face very stiff opposition from Paris to any modification of the Rhineland settlement. In these circumstances he had little choice but to look once more to Britain for support, and, as he told the foreign affairs committee of the Reichstag in June 1926, he had some reason to believe that his hopes in that respect were not entirely without foundation. Recalling a conversation with Chamberlain in London six months earlier, Stresemann told the committee that the foreign secretary had arranged for a portrait of Castlereagh to be hung in the room at the Foreign Office where the Locarno treaties were to be signed. 'I received a definite hint', he continued, 'that this diplomat had supported in the name of England France's liberation from occupation, and that he [Chamberlain] now had the intention of following the same policy with regard to Germany.'[41]

As Stresemann anticipated, Chamberlain was prepared to consider a gradual and even accelerated withdrawal of Allied forces from the Rhineland in order to further the process of appeasement. However, although he occasionally supported the German case over troop reductions, a matter in which he once confessed to Stresemann he had a 'very bad conscience',[42] Chamberlain did not accept the German thesis that complete evacuation either could or should be dealt with in isolation. In his view the Rhineland and reparations were essential features of the more general and inclusive settlement towards which he was working. Sure in the knowledge that the Germans would seek to open the Rhineland issue as soon as they had taken their seat on the League Council, Chamberlain had by August 1926 determined on a broad strategy which governed his policy over the Rhineland until the fall of the conservative administration in May 1929. 'While I have set myself no rigid programme,' he wrote to the British ambassador in Paris,

> it seems to me that the least difficult line of approach will be to aim first at a reduction in the number of occupying troops, secondly at the evacuation of the Saar, and finally at a shortening of the period of occupation. At the same time I have no illusions as to the difficulty of inducing the French Government to follow us along these lines unless they receive an adequate *quid pro quo*, and I should be astonished if the pressure of German opinion upon the German Government does not make the task even harder for France than it need be. Nevertheless, I am not without hope that French statesmen will see that for success in dealing with the economic difficulties of France they require political appeasement and a spreading conviction in Europe and elsewhere that the danger of new quarrels is averted for our time at least.[43]

As noted earlier, however, Chamberlain's attention after 1926 was largely focused on extra-European issues, and this fact, coupled with the opposition he faced from both the War Office and the Treasury to any unilateral withdrawal of British troops, meant that progress was bound to be slow and problematical. It was certainly the case that British influence helped to secure the withdrawal of 10,000 troops from the Rhineland in 1927, but, as David Dutton has noted, Chamberlain's efforts on that occasion marked the 'limit of Anglo-German co-operation' over the Rhineland, which throughout the period 1926–9 remained an issue upon which he was unwilling to 'press the French government too hard'.[44] Thus, although he recognized Stresemann's difficulties, Chamberlain would not permit a German diplomatic success over the Rhineland unless the French received satisfaction over reparations. He was thus inclined to allow the initiative over the scale and timing of troop evacuations to rest with France. Moreover, although he might have reposed a certain amount of personal trust in Stresemann, Chamberlain never overcame his fundamental suspicion of Germany's ultimate aims, a fact that was compounded by his profound sense of loyalty towards France. Ironically his suspicions became more pronounced after the promising developments of 1925–6. By August 1928 his frustration led him to compare Stresemann's policy to that which had been pursued by the Kaiser before 1914. 'Notwithstanding all that has been done to alleviate her difficulties since Locarno,' he complained indignantly, 'she [Germany] continues to parade her grievances and now to suggest that the Allied Powers were failing in the undertakings given to her at Locarno.'[45] In the spring of 1929 he told Mussolini that it would be unwise to trust 'too implicitly' in the improvement of relations between Germany and the western powers that had occurred since Locarno. 'Only the future would show', he advised the Italian leader, 'whether Germany would really accept her present position, or whether she would once again resort to arms and stake everything on the hazards of a new war.' Vigilance thus remained the order of the day, and it was imperative for Britain, France and Italy to stand together in order to guide the Germans further along the path of peace and conciliation. Germany, he feared, was 'still restless, still prone to suggest that her good behaviour must constantly be bought by fresh concessions'.[46] Shortly before Chamberlain's meeting with the Duce, Stresemann himself had made some equally revealing statements in a letter to his former collaborator Lord D'Abernon. Commenting on a recent article by D'Abernon entitled 'Back to Locarno', Stresemann wrote that he would be happy indeed if European statesmen once more found it possible to embrace the 'spirit' in which the treaties of 1925 had been negotiated. Unless a 'miracle' occurred soon, however, he feared that it would be too late. Stresemann was particularly scathing about the lack of progress over the Rhineland. France, he argued, simply wanted to use the issue as a means of blackmailing Germany over reparations. Britain, too, could and should have done more. In a tone which barely concealed his bitterness he concluded: 'If Britain, instead of her complete indifference towards these questions, had energetically used her influence with France to secure the evacuation of the Rhineland, then German public opinion and its attitude towards Britain would today be different.'[47]

Faced with French intransigence on the one hand and the British inclination to let France make the running on the other, Stresemann was ultimately forced to bow to the pressure of circumstance and agree to a linkage between further Allied concessions over the Rhineland and a new reparations schedule. During the first Hague Conference of August 1929 Stresemann accepted a revised settlement, the Young Plan, while Briand, himself under pressure from the new British labour government, reluctantly agreed to the complete evacuation of the Rhineland by mid-1930. Superficially the results of the conference appeared to represent a reasonable compromise between France and Germany in a form eminently consonant with the British concept of a general settlement. The negotiations, however, had been exceedingly difficult and in many respects their outcome did not augur at all well for the future. Not only had the British alienated the French with their insistence on a modification of the financial settlement to their own advantage and their support for Germany in the evacuation question, but the Germans themselves, realizing that a better deal could hardly be expected at present, had nonetheless attempted to make their agreement contingent on a series of further concessions. Moreover, Stresemann's acceptance of the Young Plan had united the various elements of the national opposition which now turned on him with a vengeance. It is with some justification therefore that Jon Jacobsen has argued that although Stresemann hoped that the Hague settlement would consolidate the Republic and its foreign policy, it ultimately proved to be the first stage in a protracted crisis which ended with the collapse of both.[48] Sensing the critical nature of the German situation at the turn of the decade, the new British permanent under-secretary of state for foreign affairs, Sir Robert Vansittart, warned in May 1930 that Germany was 'on the threshold of a new period' in which 'she may be sorely tempted to apply the old methods of diplomacy if she finds the new ones of arbitration and conciliation eventually ineffective for changing the *status quo* to her purpose'.[49] Before long it would become clear that these temptations were too strong for the leaders of the beleaguered Republic to resist.

Hiatus, 1930–1933

With the onset of the new decade the policymakers in Britain and Germany were forced to adapt to rapidly changing circumstances both at home and in the international arena. Following Stresemann's death in October 1929, the British embassy in Berlin anticipated no new departures in German foreign policy, which now passed into the hands of Julius Curtius. Germany's acceptance of the Young Plan meant that financial considerations would necessarily command the attention of her leaders and that it was therefore 'probable that internal affairs will loom more largely than for a number of years'.[50] By 1930, however, the picture was radically different as the first repercussions of the depression began to make themselves felt in Europe. The worsening economic situation and in particular the final withdrawal of

Allied troops from the Rhineland resulted in an explosion of German nationalist feeling and thrust the question of treaty revision to the forefront of the agenda of every political party during the election campaign of June–September 1930.[51] Alarmed by the staggering electoral success of the national socialists, Curtius and Heinrich Brüning, chancellor since March 1930, jettisoned Stresemann's policies and adopted a more aggressive and confrontational stance which, they hoped, would solve Germany's internal and external problems simultaneously. In an ill-fated attempt to pursue 'domestic policy through foreign policy',[52] the German leaders sought to secure a favourable solution of the reparations and disarmament questions by exploiting and even deliberately intensifying the impact of the economic crisis in Germany. This so-called *Durchhaltepolitik* ('stick-it-out policy') was meant to convince the British and Americans of the folly of making further financial demands on Germany at such a critical juncture and thus confront them with the choice 'between settlement or the threat of impending collapse of the German economy and utter domestic chaos'.[53] At the same time, by staking everything on the achievement of a striking diplomatic success, Brüning hoped to consolidate his position at home, thereby paving the way for far-reaching reforms and the final overthrow of Versailles. In practice, however, this strategy had catastrophic repercussions on Franco-German relations, alarmed the British, alienated the United States and ultimately played into the hands of Brüning's domestic opponents who, pointing to the lack of further concessions, continued to pillory his government at every available opportunity. Although reparations were finally cancelled during the Lausanne conference in June 1932, Brüning thus eventually became a 'victim of the very unrest he sought to exploit'.[54]

Six years later, in the immediate aftermath of the Munich crisis which had brought Britain and Germany to the brink of war, Sir Alexander Cadogan perhaps understandably lamented the fact that more had not been done to assist Brüning in his struggle against Hitler in the early 1930s.[55] However, given Britain's own concerns at that time, notably the onset of the financial crisis, the preparations for the forthcoming Geneva disarmament conference and the disturbing spectacle of Japanese aggression in China, it was clearly impossible for British leaders to focus their attention on German issues. Moreover, although they had been the most vociferous critics of Chamberlain's 'francophile' policy in the later 1920s, and despite their apparently more accommodating attitude towards German grievances, the labour leaders, MacDonald and Henderson, still sought to act as 'honest brokers' between Berlin and Paris and thus continued to work towards that same general European pacification that had been the goal of all British governments since 1919.[56] As long as German policy appeared to be directed towards similar ends, and provided that the Germans were prepared loyally

to cooperate on the basis of gradual and limited change secured by negotiated settlements acceptable to all, they could generally expect a sympathetic
hearing in London. However, if and when they sought to force the pace of
revision through unilateral action which threatened to disrupt the process
of appeasement, as was the case in 1931 with the proposed Austro-German
customs union,[57] the British closed ranks with the French and Italians to
thwart any such potentially dangerous aspirations. Equally, although in
the early 1930s the British had certainly wished to bolster Brüning and his
successors against the Nazis, the simple fact was that as time progressed
internal conditions in Germany increasingly gathered a momentum of their
own which no foreign power was materially able to influence, still less
arrest. In these circumstances the authorities in London watched in a state
of virtual powerlessness as the last vestiges of German democracy crumbled
in the second half of 1932.

Leviathan and Behemoth, 1933–1939

If the British could draw any comfort from Hitler's accession to power in
January 1933 it perhaps lay in the fact that for years he had made no secret
of his desire for a close understanding with the British Empire. In his
writings of the 1920s, and in his first forays into the realm of diplomacy,
Hitler emphasized the crucial role allocated to Great Britain in his foreign
policy programme and his fervent wish for an Anglo-German alliance.
Other aspects of that programme, however, were patently inadmissible as
far as Britain was concerned. Indeed, the purpose to which Hitler would
seek to put an Anglo-German alliance was far removed from British visions
of a stable European equilibrium, multilateral cooperation and the maintenance of peace. In short, Hitler proposed to secure alliances with Britain
and Italy, paralyse France either by drawing her into an agreement of
dubious value and unspecified duration on the basis of common hostility to
Bolshevism or, failing that, by eliminating her as a European power factor,
following which the resurgent Reich would fall on the Soviet Union and
establish a colossal German empire stretching from the Rhineland to the
Ural mountains. For some Britons the prospect of a partnership with the new,
dynamic national socialist Germany certainly held a compelling attraction. In Whitehall, however, where anti-Bolshevik sentiment, racial considerations, feelings of 'guilt' over the 1919 peace settlement and a sneaking
admiration for even the most lunatic aspirations of Hitler's movement were
rarely permitted to cloud the judgement of ministers and officials, there was
little dispute about the nature and magnitude of the dangers ahead. In

German eyes an Anglo-German alliance that would permit German hegemony on the continent and 'give her a free hand in Europe in return for German non-interference in the rest of the world'[58] would, as Hitler told a British visitor in February 1935, constitute the 'cornerstone upon which the old world would preserve itself'.[59] For the Foreign Office, however, the Nazi leader's vision amounted to nothing more than 'the old story of the separate settlement behind the back of France and the division of the world between Leviathan and Behemoth of 1899'. The sequel, wrote Victor Perowne in May 1935, 'is the swallowing of Leviathan by Behemoth'. 'In fact', he continued, 'the subconscious ideas even of those Germans who profess most loudly to believe in a German–British–American domination of the world . . . is that Great Britain would only be left undisturbed so long as Germany had her hands full elsewhere . . . so far as we are concerned, it would be the "miserable kindness of Polyphemus to Ulysses: you only keep me to be devoured last"'.[60]

The British have often been criticized for underestimating the threat posed by Hitler and for failing to make timely preparations in an effort to contain him. It should be remembered, however, that the emergence of a strong government in Germany was not entirely lacking in appeal following the experiences of the early 1930s. Moreover, the slogan 'better Hitler than Stalin' enjoyed a resonance in many western circles long before it became the vogue among the fearful following the outbreak of the Spanish Civil War. Even in the Foreign Office, where a close watch had been kept on the rise of the NSDAP, there were men of experience and integrity who for a few fleeting moments in early 1933 were inclined to wonder whether National Socialism might not yet develop into 'an idealistic and constructive system', the initial excesses of which would pale into insignificance when compared with the catalogue of outrages perpetrated by the Bolsheviks since 1917.[61] Vansittart, however, harboured no such illusions. On 7 July 1933 he wrote:

> We cannot take the same detached and high brow view of Hitlerism as
> we can of Bolshevism or Fascism, precisely because they are not really and
> vitally dangerous to us, and Hitlerism *is* exceedingly dangerous. Fascism
> has never presented the least danger to this country, and Russia has been
> too incompetent a country to be really dangerous even under Bolshevism.
> But Germany is an exceedingly competent country, and she is visibly being
> prepared for external aggression . . . I do not think anything but evil and
> danger for the rest of the world can come out of Hitlerism, whichever way
> the dice fall in Germany.[62]

Three months later Hitler gave the most concrete indication to date of his determination to rearm and to tolerate no limitations on his freedom of action by withdrawing simultaneously from the League of Nations and the disarmament conference that had been in session since February 1932. Following on the heels of the Manchurian crisis, the German move, although not entirely unexpected, underscored for the British the urgency of a comprehensive review of their own defence policy and the need to make good the deficiencies that had been allowed to accumulate since 1919. When in March 1934 the defence requirements committee declared Germany to be the 'ultimate potential enemy' against which long-term defence planning should be directed, it was clear that the policy of ignoring German rearmament was in the long run no policy at all and carried with it great dangers. During the summer and autumn the British were gradually forced to the conclusion that, sooner or later, they would have to adopt a definite attitude towards German breaches of the military clauses of the Versailles Treaty, and that in view of their reluctance to assume additional security commitments they were left with little alternative but to attempt in concert with the other powers to arrive at a mutually satisfactory arrangement with Germany before she became too strong.[63] This calculation lay at the heart of the Anglo-French offer made to Germany in February 1935.

The terms of that offer reveal much about Britain's strategy in dealing with the German menace during the mid-1930s. Essentially the British wished to barter away certain parts of the 1919 settlement and to receive in return binding assurances from Berlin of future good behaviour. Thus, under the scheme presented to him in early 1935, which provided for Anglo-French recognition and legalization of a limited amount of German rearmament, Hitler was expected to agree to a series of conditions which would oblige him to respect the territorial status quo in eastern and southeast Europe, participate in multilateral security pacts, accept an international armaments convention, return to the League of Nations and append his signature to an agreement which would extend the provisions of Locarno to cover air attack. It was hardly surprising therefore that the German leader showed no interest in the proposals apart from using the idea of the air pact to suggest an exchange of views with the British, supposedly for exploratory discussions but in reality to dangle before them the prospect of an Anglo-German condominium. Moreover, even before the visit to Berlin of Sir John Simon and Anthony Eden took place, Hitler had effectively wrecked the Anglo-French plan by announcing the existence of the *Luftwaffe* and the reintroduction of conscription on 9 and 16 March respectively. In the presence of the British ministers Hitler made quite clear his preference for 'uncomplicated' bilateral treaties and for an exclusive partnership which was primarily designed to allow him to shatter the very status quo that the British were so concerned to preserve. In these circumstances it was hardly surprising that little headway was made during the discussions on the thorny issues of security pacts, armaments agreements and the German attitude towards the League. The lack of progress, however, had at least shown where the fundamental problem lay, even if at the time its implications were not fully appreciated by either side. For in March 1935, in the first, and indeed only, direct negotiations between a British foreign secretary and Hitler, the British insistence on collective security, arms control, the inviolability of international frontiers and the need for gradual, peaceful and limited change had clashed with the German leader's determination to retain absolute freedom of action, rearm as he pleased and, in time, to expand at the expense of his east European neighbours.

Despite the cool reception of his bid for an Anglo-German understanding, Hitler was not unduly disappointed with the outcome of the British visit.[64] For his part Simon came away feeling that although the results were generally unsatisfactory, the conversations had at least served to clarify the German attitude. As long as Hitler desired good relations with Britain, which the visit had clearly demonstrated, he was most unwilling to abandon all hopes of a general agreement and to close ranks against Germany 'until this becomes *absolutely* inevitable'.[65] Eden, however, was more pessimistic. He felt that the experience had shown that the basis for any general settlement was now far more limited than it had been in the spring of 1934, and, moreover, that Germany had made crystal clear her refusal to make an active contribution to European appeasement.[66] The British ambassador in Berlin, Sir Eric Phipps, was of similar opinion. Reviewing the European scene in late March he wrote to Vansittart:

> I cannot pretend to be an optimist for looking round Europe I see
> a welter of conflicting opinions, policies and emotions, opposed to which
> we find our dynamic Hitler, untrammelled by electoral or parliamentary
> considerations, who really knows what he wants and means to get it, whose
> will is law, so long anyhow as the Army is with him which it now certainly
> is, and who, by saying a word, can hurl this united and efficient people in
> any given direction at five minutes' notice. Surely in these circumstances
> optimism would imply folly?[67]

Such views, however, seemed singularly misplaced when only three months later the Anglo-German Naval Agreement was signed in London. The culmination of a series of German overtures dating back to late 1933 and a British desire to set limits to that area of German rearmament that was still negotiable after the 'Saturday surprises' of 9 and 16 March, the treaty restricted the size of any future German fleet to 35 per cent of the total tonnage of the Royal Navy. More importantly, however, its significance was misinterpreted by the Germans, and particularly by Hitler who convinced himself that it marked the first step towards a much closer political collaboration between the two powers. Indeed, even the German naval leadership, which was generally satisfied with the results, was prepared to admit that the principal advantage lay in the fact that a 'political understanding with Great Britain has been initiated by the naval settlement'.[68]

However, it was wholly misleading to speak of the initiation of any such understanding. Whereas the Germans had conceded Britain's claim to naval supremacy in the expectation that 'the British should likewise recognise Germany's essential interests as a continental Power',[69] Britain's willingness to enter into the agreement was most certainly not intended as a green light for German ambitions in eastern Europe. The chief motivation had been to secure, at relatively little cost, a vital interest freely offered by the Great Power from which the British believed they had most to fear. From this point of view there was undeniable force in Eden's declaration to a disconcerted Pierre Laval that, practically speaking, 'no British Government could have done otherwise'.[70] Other factors, too, had played a part in the British decision, not least the hope that the treaty would prepare the ground for Germany's participation in a general naval agreement and, more broadly, for her collaboration on other outstanding problems. Thus, while the British certainly hoped to initiate a degree of cooperation with Germany, the nature of that cooperation was far removed from Hitler's conception of an alliance designed to ease his path to the east. When over the next year this became increasingly evident, the naval agreement lost much of its value for the Nazi leadership. Indeed, as early as mid-October 1935 the counsellor of the German embassy in London was speaking of the 'considerable disappointment in high circles' at the failure of the naval treaty to produce any improvement in relations.[71]

By that time the international situation had been transformed by Mussolini's invasion of Abyssinia and the deepening crisis between Italy and the League of Nations. The Abyssinian conflict provided Germany with a convenient excuse for her continued refusal to negotiate over arms limitation and multilateral security arrangements, areas in which she essentially wished to see no progress. Although Hitler was faced with the possibility of an armed clash between the two powers which, according to the thesis of his book *Mein Kampf,* were to have constituted the principal allies of the Third Reich, there were clearly advantages to be drawn from the new situation, not least with regard to the operation of the Treaty of Locarno of which Britain and Italy were co-guarantors. It was no surprise therefore that Germany chose to avoid any appearance of taking sides in the dispute, preferring to wait and see how it would affect European alignments. The situation created by the Italo-Abyssinian dispute, coupled with the menace of a dissatisfied Germany backed by increasing military might, underlined for Great Britain the importance of rapid and extensive rearmament and, if possible, some form of European détente. In the circumstances prevailing at the turn of 1935–6 this involved in the first instance the placing of relations between Britain, France and Germany on a new and more stable footing. Three weeks after the Italian invasion, Ralph Wigram, head of the central department at the Foreign Office, hinted at a further drive in this direction, writing to Phipps that the wind appeared to be 'setting towards some type of accommodation with Germany'.[72] Over the following months the political and economic experts in Whitehall were engaged in the compilation of several detailed analyses of the German problem which were designed to assist in answering two crucial questions, namely was a satisfactory settlement with Germany attainable, and, if so, what form should it take?[73] Much of this material was later used by Vansittart in the drafting of an important paper on policy towards Germany which was circulated to the cabinet in February 1936.

Vansittart was careful to avoid any confident predictions as to the prospects of a workable agreement with the Nazi regime, and the generally pessimistic tone of his memorandum accurately reflected the mood of the Foreign Office as a whole. The permanent under-secretary of state admitted to a belief that 'the present rulers of Germany are bent upon eventual adventures which will be almost certain to unleash a European war' and suspected that Hitler would seek to expand both in Europe and in Africa. On balance, however, and mindful of the pressures of public opinion and inadequate rearmament, he felt that it was worthwhile making a serious attempt to curb German ambitions if possible and thus 'to secure peace for the world by postponing a crisis; for the essential thing is that we should gain time, and things postponed have a way of not happening'. Vansittart concluded that any eventual settlement would have to be made at Geneva, that Germany could only be permitted to expand in Africa, that Britain and France would therefore have to pay for such expansion through a colonial settlement, that economic assistance to Germany must be preceded by binding political guarantees, and, most important of all, that Britain must make rapid strides in her own rearmament in order to improve her bargaining position. He further advised that the best method of approach would be to introduce the idea of a general settlement by initiating discussions on one particular aspect of the security or armaments problems, such as the air pact and air limitation or the demilitarized Rhineland zone, which, he was convinced, would have to disappear as part of any agreement.[74] By early March 1936 it had been decided that the prospect of an adjustment in the status of the Rhineland would be offered in the hope of opening fruitful discussions with Berlin.

As had happened twelve months earlier, however, a unilateral act by Hitler, another 'Saturday surprise', left the British negotiating strategy in tatters even before it had had a chance to be implemented. The reoccupation of the demilitarized zone on 7 March 1936 not only transformed the strategic balance in western Europe, with all its ominous implications for France's allies in the east, but, in Eden's words, also constituted a 'grave setback to the policy of a European general settlement' by depriving the British of a useful bargaining counter in their intended discussions with Germany.[75] It was in these depressing circumstances that the British search for stability and pacification suffered a further setback with the outbreak in July 1936 of the Spanish Civil War. The impact on Hitler of the developments in Spain should not be underestimated. In the six months that followed he signed the October Protocols with Italy and the Anti-comintern Pact with Japan, the only powers that, in his opinion, could be relied upon to oppose the Bolsheviks, wrote his memorandum on the Four Year Plan, which was designed to make Germany ready for war by 1940, increased the term of German military service to two years, and indulged in a series of menacing denunciations of the USSR, culminating in a violent harangue to the party faithful at Nuremberg in September.

Britain's decision to pursue a policy of non-intervention in Spain was a source of profound concern to the German chancellor, who was at a loss to comprehend how the once mighty empire could react with such indifference to this flagrant challenge from Moscow. Britain's position over the Spanish affair, the weakness and indecision that had been revealed by her policy during the Abyssinian crisis, and, not least, her marked disinclination to share the benefits of German power, had important repercussions for the development of Hitler's policy towards Britain. By aligning himself with Britain's other potential enemies, Japan and Italy, by stepping up the demand for the return of the German colonies and by emphasizing the need for Anglo-German solidarity against Bolshevism, Hitler now hoped to secure by pressure the partnership that his conciliatory attitude had hitherto failed to deliver.[76] In August 1936 he appointed as the new German ambassador to the Court of St James his closest foreign policy advisor, Joachim von Ribbentrop, whose diplomatic activities since 1933 had been devoted almost exclusively to the promotion of Anglo-German friendship. Shortly before his departure for London, Ribbentrop was received by Hitler who made to him the following revealing statement:

Ribbentrop . . . get Britain to join the Anti-Comintern Pact, that is what I want most of all. I have sent you as the best man I've got. Do what you can . . . but if in future all our efforts are in vain, fair enough, then I'm ready for war as well. I would regret it very much, but if it has to be, there it is. But I think it would be a short war and the moment it is over, I will then be ready at any time to offer the British an honourable peace acceptable to both sides. However, I would then demand that Britain join the Anti-Comintern Pact or perhaps some other pact. But get on with it Ribbentrop, you have the trumps in your hand, play them well.[77]

For all Ribbentrop's supposed limitations, and in spite of his considerable exertions in seeking to carry out these instructions, the gulf between the British and German positions was so wide that there was never the slightest possibility of a successful outcome of his mission. In February 1938 he returned to Germany to assume the post of foreign minister not only consumed with hatred for the British but also with a chillingly rational appreciation of what course Germany must follow if she were to realize her destiny. In October 1937 he had told the Italian leaders that a conflict with the western powers was 'inevitable'.[78] From that point onwards he did his best to engineer one while Germany still enjoyed the advantages of superior rearmament and more powerful, if somewhat unpredictable, allies.

When Neville Chamberlain succeeded Baldwin in mid-1937 the hopes that were generated in Nazi circles that the new premier would be more attuned than his predecessors to the attraction of an exclusive arrangement with Germany were soon disappointed.[79] Determined to take the initiative in foreign affairs, and in particular to explore the possibilities for agreement with the Germans on lines which were essentially no different to those that had been proposed in 1935 and 1936, Chamberlain found himself confronted with the familiar problem of how to reconcile Germany's yawning appetite for territory with Britain's position as a European and imperial power. The Foreign Office experts, of whose cautionary counsel he soon wearied, did not so much disapprove of Chamberlain's intentions, which were entirely laudable, but merely pointed to the fact that he was unlikely to succeed where they had twice failed.[80] In March 1938, after months of deliberation, and following what he erroneously perceived as the inauguration of a fairly promising Anglo-German dialogue as a result of Lord Halifax's conversations with the German leaders in November 1937, Chamberlain offered Hitler a colonial settlement in return for which the Führer was asked, *inter alia*, to undertake to respect the territorial status quo in central Europe. Hitler, however, showed not the slightest interest in the proposal and thus condemned to oblivion a third British attempt to tie his hands on the continent by offering concessions in other areas. Despite his statement to Halifax at Berchtesgaden that the colonial question was the only problem currently burdening Anglo-German relations,[81] the former German colonies only interested Hitler in 1937–8 as a means of forcing the

British finally to concede his demand for a free hand in eastern Europe. For once the rather gullible British ambassador, Sir Nevile Henderson, who had replaced Phipps in May 1937, did not permit his view of the situation to be clouded by the vague schemes for 'friendship', coupled with perceptible menaces, with which the Nazi leaders, particularly Goering, had continually pumped him since his arrival in Berlin. Following Hitler's rejection of the colonial offer during their interview of 3 March, Henderson wrote that the chancellor's attitude 'clearly shows how unpromising is the policy of those who think that he may be deflected from his aims in Central Europe by French and British expressions of disapproval. If [the] offer of British friendship and [the] prospect of a colonial settlement are not sufficient to deter him or to secure even a temporary halt, how much less effective is likely to be an ambiguous warning which is not backed up with a show of force'.[82] Eight days later, as if to prove the point, Germany annexed Austria.

As far as the British were concerned, it was not the fact of the *Anschluss* that perturbed them so much as the brutal manner in which it had been effected. Towards the close of 1937 both Halifax and Eden had made statements to Hitler and Ribbentrop respectively which appeared to indicate that Britain was not fundamentally opposed to an eventual Austro-German union, provided that it was brought about by peaceful means.[83] With Czechoslovakia, however, to which all eyes now turned, it was an entirely different situation, not least due to the fact that the Czech republic was an ally of France. A combination of suspected German designs on Czechoslovakia, freely admitted by Göring to Group Captain Malcolm Christie in February 1937,[84] the strategic implications of the German annexation of Austria, and the Franco-Czech alliance, which had been contracted in the early 1920s when Germany was still on her knees, conjured up the nightmare scenario of a general European war in which Britain could not afford to remain a passive spectator. Chamberlain and his colleagues on the foreign policy committee were thus understandably united in the conviction that the best course would be for the Czechs to seek to make as reasonable a settlement as possible with Hitler before the situation deteriorated any further. In the meantime British policy 'should be to keep Germany guessing at what our action in any particular emergency was likely to be'.[85] Almost simultaneously in Berlin, however, the leader of the Sudeten Germans, Konrad Henlein, was being instructed by Hitler, who aimed at nothing less than the annihilation of Czechoslovakia, 'always [to] demand so much that we can never be satisfied'.[86] There was thus no possibility of any 'reasonable' settlement in the long run; nor after the 'May crisis', following which Hitler decreed that Czechoslovakia must be reduced no later than 1 October, was there much time for anything apart from a frantic exercise in crisis management.

This is not the place to examine why the Czech crisis of 1938 did not result in a general European conflagration. Of far greater significance from the point of view of Anglo-German relations is the fact that Munich taught Hitler a few salutary lessons. Chief among these was that his conviction, expressed in November 1937 during the Hossbach conference, that Britain was too weak and preoccupied with problems connected with the empire to involve herself in a conflict in central Europe, indeed that as far as Czechoslovakia was concerned she was reconciled to the fact 'that this question would be cleared up in due course by Germany', was well wide of the mark.[87] Seething with rage at Britain's interference in an area which, in his opinion, was of no concern to her, Hitler calculated after Munich that he might after all have to fight Britain if he was to fulfil his dream of a 'Greater German Reich'.[88] For Chamberlain, Munich was both a glittering, if transitory, personal success and a source of anxiety for the future. 'Edward, we must hope for the best while preparing for the worst', he is famously quoted as saying to Lord Halifax.[89] These preparations took the form of accelerated rearmament, an effort in January 1939 to improve Anglo-Italian relations and a rather more successful attempt to strengthen ties with France. At the same time, however, Chamberlain remained determined to explore any possible avenues of negotiation with Germany.

The prime minister's hopes, however, were abruptly dashed when in March 1939 Hitler occupied Prague and in the process symbolically ripped to shreds both the Munich agreement and the Anglo-German declaration of 30 September 1938 in which he had solemnly agreed with Chamberlain to help promote appeasement in Europe.[90] The British guarantee to Poland which followed the seizure of Prague and the ultimately unsuccessful search for a Russian alliance over the summer were designed specifically to deter the German dictator from continuing with his programme of conquest which now threatened completely to negate all notions of stability, cooperation and a balance of power in Europe. Shortly before the outbreak of war, Hitler appeared finally to have grasped the point that Vansittart and his closest collaborators had reluctantly but inevitably been forced to admit since mid-1937. In conversation with Henderson on 23 August 1939 the chancellor declared that he was now 'finally convinced of the rightness of views held formerly to him by others that England and Germany could never agree', an unmistakable reference to the malignant urgings of Ribbentrop. The responsibility for the present crisis, he continued, rested squarely with Britain and 'nothing short of [a] complete change of her policy towards Germany could now ever convince him of [the] British desire for good relations'.[91] When shortly afterwards Germany invaded

Poland the British responded in the only manner left open to them if they were to have any hope at all of influencing the future destiny of Europe.

Conclusion: the 'necessary war'?

In 1930 Austen Chamberlain published an article entitled 'Great Britain as a European Power' in which he argued that Britain occupied a 'semi-detached' position in relation to the continent.[92] Such an assertion, implying as it did the importance of Britain's larger role as the hub of a world empire, was perhaps understandable given the time and circumstances in which it was made. Even then, however, it represented something of an illusion. It was certainly undeniable that the British Empire of the 1920s appeared to enjoy an unrivalled position among the nations, having only recently emerged victorious and substantially enlarged as a result of a protracted and bitter struggle against Germany. Nevertheless, irrespective of the rise of other potential threats to Britain's world position in the shape of Japan and the United States, and the recasting of an old adversary in its new guise as the centre of 'world revolution', it still remained an axiom of British foreign policy that peace in Europe and a stable equilibrium between the continental powers were essential prerequisites for the pursuit of trade and commerce, the lifeblood of the empire and the guarantee of continued prosperity. After all, it had been in order to safeguard these larger interests, rather than simply to protect the British mainland by turning the Germans out of Belgium, that Britain had gone to war in 1914. Despite four years of carnage, however, the British, themselves exhausted, were still left with a 'German problem' after 1919, and, worse still, with some unresolved disagreements with their major continental partner as to how best to deal with it. Having contented themselves that the German naval and imperial threat had been eliminated, and with German power in Europe reduced to a negligible level, it was easy for British statesmen to counsel moderation and conciliation where it suited their own interests. In any case, they certainly found it much easier than the French, who accused them of an ignorance of the German 'psyche' and, on a less emotional level, of a blindness to the dangers of leaving Germany not only with a capacity for revival but also nurturing an acute sense of grievance.

Whereas after 1919 France chose the path of military alliances, economic strangulation and the strict enforcement of the Versailles treaty in her attempt to contain Germany, the British chose, or, it has been suggested, took a further step along, the road of appeasement.[93] For two decades they patiently sought an elusive 'general settlement' which sought to combine reconciliation between the European powers with a process of gradual, mutually acceptable and honourable revision of the peace treaties. In a British Foreign Office paper of April 1926 this even-handed approach was described as 'preaching the gospel of reasonableness', a process in which the British, so it was claimed, 'were always ready to join our allies in insisting upon Germany fulfilling her obligations as far as they were consistent with her capacity and with common-sense'. Beyond that, however, 'we would not go; and, above all, we insisted that we Allies were bound equally with Germany by the terms of the treaty we had signed. This was our policy in great matters and in small'.[94] In the broadest terms this 'lesson' was directed in varying degrees towards both France and Germany from 1920 to 1933 and almost exclusively towards Germany following the advent of Hitler.

During the 1920s and 1930s, however, the one condition that was essential to the success of the various British schemes for any such 'general settlement' was conspicuous by its absence. Austen Chamberlain hit upon this crucial point in December 1927 when, following the successful resolution by the League Council of a rather ugly looking dispute between Poland and Lithuania, he wrote with obvious satisfaction to his sister that 'there are few things that France, Germany and Great Britain cannot do when united'.[95] Yet during the inter-war years that vital consensus was almost entirely lacking, and even in the mid-1920s, at the time of Locarno and the German entry into the League, it remained more apparent than real. In the increasingly strained international circumstances of the 1930s the British search for a European settlement became ever more urgent, its realization, however, ever more elusive. The French, horrified by the scale of Germany's resurgence and consumed by their own domestic problems, responded somewhat paradoxically to the Nazi threat by allying with the Soviet Union and occasionally exploring the possibilities of a direct Franco-German rapprochement, much to British chagrin. Moreover, British hopes for European pacification were further confounded by the fact that the most important link in the chain, Germany, was internally unstable for protracted periods in the 1920s and, ironically, almost too sure of her own destiny when delivered into the iron grip of Hitler and his followers. Although Anglo-German relations had effectively been subsumed in the numerous disputes that arose between Britain and France between 1919 and 1923, a workable *modus vivendi* might just have been possible with the relatively moderate Weimar governments of the mid-1920s. It became rather less of a practical proposition in the early 1930s when Brüning, von Schleicher and von Papen pursued increasingly reckless policies in a confused attempt to take advantage of the depression while simultaneously striving to avert catastrophe at home. Once Hitler was at the helm, the sheer vastness of his ambitions, which cut clean across the imperatives of Britain's European policy, rendered it an impossibility.

And what of Germany? In recent years it has been the fashion to detect elements of continuity in the international policies pursued by Bismarck, Wilhelm II, the leaders of the Weimar Republic and Hitler. The ideas advanced in this essay, however, at least insofar as they concern the aims and methods of Weimar and Nazi foreign policy, suggest that any such linkages should only be inferred following careful consideration of the issues. It would palpably be fatuous to deny any similarities between the aims of Stresemann and Hitler. Both wished to reassert Germany's status as a Great Power, if not as a World Power; both aimed to free Germany from the shackles of the Treaty of Versailles; both had designs in eastern Europe; and both desired cooperation with Great Britain. Indeed, perhaps the similarities go even deeper. It may well be that Stresemann was forced to conceal his real ambitions during the 1920s. It is certainly indisputable that he was compelled to operate in an environment dictated by the constraints imposed on Germany by the 1919 peace settlement, which he had nevertheless succeeded in undermining in several important respects by the time he departed the stage.

Hitler, however, was a completely different phenomenon and one who, within months of coming to power, systematically began to prepare Germany for a merciless war of conquest and racial extermination against Stresemann's erstwhile associate, the Soviet Union. Such were his achievements in that respect that Sir Eric Phipps was to write as early as November 1935 that 'Germany may be said without exaggeration to be living in a state of war'.[96] In the summer of 1936 Vansittart identified the 'new' Germany, for 'new' it undoubtedly was, as 'the most formidable proposition that has ever been formulated', and described its people as being in 'strict training now, not for the Olympic Games, but for breaking some other and emphatically unsporting world records, and perhaps the world as well'.[97] Eight months later he condemned German policy as one of 'violence and robbery', adding that Britain and Germany were separated by 'a fundamental difference of conception, of morality'.[98] By late 1937 none of the German experts in the British Foreign Office seriously believed in the possibility of a lasting settlement with Hitler; nor did some senior ministers, including Eden and Halifax.[99] On examining the voluminous archives of the Foreign Office central department, one is struck by the absence of any assessments of the prospects for Anglo-German relations or any analyses of German aims during the 1920s which are so darkly pessimistic, condemnatory in tone and so teeming with foreboding and prophecies of catastrophe as those written after 1933.

The simple fact was that unless the British were prepared fundamentally to break with their traditional concepts and sanction German mastery of the continent, or unless by some miracle Hitler could be transformed into a 'good European', a second conflict between the two powers became increasingly likely as Germany regained her strength and began to flex her ample muscles in central Europe. When the final crisis came in September 1939 the mood in Whitehall was almost one of relief that the unbearable tensions of the preceding six months were finally at an end. 'Lord Halifax seemed relieved that we had taken our decision', wrote Ivone Kirkpatrick twenty years later. 'He called for beer, which was brought down by a sleepy Resident Clerk in pyjamas. We laughed and joked and when I told Lord Halifax that news had just come in that Goebbels had prohibited listening to foreign broadcasts, he retorted: "He ought to pay me to listen to his."'[100] Meanwhile, in the Reich Chancellery in Berlin, the atmosphere was far from jocular. After listening to a translation of the British ultimatum, Hitler, who had never wished to fight Britain and who now found himself involved in a general war facing the wrong enemies at the wrong time, spent a few moments in quiet contemplation following which he turned to Ribbentrop and said simply: 'What are we going to do now?'[101]

Notes

1. Klaus Hildebrand, *Das vergangene Reich: Deutsche Aussenpolitik von Bismarck bis Hitler, 1871–1945* (Stuttgart, 1996), p. 390.

2. This became all the more urgent when during 1921 the British economy fell into recession. In May of the following year the view was advanced in the Foreign Office that a stable, independent and prosperous Germany was 'the essential and central requirement of British policy, the first condition to which our national recovery is subject'. Minute by Waterlow, 9 May 1922, cited in Francis D. Magee, 'The British Government, the Last Weimar Governments and the Rise of Hitler, 1929–1933' (unpublished PhD thesis, University of Leeds, 1991), p. 14. I should like to express my warm thanks to Dr Magee for permitting me to consult his thesis in connection with the preparation of this essay.

3. S. Roskill, *Hankey: Man of Secrets*, Vol. II, *1919–1931* (London, 1972), pp. 149–50.

4. *Akten zur Deutschen Auswärtigen Politik 1918–1945, Serie A*, eds Walter Bußmann, Jacques Bariéty *et al.* (14 vols, Göttingen, 1982–95) (hereafter ADAP, A), III, no. 277.

5. F.S. Northedge, *The Troubled Giant: Britain Among the Great Powers, 1916–1939* (London, 1966), p. 171.

6. Sally Marks, *The Illusion of Peace: International Relations in Europe, 1918–1933* (London, 1976), p. 42.

7. ADAP, A, VI, no. 104.

8. Public Record Office, London (hereafter PRO), C2758/2758/18, F[oreign] O[ffice] 371/8807, D'Abernon to the Foreign Office, 7 Feb 1923.

9. ADAP, A, VI, no. 246.

10. Alan Sharp, 'Lord Curzon and British Policy towards the Franco-Belgian Occupation of the Ruhr in 1923', *Diplomacy and Statecraft* 8 (1997), p. 94 n. 3.

11. Northedge, *The Troubled Giant*, p. 187; David Gilmour, *Curzon* (London, 1994), p. 588. For the text of the 'Curzon Note' see *Documents on British Foreign Policy 1919–1939, First Series*, eds E.L. Woodward, Rohan Butler *et al.* (27 vols, London, 1947–86) (hereafter DBFP, I), XXI, no. 330. By November 1923 the dollar–mark exchange rate was 1 : 4,200,000,000,000.0 whereas the previous January it had been 1 : 17,972.0. Gordon A. Craig, *Germany, 1866–1945*, 8th edn (Oxford, 1992), p. 450. In view of the German economic crisis and the parlous state of Anglo-French relations it can readily be appreciated why the British Foreign Office later described the situation of autumn 1923 as 'perhaps the darkest moment in the history of Western Europe since the conclusion of the war'. See *Documents on British Foreign Policy 1919–1939, Series IA*, eds W.N. Medlicott, Douglas Dakin *et al.* (7 vols, London, 1966–75) (hereafter DBFP, IA), I, no. 1.

12. Bundesarchiv Berlin-Lichterfelde (hereafter BA-Berlin), R[eichskanzlei]43 I/59, 'Über die Lage in England' (unsigned memorandum), 20 Sept 1923.

13. For recent contributions to the debate see Hildebrand, *Das vergangene Reich*, pp. 438ff.; Constanze Baumgart, *Stresemann und England* (Köln, 1996), pp. 296ff.; Jonathan Wright, 'Stresemann and Locarno', *Contemporary European History* 4 (1995), pp. 109–31.

14. Marshall Lee and Wolfgang Michalka, *German Foreign Policy 1919–1933: Continuity or Break?* (Leamington Spa, 1987), p. 77.

15. On Hitler's reaction to the Ruhr crisis and its impact on his plans for an alliance with Britain see Axel Kuhn, *Hitlers aussenpolitisches Programm: Entstehung und Entwicklung, 1919–1939* (Stuttgart, 1970), pp. 87ff.

16. Gustav Stresemann, *His Diaries, Letters and Papers*, ed. and trans. Eric Sutton, Vol. 2 (London, 1937), p. 225. Stresemann also believed that Britain's support for Germany's entry into the League of Nations was partly conditioned by a desire 'to counteract France's hitherto predominant influence on that body' (p. 504).

17. Robert C. Self, ed., *The Austen Chamberlain Diary Letters: The Correspondence of Sir Austen Chamberlain with his Sisters Hilda and Ida, 1916–1937*, Camden Fifth Series, Vol. 5 (Cambridge, 1995), p. 266.

18. David Dutton, *Austen Chamberlain: Gentleman in Politics* (Bolton, 1985), p. 239.

19. See, for example, Anthony Adamthwaite, *Grandeur and Misery: France's Bid for Power in Europe, 1914–1940* (London, 1995), pp. 121–2.

20. Stresemann, *Diaries, Letters and Papers*, Vol. 2, p. 263.

21. Baumgart, *Stresemann und England*, p. 263.

22. Richard Grayson, *Austen Chamberlain and the Commitment to Europe: British Foreign Policy, 1924–29* (London, 1997), pp. 56–7, 63, 128; Sir Charles Petrie, *The Life and Letters of the Right Hon. Sir Austen Chamberlain K.G., P.C., M.P.*, Vol. 2 (London, 1940), pp. 270–1. In a letter to Lord Crewe of 16 Feb 1925 Chamberlain had written that the Polish Corridor was an issue 'for which no British Government ever will or ever can risk the bones of a British grenadier' (p. 259).

23. Jon Jacobsen, *Locarno Diplomacy: Germany and the West, 1925–1929* (Princeton, NJ, 1972), p. 30.

24. This view is most persuasively argued in Franz Knipping, *Deutschland, Frankreich und das Ende der Locarno-Ära, 1928–1931: Studien der internationalen Politik in der Anfangsphase der Weltwirtschaftskrise* (München, 1987).

25. Grayson, *Austen Chamberlain and the Commitment to Europe*, p. 67.

26. DBFP, IA, V, no. 79.

27. Self, ed., *The Austen Chamberlain Diary Letters*, p. 312.

28. Ibid., p. 266.

29. See Frank Magee, '"Limited Liability"? Britain and the Treaty of Locarno', *Twentieth Century British History* 6 (1995), pp. 1–22.

30. DBFP, IA, I, appendix.

31. Jacobsen, *Locarno Diplomacy*, p. 127, n. 72.

32. Magee, 'The British Government', p. 16.

33. *Akten zur Deutschen Auswärtigen Politik 1918–1945, Serie B*, eds Hans Rothfels, Maurice Baumont *et al.* (21 vols, Göttingen, 1966–83) (hereafter ADAP, B), VI, no. 166. For further indications of Chamberlain's frustration with the Germans after Locarno see Baumgart, *Stresemann und England*, pp. 268–9; Dutton, *Austen Chamberlain*, p. 264.

34. ADAP, B, IV, no. 11. In October 1927 Sthamer confirmed his own suspicions, noting with resignation that 'We have recently become relatively uninteresting here'. Jacobsen, *Locarno Diplomacy*, p. 127.

35. ADAP, B, IX, no. 98.

36. Baumgart, *Stresemann und England*, pp. 262–3; ADAP, B, VI, nos. 166–7.

37. ADAP, B, V, no. 236.

38. See Dutton, *Austen Chamberlain*, pp. 279–80. The previous year Chamberlain had raised suspicions in the Wilhelmstrasse of secret Anglo-French agreements by referring not to the 'Locarno powers' but to the 'entente cordiale' during the visit to Britain of Doumergue and Briand. Baumgart, *Stresemann und England*, p. 272.

39. Stresemann, *Diaries, Letters and Papers*, Vol. 2 p. 204; ADAP, B, XI, no. 144.

40. Stresemann, *Diaries, Letters and Papers*, Vol. 2 pp. 503–5.

41. DBFP, IA, II, no. 93. Stresemann also claimed to have received reliable information to the effect that the British had recently 'made it known in Paris that, after Germany's entry into the League of Nations, they do not consider the then existing situation of political co-operation with Germany to be consistent with the continuation of a garrison in the occupied territory, and that such a state of affairs is on the contrary abnormal'.

42. Stresemann, *Diaries, Letters and Papers*, Vol. 3, p. 119.

43. DBFP, IA, II, no. 153.

44. Dutton, *Austen Chamberlain*, pp. 265–6.

45. DBFP, IA, V, no. 135.

46. Jacobsen, *Locarno Diplomacy*, pp. 245–6. Not surprisingly, Chamberlain's suspicions of Germany were increased dramatically by Hitler's actions after 1933. By the time of his death in 1937 he had written pamphlets entitled 'Keep out the German Spies', 'The Hitler Hate' and 'The Menace of German Rearmament' which had been sent to all corners of the British Empire. BA-Berlin, R 43II/1436, Dellluft [?] to Hitler, 23 Aug 1937. I am most grateful to Lorna Kals for drawing my attention to this reference.

47. ADAP, B, XI, no. 144.

48. Jacobsen, *Locarno Diplomacy*, p. 355.

49. DBFP, IA, VII, appendix.

50. Ibid., no. 23.

51. Marks, *The Illusion of Peace*, pp. 112–13.

52. Sten Nadolny, *Abrüstungsdiplomatie 1932/33: Deutschland auf der Genfer Konferenz im Übergang von Weimar zu Hitler* (München, 1978), p. 143, cited in K. Hildebrand, *Reich–Nation State–Great Power: Reflections on German Foreign Policy, 1871–1945* (London, 1995), p. 20.

53. Lee and Michalka, *German Foreign Policy, 1919–1933*, p. 121.

54. Ibid., p. 122.

55. Magee, 'The British Government', p. vi.

56. On British policy towards Germany during the early 1930s see ibid., *passim*; David Carlton, *MacDonald versus Henderson: The Foreign Policy of the Second Labour Government* (London, 1970), pp. 33ff.; Edward W. Bennett, *German Rearmament and the West, 1932–1933* (Princeton, NJ, 1979), chs 2, 5 and 8.

57. On the genesis of the crisis and the British reaction see Frank Magee, 'Conducting Locarno Diplomacy: Britain and the Austro-German Customs Union Crisis, 1931', *Twentieth Century British History* [forthcoming].

58. *Documents on British Foreign Policy 1919–1939, Second Series*, eds E.L. Woodward, W.N. Medlicott *et al.* (20 vols, London, 1946–84) (hereafter DBFP, 2), XIII, no. 204.

59. PRO, FO 800/290, Lothian to Simon, 17 Feb 1935.

60. PRO, C3943/55/18, FO 371/18840, minute by Perowne, 17 May 1935, on Phipps to Simon, 15 May 1935.

61. Magee, 'The British Government', p. 423.

62. PRO, C5963/319/18, FO 371/16726, minute by Vansittart, 7 July 1933, on Rumbold to Simon, 30 June 1933.

63. This point had already been made with some force in a Foreign Office memorandum on the implications of German rearmament in March 1934: 'Part V is, for practical purposes, dead, and it would become a putrefying corpse which, if left unburied, would poison the political atmosphere of all Europe. Moreover, if there is to be a funeral it is clearly better to arrange it while Hitler is still in a mood to pay the undertakers for their services' (DBFP, 2, VI, no. 363).

64. Paul Schmidt, *Statist auf diplomatischer Bühne 1923–45: Erlebnisse des Chefdolmetschers im Auswärtigen Amt mit den Staatsmännern Europas* (Bonn, 1949), p. 304.

65. PRO, FO 800/290, Simon to Phipps, 5 April 1935.

66. DBFP, 2, XII, no. 656; PRO, C3379/55/18, FO 371/18837, Loraine to Oliphant, 5 April 1935.

67. Churchill College Archive, Cambridge (hereafter CCA), Phipps Papers, PHPP I, 2/17, Phipps to Vansittart, 28 March 1935.

68. *Documents on German Foreign Policy 1918–1945, Series C*, eds Paul R. Sweet, The Hon. Margaret Lambert *et al.* (6 vols, Washington, 1957–83), IV, no. 275.

69. DBFP, 2, XIII, no. 351.

70. Ibid., no. 363.

71. PRO, C7192/1697/18, FO 371/18878, FO minute [Mr Craigie], 22 Oct 1935.

72. CCA, Phipps Papers, PHPP I, 2/25, Wigram to Phipps, 25 Oct 1935.

73. See esp. DBFP, 2, XV, appendix (i).

74. Ibid., appendix (iv).

75. PRO, Cab 24/261, C.P. 73 (36), memorandum by Eden, 8 March 1936.

76. On the development of Hitler's views towards Britain in 1936 see G.T. Waddington, '*Hassgegner*: German Views of Great Britain in the Later 1930s', *History* 81 (1996), pp. 27–31.

77. Wolfgang Michalka, *Ribbentrop und die deutsche Weltpolitik, 1933–1940: Aussenpolitische Konzeptionen und Entscheidungsprozesse im Dritten Reich* (München, 1980), p. 155, cited in J. Noakes and G. Pridham, eds, *Nazism 1919–1945*, Vol. 3, *Foreign Policy, War and Racial Extermination: A Documentary Reader*, 2nd edn (Exeter, 1988), p. 673.

78. Galeazzo Ciano, *Ciano's Diary, 1937–1938*, trans. Andreas Mayor, ed. Malcolm Muggeridge (London, 1952), p. 24. For Ribbentrop's policy recommendations towards the close of his London mission see *Documents on German Foreign Policy 1918–1945*, Series D, eds Raymond James Sontag, John W. Wheeler-Bennett *et al.* (13 vols, London, 1949–64) (hereafter DGFP, D), I, no. 93; Annelies von Ribbentrop, *Die Kriegsschuld des Widerstandes: Aus britischen Geheimdokumenten 1938/39* (Leoni am Starnberger See, 1974), pp. 61–74.

79. See DBFP, 2, XVIII, no. 302.

80. W.N. Medlicott, *Britain and Germany: The Search for Agreement, 1930–1937* (London, 1969), p. 31.

81. DGFP, D, I, no. 31.

82. DBFP, 2, XIX, no. 610.

83. DGFP, D, I, nos. 31, 50.

84. CCA, Christie Papers, CHRS 180/1/5, record of a conversation with Goering, 3 Feb 1937.

85. PRO, Cab 27/623, F.P.C. 27 (38), meeting of 21 March 1938.

86. DGFP, D, II, no. 107.

87. Ibid., I, no. 19.

88. Josef Henke, *England in Hitlers politischem Kalkül, 1935–1939* (Boppard am Rhein, 1973), pp. 187ff.

89. D.N. Dilks, 'Appeasement Revisited', *University of Leeds Review* 15 (1972), p. 44. For an excellent analysis of the German policy of Chamberlain's administration see the same author's '"We must hope for the best and prepare for the worst": The Prime Minister, the Cabinet and Hitler's Germany, 1937–1939', *Proceedings of the British Academy* 73 (1988), pp. 309–52.

90. *Documents on British Foreign Policy 1919–1939, Third Series*, eds E.L. Woodward, Rohan Butler *et al.* (10 vols, London, 1949–61), II, no. 1228.

91. Ibid., VII, no. 248.

92. Dutton, *Austen Chamberlain*, p. 259; p. 293, n. 6.

93. See, for example, P. Schroeder, 'Munich and the British Tradition', *Historical Journal* 19 (1976), pp. 223–43.

94. DBFP, IA, I, appendix.

95. Self, ed., *The Austen Chamberlain Diary Letters*, p. 320.

96. DBFP, 2, XV, no. 213.

97. Ibid., XVII, appendix (i).

98. Ibid., XVIII, no. 466, note 2.

99. See, for example, *Foreign Relations of the United States, Diplomatic Papers 1937 (In Five Volumes) Department of State Publication* 5435 (Washington, 1954), I, pp. 74–7, 85–6; DBFP, 2, XVIII, no. 623; *The Diplomatic Diaries of Oliver Harvey, 1937–1940*, ed. John Harvey (London, 1970), p. 69; Brotherton Library, University of Leeds, Halifax Papers, microfilm 1618, Halifax Papers, undated memorandum by Halifax on his visit to Germany, 17–21 Nov 1937.

100. *The Inner Circle: Memoirs of Ivone Kirkpatrick* (London, 1959), p. 144.

101. Brotherton Library, University of Leeds, Records of the State Department Interrogation Mission to Germany 1945, microfilm 2250, interrogation of Paul Schmidt, p. 1679; Schmidt, *Statist auf diplomatischer Bühne*, p. 464.

MAPS

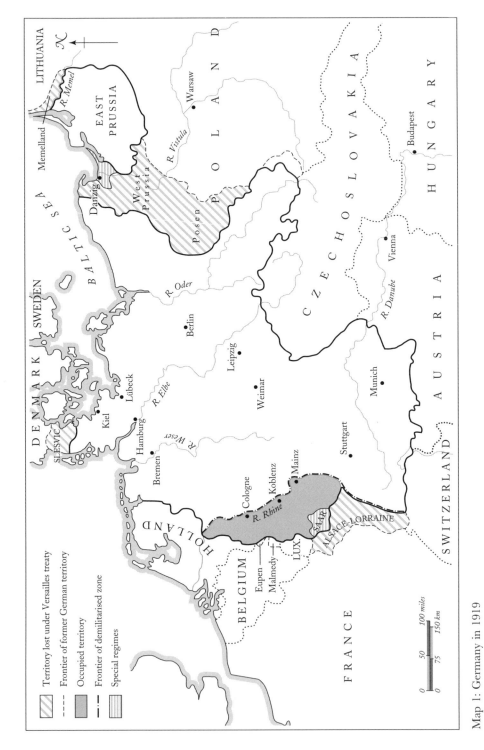

Map 1: Germany in 1919
Source: William Carr, *A History of Germany 1815–1990,* 4th Edition (London, Arnold), 1991.

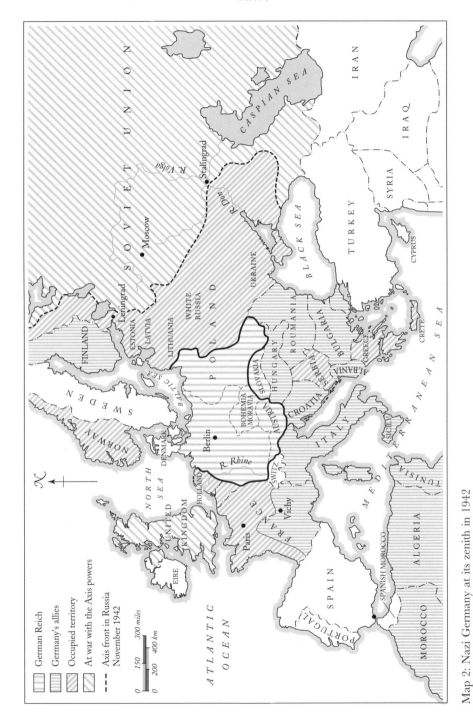

Map 2: Nazi Germany at its zenith in 1942

Source: William Carr, *A History of Germany 1815–1990*, 4th Edition (London, Arnold), 1991.

German Reich
Germany's allies
Occupied territory
At war with the Axis powers
Axis front in Russia
November 1942

0   150   300 miles
0   200   400 km

GLOSSARY

Abitur	secondary school leaving certificate
ADAP	Akten der Deutschen Aussenpolitik
ADGB	Allgemeiner Deutscher Gewerkschaftsbund (General Federation of German Trade Unions)
Alte Kämpfer	old fighters
Angestellte(n)	salaried employee(s)
Anschluss	unification with Austria
Ausländer	foreigner
Auswärtiges Amt	foreign office
autobahn	motorway
BA	Bundesarchiv
Beamte	state official
Betriebsgemeinschaft	works community
Bildungsbürgertum	educated and professional middle classes
Bundestag	lower house of the parliament in the Federal Republic of Germany
BVP	Bayerische Volkspartei
CAB	Cabinet Office
CCA	Churchill College Archive, Cambridge
DAF	Deutsche Arbeitsfront (German Labour Front)
DBFP	Documents on British Foreign Policy
DDP	Deutsche Demokratische Partei (German Democratic Party)
Deutsche Gesellschaft für Rassenhygiene	German Society for Racial Hygiene
Deutschvölkischer Schutz- und Trutz-Bund	German People's Protection and Defiance League
DGFP	Documents on German Foreign Policy
DNVP	Deutschnationale Volkspartei (German National People's Party)
DVP	Deutsche Volkspartei (German People's Party)

Einsatzgruppen	task forces
Erbhofgesetz	Law on Hereditary Farm Entailment
FO	Foreign Office
FRG	Federal Republic of Germany
Führer	leader
Führergestalten	those born to rule
Führerprinzip	leader principle
Gauleiter	district leader
GDR	German Democratic Republic
Gestapo	*Geheimstaatspolizei* (secret state police)
Gleichschaltung	co-ordination
GNP	Gross National Product
Götterdämmerung	twilight of the Gods
Großdeutsch	Greater German
Grossraumwirtschaft	closed economic bloc
Hilfswerk 'Mutter und Kind'	Relief Organization Mother and Child
Historikerstreit	'Historians' quarrel'
ISK	Internationales Sozialistisches Kampfbund (International Socialist Fighting League)
Jüdisches Frauenbund	Jewish Women's League
Junker	Prussian aristocrat
Kaiserreich	German Empire of 1871–1918
Kentrallverband Jüdischer Studenten	Central Union of Jewish Students
Kinderreich	with many children
Kleindeutsch	lesser German
KPD	Kommunistische Partei Deutschlands (Communist Party of Germany)
Kreisleiter	regional leader
Kriegsmarine	navy
Kristallnacht	crystal night
Kulturkampf	struggle between the *Kaiserreich* and the Roman Catholic Church
Länder	individual German states
Lebensraum	living space
Leistung	achievement
Luftwaffe	air force
Machteroberung	conquest of power
Machtergreifung	seizure of power

Meisterbrief	master artisan's certificate
Ministeramt	ministerial office
Mitteleuropa	central Europe
Mittelstand	middle class
Nationale Erhebung	national renaissance
NATO	North Atlantic Treaty Organization
NB	Neue Beginnen (New Beginning)
NSDAP	Nationalsozialistische Partei Deutschlands (National Socialist Party of Germany)
NSF	Nationalsozialistische Frauenschaft (National Socialist Women's Organization)
NSV	Nationalsozialistische Volkswohlfahrt (National Socialist Public Welfare)
Ossis	colloquial name for East Germans
Ostpolitik	Eastern policy
Paulskirche	St Paul's Church
Preußische Landesverband Jüdischer Gemeinde	Prussian Land Union of Jewish Communities
PRO	Public Record Office
Realpolitik	realist politics
Regierungsrat	government adviser
Reich	empire
Reichsnährstand	Imperial Food Estate
Reichsbank	national bank
Reichsbischof	imperial bishop
Reichsherrlichkeit	imperial grandeur
Reichstag	lower house of the German parliament
Reichswehr	imperial army
RM	Reichsmark
Rote Frontkämpferbund	Red Frontline Struggle League
SA	*Sturmabteilung* (storm troopers)
SAP	Sozialistische Arbeiterpartei (Socialist Workers' Party)
SD	Sicherheitsdienst (security service)
SED	Sozialistische Einheitspartei (Socialist Unity Party)
SPD	Sozialdemokratische Partei Deutschlands (Social Democratic Party of Germany)
SS	*Schutzstaffel*
Stasi	East German secret police

Stufenplan	a plan in stages
UN	United Nations
USPD	Unabhängige Sozialdemokratische Partei Deutschlands (Independent Social Democratic Party of Germany)
Volk	people
Volksgemeinschaft	people's community
Volksgenossen	people's comrades
Volkswirtschaft	national economy
Vormärz	period before the 1848 revolutions
Waffen-SS	military section of the SS
Wehrmacht	armed forces
Wehrwirtschaft	defence-based economy
Weltanschauung	world-view
Weltpolitik	world policy
Wessis	colloquial name for West Germans
Zeitgeist	spirit of the times
Zentrum	centre
Zollunion	customs union

INDEX